tan Social And Cultural T
765.00.0974

780415375665

).00 Indian.Rs

Saeed Book Bank

Importers & Distributors, Booksellers & Publishers

F-7, Jinnah Super Market, Islamabad-Pakistan.
Tel : 92-51-2651656-9, Fax : 92-51-2651660
E-mail : sales@ saeedbookbank.com
Arbab Road, Peshawar Cantt. Pakistan.
Tel : 92-91-5273761, 5285724
Fax : 92-91-5275801, 5274081
E-mail : sbb @ pes.comsats.net.pk
Web : www.saeedbookbank.com

Pakistan

Muslim societies are presumed to be stagnant and resistant to change. Yet the reality is quite the contrary. Pakistan is a pivotal Muslim nation. It exemplifies the scope and direction of social change in a Muslim society. This book shows how modernization as well as Islamization are simultaneously acting as processes of social transformation in Pakistan, along with population growth, urbanization and economic development. It offers an insightful view into Pakistan, exploring the wide range of ethnic groups, the countryside and cities, religion and community, and popular culture and national identity. It concludes by discussing likely future social developments in Pakistan, engaging students and academics interested in Pakistan and multiculturalism. Overall, this book is a comprehensive examination of social and cultural forces in Pakistani society, and is an important resource for anyone wanting to understand contemporary Pakistan and the Muslim world.

Mohammad Abdul Qadeer is Professor Emeritus, School of Urban and Regional Planning, Queen's University, Canada; where apart from teaching for thirty years, he was the director of the school 1986–96. He has taught at two Pakistani universities and has been a consultant to UN agencies, the Government of Pakistan and various Canadian bodies. Among his publications are two books entitled *Urban Development in the Third World. Internal Dynamics of Lahore, Pakistan* and (co-authored) *Towns and Villages in Canada.*

Routledge Contemporary South Asia Series

1   Pakistan: Social and cultural transformations in a Muslim nation
Mohammad Abdul Qadeer

Pakistan

Social and cultural transformations
in a Muslim nation

Mohammad Abdul Qadeer

Routledge
Taylor & Francis Group

LONDON AND NEW YORK

FIRST INDIAN REPRINT 2007

First published 2006
by Routledge

2 Park Square, Milton Park, Abingdon, Oxon OX14 4RN

Simultaneously published in the USA and Canada by Routledge

270 Madison Ave, New York, NY 10016

Routledge is an imprint of the Taylor & Francis Group, an informa business

© 2006 Mohammad Abdul Qadeer

Typeset in Times New Roman by
Bookcraft Ltd, Stroud, Gloucestershire

Printed and bound in India by
Replika Press Pvt. Ltd.

British Library Cataloguing in Publication Data
A catalogue record for this book is available from the British Library

Library of Congress Cataloging in Publication Data
Qadeer, Mohammad A.
Pakistan: social and culture transformation in a Muslim nation/
Mohammad A. Qadeer.
    p. cm. – (Routledge contempory South Asia series; 1)
    Includes bibliographical references and index.
    ISBN 0–415–37566–5 (hardback : alk. paper) I. Social change–Pakistan.
    2. Islam and culture–Pakistan. 3. Pakistan–Social conditions–20th century. 4. Pakistan–Social conditions–21st century. I. Title. II. Series.

HN680.5.A8Q33 2006
306.095491'0904dc22   2005036258

ISBN 10: 0–415–37566–5 (hbk)
ISBN 13: 978–0–415–37566–5 (hbk)
ISBN 10: 0–203–09968–0 (ebk)
ISBN 13: 978–0–203–09968–1 (ebk)

To the two families that are my anchors to
  the past, present and future:
My parents, brother and sister,
My wife and children, Susan, Nadra, Ahmer and Ali

PAKISTAN

Contents

Illustrations

Figures

Tables

Glossary and abbreviations

Ahl-i-Hadith	a puritanical Islamic sect
Ajrak	printed cotton shawl of Sindh
Amirul-Momneen	commander of the (Muslim) faithful
Anjuman	voluntary association or group
APWA	All Pakistan Women's Association
Babu train	commuter train ferrying clerks and workers
Bara	smuggled goods market
Barani	rain-fed dry lands
Basant	spring festival of kites
Biradari	an endogamous group claiming common lineage (clan)
Burqa	full body coverall with a face veil
CENTO	(Central Treaty Organization) American sponsored regional defense pact for the Middle East in the 1950s
Chador and Chardewari	(literally meaning: women's shawl and four walls of a home) metaphorically it means the inviolability of a woman's modesty and a home's sanctity
Chowkidar	watchman or security guard
Fatwa	Islamic legal opinion meant to be enforced
Fahashi	obscenity
GDP	Gross Domestic Product
GIKI	Ghulam Ishaq Khan Institute
Goth	small village of Sindh
Hari	bonded tenant
Haveli	a mansion
IJT	Islami Jamiat-i-Tulaba, students' wing of Jamaat-i-Islami
IMF	International Monetary Fund
Jagir	land grant and revenue estate
Jagirdar	landlord – revenue contractors with tenants in servitude
Jajmani system	caste based Indian system of bartering services
JI	Jamaat-i-Islami, an Islamic political party
JUI	Jamiat ul-Ulema-e-Islam, an Islamic political party
JUP	Jamiat ul-Ulema-e-Pakistan, an Islamic political party

Jehaz	dowry
Kaliwal	co-villager or member of a local community
Kammi	low-caste artisan or servant customarily attached to a landowner
Katchi Abadi	squatter settlement, neighborhood of dubious tenure
Khel	subdivision of tribe living in close proximity (clan)
Kothi	bungalow with a lawn
Khalifa	temporal and spiritual leader of Muslim community
Kunda	unauthorized hook for tapping electricity from overhead lines
Kurta	open-collar long shirt
Lassi	yogurt drink
LUMS	Lahore University of Management Sciences
Madrassah	Islamic school, primarily for religious learning
Mahr	bridegroom's dower for bride
MMA	Muttahida Majlis-i-Amal, united Islamic alliance
Mohallah	traditional residential neighborhood
MQM	Muhajir (later Muttahida) Quami Movement, a political party
MRD	Movement for Restoration of Democracy (1980s)
Mucca	fist
Muhajir	Muslim refugee from India, mostly refers to Urdu-speaking persons
Musawat-I-Mohammadi	the Prophet's egalitarian system
Mushaikh	spiritual guide
Nang	code of honor
Nizam-e-Mustapha	the Prophet's ordained system of rule
NWFP	North Western Frontier Province
Pacca	permanent structure of brick and cement
Patwari	official responsible for land records of a village
Pir	spiritual healer and guide
PML	Pakistan Muslim League
PML (N)	Pakistan Muslim League (Nawaz)
PNA	Pakistan National Alliance
PPP	Pakistan People's Party
Purdah	custom of veiling women
Qabza group	gang that appropriates property by strong-arm methods
Quarter	one- or two-room modest dwelling
Riasti	inhabitants of former princely states
Sajjada Nashin	custodian of a shrine
Seypi	customary system of services being provided for share from crops
Shalwar	baggy pants
Sharia/Shariat	rule of Islamic laws

Sipah-I- Mohammadi	(literal meaning, soldiers of Mohammad), Shia militant force
Sipah-I- Sahaba	(literally means soldiers of the Prophet's companions) Sunni militant force
Tandoor	clay oven to bake bread
Taulka	subdivision of a district in Sindh
Tehsil	subdivision of a district in the Punjab and the NWFP
Ulema	scholar of Islamic jurisprudence
Walwer	Pashtoon custom of bridegroom bringing dowry for bride
WAPDA	Water and Power Development Authority
Zamindar	landlord
Zat	caste or clan identity of an individual

Preface

Poverty is often equated with social stagnation. Particularly, poor countries are assumed to be static and unchanging, needing international advice and guidance. Recently this argument has been extended to include culture as a force of resistance to change. Islamic countries in particular are presumed to be tradition-bound and resistant to modernization and democracy. Yet a dispassionate look shows that the developing societies have been changing rapidly in the postcolonial era. The change may not fully conform to the theories and expectations derived from Western experiences, but the developing societies are carving out their own paths of change. Pakistan is both a low-income and a Muslim society where social change is not only palpable, but also takes multiple directions. Some institutions and practices follow the path of modernization, even westernization, while others reinvent indigenous ways and revive Islamic traditions.

Pakistani society has burst out of its agrarian roots. Not only has it been urbanizing rapidly, but urban modes of living have also been sweeping all across the country. An urban ethos and rising expectations are permeating remote regions of the country. In about five and a half decades of independence, it has evolved from a coherent but custom-bound and somnolent social system to a fragmented, mobile and materialistic society. In the process moral order and social institutions with agrarian roots have been split asunder. Social consensus about values and norms has been giving way to contradictory mores and institutional lags. Traditional society has passed but the new one is struggling to take hold. A state of ideological divisions and moral uncertainty prevails. In this void, revivalist Islam has risen to challenge material modernization and amoral globalization. Three processes, modernization, indigenization and Islamization, are competing in the socio-cultural space, giving rise to divergent lifestyles.

All in all, Pakistani society is far from being stagnant. It is poor but changing so rapidly that it is divided and turbulent. This book aims at analyzing and composing the story of its social change since independence. It is an account specifically focused on the internal dynamics of Pakistani society and culture in the postcolonial period of the last five decades. It is a contemporary social history.

Social history is a neglected field in Pakistan, though political and economic histories are plentiful. Although there are numerous sociological surveys of villages and cities, anthropological profiles of tribes and ethnic groups as well as studies of demographic trends and socioeconomic development, there is no systematic account of the evolving social institutions and cultural patterns. This book aims at initiating a social-historical line of inquiry.

Drawing on the treasure trove of the aforementioned studies, this book composes an integrated picture of social organization and cultural norms in Pakistan. It follows an institutional approach, tracking the evolving structures and underlying processes of urban and rural social organizations as well as Islam, family, community, class, civil society and everyday life as social institutions. It also explores the relationships between social organization and culture on the one hand, and political developments, economy and ideology on the other. The book focuses on these institutions as they are lived and not so much as imagined, though it illuminates empirical trends with theoretical insights.

A word about sources of information is necessary. I have relied on published data whenever available. Census of population and housing is one such source. Pakistan's censuses have been irregular. They are meant to be taken every ten years, but after two decennial censuses in 1951 and 1961, a population count was carried out in 1972 after the suspension of the census in 1971. The next census in 1981 covered both demographic and housing variables, but then political hiatus postponed the next census of 1991 until 1998. Topics covered and categories of data collection have not been consistent over time. There is a bias towards underestimation. My observations and interpretations take into account these limitations. National sample surveys reported by the Federal Bureau of Statistics are additional sources of data about social trends. Social surveys and information presented in national and provincial assemblies complement the aforementioned sources of quantitative data.

Many observations have been culled from content analysis of news, opinions and statements in magazines and newspapers. In the post-1990 period, websites and electronic sources have become an increasingly good source of information. Books, research reports and case studies have also been used whenever appropriate. My personal experiences of growing up, teaching and working in Pakistan have enriched my understanding of the cultural patterns and social changes. I have often illustrated observations with my personal vignettes. Altogether I have a fair degree of confidence in my observations and conclusions, which are based on multiple sources of information.

This project has been brewing in my mind for almost a decade. I started keeping notes and journals in the 1970s. My visits to Pakistan included long discussions of social-cultural and, of course, political events with friends, colleagues and relatives. Many of them may find their views and insights reverberating in this book. I have lost track of what I have drawn from them. Yet I am grateful all the same. My academic home, the School of Urban and Regional Planning, Queen's University, Kingston, Canada, has been a congenial and supportive place to nourish my intellectual interests. The School has also assisted me with a small grant for the typing of the final manuscript. All this help is acknowledged with gratitude.

I owe a heavy debt of gratitude to many individuals. Anwer Ahmed of Toronto has read and commented on every chapter. His comments and reassurances have sustained me through high and low periods. Hasan Gardezi, though a friend, has been my informal academic referee for this book. His insightful comments have helped me clarify many points. Tanveer Asghar analyzed data and did a content analysis of Pakistani newspaper headlines. Thanks, Tanveer. Tariq Ahsan reviewed the first four chapters. His suggestions helped clarify many points. Fayyaz Baqir has been an invaluable source of information about southern Punjab, Northern Areas and Balochistan. His comments on chapters six and seven gave me confidence in my observations. Pakistan's veteran journalist and a friend of many years, Khalid Hasan, reviewed chapter seven and wrote a column about its findings. His support is much appreciated. Azhar Butt has been a lifelong companion on my intellectual journey. A lot in this book germinated in our long, exasperating for our families, and absorbing conversations extending over almost our whole adult lives. Thank you Azhar, I hope I have put to good use those interminable discussions. I have similar feelings and sense of gratitude for Zafar Rathore. Many others have contributed in sharpening my observations and impressions, yet my brother Mohammad Rauf and deceased sister- and brother-in-law, Khalida Zain and Dr Zain-ul-abedin, stand out.

Finally, without my family's active support, this project may not have been completed. My sons Ali Qadeer and Ahmer Qadeer read many chapters and pointed out ambiguities. Similarly, my daughter Nadra Qadeer's comments have undoubtedly kept me aware of the language appropriate for discussing gender issues. Almost all writers acknowledge the help of their partners. Susan, my wife, has done much more than holding up my sagging confidence. She has been the first reader of successive drafts and editor of my grammatical lapses. She has also often helped in clarifying my vague ideas. Her contributions have been highly crucial in carrying through this undertaking. Thanks are not enough to express my feelings.

Jackie Bell, my colleague from the School at Queen's University, has copy-edited the final draft and brought it in line with the publisher's style manual. Her help is gratefully acknowledged. Jo-Anne Rudachuk of the same school has typed the final draft. Thanks, Jo-Anne.

Yet it goes without saying that I bear the sole responsibility for any shortcomings of this book. I just consider myself lucky to have such caring friends and family.

Mohammad A. Qadeer September 2005
Professor Emeritus, Urban and Regional Planning
Queen's University, Kingston, Canada

1 Changing Pakistan

The beginnings

On the steamy afternoon of August 14, 1947, the last viceroy of British India, Lord Mountbatten, flew into Karachi to address the newly formed Constituent Assembly of Pakistan, the homeland carved out of British India for Muslims. This ceremony marked the culmination of almost half a century of Indian Muslims' struggle to free themselves from colonial rule and avoid being swamped by the Hindu majority in an independent but singular India. Lord Mountbatten handed the reins of government to Mohammad Ali Jinnah, popularly known as the supreme leader (Quaid-i-Azam), who, as the leader of the Muslim League parliamentary party, was nominated to be the first governor general of the new state of Pakistan. That afternoon's handover of governmental authority launched Pakistan as a nation state as well as a society.

Pakistan was a new society in 1947. Prior to this, its constituent provinces or regions had not existed as a single unified social, economic, or political unit, although they had historical bonds and cultural affinities among themselves. Each of its five provinces – that is, Punjab, the North Western Frontier Province (NWFP), Balochistan, Sindh, and East Bengal – was a distinct ethnolinguistic region. Each one had a long history and a founding legend that harks back to antiquity. The British consolidated them, individually, out of tribes, territorial communities, and princedoms in the late nineteenth century.

Although the provinces had few lateral bonds or institutions, they shared Islam, the religion of the majority populations, and a sense of community and common identity fostered by the long political struggle for independence. The sense of a national community crystallized from the political awakening and was cultivated by poets and journalists of, particularly, the vernacular press.[1]

With the exception of East Bengal, the other four provinces also formed a contiguous landmass, shared a watershed, and had a common inheritance in the historical Indus Valley civilizations. Their shared geography has occasionally been made the basis for claiming a unity of people's temperaments and social values, as reflected in the notions of "Land of Sindhu" and "The Indus man."[2]

Yet the most significant factor in their coming together for political union was the rising tide of modern nationalism. Muslims of these provinces had cast their lot together and chosen to be one nation in the decolonized India.

State and society

Pakistani society largely emerged after the formation of the nation state. It did not preexist as a coherent structure, although some consciousness about common social institutions had evolved in the course of the struggle for independence. The provincial societies (henceforth called "communities" in order to differentiate them from the national society) were, of course, fully organized historical formations. They constituted the building blocks of the emerging Pakistani society. Integration of the provincial communities has been one of the abiding themes of national development and a crucial process of Pakistan's social history.

The state as the precedent for society has given preeminence to political and governmental institutions in Pakistan's social development. Pakistan's social and cultural history evolves along with the country's political developments and state policies. Cyclical changes of government from elected to military rule, person-centered politics and corruption, economic plans and foreign indebtedness, for example, affect the social structure and moral order. Yet the relation between the state and society is not entirely one-directional; the path of social change also curls back from society to the state.

Political parties recapitulate the clannish ethos under the personal tutelage of a leader, the military and civil services feed off tribal sentiments, and private riches come from cashing in on public authority. These are some of the ways in which social organization and cultural institutions affect the state. Pakistan's state and society have evolved in tandem – only the state often leads the way.

Pakistan has had a strong state and a weak society for almost four decades. Since the 1990s, the pendulum has begun to swing the other way, particularly with the rise of Islamic groups of considerable "street power." These shifts in state–society relations have a direct bearing on the development of society and culture.

Presently, I shall focus on the formation of the national society and its evolution. I am aiming to probe the social and cultural changes that have swept through Pakistani society since its independence. For this purpose, the state as a lead institution becomes a gateway into the social system. The path of sociocultural changes parallels the course of the state's evolution. In Chapter 2, these changes have been periodized in correspondence with the phases of the state's development.

My focus will primarily be on changes in social institutions such as the family and clan, community in urban and rural settings, social class, lifestyles, education, and religion, as well as everyday life. How have social class, caste, or clan structures changed? What role has religion played in cultural development and why has religion, as a social institution, gained strength? How have traditions and modernity, using the terms currently in vogue, interwoven with each other? How have social relations changed? What has modern technology done to social organization? Such are the questions that interest us. This is the terrain of social history that will be charted in this book.

Of course, political ideologies and processes affect social institutions and are thus woven into social history. Yet political history *per se* is not the focus of this book. I will examine political events, ideologies, and personalities primarily to trace their influences over social and cultural patterns, but will try not to be entrapped by their account.

Pakistani society

Over the years, an upper-tier national social organization has evolved, comprising provincial and regional communities. This is Pakistani society coinciding with the nation state. Its formation has not been without setbacks, as the violent separation of East Pakistan (1971) shows. As the state's institutions are located primarily in the western provinces, – in the Punjab and Sindh in particular (Karachi was the first capital of the new nation) – the emerging national society is also centered on the social institutions and cultural practices of these provinces. East Bengal, although the most populous province, was on the periphery of the emerging Pakistani state and society from the beginning. It had little influence on the formation of Pakistani society. Its separation legitimized and consolidated what had been the *de facto* basis of Pakistani society. Surprisingly, the separation of East Pakistan had little effect on everyday life in Pakistan.

National society and provincial communities

This book is about changes in Pakistani society and culture. By referring to Pakistani society and culture in the singular, I am assuming that overarching national social institutions and cultural patterns have not only evolved, but also continue to spread and change. This assumption does not rule out the existence of provincial and (subprovincial) regional communities and (sub)cultures. It only recognizes that a layer of national values, beliefs, sentiments, and institutions envelops the otherwise distinct and persistent regional social organizations and subcultures. As will become evident later, this assumption is amply supported by evidence. Yet it is not meant to contradict the regional claims for social, cultural, and linguistic distinctions, be those at the provincial scale such as Punjabi, Pashtoon, Sindhi, and Balochi or lower down the community hierarchy in the form of Sariaki, Pothohari, Hazarawal, Muhajir, Makrani, Kashmiri, Hunza, etc., at the regional or district levels.

Pakistani society is rooted in the social structures and cultural norms of provincial/regional communities, such as clan, religion, bazaar economy, corporate sector, ethnicity, class, occupation, and economic status as well as gender. The rural–urban divide and the modern versus traditional dichotomy are found throughout these structures and institutions. We will examine how these institutions and structures have changed; what phases and tendencies characterize these changes? How will social components of provincial (regional) communities dovetail with each other to form the national social organization? Equally important is the question of "why" these changes happen, namely what internal and external forces propel changes of social organizations and cultural institutions?

Our immediate task is to sketch the "contours of change" in Pakistan's society and culture over the 55 years of its existence as a nation. Pakistan has changed sociologically and culturally, although it has remained anchored in its historical inheritance. Before analyzing the directions and bases of social changes, it may be worthwhile to sketch broad contours of Pakistani society, not as a "fixed" structure – no society is – but as a changing and evolving system. This sketch will be drawn primarily with the help of social and economic indicators. These measures will not only illustrate, albeit in gross terms, the magnitude of social change in Pakistan, but they will also identify structures and geographies of resistance.

Pakistan: an ancient land and a new country

Sir Mortimer Wheeler, the British archeologist, entitled his book *Five Thousand Years of Pakistan*, for a country formed in 1947. Pakistan undoubtedly is one of the oldest inhabited regions of the world. Paralleling Mesopotamian, Egyptian, and Chinese civilizations, the Indus River Valley, the heartland of Pakistan, supported planned cities and a thriving commercial economy for millennia BCE. The country may be new in name and political organization, just as Germany and other European countries were new nations in the nineteenth century, but its cultural and social roots reach back to antiquity. There are parcels of land in Pakistan that have been farmed uninterrupted for thousands of years.

This long territorial history is equally manifest in the cultural traditions and community life of Pakistan's villages and towns. The Muslim nationalism that gave birth to Pakistan as a twentieth-century nation state is layered over ancient communities and territorial societies that evolved from the mingling of Aryans, Greeks, Arabs, Mongols and various tribes of Central Asia and Persia, who periodically came as invaders and migrants but settled and assimilated in the prosperous agrarian communities of the Indus Valley.

The "land" in its territorial and cultural meanings is the anchor of Pakistan's national identity and society. Its centrality in defining Pakistan as a nation is expressed in Pakistan's national anthem, which begins with a three-line ode to the land of Pakistan:

> Blessed be the sacred land,
> Happy be the bounteous realm, and
> Symbol of high resolve, land of Pakistan.

For the past millennium the Muslim majority has imprinted this "land" with an Islamic ethos, and thus Pakistan's society and culture are suffused with Islamic themes, values, and symbols. Yet historical beliefs and local traditions coalesce and collide with the juristic norms and universal symbols of Islam in an ongoing process of cultural fusion. Economic development and modernization are relatively recent processes inducing new forms of cultural change and social transformation.

The "land"

Land being so central to the project of constructing a nation, Pakistan's national state was initially organized on two territorial clusters, where Muslims were in the majority, namely, four provinces in the western wing and the split off East Bengal joined with a district of Assam to form the eastern wing. What has eventually remained of Pakistan, after the separation of the eastern wing, is an area of about 796,100 sq km forming an approximate parallelogram from the Himalayas in the north to the Arabian Sea in the south, from the mountainous offshoot of the Himalayas and the Hindu Kush forming the border with Afghanistan and Iran in the west to the politically demarcated line partitioning the Punjab province and delineating Sindh's boundary with India in the east. In addition, about one-third of the disputed state of Jammu and Kashmir, forming Azad Kashmir and the Northern Areas, is also territorially and politically attached to Pakistan.

In terms of area, Pakistan ranks 36th among the nations of the world. It is not in the class of big countries such as the USA, Russia, or India, but its territory is four times that of the UK and almost twice that of Germany. Within Pakistan, Balochistan is the largest province in terms of area (347,190 sq km) but has the smallest population (about 7 million in 1998). The Punjab, with 55 percent of the nation's population (73 million), is the second largest in area (205,344 sq km). Its combination of land and population makes it the hub of Pakistan's society and culture. Sindh has an area of 140,914 sq km and a population of about 26 million, but it is its megacity Karachi, the national port and premier industrial and commercial center, that makes this province central to the economy and society of Pakistan. Historically, NWFP and Balochistan are tribal societies with frontier traditions. Both provinces also have designated "tribal territories" which are self-administered, ruled by customary laws, and are bearers of distinct subcultures. These two provinces have been the historic gateways to India from central and western Asia. Their geostrategic position and strong martial traditions are the bases of their political and cultural role in Pakistan. Azad Kashmir and the Northern Areas are nominally autonomous territories, whose status remains to be decided after the resolution of the Kashmir dispute with India. Yet for all practical purposes they are parts of Pakistan.

Each of the four provinces, the federal territories, and the Northern Areas is a distinct cultural area of diverse local communities, social mores, and dialects, even languages. This diversity of social and cultural attributes makes the "land" all the more critical as the unifying force at the national level, both symbolically and territorially.

Pakistan's lands are basically semiarid, but waters of four rivers (the Indus and its three eastern tributaries) irrigate them. A network of dams, weirs, canals, and field channels, built by the British in the early twentieth century and expanded since independence, has transformed the landscape of the plains in the Punjab and Sindh. Canal irrigation has turned these dry and dusty lands into the national granary. The variety of Pakistan's landscape is striking. From some of the loftiest mountains, K2 and Nanga Parbat in the northwest, to some of the flattest alluvial plains of the world, combined with deserts, plateaus, hills, and mangroves, Pakistan has all of them.

About 59 percent of Pakistan's land area consists of the mountainous tablelands of Balochistan, NWFP, and the northern and western fringes of the Punjab and Sindh provinces. The plains of Pakistan resemble the North American prairies in flatness and vastness. They extend over an area of about 300,000 sq km with a gradient so gentle that the northern uplands, 1,600 km from the sea, are only 250 m above sea level. With most of the population concentrated on flat lands, a typical Pakistani is a person of the plains, steeped in legends and memories of rivers and deserts and wheat fields. Highlanders and coast dwellers are on the margins of Pakistan's landscape of imagination and identity.

132.35 million at the time of the 1998 census. Over a period of 55 years, the population has more than quadrupled. This magnitude of population growth has transformed Pakistan. Within the life of one generation, somnolent villages have become noisy and crowded towns, leisurely cities have turned into sprawling megalopolises and what were assumed to be plentiful gifts of nature, land, water, forests, and clean air, are now perennially scarce.

Population growth has not only changed the landscape and the size of cities and villages, but has also altered the social organization of Pakistan. Families and clans are more spread out and their kinship ties have loosened. People are moving out of ancestral occupations and places in pursuit of economic and cultural opportunities unavailable at home. Community life is losing the intensity that comes from the face-to-face relations of many generations. Population growth is one of the driving forces of social change.

Demographic factors have also affected the ethnic and regional composition of Pakistani society. It is a country where one province, Punjab, has the majority of the population, although its share has slightly declined from about 61 to 56 percent over a period of five decades. Its demographic predominance colors Pakistan's society and polity. Sindh and Balochistan have increased their share in Pakistan's population a little; Sindh's share increased from 18 to 23 percent and Balochistan's from 3.5 to 5 percent. The proportion of NWFP's population has remained almost constant at 13.5 percent, with minor fluctuations around this mean from census to census.

A typical Pakistani would be a child or youth, as 43 percent of Pakistan's population are below 15 years of age. This ratio has not changed significantly in the last 50 years and even provinces differ only marginally in this respect. All parts of the country have large proportions of dependent population. Pakistan is also a country where males outnumber females by 108 to 100, although this gender ratio has come down from 116 to 100 since 1951 suggesting some improvement in the health conditions of mothers and female children.

Historically, Pakistan has been a rural society; the overwhelming proportion of its population lived in villages and tribal settlements. At the time of independence, only 17 percent of the population lived in urban areas, defined as places with a population of 5,000 or more with some form of local government. With accelerating urbanization, by the beginning of the twentieth century almost 37 percent of the population lived in cities and towns. The urban population edges up to being in the majority (56 percent), if the population living around cities and in densely populated districts is taken into account.[3]

Demographic processes propel social change, yet they in turn are affected by changing mores and behaviors. Some significant behavioral changes are evident from demographic indicators. Pakistan remains a country of high birth rates, despite an observable drop in the fertility of its population. Its crude birth rate was estimated to be about 42 per 1,000 during the period 1962–5, which has come down to 36 by 2001. More striking is the drop in the mortality rate, although they both still remain high by international criteria. The crude death rate was about 30 in the late 1950s and has come down to 8 by 2001. The large gap between the birth and death rates is the primary cause of the population explosion in Pakistan.

Life expectancies at birth have increased, rising from 48 years for males and 45 years for females in the early 1960s to 63 and 65 years respectively in 2001. Slightly higher life expectancy for females is an indicator of improving health services for women and changing social values. It goes without saying that social progress is not uniform across the country. There are significant variations between provinces, and within provinces between districts and social classes, on all these criteria. Urban areas lead in these changes, as do the provinces with high levels of urbanization. The prolongation of life can be witnessed in Pakistan's capital, Islamabad, where retired but sprightly officers well past their sixties are predominant among morning walkers. This is, of course, a thin slice of Pakistan's society, but it is a part all the same.

Ethnic mix

Pakistan's rich history is reflected in the racial, linguistic, and cultural diversity of its population. Periodic waves of invaders from central Asia introduced new racial and cultural strains in the indigenous population of the area. Although the newcomers were assimilated in local communities, their ancestral origins morphed into ethnic and caste identities, such as Khans, Rajputs, Mughuls, Qureshis, Sayyids, etc. The variations of skin color and physical features evident in Pakistan's population can be traced back to the diversity of its racial and geographic origins. The combination of physiognomic, cultural, and linguistic differences has laid the groundwork for ethnic diversity in Pakistan. These differences were further sharpened by the British colonial policy of classifying people by ethnicity and caste.

Ethnically, Pakistan's population falls into six major groups, each coinciding with a cultural/linguistic area, namely those whose mother tongue is Sindhi, Balochi, Pushto, Punjabi, Saraiki, or Urdu. Classified by the criterion of mother tongue, as per the 1998 census, the largest ethnolinguistic group was Punjabis (44.2 percent), followed by Pashtoons (15.4 percent), Sindhis (14.1 percent), Saraiki (10.1 percent), Urdu speakers (largely Muhajirs, 7.6 percent), and Balochis (3.6 percent). There are many minor ethnolinguistic groups in the Northern Areas, Azad Kashmir, and within the major ethnolinguistic areas.

Being a region of isolated valleys separated by the high Himalayas, the Northern

Area is the home of about eight ethnic groups speaking five languages in their respective communities, for example, Shina, Balti, Brushiski, Wakhi, and Khower. Kashmiri is a language spoken in Azad Kashmir and parts of the Punjab and Northern Areas. Balochistan has Brahvi as a distinct language within the Baloch ethnic area. Pothohari is both a region and a dialect bordering on a language in the Punjab.

The point of this description is to underline the pluralism of Pakistani society. How ethnicity and nationality dovetail with each other is a question that will be discussed in Chapter 4. Presently, the focus is on projecting a picture of the ethnic diversity in Pakistan.

Poverty and economic development

Poverty is endemic in Pakistan. It defines the country as a poor nation. About one-third of Pakistan's population live in poverty at the beginning of the twenty-first century, although the incidence of poverty has decreased since independence.[4] Mass poverty in Pakistan coexists with the affluence and even opulence of landowners, businessmen, professionals, and the political and bureaucratic elite. Cities like Karachi, Lahore, Peshawar, Islamabad–Rawalpindi and even places such as Faisalabad, Quetta, and Multan have fancy restaurants, five-star hotels and car-choked streets. Yet the same cities have squatter settlements, lacking in water supply and sanitation, where 20–40 percent of their population live.

Contrasts in the standards of living of the lower- versus upper-class households are etched in the urban landscape. Although poverty has shown a downward trend, social disparities remain very wide and very notable. The poorest 20 of percent households have marginally increased their share of the national income from 6.4 percent in 1963–4 to 9.2 percent in 1993–4, although the rate of increase fluctuated up and down over this period. Yet the highest 20 percent of household income earners continue to take almost 40 percent of the national income, losing only three to five percentage points in the comparable period. At the end of the twentieth century, about 30 percent of Pakistan's population still lived at below $1 per day.

The poverty of people is a reflection of low production and economic underde-velopment. Pakistan is a low-income country. Its per capita GNI (gross national income) of $420 in 2001 places it 102nd among the 133 countries whose economic performance is tracked by the World Bank.

Pakistan's economic development is marked by a steady progress that has not yet turned into the "take-off" phase. Its per capita income in constant prices (1980–1 base) rose from Pakistani Rupees (Rs) 1,760 in 1959–60 to 4,589 in 1996–7. Over about 40 years, Pakistan's per capita income increased 2.6 times, making allowance for the population increase as well as inflation. Roughly, an average Pakistani is almost three times richer than she or he was in the middle years of the twentieth century. Such gains are visible in people's consumption of food, in their dress, and housing. It was not uncommon to see barefoot children, even adults sometimes, in the 1950s and 1960s. By 2001 it was a very rare sight. Similarly, in the irrigated lands of Punjab, mud houses have almost disappeared in villages.

Such are the visible changes. Undoubtedly, the economic floor for a majority has risen a bit but not enough to spare the country from mass poverty.

Economic development is manifested in the factories that have sprung along roads radiating out of cities, in national food self-sufficiency, and in the growth of the professional and commercial classes. It can be seen in the crowded airports, glittering shopping strips, palatial bungalows, and sprawling cities. Yet the development is unevenly distributed, regionally and socially.

Much of the economic progress is concentrated around major cities. The Karachi–Hyderabad corridor in Sindh and the Lahore–Faisalabad–Gujrat triangle in central Punjab have developed as has the Peshawar Valley. Southern and western Punjab, interior Sindh, southern NWFP, and Balochistan as well as sections of the tribal territories have not equitably shared in the economic development, although winds of change have swept through there as well.

Economic development has proceeded in planned steps through nine five-year plans, aided and advised by international agencies. The development has a large element of deliberate policy choices and foreign aid. The outcome of this effort is reflected in the fact that Pakistan's economy has undergone a structural change, its base evolving from almost complete concentration in the primary activities to increasing reliance on secondary and tertiary production.

Agriculture contributed about 53 percent of GDP in 1949–50 but its share dropped to 25 percent by 2001, although the "green revolution" of the 1970s had increased its productivity significantly. The industrial sector grew from 8 percent of GDP in 1949–50 to about 25 percent in 2001. Similarly, the services, the tertiary sector, contributed 39 percent of GDP in 1949–50 and their share has risen to about 51 percent in 2001.[5] These shifts in the composition of the GDP indicate a significant change in the occupational structure of the national labor force. This change is the harbinger of a major restructuring of society and culture. It needs to be reiterated that these shifts in the economic and occupational structures are not evenly distributed across provinces, and within provinces among regions. Various parts of the country have changed in the same directions but at different rates and to varying magnitudes.

Social development

On the UNDP's Human Development Index, Pakistan ranks quite low, 138th among 173 countries. Undoubtedly, as a society, it falls short in the provision of educational, health, and welfare services for its people. It is a country of large social deficits. Yet this does not mean that there has not been any development of the social infrastructure nor any change in the well-being of the population.

Pakistan has certainly advanced socially, albeit not enough, both by people's expectations and global standards. It is a very different country in terms of health, education, nutrition, and housing from what it was when the British left in 1947.

Infant mortality has been very high in Pakistan, an indicator of poor maternity and pediatric services, unsanitary living conditions, and poverty. The infant mortality rate was about 222 per 1,000 live births in 1901–10. It came down to 131 per 1,000 by 1961, dropping further to 103 per 1,000 by 1989–94, and fell more rapidly in the 1990s to 82 per 1,000 by 2000.[6] Of course, it is still far from the range of 5–10 per 1,000, characteristic of prosperous and modern societies.

The number of qualified doctors is an indicator of the quality of health services in a country. Pakistan had few doctors at its inception (1,360 in 1948) but their numbers increased more than fiftyfold in about 50 years to 74,229 in 1996. From one doctor per 22,800 persons in 1948, the ratio changed to 1 doctor per 1,760 persons in 1996. In the 1990s, unemployed doctors were demonstrating periodically for jobs. This is a striking improvement in the availability of physicians although on other indicators of health facilities, such as hospital beds, public health, etc., progress has not been as remarkable.

Educational facilities, too, have registered significant increases. The number of primary schools increased from 8,413 in 1947–8 to 150,963 by 1996–7, almost 17 times in about 50 years. Similarly, secondary schools increased by 24 times, from 408 in 1947–8 to 9,808 by 1996–7. Girls' primary and secondary schools have also increased in parallel. The same or larger magnitude of changes can be recounted for universities, professional colleges, and technical institutes. Women's educational institutions have also increased considerably, although they have lagged behind when compared with those for men.

Similarly, notable progress has been made in advancing literacy among the population, although much still remains to be done. The proportion of literate males (males 10 years or older and able to read with understanding) was estimated to be 16 percent in the 1960s and now it has climbed to 57 percent. Female literacy rates lag behind but they are also improving, with about 33 percent of women being literate. Although still a long way away from the goal of universal literacy, the rise in the proportion of the literate in the population underlines changing social conditions.

To get a snapshot of the changes in people's welfare, the availability of food staples and some consumer items could be examined. Wheat is the staple of Pakistan's diet. Historically, the wheat harvest determined the yearly prospects of people's welfare. Thus, its output is a baseline measure of the market conditions for the poor. The output of wheat increased almost fivefold, from 3.35 million metric tons in 1947–8 to 16.65 million metric tons by 1996–7. The production of rice increased six times from 0.69 million metric tons in 1947–8 to 4.30 million metric tons in 1996–7.

Probably the most notable success story of the agricultural revolution in Pakistan is the production of fruits and vegetables. From relatively meager supplies in the early years, fruits and vegetables have become plentiful and many new varieties have come into the market. One illustrative example is that of the production of strawberries, which were almost nonexistent in the Pakistan of the 1950s and 1960s. By the 1990s, strawberries were piling on sidewalks, during the season, wanting for customers. Fruit production has increased by 231 percent in the 25 years spanning from 1970 to 1995. What this potpourri of figures suggests is that

Pakistan has been making progress in producing basic commodities for consumers.

Economic development has certainly expanded the ranks of the middle classes and has made some dent in living standards. One indicator of the expanding middle class is the ownership of motorcycles and scooters. Over the 50-year period from 1947 to 1997, the number of registered motorbikes/scooters increased from a mere 3,618 to 1.7 million, a staggering increase in this middle–lower-income mode of transport. The signs of development are all around. Roads are choked with traffic, brick or concrete houses are more common than mud homes, electricity and telephone facilities are now available in villages, and airports are jammed with travelers. Most of these facilities were the prerogatives of a select few at the time of independence.

Building national society and culture

The foregoing snapshot of social and economic development is meant to underline a simple fact: Pakistan's society and culture have changed notably since independence. Modern institutions and organizations have permeated the traditional agrarian communities and tribes. People are more mobile, relatively more dependent on cash transactions, and subject to global technological influences and trends in consumption. Yet, family and, to a lesser extent, blood bonds remain the core social institutions.

Radio, television, and videos have penetrated the remote corners of the country. In the 1990s, telephones were available in almost every part of the country. Western influences are visible in music, architecture, arts and crafts and even food. Pizza, hamburgers, and fried chicken have filtered down to the second- and third-tier cities. Eating out is a popular pastime. Well-fed people of large girth are not uncommon but they coexist with swarms of small children and young women begging for food. Traditional customs and religious piety have come back with renewed vigor, even among the urban professional and business classes. Proportionately more women are working for remuneration in public life, but conservatives rail more vociferously against their freedom.

Today's Pakistan is different in many ways from what society was in 1947, yet it is not a new society. It maintains a continuity of traditions. Values and institutions remain tethered to their historical roots. This interplay between continuity and change is not unique to Pakistan. It is the story of all countries. It is the phenomenon of "the more things change, the more they remain the same." This adage underlines the complexity and circularity of charting social change. It also underlines the tack I will take in examining the changing society and culture of Pakistan. How do the dynamics of social change unfold, whom do they sweep up, whom do they leave behind, and why? These are some of the questions that frame the narrative of this book.

Organization of society

While recognizing a variety of ways in which the term "society" can be used, in this book it is defined as the institutionalized "modes of conduct," as Anthony Giddens says, or organized and structured social relations forming a nation.[7] The evolution of Pakistani society parallels the ideological and constitutional development of the state and the government.

Independence ushered in the process of developing a national society and culture.[8] New national institutions and organizations of all kinds emerged within two decades of independence, for example, Pakistan Science Congress, Writers Guild, Institute of Engineers, National Union of Journalists, Cricket Control Board, the Olympic team, etc. Urdu was proclaimed as the national language, educational and religious institutions were reorganized along national lines, and a radio broadcasting network was established. Newspapers, sports teams, labor unions, chambers of commerce and industry, and a national-level women's association (APWA) were organized on an all-Pakistan basis. Provincial bodies and interest groups linked with one another to form national organizations. These are the organizational and institutional foundations on which a national society and cultural system have gradually emerged.

Similarly, national symbols and sentiments found roots in all parts of the country. Noor Jehan's, Pathana Khan's, or Abida Parveen's songs enthralled Punjabis and Balochis equally. Pictures of cricketers Fazal Mahmood or Imran Khan hang in the shops of Gilgit or Thatta.

Pakistan has emerged from an imagined community to a lived-in society. I will elaborate on these processes and organizations later and examine how far they have or have not integrated provincial and regional interests. Presently it is enough to point out that the framework of a national society has emerged to overarch the provincial communities.

National society and culture are, of course, composite structures. There are contradictions between national and provincial interests, particularly in matters relating to language, ethnicity, identity, and power. There are small political groups and movements agitating for Pakhtonistan, Sindhudesh, or Baloch liberation. Nevertheless, such provincial or regional sentiments swirl within the national cultural pool.

Overall, regional communities and cultures have a greater influence over the family, marriage, kinship, and everyday life than national society, whereas national institutions and values have a more significant role in the arts, literature, education, politics, defense, and the economy.

National and regional cultures have, at various times, interwoven and competed with each other. In times when centralization is the ideological thrust, national themes and institutions are in the ascendancy, but when the pendulum swings toward decentralization, regional and ethnic societies and cultures reassert their autonomy. The political ideologies and movements that shift the balance between national and regional social and cultural systems are the markers of Pakistan's social change. They divide the history of social change into three periods of distinct social and cultural organizations. I will discuss in detail the periodization of Pakistan's political and social development in Chapter 2 . Presently, this sketch of the social and cultural changes in Pakistan will be concluded with a discussion of the external and internal processes that are driving these changes.

Processes of social change

Pakistani emigrants settled in London, Toronto, or Dubai are often surprised at the changes in the daily life of their friends and relatives back home even if it has been just a few years since their last visit. Social change is palpable to individuals and is evident in the indicators recounted above. What is not so obvious is the direction the change is taking. Is it a march toward modernism, oscillations from the traditional to modern ways and back, or a fracturing of a coherent social system? Of course, these questions will engage us in the rest of this book, but presently another question is more pressing, namely, what processes and forces are driving the change?

Historical events, external economic and political forces, technological advances, internal political and social dynamics, and the diffusion or invention of new ideas and practices are some of the known "causes" of social and cultural changes. Much theoretical heat is generated by arguments about what constitute the "primary" forces of social change. Is this change instigated by the evolution of production, technology, ideology, and worldview; by liberty, and individualism; by the free market and unleashing entrepreneurship; by the inexorable logic of the global system; or by the dialectics of dependency and self-sufficiency? The point is that there is a very rich menu of theories to choose from in seeking explanations of social change in Pakistan. Yet the challenge lies in uncovering the structure of Pakistan's social change.

I want to proceed from the inside out, by focusing on processes and forces inducing change from within the society and then account for the role of external forces that may have initiated, catalyzed, complemented, or impeded the internal changes. My approach is clearly tilted toward the internal dynamics perspective. With this in mind, the following are brief accounts of the significant processes that have promoted social change in Pakistan.

Independence

Independence (1947) from the British Empire was a seminal event in the history of Pakistan. It scrambled the historical social order and opened up opportunities for business, politics, and jobs that had been blocked for Muslims. Independence brought a large-scale emigration of Hindus and Sikhs out of Pakistan, thereby removing large swaths of the middle and upper strata composed of businessmen, professionals, bankers, and farmers. Their departure left holes in local social structures.

Muslim immigrants coming from India filled some of these slots. The social structure was realigned, eroding religious and caste monopolies and releasing the entrepreneurial spirit. The Punjab and the Karachi–Hyderabad region of Sindh were at the epicenter of this change. The Frontier and Balochistan provinces were affected to a lesser extent.

Independence stimulated people's ambitions and raised their expectations. There was a threshold change in the social psychology and moral order.

Independence was essentially a one-off event. It unleashed other processes among which the seven outlined below stand out as particularly relevant to social and cultural change in Pakistan. They operate in combination with one another, not independently, both mutually supporting and impeding each other in a truly dialectical way.

Population growth

Increase or decrease of population has all kinds of social and cultural consequences. When population grows rapidly, as has happened in Pakistan, the impacts are almost volcanic. For example, a large increase in the population over a short period has swollen the number of children and youth who have to be fed, clothed, educated, and gainfully employed. At the societal level, such burgeoning social needs have resulted in the perpetuation of poverty, unemployment, and turbulent youth. The changing composition of the population also poses challenges for the established political order and adds to the urgency of building a responsive system of governance. These challenges may not be met but they continue to shake the social order.

Population growth also realigns family and marriage institutions, affects kinship ties, and class hierarchies. All this has happened in Pakistan. The population explosion in Pakistan has precipitated environmental and resource scarcities, such as those of land, water, energy, and air quality. It has changed the landscape.

Social changes brought about by population growth will be examined in detail later. Presently it is enough to point out the significance of demography as a process of change. However, it may also be noted that population growth itself is the result of other forces, such as advances in medicine and public health and changes in social attitudes, and religious and moral values, etc. Like peeling an onion, the exploration of "causes" can lead one from layer to layer. The social and technological factors are inextricably bound up with the demographic changes. Awareness of this fact informs our analysis.

Urbanization and urbanism

Another process inducing social change is urbanization. Villages have turned into cities and cities have spread out to become megalopolises. These are the physical expressions of urbanization, which is defined as the concentration of a large number of people in areas that have some form of local government and community services.[9] A relatively high density of population is the defining characteristic of urbanization.

The concentration of population, a physical attribute of urbanization, is feasible primarily in areas specializing in secondary and tertiary activities. It is intertwined with urban social organizations and municipal institutions. Urbanization overlaps with urbanism as a way of life and community structure. The spread of urban ways of life beyond cities carries urbanism into villages.

Urbanization also refers to the proportion of a country's population that lives in urban areas, or, in other words, is engaged in commercial, administrative, and/or industrial activities and follows corresponding cultural norms and behaviors. It stands for the commercial and industrial mode of production.

Pakistan is being swept both by urbanization in the sense of an increasingly larger proportion of the population living in urban areas, and by the spread of urbanism in the countryside. Both aspects of this process are transforming social life in Pakistan. Urbanization in Pakistan is fueled by population growth, but its structure and form are determined by the processes of industrial development, economic growth, and the communication revolution, thereby connecting this process to other forces of social change.

Economic development and modernization

National income (gross national product – GNP) increases with the broadening of productive capacities and by improving the efficiency of the production of goods and services and their equitable distribution. One explicit objective of national independence is to raise national income and improve people's living standards, or, in other words, to break the historical vicious circle of poverty. This is the process of economic growth.

Economic growth is the primary goal of national development. Pakistan has embraced this goal wholeheartedly and pursues it in a planned and deliberate manner. It has followed nine five-year plans implementing programs and projects in almost every sector of the economy and society, be it industrial development, irrigation, health, education, or housing. Economic development cannot but promote social transformation. It brings about institutional restructuring and cultural change. The combination of economic development and sociocultural transformation has been called modernization. The meanings and scope of modernization will be discussed in the next chapter, but at this stage it is enough to point out that it is a multifaceted process of sociocultural change.

Economic development in Pakistan, although not proceeding at a consistent and satisfactory pace, nonetheless has promoted new industries and extensively commercialized agriculture. Technological advancement is the hinge of economic development. Pakistan's large farms have been mechanized (use of tractors) and chemicalized (reliance on fertilizers, miracle seeds, and pesticides), its industries have multiplied with the introduction of new manufacturing activities, and now information technology is taking hold. Technological advances in particular and economic development in general have introduced new occupations and changed patterns of consumption. All in all, the material and technological bases of society are changing, leading to the realignment of the social organization of production. It is even affecting people's attitudes and values. Borrowing a Marxist formulation, the changes in the material base of Pakistani society are affecting its superstructure of social institutions and cultural patterns.

Social mobility and migration

Modernization and mobility of people, although distinct, are mutually reinforcing processes. Mobility is a potent force of social change. It can take many forms: emigration and immigration from and to Pakistan, movement of workers and families from one region or town to another, migration from rural areas to cities, transfers and postings of employees away from their hometowns, circular movements between hometowns and places of work on a seasonal or cyclical basis, change of residence within the same city, and so on.

These are examples of geographic mobility but they have their social and cultural counterparts. People change occupations, gain (or lose) in social status, or take on new values, beliefs, and lifestyles. Put together, these constitute a river of sociocultural change.

Social mobility has breached the "fortress of tradition" in Pakistan. It began with independence and the exchange of populations. Post-independence economic development and urban growth drew a large number of people from NWFP and Punjab to Karachi. Rural–urban migration has swept through almost all the cities of Pakistan, for example, Faisalabad, Multan, Islamabad, Peshawar, and Quetta. The military and civil establishments rotate their officials through many parts of the country during their careers. In the 1990s, almost four million Afghans came as refugees to Pakistan. These refugees have not only changed the demography of NWFP and Balochistan, but have also contributed to the rise of Islamic militancy in the country. Cumulatively, various forms of mobility have transformed the life and culture of local communities.

More than a million workers and professionals travel for jobs to the Gulf, Saudi Arabia, Libya, and Japan and almost an equal number have migrated to the UK, USA, Canada, and Europe. These temporary or permanent émigrés have become a major export (labor) of Pakistan. Their remittances and family and kin bonds have been a major force of social change, even in remote villages. They have also contributed to the revival of many traditional beliefs and practices. The expatriate Pakistanis in Arab countries particularly have brought back austere practices of Wahabism.

These population movements, temporary and permanent, are resulting in the restructuring of families, changes in marriage patterns, lifestyles, and cultural norms. I will follow the trail of mobility as a force of sociocultural change and resistance in this book; presently it is just tagged as a process of change.

Communication and information

Advances in communication and information dissemination, such as television, videos, Internet, and CDs, have increased the circulation of ideas, symbols, and images across national and regional borders. People have access to new sources of news, facts, and entertainment. These media help rationalize, redirect, or impede changes that are underway through economic and social development.

Bollywood music, BBC news, and American movies along with Pakistan Television's drama serials enthrall people in remote corners of the country. Family members spread across the world are accessible on telephone from most parts of the country. Both the medium and the message are raising new expectations, reviving old beliefs, and realigning cultural values. The social impact of communication and media has seeped deep into social and cultural institutions, paradoxically reviving traditions as well as introducing new practices. Like other processes, communication and information media are bound up with other socioeconomic forces, thus making them a strong current of social change.

Internationalism and globalization

Contemporary societies are enmeshed in the international system of trade and aid as well as supranational laws and regulatory regimes. These external forces play a significant part in the development of contemporary societies. Pakistan joined the US-sponsored regional defense pacts, SEATO and CENTO, as early as 1954–5. It also became a major recipient of foreign aid. Its dependence on international aid exposed its society to US and UN influences and regulations. For example, since the 1980s the agenda of the World Bank and the IMF has been the privatization of public services, market-based exchange rates, and free trade. These policies are pushed through the conditions attached to loans. They have not only influenced Pakistan's economic and fiscal policies but have also affected differentially the quality of life in villages and towns. Their influences permeate from the economic sectors to the social structure and cultural practices.

Similarly, international conventions and laws, such as those regulating endangered species, environmental pollution, nuclear energy, free trade, human rights, etc., filter down to the national level affecting public policies, cultural norms, and social relations. These external ideas and rules become agents of social change.

External relations in general have profound impacts on the political, religious, and intellectual life of a society. Pakistan's relations with India, for example, have greatly influenced its ideology, national attitudes, and social psychology as well as intergroup relations. Similarly, its involvement in the US-backed Afghan resistance to the Soviet occupation has brought terrorism and sectarian strife in Pakistan's relatively peaceful religious life. Pakistan's strong identification with the Islamic world has also been a source of new ideas and practices.

Recently, internationalism has taken a new turn. It has expedited the erosion of national controls over the movement of capital, trade, technology, and information across international borders. Globalization, the process that interlinks economies, markets, and institutions, is reorganizing production activities at the international level, wherein enterprises, investments, and goods and services move from location to location across national boundaries in pursuit of profits and freedom from regulations. It is an era of increasing contacts across national boundaries in the economy, technology, and culture. It is affecting all countries of the world; some are, of course, more helpless in the face of these global forces than others. Pakistan's economic dependence has made it particularly vulnerable to the process of globalization. One year its textile industry is booming, the next year it is in a deep slump as global buyers cultivate lower-cost suppliers in Bangladesh. Globalization is beginning to determine the economic fate of local communities and households. It has so far brought considerable uncertainty and disparity in people's daily life. Yet it has become a force of accelerating cultural change.

The above-described six processes are themselves composed of many forces, yet they form systematic factors operating in almost all societies. Apart from them, there are a few Pakistan-specific events and factors that have influenced the course of the nation's social history, which should also be mentioned.

Islamism as an ideology and social movement

Pakistan has a special relation with Islam as an ideology. Its founding ideology of Muslim nationalism puts Islam at the core of its national consciousness and moral order. Pakistan has been struggling to balance its Islamic commitments and the demands of the contemporary industrial-urban society. It has experimented with various constitutional formulae in successive phases of the evolution of its state and society. Since the 1980s, the rise of political Islam and global Islamic movements have become potent forces in the reorganization of Pakistani society. They constitute a distinct complex of ideological and moral forces promoting new behaviors, norms, and institutions in Pakistani society. The Pakistan of 2001 is a society where mosques and shrines are full, radio and television are saturated with Islamic themes, and marches and meetings of Islamic causes can attract hundreds of thousands of people. Undoubtedly, it is a society distinctly more religious than what it was in the 1960s and 1970s. Islamism as a force of social change is a distinct phenomenon in Pakistan.

Historical and contingent factors

There are historical events – one-of-a-kind factors and personalities – that play a significant part in changing a society and its culture. Pakistan has had its share of such factors. The wars with India (1965 and 1971), the ousting of the Afghan king, the separation of East Pakistan, the failure of the one-unit experiment, floods and droughts, and Bhutto's populism are such contingent factors that have affected the trajectory of social change in Pakistan. Their influence will be appropriately noted wherever applicable.

At this stage, the scope of our narrative has been outlined. I have also reviewed the processes that underlie the interplay of continuity and change in Pakistani society. Our next task is to trace the historical phases in which Pakistan's political and social developments can be divided.

2 Patterns of social change

Models of change

History is an account of change. A princess' marriage is of little interest *per se*, but it becomes history if the marriage seals a bond between two dynasties. Normal and routine events are not significant historical facts. What makes an event historical is its contribution to changing the course of events that follow. Also, history goes deeper then mere occurrences. It attempts to find an order or hinge that links together disparate events and phenomena. The search for underlying trends is the province of historians and social theorists. By discovering patterns in a multitude of events, historians and theorists attempt to explain the bases of social change. The objective of this chapter is to lay out a framework for studying patterns of change.

The most widely held view is that human societies march along a linear evolutionary path: their economic production evolving from hunting/grazing to farming and manufacturing; political institutions developing from tribes to monarchies and democracies; social organizations turning from patriarchal to individualistic in orientation, and settlements growing from rural to urban in structure. Ibn Khaldun, Herbert Spencer, Auguste Comte, and Max Weber, among others, subscribe to the linearity of human history. Oswald Spengler, Karl Marx, and Arnold Toynbee find human societies following cyclical, evolutionary, or dialectical paths of development.[1] Recent theoretical formulations place economic organization at the center of the process of change. Economic development is conceived to be the driving force of change. Its advent as a discipline has lent further support to the "linearity" model of one formulation or another.

National economies grow by diversifying from agriculture to manufacturing and service/information industries, but this occurs as part of a broader process of evolution from agrarian to industrial and postindustrial societies. National development is expected to follow predetermined "stages of growth" (as per Walter Rostow) or alternatively a path that leads from tribal or feudal to capitalist and eventually socialist modes of production in Marxist perspectives.[2]

Between these two polar views have grown numerous hybrid models, for example, dependency and the world system theories, dualism, the convergence hypothesis, and, lately, environmental determinism. Yet the point that is common in these theories is that social change is not a random process but follows discernible patterns, despite disagreements about the form they may take. Presently the question is how to proceed in looking for the patterns of social change in Pakistan or, in other words, what concepts and models will inform our observations of Pakistani society?

Development and modernization

Like most postcolonial societies, Pakistan has embraced development as its primary national goal. At the core of the concept of development is the idea of economic growth, whereby the real per capita income of a country increases over a period of time, without increasing the number of people below an absolute poverty line and not widening inequalities further.[3] It may be noted that the contemporary concept of economic development includes some notions of social equity and reduction of poverty. Thus, inherent in the goal of development are social objectives calling for institutional reforms which now include responsive governance, democracy, and human rights. Amartya Sen has even redefined development "as a process of expanding real freedoms," including freedom from deprivation and entitlement to education, health, and human rights.[4] Thus, these freedoms become normative markers of the path of development and indicators of social change.

Modernization theories reflect this expansion of the scope of the development discourse by bringing social change to the core of the idea of development. It is a process that transforms human societies technologically, socially, economically, and even environmentally. It results in the application of science and technology to production and management activities to increase efficiency, in the division of labor and occupational specialization, in the restructuring of economic organization, in the emergence of interest-based associations and communities, in constitutional governments (in contrast to hereditary authority), and in knowledge and achievements, rather than family and caste/clan standings determining the status of an individual. These characteristics take the form of tendencies rather than categorical features, thereby making modernization as much a state of becoming as of being.

Modernization initially occurred in Europe and North America, therefore its institutional forms bear a stamp of westernism. It is often used synonymously with the emergence of Western social institutions and cultural practices in a developing country. Yet conceptually modernization is independent of westernization. It is a process of change leading to the promotion of the above-described norms and institutions.

Many modern products and mores were initially forged in Europe and North America. The Western packaging of modern institutions makes their diffusion in the Third World synonymous with the spread of westernism. For example, modern medicine cannot be practiced without hospitals, laboratories, public health laws, and patients' rights. Obviously, there are ready-made Western forms of these institutions and practices which are often deliberately adopted by developing countries. Thus, the adoption of modern technologies and institutions appears to be a process of westernization. Yet the culture of the adopting society modifies and realigns the meanings and functions of such adoptions. That is why modernization is considered more a matter of goals and scope of social change than of particular institutional forms.

Gunnar Myrdal in his seminal study of South Asia, including Pakistan, postulated "modernization ideals" as the criteria for assessing the region's development. These ideals are a set of goals, norms, and attitudes, namely, rationality of decision-making, raising of productivity and levels of living, social and economic equalization, improved institutions and attitudes including efficiency, diligence, orderliness, punctuality, frugality, energetic enterprise, etc.[5] He considers modernization to be qualities suffusing social institutions and economic organizations and not a packaged way of life. These qualities can also be incorporated in traditional social institutions. A society's movement towards these ideals is the measure of its modernization. This is the argument recent modernization theories have begun to advance.

Pakistan's development, since the mid-twentieth century, has substantively transformed social life both through national policies and by people's choices. Led by economic growth, development in Pakistan has promoted modernization on a broad front. Ask a Pakistani about his or her ambitions; the answer invariably will be educating children to be professionals (such as doctors or engineers), having a nice house, and enjoying modern amenities. People count refrigerators, motorbikes, telephones, and television as their proud possessions and symbols of modern living.

This "material" culture is undoubtedly heading towards modernization. It is in matters of nonmaterial institutions and customs that the ideals of modernization may not be fully imbibed or accepted. For example, the modernization of consumption patterns stands in contrast with the strengthening of traditional practices in dowry, gender relations, religious revival, and politics. These divergent trajectories of change in different social institutions make Pakistan's development difficult to fit in linear evolutionary models. In Pakistan, tradition and modernity interweave in myriad ways to propel social change.

Tradition and modernity

Modernization theories envisage societies traversing the path leading from traditional to modern modes of living. Daniel Lerner's phrase "the passing of the traditional society" graphically captures this viewpoint.[6] Yet the development of most postcolonial societies has not followed a straight path. Like Pakistan, most societies found that traditions are very resilient; they evolve and reassert in new forms. Joseph Gusfield debunked the counterposing of tradition and modernity as opposites even in the early days of modernization theories.[7]

Ernest Gellener calls the relationship between traditions and modern institutions "post-traditional" and found that traditions can promote modern advances as much as they can impede the diffusion of modern ideas and practices. Recent theorists of modernization – Clifford Geertz, John Lewis, and Samir Khalaf, for example –

view the relationship between tradition and modernity as dialectical and adaptive and not unidirectional.[8] Certainly, Pakistan's experience bears out that traditions do not just die out in the face of modern forces. They are reinvented and reincorporated to meet new challenges.

Reinvention of tradition and social change

Tradition is not invariably a force of resistance to the ideals of modernization, as it is popularly made out to be. It tends to be conservative in outlook, but under some conditions it can become a platform for inducing the desired change. The outcome depends on the structure of the traditions and the meaning and functions of envisaged change.

Tradition is defined as any human practice, belief, value, institution, or artifact handed down from the past to the present.[9] Undoubtedly, some traditions are more central to a culture than others. Some come down from the distant past and others are transmitted across just one generation. Similarly, some traditions are limited to a particular region or caste/clan, while others are shared by all members of a society. Given all this variety in their make-up and scope, it is obvious that traditions cannot be uniformly contrary to the ideals of modernization. After all, they are the "guide" by which people live.

In fact, traditions are seldom static. Almost every generation reinterprets traditions and invents or constructs rules or practices to inculcate certain values justified on the "'pure" past.[10] Pakistan's Islamic revival (1980s onward) and the USA's evangelic neoconservatism are two examples of reinvented traditions.

All in all, tradition and modernity are neither monolithic structures nor mutually exclusive. They coalesce and collide in several ways. How is Pakistan's drive to modernization resisted and assisted, in different sections of the culture, by traditions? This quest guides our investigation.

Observing the patterns of change

Social change is a continuous phenomenon, sometimes moving imperceptibly for decades and then suddenly bursting out in a revolutionary upheaval. Its flow is usually encapsulated in discrete periods of distinct societal events and pervasive cultural themes. This is the historian's craft of periodization. Our narrative also relies on this technique of organizing observations. The roots of Pakistan's traditional society can be traced to the Indus Valley civilization, but its contemporary form has emerged from the fusion of the cultural influences of Afghan–Mughul and British rules, and the contributions of the nineteenth-century regional regimes of Sikh–Talpur/Mirs and Kalat Confederacy in various parts of present-day Pakistan.

Pakistani society as a social formation came into being in 1947, although its component communities have existed for millennia. The state of Pakistan is the midwife in the birth of Pakistani society. This fact is critical for studying the development of society in Pakistan.

The various phases that characterize the history of the national state also mark distinct periods in the evolution of Pakistani society. Social and cultural changes in Pakistan are intertwined with political and constitutional developments. Thus, our task essentially is to identify the phases through which the state has passed and identify corresponding social and cultural changes.

Periodization of Pakistan's political and social history

In its 55 years of independence, Pakistan has had three long stints of military rule for a total of 26 years. Its elected governments have been coalitions of provincial and ethnic interests gathered in political parties of shifting ideologies and disloyal leaders. In about 29 years of democratic rule, there were 19 prime ministers, some lasting only a few months and others forming governments twice. These cycles of governance, long military rules alternating with elected governments of short tenure, have affected the development of the state and consequently society.

From the sociocultural perspective, Pakistan's history can be divided into three periods. Each period corresponds to particular ideological themes and power configurations of the governments of the time. Furthermore, each period manifests a distinct emphasis on a particular set of values, ideologies, social relations, and citizenship. The three periods are (1) 1947–71, which focused on attempts at nation building and modernization; (2) 1972–7, marked by populist egalitarianism; and (3) 1977–present, a period of Islamization and globalization. In the following sections, the defining characteristics of each period will be described.

Period 1: nation building and modernization – 1947–71

This was the formative period of Pakistan's national society. Two themes define this period: (1) organizing and consolidating both the state and society and (2) modernizing the economy and culture. Underlying both these themes was the goal of building a modern nation.

The period began with the founder and the supreme political leader of the Muslim League, Mr Jinnah, briefly becoming the governor general of the new country. He aimed for a democratic and constitutional state on the European model and a nondenominational society. After struggling for a separate homeland for Muslims, at the moment of his triumph Jinnah articulated for Pakistan the vision of a secular state where "Hindus would cease to be Hindus and Muslims would cease to be Muslims…in the political sense as citizens."[11]

The notion that citizenship is based on territorial and historical bonds and not just on religious affiliations may have lost its authoritative advocate with Jinnah's death in September 1948, but it continued to define social life in Pakistan. In its early years, Pakistan was a pluralist and tolerant society, notwithstanding the bloody communal riots and ousting of minorities in the moral and social breakdown of partition. As an Anderson's "imagined community," Pakistan began its national journey with aspirations of economic and social progress along the path of modernity.[12] Jinnah's secularist enunciations expressed those aspirations. These goals brought the urban professional and "officer" classes to the forefront as the power wielders in the first period of Pakistan's social history.

Pakistan's independence came wrapped in communal riots and the ethnic cleansing of Muslims, Hindus and Sikhs from the parts of the divided Punjab province that had gone to India and Pakistan respectively.[13] Refugees streamed across the newly delineated international border between the two countries, in both directions, leaving behind their homes, farms, and businesses. Almost three million Hindus and Sikhs left Pakistan and in all about five million Muslims came from India to settle in Pakistan. This tragic and momentous exchange of populations shook the foundations of Pakistan's social structure.

Almost overnight, Pakistani Punjab and the cities of Sindh lost most of their middle and upper social strata. Muslim refugees arriving from India were allotted properties left by Hindus and Sikhs in exchange for what they had surrendered in India. These cataclysmic events and consequent migrations churned up the social structure, uprooted local traditions, and eroded community norms. The replacement of Sikh landlords by migrants from East Punjab, for example, resulted in realigning tenant–landowner relations, revising community norms and caste/religion-based division of labor. Similarly, the prestige and status of village elders, based on historic social structure and traditions, had no meaning for refugee youths, resulting in the erosion of social control and community solidarity. It took almost a decade for local communities to restructure and evolve a new normative balance. The increase in social mobility of unprecedented magnitude was the immediate impact of the partition of India and the establishment of Pakistan.

Migration realigned the power structure. At the national level, the leaders of the Muslim League, who were mostly rural landlords and city lawyers, became the ruling elite along with civil and military officers. They espoused liberal values and aspired to modern lifestyles. They lived in bungalow estates in cities, separated from the kinship compounds of old neighborhoods where the majority of the population lived. Their wives and daughters, often, did not observe *Purdah* (the custom of veiling the face) or secluded themselves inside their homes. They pursued material comforts and their personal lives were molded around mores of secular lifestyles. By and large, the example set by the elite in the newly independent Pakistan was that of living in modern ways. Similar expectations were entertained by the masses. Thus Pakistan began its journey of development aiming for modernization and material progress.

The *raison d'être* of Pakistan was to safeguard Muslim political, cultural, and economic interests. The idea of a national state for the Muslim minority in India was interpreted by some leaders as that of establishing a state ruled by Islamic laws. This notion floated around as one of the ideas for the creation of Pakistan. After independence, it surfaced to contest the ideal of a secular national state and society. Conservative Muslims, Islamic political parties, and social movements, which had been defeated by the Muslim League in the decisive elections of 1945, rallied around the "promise" of an Islamic state after independence. Thus, the groundwork was laid for an ongoing contest between the ideals of modernism and the conservative Islamic order in Pakistani society. The social history of Pakistan has been molded by this ideological struggle.

In the first period, Islamists could not come to the forefront. The challenges of building a state from scratch required persons of modern outlook and talents. Most of the Muslim League leaders, although Muslims, were not committed to the creation of a "theocratic state." Yet in the long drawn-out political log-rolling for the constitution of Pakistan, Islamists scored an early victory with the adoption (in 1949) of the Objectives Resolution by the Constituent Assembly. It proclaimed that

> Whereas sovereignty over the entire Universe belongs to Allah Almighty alone... He has delegated sovereignty to the State of Pakistan through its people to be exercised within the limits prescribed by HIM as a sacred trust.

By acknowledging Islamic identity for Pakistan, modernists felt that the constitution could still be based on the principles of a liberal democracy. The making of the constitution became the first battleground among competing political interests and divergent ideas of Pakistan.

Provincial autonomy with decentralization of authority was the logical structure for a country composed of ethnically distinct regions and divided into two separate wings 1,000 miles apart. Yet, national unity and social integration were held to be synonymous with a highly centralized state. Islamic order was viewed as the overarching unifying force that would counter claims of regional autonomy. The idea of Islamic unity became the rationale for proponents of a unitary state. It pitched nationalists and Islamists against advocates of regionalism and a decentralized state. Thus, a near stalemate developed in the process of constitution-making. For the initial ten years, Pakistan experienced periodic constitutional and political crises resulting in unstable governments, unresolved ideological conflicts, ethnic confrontations, and a long hiatus in constitution-making. The constitutional crises alienated the Bengalis of East Pakistan.

Between 1947 and 1958, there were seven changes of government, two suspensions of the Constituent Assembly (national parliament), the demise of the Muslim League as an effective political party, and the rise of civil and military officers as power brokers. Ghulam Mohammad, a finance ministry officer, quickly rose to become the virtual ruler of Pakistan as the governor general in 1951, only four years after independence. From then on, military and civil officers practically ran the government until the break-up of Pakistan in 1971.

By 1958, Pakistan's parliamentary institutions were paralyzed and politicians had been thoroughly discredited. Ayub Khan, the army's commander-in-chief, in collaboration with the governor general, Iskander Mirza, staged a military coup and disbanded the national and provincial assemblies as well as the elected government. Pakistan passed from a parliamentary state to a military dictatorship without much public protest. Military rule was the culmination of the military and civil service officers' drive to take the reins of government and guide the nation's destiny. The military rule initially met with public acceptance. It brought a hope of order and stability after the popular disenchantment with parliamentarians' shifting alliances and frequent changes of government.

From the sociological perspective, the military rule symbolized the triumph of the modernist perspective and centrist state over regional or ethnic interests and traditional Islamic values.[14] The elite civilian and military officers had long regarded politicians as opportunists and parochial, motivated by ethnic or personal interests, and lacking in administrative skills. They viewed themselves as the "steel framework" that held Pakistan together and regarded themselves as qualified for governance and management. Now they took on another mission, namely the economic and social development of the country.

In the second half (1958–71) of period 1, Pakistan's determined attempt to pursue economic development and modernization, was led by the military governments of Ayub Khan, first as martial law administrator and later as an "elected" president backed by the army for ten years (1958–68). During this period, two five-year plans were implemented to promote industrial and agricultural development and accelerate the growth of national income. It was a period of rapid economic growth, averaging about six percent per year growth in GDP, and the emergence of the spirit of "rising expectations" among the masses. New industries developed in cities, agriculture was transformed from a household economy to a miracle seeds- and fertilizer-based enterprise of the "green revolution."

The family planning movement, land reforms, and enactment of social legislation for women's rights initiated modernist thrusts in Pakistani society. Such internal changes were complemented by the increasing American influence in Pakistan's affairs as a result of its joining the US-sponsored regional military alliances. In the early 1960s, Pakistan was a place with a modern feel and Western ambitions under military rule.

As the recent history of Pakistan indicates, it is a country where no victory is complete and no defeat is final. The dominant ethos of one period is displaced in the next by the ideology and outlook that had been cast aside earlier. Yet the wheel turns again in the next round. Also, temperamentally, Pakistanis are irrepressible people. They tire of ineffective, unresponsive, or repressive rulers rather quickly and are not reluctant to give vent to their frustrations through protests and agitations. The first period was an era of the unitary state. The government was highly centralized and both the political andl cultural autonomy of the provinces were subordinated to the authority of the national government.

East Pakistan was peripheral to Pakistan's power structure. The ruling elite viewed the Bengalis' demands for provincial autonomy and economic parity as threats to Pakistan's integrity. The merger of the four provinces of the western wing (one unit) as a counterweight to East Pakistan also brushed aside ethnic identities and regional traditions. The war with India in 1965 aroused feelings of national unity and gave Ayub Khan's military government momentary popularity, but when the political and economic costs of the war came home, people rose in protest bringing down his government and the modernist momentum with it.

After ten years of Ayub's centralist rule, suppressed regional and ethnic interests reasserted themselves. They joined forces with the popular discontent over the increasing social inequalities to bring down the centrist state.

Altogether, the anti-Ayub agitation was a historic event in Pakistan's history. It interrupted the march of modernism and recalibrated the balance between regional communities and national society. It shifted the political power away from civil and military officers to political leaders, although another army chief had to take over immediately to fill the power vacuum left by Ayub's hurried resignation.

General Yahya's two-and-a-half-year rule (1969–71) was an interregnum between the two epochs of Pakistan's history. It was largely a period of undoing the structures and institutions of the unitary state created under Ayub's leadership. The four western provinces were restored. Ayub's 1962 constitution was discarded. Elections for a new assembly were held in 1970, producing two irreconcilable political parties as winners in the two wings of the country. Some social reform legislation, anathema to Islamists, was suspended. Another war with India (1971), following a year of bloody attempts by the army to contain Bengali rebellion, ended in the defeat and dismemberment of Pakistan. East Pakistan became the independent country of Bangladesh. The rump Pakistan emerged as a new country of revised geography, ideology, and social organization.

Period 2: populist egalitarianism 1972–7

Pakistan was remade by the rebellion in East Pakistan and the war with India in 1971. It came out of this conflict a shrunken country, reduced to the four contiguous provinces of its western wing, and a humiliated nation that had lost the war to its historic adversary, surrendering 93,000 soldiers as prisoners of war. Of course, the seeds for this harvest of failures had been planted in Ayub's "decade of development" and even further back by the paralysis of the electoral democracy in the 1950s. The socioeconomic transformations of the first period laid the groundwork for the emergence of new political forces, some reinvigorating the by-passed ideologies and others promoting new interests.

The social agenda of Pakistan had remained crammed with competing ideologies and unresolved issues of economic and political disparities in the 1960s, such as unitary or federal state, elite rule versus the claims of the rising industrial and commercial classes, military/civil officers' versus politicians' roles in governance, Karachi–Punjab domination versus Sindhi/Balochi and Pashtoon representation in national affairs, class conflicts and ethnic disparities, the traditionalists versus modernists divide, and continuing confrontation with India, including the Kashmir question. These persistent questions were complicated by the sharpening social disparities and the skewed distribution of the gains of development.

Ayub's authoritarian government suppressed many of these issues but they simmered below the surface. Zulfiqar Bhutto, Ayub's protégé and favorite minister for almost eight years of his ten-year rule, ignited the simmering discontent into a mass agitation that brought down the military-backed Ayub government (1969).

In Pakistan's history, Ayub's resignation was a seminal event. It established the power of street protests as a check of the last resort on authoritarian, ineffective, or corrupt governments. Elections for the revived assemblies (1970) were followed by Bhutto's emergence as a charismatic leader of Punjab and Sindh, the heartland of the new Pakistan (1971).

The new but reduced Pakistan rose on a wave of people's power ultimately expressed through elections. Bhutto shrewdly seized the opportunity by positioning himself and his Pakistan People's Party (PPP) at the forefront of the people's agitation. His slogan of *roti, kapra, aur makan* (food, clothes, and homes) captured in stark terms the common person's claim to the basic necessities of life. It was a revolutionary idea that extended the meaning of political independence into the economic and social realms. It introduced a new theme in the ideology of Pakistan.

Pakistan's traditional divisions of status and power were questioned and its social structure was shaken. Political parties of all persuasions accepted economic and social justice as a goal. Gone were the days when Maulana Maudoodi, founder of the Jamaat-i-Islami, could say that God made five fingers different from each other and so are humans, all are not equal. Citizens' rights found a place in Pakistan's narrative. Social justice burst into the public consciousness.

Bhutto can be credited for articulating egalitarianism as the promise of a restructured Pakistan. His party's program wove together the diverse religious, economic, and social strands of people's expectations in a catchy slogan: "Islam is our religion, socialism is our creed, and democracy is our system." The second period (1971–7) is essentially an era of Bhutto's rule, ideology, and even whims.

The defeated and dispirited Pakistan of 1971 had to be put together anew. As the leader of the majority party (PPP), Bhutto was thrust into the role of the nation's savior. He christened himself as "Qaid-i-Awam" (supreme leader of the people) echoing the venerated status of Mr Jinnah, the "Qaid-i-Azam." Ironically, Bhutto began his rule as the chief martial law administrator to inherit General Yahya's military government, although soon after he became the president and eventually the prime minister after the unanimous approval of a new constitution of a parliamentary form of government by the national assembly in 1973.

From the sociological and cultural perspectives, period 2 encouraged workers and peasants to assert their rights. Bhutto voiced their deprivations and explicitly favored their needs as citizens of equal standing in the nation. Nevertheless, much of the talk of equality remained just that – a rhetorical flourish – yet these notions caught the people's imagination. The egalitarian spirit of the 1960s infiltrated into Pakistan, installing a new moral economy. People who were almost invisible began to claim entitlement to a fair share of the fruits of independence. New claimants to power and privilege came on the scene and the relative standings of various groups and classes were shaken. The Pakistan People's Party's (PPP's) lower-middle-class cadres became power brokers and appropriated lucrative food distribution agencies (ration depots), public lands, and subsidized housing. All in all, the social structure of Pakistan began to be realigned. A new elite class emerged and the mode of operation in the public realm was redefined.

Driven by the PPP's policies of nationalizing major industries and financial institutions, economic development in this period slowed down initially but picked up pace after 1974 to register an overall GDP growth rate of 4.4 percent per year on average. It was largely propelled by public investments, private investors being apprehensive about nationalization drives, and most of the growth occurred in the service sector. Private entrepreneurs turned to small industries and bazaar (informal) businesses, dividing their assets among family members to remain below nationalization thresholds.

By 1976, access to public authority had become the route to private fortunes. Similarly, public employment expanded turning into another source of patronage for PPP supporters. Social consequences of these structural changes in the economy took the form of divisive fissures within the middle and lower classes between PPP supporters and opponents.

Bhutto cultivated relations with Islamic countries and tilted Pakistan's foreign policy partially away from its long dependence on the USA. Close relations with Iran, the Gulf states, and Libya opened avenues for employment abroad. A steady stream of Pakistani labor started going to these states for jobs. This circulatory migration grew over time to become a major source of foreign exchange earnings and family incomes. The remittances of these workers transformed the social life of villages and towns.

Culturally, vernacular speech and local dress rose in standing and prestige. Sindhi *kurta* (long shirt) and *shalwar* (baggy pants) could be found in places where previously a suit and tie were the prescribed dress. Bhutto himself swapped his Savoy suits and Italian shoes for the Sindhi farmer's attire when he had to address public meetings. Folk music and culture were promoted and patronized. It was no longer uncouth to speak in regional languages in halls of power and culture.

The PPP government under Bhutto had two distinct phases. From 1972 to 1974 was a phase of social reforms. Apart from the new constitution, necessary for the shriveled Pakistan, a series of measures were taken to expand the scope of land reforms, to extend labor rights, to reorganize educational institutions by national-izing private schools and colleges, to bring key industries and banks into public ownership, to promote rural development, and to resettle the landless and squatters. These measures held out the promise that there would be some redressing of the imbalance between the rich and the poor, although the needs of the poor outstripped resources by a long yard. These enactments were emblems of Bhutto's Islamic socialism.

In quick order, a new spirit of individual dignity was infused. A common refrain among the upper classes during those days was, "Bhutto has emboldened the servants." The servants may not have gained much but they certainly were more aware of their rights. Yet this awareness remained largely unfulfilled. It did not translate into tangible gains for the poor. Soon Bhutto's drive for absolute control got the better of his policies. He alienated his supporters and persecuted his opponents. The second half of his regime was devoted to rolling back the spirit of the people's assertiveness that he had ignited.

The second phase of Bhutto's period (1975–7) witnessed a resurrection of Pakistan's persistent contradictions. Small provinces were once again alienated by the federal manipulations of their governments and by military expeditions. Muhajirs (Urdu-speaking migrants from India) and Sindhis rioted against each other's privileges. Ethnic confrontations were precipitated around job quotas, cultural and linguistic rights, and political power. Industrial labor's assertiveness was suppressed with arrests, shootings, suspensions of unions, and political repression. "There were 15 incidents of police firing on striking workers in 1972, 26 in 1973, and 32 in 1974."[15] The security of civil service jobs was removed making public officials vulnerable to political pressures. Mohammad Waseem sums up the thrust of the latter part of Bhutto's era in this observation: "by weakening the old clientele structures ...Bhutto had created a certain 'freeing effect' on the large rural and urban masses whom he subsequently tried to contain through police and other law enforcing agenies."[16]

Thus, what began as a promising era of social and cultural restructuring ended up reinforcing the ethnic, provincial, and class conflicts that had kept Pakistan internally divided and externally dependent. Bhutto's personal and ideological contradictions betrayed a promising social change. Yet one enduring legacy of this period is the incorporation of people's rights and social justice in the national agenda. After Bhutto, no party or leader could expect to gain public support without acknowledging the rights of the poor.

The beginning of the third phase of Pakistan's social evolution can be conveniently marked with the end of Bhutto's regime, although the era of populist egalitarianism had begun to unwind much earlier. Bhutto quickly amassed a large debt of alienation and opposition with his combative approach. Family entrepreneurs and bazaar merchants were angered by the nationalization of flour, rice, and cooking oil mills (1976). Pashtoons, Muhajirs, and Balochs had been in a veritable revolt against his repressive policies. The military felt manipulated by his interference in its internal organization and by his attempts to create a parallel security force. The left-leaning members of his own party were persecuted for opposing his tilt towards landlords and notables. Professionals and public officials resented their loss of job security and subordination to the party cadres.

All in all, Bhutto's espousal of the common people's welfare, although inspiring, was counterbalanced by his authoritarian ways. The social forces engendered by his poorly executed reforms provoked reactions from contending interests. The egalitarian thrust and modernist outlook were trumped by the hostility of the middle classes, ethnic minorities, and the disappointed working poor.

These diverse groups rallied together under the banner of Islamic order to form an electoral alliance, Pakistan National Alliance (PNA), for the national elections (March 1977). The elections ended in dispute and confusion. About four months of street protests and mass agitation gave the military an excuse to stage a coup. General Zia-ul-Haq, Bhutto's handpicked chief of the army, overthrew him and installed the third martial law government in Pakistan's history on July 5, 1977. This was the counterrevolution to the radicalism of the 1960s.

Period 3: reinvented traditions, Islamization, and globalization – 1977–present

The military government of General Zia gave another spin to the wheel of Pakistan's ideology. It set sights on establishing the Nizam-i-Mustafa (The Prophet's order), promising Islamization of Pakistani society and state. Thus began the third phase of Pakistan's social history, which continues to the present, melding traditions with Islamic precepts, with varying intensity and purpose.

The third period is characterized by a tilt towards the conservative ethos of the Islamic order on the one hand, and increasing integration of Pakistani society in the global circulation of people, technology, and finance, on the other. Just as the preceding period was defined by populist rhetoric about people's rights, this period was an era of neotraditionalism and the military's domination over national affairs.

The PNA's agitation proved to be the spark that lit the fuse on the simmering discontent of businessmen and the dispossessed industrialists. This bazaar coalition of traders, upper, and some sections of urban middle classes brought down Bhutto's regime and revived military rule. These groups, petite bourgeoisie in Marxist terms, were conservative in outlook but pragmatic in approach. They demanded law and order and wanted to preserve the traditional social hierarchy, yet they had no reservations about adopting modern material progress.

The third period has been imprinted with General Zia's overriding concern to maintain his rule and invest the military with controlling authority in Pakistan's affairs. Given the modernist orientation of the army, Zia was expected to be a promoter of modernism.[17] Yet as his promised 90 days' rule stretched to ten years, he sought legitimacy for his rule by casting himself in the role of the builder of the promised Islamic order.

A two-pronged approach combining punitive provisions of orthodox Islamic jurisprudence and market-oriented economic and social policies constituted General Zia's Islamic system. The goal of enacting Islamic order was also the justification for suppressing dissent and discouraging demands for democracy. The Hudood Ordinance (1979) instituted stoning, flogging, and amputations as punishments for drinking, thefts, adultery, etc., although such medieval punishments were not applied in practice. By putting them on the books, General Zia earned the support of conservative Islamists and repressed any dissent. A parallel legal code and judicial system, called *Sharia laws* (Islamic jurisprudence) was introduced. Islamic wealth tax (Zakat) and farm levy (Usher) were legislated (1979). The law of evidence was amended, reducing a woman's evidence in financial transactions to half the weight of a man's. The Ahmadis, a much-maligned Muslim sect that had been legislated to be non-Muslims, initially by Bhutto in his desperation to establish his Islamic credentials, were further prohibited from practicing any Islamic rituals. The unfolding Islamic order was harsh on women and minorities.

General Zia's regime reprivatized nationalized industries and banks. With economic and financial incentives, it fostered a new group of entrepreneurs who became stakeholders in the new social order. Out of this new class have come the industrial-political houses of Nawaz Sharif, the Chaudhries (of Gujarat), and General Akhtar's family, who, in the span of a few years, joined the ranks of the super-rich in Pakistan. Military rank and connections became the currency of influence and privilege.

During General Zia's regime (1978–88), the military came to be the dominant social institution in Pakistani society and state. Its budget became the single largest item in national expenditure. Military officers, both retired and in active service, were regularly inducted into the civil administration, and retired military personnel were entitled to about 33 percent of the jobs in the lower ranks of public agencies. The military acquired choice urban lands to distribute among its officers. Mohammad Waseem comments that "the Zia regime was the first truly military regime in Pakistan...it wholly depended on the military...and showered patronage on its personnel to offset the absence of any support base in the wider society."[18]

During Zia's regime, international events also favored the rise of Islamic groups and conservative ideologies. Afghanistan exploded into a communist coup, which in turn led to Soviet Russia's invasion. This gave an opportunity to the USA to "bleed" Russians in a guerrilla war turning Afghanistan into their "Viet Nam." Pakistan became the strategic partner of the US and turned into a base for Afghan Mujahideen (holy warriors). This role sustained General Zia's regime and strengthened the Islamists' positions in Pakistani society.

The Soviet invasion and the civil war that followed its retreat from Afghanistan in 1988 sent waves of Afghan refugees to Pakistan. Thus began the intertwining of Pakistan and Afghanistan's political and social destinies, sometimes bringing them closer and at others pulling them apart, and mutually reinforcing each other's traditional proclivities.

Another social impact of Pakistan's involvement in Afghanistan has been the virtual fading of the border between the two countries and the flow back of drugs, criminals, guns, and zealots into Pakistan. All this traffic started in General Zia's regime and continued under Benazir Bhutto and Nawaz Sharif's "democracies" right up to the third round of military rule under General Musharraf (1999). The Afghan war fostered Jihadi culture and militant orthodoxy in Pakistani society.

Pakistan's ideological swings did not result in enduring victories of one set of ideas over others. Ideologies remained largely on the rhetorical plane, whereas daily life and social institutions continued to function in their set ways. The ideological order of the day, Zia's Islam or Bhutto's socialism, essentially captured public space and privileged its supporters.

The idea of instituting an Islamic order was one of the themes in Pakistan's nationalism. Zia's military rule hitched itself to this theme and aligned itself with Jamaat-i-Islami and Islamic priests. By 1978, the military's intellectual orientations had changed. Its modern outlook had worn off. It had been imbued with the spirit of Muslim nationalism regarding itself as the defender of Islamic ideology. Its officers came from the ranks of the emerging middle/lower-middle classes, largely of the rural northwestern Punjab and NWFP. They grew up with vernacular beliefs and Islamic ideals,[19] yet also aspired to modern lifestyle and material progress. They tended to be conservative with strong Islamic colorations but their career ambitions and expectations of living conditions were modern.

The third period fortuitously coincided with the oil-induced economic growth of the Gulf states. Pakistan's workers and professionals found jobs in the Middle Eastern countries and thus further increased the circulatory migration of expatriates. Their remittances lifted the rate of economic development in Pakistan. GDP growing at more than 6 percent per year in the period 1978–88. The manufacturing sector expanded at the phenomenal rate of 8–9 percent per year, primarily stimulated by the demand for consumer goods. The Afghan war and the flow of American aid also stimulated the economy. Pakistan was turning into a consumer society, particularly under the influence of remittances.

Television sets adorned village homes that did not have electricity, restaurants appeared in small towns where none existed before, cars began to choke cities. A segment of society led a life of opulence, although little impact was made on mass poverty. All in all, the period of Zia's rule witnessed Pakistani society operating on two different tracks. At the rhetorical and symbolic plane, it tilted towards the Islamic and vernacular ethos, while in social practice and in life routines it was driven by consumerism and material advancement. This duality began under Zia's rule and it has become a defining condition of contemporary Pakistan.

Politically the third period has been an era of military rule, directly and indirectly. Yet the duality of Pakistan's value structures permeates political institutions too. Despite the dominance of the military and the pull towards absolutism, the drive for democracy and representative rule has been irrepressible. Zia's Islamic punishments, lashings, hangings, and *Qisas* (pre-emption) did not deter popular protests. His attempts to transform Pakistan from "a congeries of conflicting mindsets and regional societies into the solitary community...(of)...an Islamic State" ran into popular opposition.[20]

By 1981, three years after Zia's coup, the country began to stir with demands for elections. True to Pakistan's history, an alliance of almost all political parties called the "movement for restoration of democracy" (MRD) was formed. It launched a protest movement that fizzled out after a few marches and arrests in major cities but caught fire in the towns of Sindh, where Sindhi youth were chafing against the federal government's domination. Thus began a cycle of protests that led to the civilianization of the martial law government through elections from which political parties were kept out, leading to a new National Assembly (1985) and installation of Mohammad Khan Junejo as prime minister.

Another military government had gone through the full circle and was heading to its culmination due to popular discontent. General Zia's tragic death in an air accident (August 1988) brought military rule to an abrupt but not unanticipated end. Before his death, Bhutto's political heir, his daughter Benazir Bhutto, had returned (1986) to Pakistan from exile and was given rousing receptions by large crowds wherever she went. Pakistan was ready for another round of democracy.

The democracy that returned to Pakistan after General Zia's death was not entirely free from military overlordship. Its domain was laid out by the military and its policies were subject to the army's veto. Military's direct or indirect involvement in the governance of Pakistan is one of the defining features of the third period, although nominally the country had elected governments for 11 years. These 11 years (1988–99) witnessed four national elections (1988, 1990, 1993, and 1997) and four elected governments, the tenure of each being cut short by the reigning president and the military. Benazir Bhutto, the chairperson of the PPP, alternated with Nawaz Sharif, a Zia protégé and the leader of the Pakistan Muslim League (PML), as the prime minister and the leader of the house in the National Assembly.

Through elections, both had parliamentary majorities and formed the government twice, one succeeding the other, and in each case their governments were dismissed and the elected assemblies terminated on charges of corruption and mismanagement. Pakistan's democratic politics in this period revolved around personal vendettas, ethnic and provincial rivalries, featherbedding and conspiring with the military against rivals. The democratic period was consumed by the confrontation between the PPP and PML, which also became a personal battle between their respective leaders, Benazir and Nawaz.[20]

From the social perspective, there was little to distinguish between the two parties. The PPP had its roots in the populist appeal to working classes, although its leadership was largely made up of rural landlords and big city lawyers. Benazir even modified the party's socialist rhetoric to win acceptance by the military establishment and the USA.

The PML had a long history of being a party of the rural elite and urban salariat class.[21] In Pakistan, the military rulers often reinvigorated it when they needed a political platform to give a civilian face to their governments.

Nawaz Sharif came on the political scene as General Zia's strap in Punjab. His party, the PML, represented the interests of urban businessmen and industrialists hurt by Bhutto's nationalization policies. The PML became the voice of the Punjab but it expanded its social base by espousing the interests of small businessmen and owner farmers and industrialists. Both parties looked to the same social classes for support, although the PPP was identified with the rural constituencies and the PML with the urban. The PPP was said to be Sindhi in origin, whereas the PML was Punjabi in identity. The two parties differed only marginally in their social class characteristics, but represented different segments of the same classes.

Ideologically, Nawaz Sharif's PML is conservative in outlook and supports the market economy and Islamic values. Benazir's PPP is historically a left-of-center party which appeals to the salaried and rural middle classes, although its leadership is increasingly made up of landlords and heads of rural clans. It combines a modernization agenda with indigenous spiritual and cultural symbols. Their differences are more of style than substance, indicative of the narrow differentiations of interests and ideology.

The democratic phase of the third period was a time of economic slowdown, partially the result of a global recession of the early 1990s. After a rocky start, Benazir's first government managed to pick up the pace of economic development. The momentum it created was built upon by the successor government of Nawaz Sharif, which expanded the scope of privatization and gave more incentives to investors. Thus, the overall rate of economic growth during 1988–98, the seventh- and eighth-plan periods, reached the range of 4–5 percent per year.

Yet both regimes were mired in corruption and accused of appropriating public resources for the benefit of their supporters. Nawaz Sharif's "yellow cab" scheme and Benazir's "green tractors" program are examples of policy measures, ostensibly aimed at stimulating economic entrepreneurship, which actually ended up benefitting their parties' clients. Defaulting on loans from public sector banks, cooperative societies, and investment institutions became a well-honed way of encashing public influence and rewarding cronies. These measures may have bought a temporary respite from economic recession but they contributed to the inflation of the national debt. Cumulatively, the economic policies of the two parties have further divided the middle and upper classes by political and personal loyalties. A culture of grab-and-own has been institutionalized by this competition to build party support.

Interestingly, Islamization was the inheritance of the PML, particularly Nawaz Sharif. Benazir Bhutto tended to be a bit liberal in her social policies and political symbolism. Yet, the PPP struck an alliance with the Jamiat Ulema-e-Islam (JUI) during the second round of its government (1996), and sponsored the Taliban in Afghanistan. Nawaz Sharif canceled the designation of Friday as the weekly holiday (that had been introduced by Zulfiqar Bhutto to appease the Islamists) because "it was an obstacle for importers and exporters." Yet, when he wanted to clip the power of parliamentary opposition and the military, he introduced the Shariat Bill, which would have concentrated all powers in his hands as the head of government, making him, and any future head, an authoritarian caliph. Islamization has served as much as an instrument of political advancement deployed strategically to promote party and personal interests as an ideological goal.

The third period was capped by another coup (1999), which was staged by the chief of army staff (COAS) General Pervaiz Musharraf. The military, which had played the role of kingmaker and arbiter of political contests during the democratic phase lasting from 1988 to 1999, took power by disposing of Nawaz Sharif's second parliamentary government. Major differences of policy emerged between the military under General Musharraf's command and Nawaz Sharif's government. A lightning attempt by Nawaz Sharif to remove General Musharraf as the COAS was foiled by the military, which countered by arresting the prime minister and removing him from power. Thus, another round of direct military rule began in 1999.

Under General Musharraf, the political pendulum swung again towards modernist symbols. Musharraf began his rule with the promise of reforming governmental institutions, reducing crime, violence, intolerance and, most of all, recovering misappropriated public wealth and holding the corrupt to accountability. He reinvigorated Pakistan's alliances with the USA and joined its coalition against terrorism and provided facilities for America's war on the Afghan Taliban. All these policies meant pulling back from the conservative bent of the Islamization process. Modernist nongovernmental organizations (NGOs) were brought forward as promoters of social reforms. Yet Musharraf's modernism did not last very long.

The politics of elections caught up with this modernist push. The national elections of 2002, meant to bring back "cleansed democracy," resulted in the emergence of a coalition of Islamic parties as the third largest bloc in the parliament and in their taking over the provincial governments of NWFP and Balochistan. The strong showing of Islamists in elections is indicative of deepening social divisions and divergent ideological and cultural pulls in Pakistan.

Overall, the third period has three features that lend it a certain degree of unity as a historical phase. First, it is an era of the institutionalization of the military's direct domination of government institutions and economy. Second, it is a period that has seen the revivalist thrust in national ideology and culture. Third, it has been a time of accelerating modernization of the material base. The society has been pulled into the global network, specifically by the expansion of the Pakistani diaspora and the increasing circulation of expatriates. Another link into global networks is Pakistan's dependence on foreign loans and international agencies.

Dance of change

The three periods marking distinct phases of the political and social history of Pakistan point out a rhythmic interplay of continuity and change. The path traced by the historical evolution is that of one step forward and another sideways, a thrust toward modernity in one period and the pull of tradition in another. This is the dominant pattern of social change, but not all aspects of social life have been affected equally, nor have all communities, regions, and classes experienced change to the same extent. With this caveat, one can identify some persistent trends of sociocultural change in Pakistan.

- People have embraced the goal of material well-being. Regardless of their beliefs and traditions, they readily adopt new technologies, particularly those bringing convenience and pleasure. This is an uninterrupted trend across the three periods.
- The shifts in the state's ideology and organization result in a realignment of the power structure, favoring some groups and classes and reducing the influence of others. Corresponding to the changes in government and ideology, there is some shift in people's expectations and beliefs.
- Some social institutions have changed more rapidly than others. Overall, the material culture has continued to change towards modernism, while the non-material aspects have witnessed a grafting of modern forms onto traditional functions and meanings.
- Islamic themes were woven into the conception of Pakistan's nationalism. They remained largely on the symbolic plane of Pakistan's public sphere during periods 1 and 2, although Islam as a religious and spiritual institution continued to be a critical element of national culture and people's identity. Yet in the third period, it has become an instrument of inventing traditions and reorganizing social life. The modernizing thrust of the early periods is yielding to invigorated Islamic ideology and practices in public space and daily life.
- Among other secular trends that span the three periods are increasing mobility, expanding integration in global networks, a greater differentiation of social classes, and the reinvention of traditions.

The three periods reflect a dialectical process between traditional society and modern technologies and practices. They delineate the broad contours of Pakistan's social history and provide a framework for the analysis of specific social institutions and cultural practices.

3   Landscape of independence

Introduction

Land is an ancient, nay original, creation. However, it is fluid and changing, being the imprint of human activities on physical space. Pakistan's landscape, like any other country's, is rooted in the lie of its land that ranges from snow-capped mountains, river valleys, and stony plateaus, to sandy deserts and coastal mangroves. Land links the landscape to its prehistoric past, but current human activities, both individual and collective, build on this base to produce landscapes characteristic of a particular time. Independence is a defining moment in the history of Pakistan's landscape.

The advent of independence in 1947 has ushered in population growth, people's mobility, political change, and economic as well as technological development on such a scale that Pakistan's landscape is "new" for all intents and purposes. In the past few decades, the physical space has been so extensively reorganized that Hindus and Sikhs, who migrated to India on partition, would find little familiar if they were to return. It is a landscape largely made after 1947.

One or many landscapes?

Is Pakistan's landscape a singular unit or a plurality of environments? The answer to this question revolves around the geography of Pakistan as a nation state and an economy. Although Pakistan is a country of distinct ethnocultural regions and a territory of divergent natural features, it increasingly functions as a unit whose various parts dovetail with each other to form a coherent habitat. On this basis, there is justification to view various regions as parts of an integrated landscape of hierarchical structure, ranging from local communities, regions of distinct ecology, and provinces to the national space.

Physiographically, Pakistan can be divided into two broad parts: the western and northern highlands, and the Indus plains.[1] Each of these parts can be further delineated into regions of distinct topography, climate, geology and ecology, such as the Karakoram and northern Himalayas, Sofad Koh and Waziristan Hills, the Balochistan Plateau, Upper and Lower Indus valleys, Punjab's Doabs, the Thar Desert, etc. Ethnolinguistic differences overlay these physiographic variations to create a mosaic of landscapes which is stitched together by the Indus River, its tributaries and irrigation canals, roads, railways, electric grid, and gas pipelines. A national network of cities, villages, and their interconnecting linkages has emerged to anchor the regional environmental systems. A pipeline blows up in Balochistan and cooking stoves in the Punjab are extinguished. Or, a lean season of snowfall in the Himalayas signals a year of parched fields in Sindh. Such are the manifestations of the interdependencies of Pakistan's landscape.

Landscape: the historical bases

Pakistan's historical image is that of vast dusty plains baked by the summer heat, dotted with muddy villages, interspersed with walled cities and crowded towns along historic caravan routes. The cool and forested Kashmir mountains and the dry and rocky highlands and hills of North Western Frontier Province (NWFP) and Balochistan form protective walls on the north and west of the plains. The latter, particularly, support tribal societies and self-ruling communities that have fascinated anthropologists and adventurers for the independence and bravery of their people.

Historically, cultivation was largely limited to the flood plains of rivers, whose banks were lined with wildwoods and bush-forming corridors of wilderness linking the mountains of Kashmir with river valleys. Up to the middle of the nineteenth century, lions could be hunted in these forests, even near the capital city of Lahore. Now it would be hard to find a partridge in these areas! All in all, Pakistan was a land of agrarian and pastoral communities sprinkled over flat and largely sandy plains, whose dryness was relieved in part by the rivers spilling out in summer from the snow melt of the Himalayas and by the annual monsoon rains.

Before the British conquest of Sindh and Punjab in 1843 and NWFP in 1849, the landscape of Pakistan changed so slowly that it appeared to be frozen in time. Invasions, floods, shifts in river courses, famines, or droughts would ravage farms, depopulate villages and towns, and disrupt trade, but then as their effects wore off, life returned to its historical roots.

British rule brought an unprecedented regime of civil and criminal laws, land settlement, local administration, and steam technology, which resulted in a major reorganization of the landscape. One of the world's largest canal networks was built in the Indus plains to irrigate barren lands; it started in the 1860s, and continued up to 1930 when the Sukkur barrage in Sindh was completed. The area thus irrigated was distributed among farmers brought in from far-off districts. Roads and railways were built to connect villages and market towns with major urban centers and ports. In sum, the ecology, settlement pattern, and land tenure of the whole country were drastically reorganized.

The Indus plains became the granary of India. In central Punjab, and upper Sindh, green fields replaced the hard scrabble. This agrarian landscape, fringed by rocky plateaus and mountainous valleys, was the heartland of Pakistan at the time of independence. Pakistan started its historical life with the imagery of a land of wheat fields and tight-knit villages, whose cities and towns were peripheral to its legends and memories.

Social geography at independence

The population of Pakistan in the year of independence was about 30 million. This is an estimate, falling as 1947 does in the middle of the decennial census period. The more accurate count of the national population was provided by the 1951 census, totaling 33.7 million with 82 percent living in rural areas and only about 18 percent residing in urban places that could be as small as towns of 2,500, provided they were incorporated as local governments. A visiting American professor's impressions of Pakistan in the 1950s are of a "village centred-land .... (whose) villages, however small in population, are internally as crowded as the bazaars of Lahore and Karachi."[2]

A village historically has been a self-contained community. It produced wheat, maize, cotton, or other agricultural products; its resident artisans supplied tools and implements to farmers, made cloth and shoes, built houses, and matched marriageable couples. Most large village communities, or clusters of small villages, had their own carpenters, blacksmiths, weavers, masons, and other hereditary occupational castes living and working in the local area.

A village economy operated internally on the customarily defined exchanges of produce and services among its members, although some mutual payments for goods and services, not regulated by the stipulated exchanges, were not uncommon. The occupational divisions coincided with social differentiations in clans and castes. Within villages, households of a clan or caste lived in close proximity, forming tight quarters. Village communities in irrigated plains are relatively large and closely spaced. In the sparsely populated dry lands of NWFP and Balochistan, villages are small and submerged in tribal territorial community and economy. These two provinces also have nomadic and migratory communities, moving with seasons from highlands to plains. Sindh's goths (village offshoots) tend to be small but customarily linked with neighboring communities to form a tribal or caste cluster.

Strategically located in the networks of villages are towns serving as commercial, administrative, religious, and spiritual centers for surrounding regions. The British divided provincial territories into administrative districts and subdivisions called *tehsils* (approximately equal to counties in size) and designated centrally located towns as headquarters of these jurisdictions. *Tehsils* and *talukas* were subdivisions within a regional district for administrative and public service purposes. District capitals and *tehsil* and *taluka* centers emerged as second- and third-tier urban settlements. Gradually, schools, colleges, hospitals, and courts opened in these places. Landlords from surrounding areas started to build second homes in these towns to be close to public officials. Commercial activities also converged on these towns, invigorating their bazaars and markets.

The provincial capitals and a few nascent industrial and commercial centers formed the top layer of the urban hierarchy. In 1951, there were only nine cities of 100,000 or more population in Pakistan. Lahore was the premier city, a provincial capital and cultural as well as education center. Development gathered momentum in Karachi after independence. On being designated as the national capital, this port city quickly became the commercial and industrial hub of the new country.

Although Pakistan was predominantly a rural country, it had a fairly well organized urban system, particularly in the plains of Punjab and Sindh. The sparsely populated NWFP and Balochistan lagged behind in urbanization. In 1951, about 88 percent of the population of these two provinces lived in villages, whereas for Sindh and Punjab, this proportion was 71 and 82 percent respectively.

Sindh made a head start in urbanization, as Karachi drew large numbers of refugees from India, many migrating with the transfer of federal ministries from Delhi. The population in the city exploded, turning it into the first city in Pakistan with one million people. Immigrants coming to Punjab were mostly Punjabi Muslims from India who replaced departing Hindus and were dispersed in villages and cities. Yet Lahore and Faisalabad took off as the commercial and industrial poles of the province.

Pakistan gave the impression of a wide open land in early years after independence, despite its network of villages, towns, and cities. A train ride out of Lahore or Rawalpindi, in the heartland of Punjab, revealed vast swaths of fields and fallow tracts with few human figures visible across the horizon. Travel to Karachi meant coming out of a train at the end, bathed in desert sand. Open country and wilderness were part of the lore of the land and not alien to the people of urban areas either. Poetry celebrated the purity of country life and romanticized the sincerity of village relations. The landscape of Pakistan's imagination idealized the peace and romance of village life.

Pakistan is a country of pluralist traditions. Each of its provinces has a distinct mix of languages and ethnic stocks. There are numerous dialects, changing almost every hundred miles.

Independence brought refugees from India who were linguistically and ethnically different from the original residents of the receiving regions. This process further extended the diversity of population and patterns of living, particularly in Sindh and Punjab. It also laid bases for the ethnic strife in the competition for jobs, political power, and state patronage. Immigrants to Karachi transformed it from a Sindhi port city to an Urdu-speaking metropolis, triggering feelings of distrust between Sindhis and Muhajirs (as the Urdu-speaking refugees from India came to be known). Sindh's ethnic and linguistic split has aligned along the urban–rural divide. Muhajirs have spread out in cities and Sindhis continue to dominate in villages and towns.

Balochistan is a multicultural province divided into regions dominated by Balochs, Barohis, Pashtoons, Jats, and small clusters of other ethnic minorities. In the 1980s, the province received a large number of Afghan refugees, tilting the demographic and social balance toward Pashtoons in northern and central districts and injecting a conservative Islamic ethos among easygoing, although tradition-bound, tribal communities.

Punjab's diversity of dialects, Saraiki and Pothohari contrasting with the heartland Punjabi, was striking at the time of independence. Since then, the increased mobility of population and the absorption of refugees from India have stimulated homogenizing tendencies both linguistically and ethnically. NWFP, although symbolically a Pashtoon region, is also a province of many ethnicities and languages, for example, Hindku-speaking people inhabit the Peshawar Valley and

Hazara district, and Saraiki speakers are found in the Derajats. All in all, Pakistan inherited a landscape of many social and ecological hues. How have the economic and social changes of the past decades affected this pluralism? This question is addressed in this chapter as well as those to follow.

National development and landscape

Independence made an immediate imprint on the landscape of the nation. Millions moved across the newly drawn border between India and Pakistan, repopulating abandoned farms and villages and crowding the towns. Karachi and Lahore had their first wave of squatter colonies, known as *katchi abadis* (temporary settlements), lining major roads and occupying public parks immediately after independence. The misery and sufferings created by the partition were palpably reflected in the plight of the homeless. The middle- and upper-class refugees, although resettled in abandoned Hindu and Sikh properties, pined for their ancestral homes and communities. Pakistan's human habitat began its historic journey with the pain of abandonment and challenges of reconstructing community life.

Refugee Rehabilitation, as it was officially called, was the process that ushered in the first wave of changes in Pakistan's landscape. It redrew property lines by adjusting refugees' claims of properties left in India against the abandoned farms, homes, and businesses of Hindus and Sikhs. It spawned new developments, such as satellite towns, housing estates, and planned suburbs around major cities. Karachi's Pir Ilahi Bux Colony, Rawalpindi's Satellite Town, and Hyderabad's People's Colony are examples of the new idiom of urban expansion forged by the demands of resettlement.

The developmental and modernization thrust of period 1 (1947–71) was based on the notion of bountiful natural resources that only need to be scientifically exploited. This notion translated in further tapping of rivers for new irrigation canals and hydroelectric works. Jinnah (1947), Taunsa (1958), Kotri (1957), Warsak (1961), and Gaddu (1962) barrages were built in quick succession. These barrages diverted river waters into canals that transformed the desert of Thal and the dry lands of southwestern Punjab and lower Sindh into lush farms.

Yet the most striking changes in the landscape came with the dams and irrigation canals built under the Indus Water Treaty of 1960 between India and Pakistan. The treaty was negotiated with the mediation of the World Bank to resolve the water-rights dispute between Pakistan and India. Pakistan was given exclusive rights over the waters of three rivers, the Indus, Jhelum, and Chenab, while ceding the waters of Ravi, Beas, and Sutlej to India. This treaty necessitated the building of eight link canals to feed water from the western rivers into the irrigation network drawing on the rivers allocated to India. It also led to the building of two large dams for the storage of water, namely Mangla and Tarbela, which were completed in 1968 and 1982 respectively.

Tarbela is said to be the largest earth dam in the world, storing 11 million acre-feet of water. With about half of Tarbela's storage capacity, Mangla is still among the big dams of the world. Dams represent a shift in Pakistan's historic water management approach, which has been based on barrages that merely divert river water to canals without large-scale storage, whereas dams have big lakes to store summer snowmelts for winter irrigation. They realign the contours of the land and affect the ecology of the whole country.

The storage lakes of Tarbela and Mangla have inundated valleys far back in the mountains and displaced thousands of people from their farms and villages. These lakes are a new experience for people from the plains who are unaccustomed to vistas of large bodies of water. These dams are also sites of major hydroelectric generating stations, which have lit up villages and towns even in remote areas and have laced the country with hydro lines.

Yet the dams also hold back the nourishing soil that Indus and Jhelum used to bring down from the Himalayas to enrich the lands along their paths. Without the replenishing of soils, Pakistan's farmland is increasingly becoming dependent on chemical fertilizers. The lakes are slowly silting up, heading toward the loss of the dams' storage capacity. The dammed rivers, Indus and Jhelum, present a sad spectacle. These mighty rivers, associated with legends of heroism and romance, have been reduced to limping streams and shallow pools.

To finish the story of the changes in the countryside due to water and agricultural development, the programs of periods 2 and 3 may be briefly recalled. After Tarbela, no big dam has been built. The second period, distinguished by the populist ideology of the Bhutto regime, witnessed the re-emergence of provincial and regional interests. The first period's centrally directed thrust for development began to break into regionally focused projects in the second period. It turned out to be the era of small dams and regional irrigation systems, for example, Bolan-Nari dam irrigated about 25,000 acres; Hub dam 85,000 acres; Tanda, Gomal, and Khanpur dams in NWFP also irrigated on similar scales. The same strategy has continued up to the present, although plans for Kalabagh and Basha dams have been on the books for almost two decades.

The changing face of the land

Although the four provinces have steadily become more interdependent for water, power, gas, transportation, and communication, they have persistent disagreements about the distribution of water and power. After 1971, it became difficult to pursue a national plan for resource development. The proposal for Kalabagh dam has been stymied on account of NWFP and Sindh's opposition, largely based on the perceived advantages for Punjab. It has not passed the stage of "studies." Even the military governments of the third period have not been able to break the deadlock among the provinces for forging a consensus about proposals for new dams. Pakistan is now faced with acute water and electricity shortages, yet a national strategy for developing these resources cannot be forged. The National Water Distribution Agreement (1991) has virtually collapsed. Outages of electricity supply and shortages of water occur frequently in cities and villages. The landscape of Pakistan has evolved from pastoral harmony to the turbulence of rising expectations and regional disparities.

Other development programs have also left their marks on the land. Initially discovered in Sui, Balochistan (1952), natural gas has become the primary domestic and industrial fuel in much of the country. A network of gas fields, pipelines, pumping stations, and storage depots has sprung up across the country. Factories and industrial estates dot the pipeline routes, injecting urban sights, blights, and smells amidst rural prospects.

The populist thrust of the second period favored the building of farm-to-market roads, thus spreading the transportation grid into remote areas. The Karakoram highway linked upper Himalayan valleys to the plains and opened a land route to China. It has had a dramatic impact on the settlement pattern of Gilgit, Chitral, and Hunza valleys. Homes and hotels have sprouted on the lofty Himalayas. Trees have been felled to clear the land for expanding villages and hamlets, leaving the mountains denuded.

Baloch tribes initially resisted the construction of roads through their territories, but the army action of 1973–4 opened the way for the construction of roads in the Sibi and Kalat districts. In the third period, the building of roads picked up pace in the province, partially to facilitate the movement of Afghan Mujahideen and refugees. A coastal road links together fishing communities and connects them to Karachi. In 1992, the construction of the first national motorway began in Punjab, marking another major step in the restructuring of space. Now Islamabad, the national capital, and Lahore are more accessible to each other than they are to some of the villages around both cities. Motorways are being built up to Peshawar and Faisalabad.

Economic and social development since independence has changed the face of the land. Gone is the somnolent agrarian look of the countryside, except in some remote areas. The hum of activity and whirl of movement pervades almost all across the land but it is more palpable in the Peshawar–Lahore–Karachi triangle. This change has come with many environmental costs: deforestation of the land; pollution of rivers, canals, and groundwater; degradation of farm land with salinity and chemicals; and the loss of agricultural land. Finally, there is a somber realization that natural resources are finite. At the beginning of the twenty-first century, Pakistan is beginning to bump into scarcities of water and farmland.[3] Yet its population is forecast to grow to about 227 million by 2020, a 60 percent increase in 18 years. It is a crowded land, particularly in the plains, which will become a crammed habitat.

Contours of inequality

Land rights define the fortunes of people in agrarian societies. Who owns the land and what rights do owners, tenants, or workers have to use land and enjoy its fruits? These norms determine their respective social status and economic well-being. Historically, Pakistan's social structure has been based on its land tenure system.

From ancient times, a king or conqueror was the ultimate owner of all lands, although his authority was delegated to appointed chiefs who collected the king's share of the produce and ruled over peasants. By the eighth century AD, Arabs and later Afghans conquered Sindh, Balochistan, and Punjab. They maintained the institution of local chiefs and grafted Islamic laws onto the customary land tenures. The chiefs could be hired and fired at a king's pleasure. They combined the functions of local rulers and king's assignees for land management. Yet, peasants and cultivators were mostly attached to land as part of village communities. In some areas, whole villages or caste groups were the collective owners of land.

The British organized an ownership-based land tenure system on these historic foundations. They conferred proprietary rights of settled land on individuals, and in some areas on families or clans collectively, as in NWFP and Balochistan, where tribes became the communal owners. Furthermore, the British land settlement also recognized inheritable tenancies with defined rights and obligations for peasant cultivators. The state's share was limited to prescribed land revenue assessed periodically by district officials. The ownership of waste and common lands was assumed by the state. The historical role of the *jagirdar* (local chief) as a revenue collector was extinguished, although loyal clan and tribal leaders were given *jagirs* as gifts, exempt from land revenue and other taxes, with limited powers to control tenants on their estates.

Zamindars (owners of estates) could be cultivator owners or have peasants as hereditary tenants with defined rights and obligations. Lands in the NWFP were parceled out among tribes, which divided their estates among *khels* (clans), whose members had equal shares of land to farm. Periodically, a *khel* may redistribute lands (the custom being called *vesh*) among its members to equalize the quality and size of farm holdings.[4] Yet, in settled areas, private ownership of land emerged as the common tenure.

Pakistan inherited a land tenure system where the size of estate became the defining criterion of the status and power of landowners. Large estates could have two layers of inheritable rights, one of owners and the other of cultivators and tenants. The rights and obligations of owners versus tenants vary from province to province and region to region, but generally the tenants are subservient to landlords economically and politically. In the same vein, owner cultivators of small farms rank lower in status and power than big landowners. There are many regional variations from this simplified model. In Sindh, *zamindars* have large holdings and greater authority over tenants. Rural social inequalities are rooted in the disparities of land ownership.

Land tenure

Small landholdings are the norm in Pakistan in general and in the irrigated plains of Punjab and Sindh in particular. The average size of a farm in Pakistan was 10.1 acres in 1960 and increased slightly to 11.6 acres by 1980.[5] It is estimated that 12.5 acres is the subsistence landholding for farming in Pakistan; 74 percent of farms were smaller than this size in 1980. Apart from the small size, farm holdings in Pakistan are fragmented due to the successive divisions of land by inheritance. About 58 percent of farms are fragmented in 3.7 discontinuous land parcels on average. Thus, a typical owner farmer is a land-poor person, thereby placing owners of even 50 acres of land among the rural elite, namely *zamindars* (landlords). Only 2–3 percent of farms in Pakistan are 50 or more acres in area, yet they command almost a quarter of the national farmland. A typical village in Punjab or Sindh may have only one or two farms of this size. Obviously, their owners will not only be rich compared to other farmers, but they would also wield political and social power. A majority of owner farmers are poor and powerless in relation to these *zamindars*. The poverty of tenants, landless peasants, or farm workers is indescribable.

Land reform for a relatively more equitable distribution of land ownership, especially to enable tillers of land to own what they cultivate, was on the national agenda up to the late 1970s. The modernization phase (1947–71) witnessed one attempt at land reforms, although many national inquiries and reports were previously prepared about the agrarian structure. Ayub Khan's government passed an ordinance, West Pakistan Land Reforms Regulation No. 64, in 1959, abolishing *jagirs* and laying down 500 acres of irrigated land as the ceiling for any single owner (with some allowance for the quality of land and orchid or horse farms), with excess acreage to be acquired for distribution among tenants and the landless. It also provided legal protection to tenants against ejection by landlords, except for stipulated reasons. It was a conservative measure, but it acknowledged the significance of equitable land ownership for economic and social development.

In the second period (1972–8), the era of Bhutto's populist egalitarianism, the redistribution of farm land was carried farther: reducing the ceiling for individual holding to 150 acres (further reduced to 100 acres in 1977) in irrigated areas; barring intrafamily "gifting" of land to bypass the land ceiling regulation; and distributing lands acquired from landlords free to tenants.[6] Land reforms had little effect in making land ownership less skewed. Only 763 landlords were required to surrender excess land totaling 1.9 million acres under the 1959 Land Reform Regulations. The more drastic reform measure of 1972 netted another 1,754 landlords, who surrendered 0.58 million acres for redistribution.[7] Big *zamindars* evaded land reform regulations by dividing their estates among kin and by bribing and influencing officials responsible for land reforms. There were many loopholes in the regulations that made it easy to bypass land ceilings.

The issue of large landholdings has been swept aside in the rising tide of commercial and mechanized farming and the ideological shift in both the development theory and in the public policies of the third period. The green revolution has turned farming into a capitalist enterprise. Farming increasingly requires investments in miracle seeds, chemical fertilizers, farm machinery, and even tubewells for the sustained supply of water. It has become an activity based on hardheaded calculations, and is no longer an inheritable calling.

Furthermore, landlord families in Pakistan are branching out in industries, businesses, and urban real estate, thereby channeling their economic surplus and social power to gain a foothold in the emerging national economy. Farmers' sons are training for professions and settling in cities, even going to the Gulf, Canada, or Europe in search of employment. The social disparities between landlords and middle-income farmers versus tenants and workers are increasing, despite general improvement in the latter's living conditions. The landlords are outpacing other classes in the race to affluence and influence.

Talking of the political economy, it may be mentioned that the collapse of the Soviet states in Russia and Eastern Europe has set back equality as a social objective. Globalization has shifted the development discourse. The World Bank and IMF are pushing for property rights, privatization of production, and market pricing of goods and services. In such an ideological environment, defenders of land reforms are in retreat. Reducing socially constructed inequalities of land ownership is not on the development agenda of Pakistan anymore. It is striking that conservative Islamists, including Jamaat-i-Islami, are ideologically opposed to limiting landholding and other provisions of land reforms. Their ideological influence has waxed strong in the third period, starting with General Zia's military rule in 1978.

General Zia renounced the possibility of any further agrarian reforms in 1979. The Islamic *Shariat* (jurisprudence) court in Pakistan pronounced in a ruling in 1989 that Bhutto's land reforms were in contravention of Islamic law. No new initiative toward equalization of land ownership has been taken in the third period. In 2003, Premier Zafrullah Khan Jamali disavowed any new land reforms.

Social contours of inequitable land distribution have been etched in the landscape. The population pressure has accelerated the process of land subdivision and is reducing the size of large estates, although keeping the family and clan concentrations of ownership. The land question has transmuted into the issue of land supply and development. Land scarcities have emerged in both, rural and urban areas.

Land loot

Land is a factor of production. It is also a primary source of unearned increases in value and rent arising from developments for which owners did not invest any capital or labor, such as land prices rising from improvements in infrastructure, neighborhood, and locality. In Pakistan, land has mostly fallen into the hands of people of influence, authority, and connections. This has happened in the new irrigated areas and expanding cities and towns. With economic development, urban property became very lucrative and privileged access to it has turned out to be a source of easy riches.

Pakistan has plentiful raw land, but much of it is not suitable for cultivation or habitation. Out of the total area of about 217 million acres, only about 50 million acres are used or usable for agriculture. The bulk of Pakistan's lands fall in the category of dry range and desert, found mostly in Balochistan province.[8] Since independence, the total cropped area has expanded by 19 million acres, largely the result of building new irrigation networks, the installation of tubewells, and the water management of *barrani* (dry but rain-dependent) tracts.

These newly developed farmlands have been distributed among resourceful farmers, military and civilian officers, and public and private corporations. A majority of settlers were persons with connections and political and administrative influence. Quotas were set aside in new barrage lands for military and civilian officers. Similarly, public lands on the border with India were given at nominal prices to retired military personnel to form a civilian defense line. Whatever quotas were set aside for distribution among peasants and ordinary farmers were in practice distributed primarily to those who paid bribes or pulled strings. One way or the other, the land distribution policies benefitted persons of influence, authority, and connections.

The allotment of new irrigated lands to settlers has not only pre-empted the opportunities of local farmers, but has also displaced historical users of those areas, such as grazers, nomadic farmers, and residents. These displacements have fostered simmering resentments between settlers and locals. In Sindh, for example, the settlement of Punjabis on new irrigated lands fanned ethnic strife. In the same vein, persons displaced by the Mangla dam were still protesting their inadequate compensations and abandonment even 40 years after the building of the dam although lands irrigated by new canals were immediately parceled out to persons of quotas. Those who benefit from, and those who bear the costs of land development turn out to be people of radically different social status. People displaced as a consequence of land development are treated as children of a lesser God. Land policies have sharpened ethnic cleavages and reinforced class divisions. The story of urban land is not much different.

The political economy of urban "plots"

Pakistan's exploding cities and urbanizing countryside have transformed land markets. Agricultural lands and open spaces on the periphery of cities, towns, and even villages are divided into lots, serviced with rudimentary infrastructure, and turned into sites for houses, shops, or factories. This process of land conversion from rural to urban use adds value and increases land prices. In rapidly growing cities and towns, the demand for urban lots, popularly known as plots, far outstrips the supply, making them a scarce commodity and pushing up their prices.

Urban plots are a major source of capital gains. They are a means of getting rich quick, particularly if located on choice sites in government-sponsored projects that have clear titles and provision of public utilities. Getting such a plot at the "allotment" price is a windfall. Officials, politicians, military personnel, journalists, etc., have had quotas of plots set aside in urban development projects while ordinary citizens have been bidding for them in auctions. This is how status, authority, and connections are converted into property and wealth.

Plot development began soon after independence to resettle refugees and to accommodate officials of the new state. Karachi, the initial national capital, was woefully short of housing and industrial sites. Its extensive public landholdings came in handy for developing residential colonies and industrial and commercial estates. Two new townships, Korangi and New Karachi, and numerous housing estates were developed under the Greater Karachi Resettlement Plan in the first period. Other cities followed suit. University Town in Peshawar, Samanabad and Gulberg in Lahore, and Quetta's Satellite Town were early public projects that subsidized professionals, administrators, and political leaders to become property owners.

These developments also popularized the *kothi* (bungalow) as the idiom of modern living. The lower-class equivalent of a bungalow is a "quarter," a single-storey structure of one or two rooms, along with a verandah with a courtyard enclosed by boundary walls. Quarter colonies are built for clerical employees and workers. By segregating land use and separating lots of different sizes, these developments resulted in separating social classes and creating sprawling cities.

In cities, the process of land development proceeds in two different modes. The first mode consists of publicly sponsored or approved land development for carving out urban plots. It is the universe of planned suburbs, housing societies, satellite towns, and new cities. The second is the process of illegal occupation, with the connivance of police, magistracy, and municipal officials, and informal subdivision of public land by dealers to settle squatters. This mode prevails in squatter settlements, *katchi abadis*, and unapproved subdivisions.

The first mode operates in the upper circuit of the urban land market for businessmen, civil and military officers and professionals, as well as overseas Pakistanis. The second mode functions in the lower circuit for the working poor and lower-middle classes. Sometimes, it is also organized on a community basis, resulting in geographic concentrations by ethnic groups, particularly in Karachi. In *katchi abadis*, usually a middleman developer organizes occupation of public land and settles squatter households for a fee or subdivides land into unapproved plots and sells them to needy households. The second mode is largely organized as a market process. Thus the rich and influential get choice plots at subsidized prices, but the poor and homeless pay, more or less, market prices. This is how resources are transferred to members of groups that wield political and official authority. There are some very insightful accounts of these processes, but I have to leave them aside to maintain my focus on the changing landscape of Pakistan.[9]

The crowning event of the first period, from the perspective of land development, was the transfer of national capital from Karachi to the proposed new city of Islamabad in 1959. Situated beside the Margala hills near Rawalpindi, Islamabad has urbanized almost the whole of Pothohar plateau and ignited the largest scramble for plots in Pakistan.

To round off the narrative of urban plot distribution, public policies and market practices of the second and third periods may be briefly described. During an era of "people's rule" (period 2), a program was started to confer ownership of the squatted land on residents of *katchi abadis*. The informal land subdivisions were to be regularized, giving legal cover to the private appropriation of public lands. Even in rural areas, three-marla (675 sq ft) plots were carved out of the village commons for distribution to the poor for housing. Yet in implementation, ward politicians and local power brokers became the arbiters of this public largesse. The upper-circuit plot allotments continued with political cadres added to the ranks of beneficiaries. Plots became the chips for buying political support and rewarding loyalty by Bhutto's government.

The politics of plots has continued in the third period. General Zia's regime opened the business of suburban development to the military and its affiliated corporations. Mostly, cantonment lands were assigned to these organizations for development and distribution. Today, in every major city, some of the most coveted addresses exist in housing societies such as Defence Societies and Askari Development that are affiliated with the army, navy, and the air force. Other government agencies, such as railways and revenue departments, have followed the military and divided some of their landholdings among their officials.

The policy of distributing small housing lots to the poor was maintained in the third period. Yet, the elite continued to get their share. Benazir Bhutto allotted 1,165 plots to parliamentarians, military officers, and party workers in her two stints as Prime Minister. Nawaz Sharif personally allotted about 2,000 plots in Lahore alone, during his tenure as the provincial chief minister.[10] All in all, subsidized plots have enriched the well-connected and powerful and reinforced the contours of the emerging class structure in Pakistan. Even the low-income housing programs or informal subdivisions become a source of "middlemen's cut" for the well-connected before reaching the poor. These modes of land distribution have shaped the internal structure of Pakistani cities and towns. They have also been instrumental in promoting urban sprawl.

The urbanization of everybody

The face of Pakistan has changed over the many decades since its independence. It has become a country of megacities, sprawling towns, and bursting villages. Its people are no longer bound to ancestral homes and clan quarters, but settle in unaccustomed places in pursuit of opportunities for personal advancement, safety, and shelter. The country has plugged into urban ways of life, known in the literature as urbanism, even in areas geographically classified as rural. Although the poor, minorities, and the people of remote regions have not shared equally in this social change, urbanization has swept the country and changed its look.

Urbanization is outwardly a process of more and more people living in cities and towns, namely places that specialize in commerce, industry, and communications, have relatively large populations, and some form of municipal or corporate government. Yet, the concentration of population in urban places also enmeshes people in relatively more formal social organizations, impersonal cultural mores, specialized economic activities, and new forms of community life.[11] This association of the physical and spatial aspects of urban places with more formalized and relatively impersonal rules of behavior makes urbanization a process of social transformation.

Urbanization, measured as the proportion of national population living in urban places, is also related to urbanism as a way of life pervading a country. Pakistan's urbanization has come about in two ways. First, from the growth and expansion of cities and towns, and second, by the build-up of population in (some) rural areas to urban densities, mainly from the explosion of cities and towns and by the implosion of rural population. The second process is unacknowledged but real. Both modes of urbanization have similar effects.

Beginning with almost one in six persons being an urban resident, Pakistan now has one in three people (32.5 percent in 1998) living in cities and towns; although if the effects of urbanization by implosion are included, the actual figure may be close to one in two and possibly a majority.

Urbanization as defined by the census has spread at varying but rapid rates in the four provinces. From 1951 to 1998, the urban population in NWFP increased from 11.1 to 16.9 percent registering the slowest rate of urbanization. Punjab's urban population rose from 17.4 to 31.3 percent. Sindh, led by the primary city, Karachi, maintained its lead by going from 29.0 to 48.8 percent and Balochistan almost doubled the proportion of its urban population from 12.4 to 23.9 percent. The number of urban places increased from 218 in 1951 to 515 in 1998, almost two and a half times the numnber in 47 years. Cities with a population of more than 100,000 multiplied from 10 to 59 in the same period. The most dramatic growth has been that of the big cities, namely Karachi, Lahore, Faisalabad, Multan, Peshawar, and Quetta. They have spread out over whole regions.

By the year 2000, nine cities had populations of over one million people. Karachi had almost 10 million people and Lahore had about six million, rivaling New York and Chicago in size. Faisalabad's growth rivals Karachi as far as rate of growth is concerned. It rose from being a market town of 180,000 in 1951 to become the textile capital of Pakistan with a population of more than two million in 50 years. Even Quetta, the crisp and cool capital of Balochistan, turned into a noisy city of a million inhabitants. Its proximity to the Afghan border brought waves of refugees from Afghanistan's wars of the 1980s, 1990s, and 2002.

Cities spill into the surrounding regions and their offshoots drive ribbons of urban development into the countryside, swallowing villages and spawning jerry-built housing colonies. Commuters converge daily on these cities in *babu* trains (popular term for trains purportedly bringing legions of clerks to their jobs) and overflowing buses from places beyond the surrounding districts. Where a city ends and the country begins is hard to demarcate.

Within cities, a majority live in crowded quarters and squatter colonies. One-fifth to one-third of big city populations live in *katchi abadis* (squatter settlements). At the same time, planned suburbs, opulent housing societies, and shopping plazas proudly supporting McDonald's and Kentucky Fried Chicken abound, particularly in big cities.

The exponential growth of cities and towns is the result of the continuing high rates of natural population growth (births minus deaths) and the in-migration of people from villages for jobs, economic development, better living conditions as well as factors that "push" rural residents out of their ancestral habitats. The phenomenon of fast urban growth is a universal process. The West went through this process in the early twentieth century and now the Third World is being swept along by it. Pakistan is in the thick of this cycle.

What is a new form of urbanization in Pakistan and many other countries of Asia is the rapid growth of the resident rural population. Villages spill out; homesteads coalesce together to form bands of settlements; homes, workshops, and bus stands emerge, one by one, along roads, cumulatively forming ribbons of exurbia. The fields do not disappear but they are interspersed with homes, paths, pools of wastewater, etc., signaling the arrival of urban sprawl.

In-place urbanization of the countryside

This process of in-place implosion of population results in the urbanization of rural areas. When the population density reaches urban levels, usually 400 persons per sq km or 1,000 persons per sq mi., the need arises for urban facilities and services. Streets have to be aligned and named. Drains have to be built and waste disposal needs to be organized on a communal basis. Water supply needs to be collectivized. All in all, at urban density levels, municipal services become necessary. These community needs are directly related to the density of development and thus they represent the thresholds at which a rural area crosses over to an elementary form of urban place. The urban infrastructure may not be provided, but its absence severely affects the health and well-being of residents. This urbanization from the bottom up gives rise to ruralopolises, a new form of diffused human settlement that has urban-level densities and requirements for corresponding utilities and services.[12]

Pakistan is a country of high rates of population growth (although the trend is downward) and its irrigated plains are under intense population pressure. This has transformed most of central Punjab, southern Sindh and the Peshawar Valley of NWFP into ruralopolises. From Peshawar to Multan (with some gaps) along Pakistan's main axis of irrigated regions, there is a continuous band of diffused settlements linked to cities, set among fields, orchards, and open spaces. Similarly, Karachi to Hyderabad is another high-density rural region, anchored in the two big cities. Here rural population densities are equal to or more than the UN norm for defining urban areas (Figure 3.1).

In 1998, about 31.3 million people lived in the high-density rural areas (ruralopolises) covering about 70,000 sq km. If this population is also counted as urban, then Pakistan is a country of urban majority (56.5 percent). This refers as much to the urbanization of landscape as it does to the population increase.

Urbanism has also permeated rural areas. The availability of radio, television, scooters, telephones, etc., and the increasing reliance on modern medicine, travel, and migration, have opened up rural social structures and changed people's behavior. Whether in physical terms or in ways of life, Pakistan has come under the influence of urbanization thus changing the landscape permanently. Today's Pakistan is a landscape of rural sprawl, tethered to some of the densest cities in the world. deserts of Sindh, highlands of Balochistan, and sections of irrigated districts that have been bypassed by roads and canals are the only large purely rural areas left.

Changing living conditions

The impact of urbanization can be seen vividly in the changes it induces in the use of land. What were essentially bare tracts of land, cultivated fields, or open spaces are built upon and turned into houses, stores, factories, schools, streets, and parks. This physical transformation is the visible change in landscape, but associated with it are radical changes in the quality of life, environment, and architecture. In

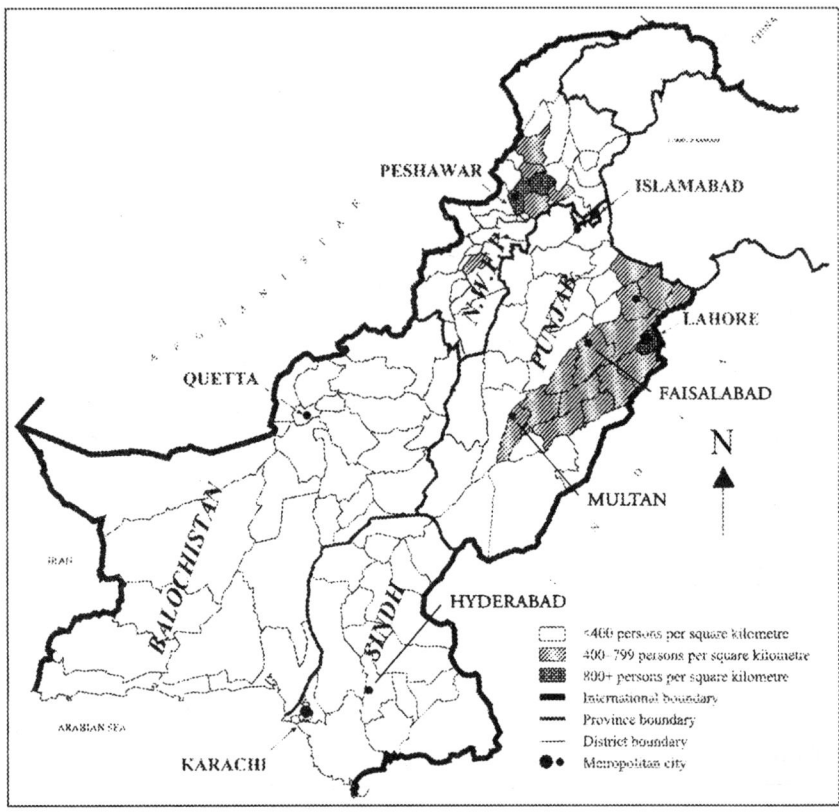

Figure 3.1 Ruralopolises: high density rural districts

fact, urbanization itself is the sum total of many processes, such as economic and social development, technological changes, and the transformation of transportation systems. Pakistan's urbanization recapitulates these processes to one degree or another. Changes in three sectors are particularly relevant to this narrative of the changing landscape, namely transportation, infrastructure, and housing.

Transportation

The compact quarters and narrow streets of Pakistani towns and cities were based on preindustrial modes of transport. By walking, riding horses, or use of animal-drawn carriages, one could cover a radius of about two to five miles for daily business. This commuting radius circumscribed the area of a settlement including fields. The automobile extended this radius, blew open the compactness of settlements, and spread cities and towns outward. But the automobile was a rare possession in the colonial era and suburban bungalows were practically the preserve of the British officials and local elite so its full impact came after independence.

Independence breached the social frontiers. The emergence of newly affluent business and professional classes precipitated the demand for modern homes in newly developed suburbs of wide streets and leafy lawns. The *kothi* and car became badges of economic success and modernism and defined the ideal of good living.

By the 1970s, Japanese motorcycles and Italian scooters became affordable for clerks, students, and deliverymen for use as personal transport. By ingenious, but precarious, balancing of passengers on the front and back of a rider, a family of five persons could be squeezed onto two-wheelers. Thus, even people of modest means gained the ability to travel distances. With about 1.7 million motorcycles or scooters and another 0.6 million cars in 1997, roughly 7–10 percent of Pakistani households had access to motorized personal transport. In 1947, only 12,749 cars were registered; the number of registered motorcycles, at 3,618, was even lower.[13] This shows a dramatic increase in people's mobility since independence.

Motorcycles eased travel in the expanding cities and towns, spreading housing in the countryside, and opening up remote areas. As a vehicle, the two-wheeler can reach places that have no roads thus bringing isolated sites within the orbit of urban development. The motorcycle revolution has fostered ruralopolises.

The poor are not untouched by the transport improvements. Suzuki vans and mini trucks, hazardously overloaded and recklessly driven, transport children to schools, factory workers to their jobs, farmers to markets, and women to saints' tombs by the millions every day. The mini van explosion started in the 1960s and has now spread all over the country. The number of vans climbed rapidly from 871 in 1961 to 92,110 in 1997 while almost an equal number of unregistered vans may be on the road. Pakistan has been turned into the land of crowded roads and chaotic traffic.

Although woefully deficient, the infrastructure of roads, utilities, and services has expanded, while the demand for transportation has ballooned. The road network has spread out more than fourfold, from 50,000 to 225,000 km in the 50 years from 1947 to 1997. The bulk of the road-building work took place after 1980.

Infrastructure

The electricity grid now covers most of the country and the number of electricity consumers has increased from 0.3 million (about 20 percent of households) in 1947 to almost 10 million (approximately 50 percent of households) in 1997, not counting hundreds of thousands who illegally tap electric lines for domestic and industrial use. A night flight over Pakistan in 1960s was a journey in the dark that was relieved only when the plane flew over cities. Now a night flight goes over rivers of lights and lakes of illumination below. The telephone was a facility reserved for the privileged up to the late 1960s. Now middle-class homes have telephones in both rural and urban areas. Cell phones and the Internet are the new symbols of status. Pakistan is acquiring the appurtenances of modern living, albeit unevenly.

Housing

Housing quality and design are among the most reliable indicators of people's living conditions and the state of habitat of an area. The living conditions in

Pakistan are being modernized incrementally year by year, mostly on individuals' initiatives in the private sector, complemented by a series of public sector programs. "Housing and Physical Planning" has been a distinct sector of Pakistan's five-year plans from the beginning. At a time when housing was not even on the agenda of the World Bank and the international development agencies, Pakistan had initiated ambitious programs for housing, water supply, and urban land development. It is not for me to evaluate these public initiatives, but to point out that deliberate efforts have been going on for the improvement of housing conditions and the physical environment that sustains modern living. Yet they fell far short of the needs.

The results of these efforts, public and private, are etched on the landscape. There are acute housing shortages, combined with notable improvements in housing quality all over the country. Palatial houses imitating Western designs (for example, replicas of the White House) have sprung up in the most unlikely places, such as small towns and tribal areas. More numerous are large newly built suburbs in cities and towns covered with the two- to three-storey houses, representing the lifelong dreams of millions to own a home with a flush toilet, concrete roof, and solid walls. Saying goodbye to mud homes and insecure tenures is a part of the revolution of rising expectations in Pakistan. These expectations have been realized for many of the middle class as well as segments of the lower-middle and working classes. Pakistani cities present a split personality; squatter settlements coexist with suburban estates reminiscent of Scarsdales and Hammerschmidts.

The results of housing "progress" are evident both visually and statistically. Burgeoning cities, exploding towns, and urbanized countryside are vivid manifestations of the increasing tempo of construction activity. My memories of the 1950s in the historic heart of Lahore are suffused with images of children in the neighborhood doing their daily chore of carrying water from the houses that had a piped water supply. Out of the nine houses in our cul-de-sac, only two had municipal water supply, three had electricity, and most had mud floors. Today, each home on that street has been renovated with concrete roofs, taps on each floor and, thanks to the installation of sewers in the old city, flush toilets. Periodic censuses of housing bear out this experience on the national level.

In 1960, out of the 6.9 million occupied houses, about 21 percent had brick or concrete walls and only 6 percent had concrete or tile roofs. Let us examine what happened over the next 20 years. Out of 12.4 million dwellings in 1980, 10 million (81 percent) had been built after independence. There was no significant difference between rural and urban areas in this regard. Pakistan could be described as a newly built habitat. About 43 percent of the national housing stock had *pucca* (brick or concrete) walls, but only 9 percent had concrete roofs. The quality of rural housing was poorer; only 30 percent had *pucca* walls and a mere one percent concrete roofs. Urban areas had a large proportion of housing with semi-*pucca* roofs (62 percent). Provinces differed in the structural quality of housing as well.

Forty-seven percent of Pakistan's housing had a water supply (mostly electrified and hand-pumps) installed within a house; urban areas measured better (65 percent) than rural (40 percent) on this score. The proportion of dwellings with electricity was 31 percent for Pakistan, 71 percent for urban, and one percent for rural housing.

By 1998, the quality of housing recorded a marked improvement. Home-building activity accelerated. Almost seven million homes were built between 1988 and 1998, mostly of the "one to two rooms plus courtyard" variety. The overall proportion of dwellings with *pucca* walls rose to 58 percent, and those with *pucca* roofs increased to 44 percent. Urban housing was structurally nearing the point of being mostly *pucca*: 86 percent with *pucca* walls and 65 percent with concrete or iron sheet roofs. Rural housing, although lagging behind the urban areas, also registered major gains in quality, and was increasingly being built with cement and bricks rather than mud and thatch. Forty-six percent had *pucca* walls and 20 percent had cement or concrete or iron sheet roofs.

The most dramatic improvements were in the provision of utilities: 75 percent of the national housing stock had piped water or hand-pumps inside the house, and 70 percent had electricity. Urban housing standards were at a point where 89 percent of dwellings had a water supply inside the house and 93 percent had electricity. The majority of rural housing also reached these standards with 68 percent of dwellings with piped water supply and 60 percent with electricity. Pakistan's housing quality had come a long way from that of the neighborhood where I had grown up in Lahore.

Pakistan's housing problems are far from being under control. The quality has improved but the supply continues to lag behind needs. Housing shortages, particularly for low-income households, are endemic. Despite a healthy annual rate of new construction, housing supply falls short by 270,000 dwellings per year.[14] *Katchi abadis* continue to multiply, accommodating 20–30 percent of the population of cities such as Karachi, Lahore, Hyderabad, and Quetta. More and better quality houses are being built, services have improved, but housing prices have outpaced people's ability to pay. This shortfall is dramatically reflected in the data on crowding in housing.

The average number of persons per house rose from 5.2 in 1960 to 6.7 in 1980 and 6.8 in 1998. This indicates that households are doubling up and two-generation families are living under the same roof. Better quality but expensive housing required pooling of resources among old and young families, reinforcing the joint family. Almost one-third of the population operates ouside the formal market. The habitat that is being built sharpens the social distance among classes. It is also a testimony to the imbalance between private consumption and collective welfare.

Habitats of memories: old and new

The landscape of Pakistan may have been urbanized, but its popular image remains steeped in the idioms of agrarian paradise: golden wheat fields swaying with the breeze, buffaloes lazing in ponds, villages overflowing with *lassi* (a churned yogurt drink) and butter, rivers that sheltered legendary romances, land that breeds purity, honor, and innocence. On the contrary, cities are places of bright lights, clever men, charming women, hard bargains, weak community, and technological wonders. A sentiment of rural romanticism forms the substratum of images in the landscape of memories. The pervasive urbanization and urbanism pitch the emerging reality against these beliefs, producing hybrid spaces, inconsistent behaviors, and a fusion of contradictory forms and functions.

One late February day in 1995, my drive across the waist of Punjab from the east to west, and then onward into NWFP, brought up the mixture of the old and the new landscapes. From Sahiwal (population 200,000) to Jhang, Shahpur, and northward to Chakwal, I passed large tracts of ripening wheat, fruit orchards, and patches of sunflower crops, filling me with nostalgia for the romance of village life celebrated in Punjabi poetry. Yet, on the same journey, I was stuck for an hour over the Chenab river bridge in the gridlock of sugarcane laden trolleys, oil tankers, trucks overflowing with bales of cotton, and buses and commuter vans brimming with passengers, all pointing to the industrial and commercial establishments that had sprung up along the length of this back road.

Similarly in the Peshawar Valley, miles away from a city, the valley floor is pockmarked, as far as one can see, with homes and huts standing in the midst of fields. Urbanization is unmistakably present all around. Its effects can be deduced from the "pee test": one is hard pressed to find a bush to pee behind in privacy, while traveling along a major road. Almost no area is now assuredly free from the human gaze. In the 1960s and even in the 1970s, most roads passed this test, but now only the very remote ones do.

The majestic high Himalayas beckon still, but now reaching them is not a scary trip in a jeep over tortuous treks. The Karakoram highway, although subject to mud slides, allows honeymooning couples to drive up to Hunza or even higher near the Chinese border. At night, electric lights in homes high up on the mountainsides twinkle like stars in the sky and the flicker of television screens dances in valley bazaars. Even this remote corner of the country has been pulled into modern ways of life. More and better housing covers the land, yet families are doubling up, as the young couples cannot afford to rent or own a home. The poor have no place in the housing narrative. It is not geography any more but social position that differentiates traditional modes of living from the modern. The affluent in villages live with almost as many modern conveniences as their counterparts in cities. Pakistan has been urbanized, physically and demographically, but its social institutions remain steeped in a rural ethos.

4 Nation and ethnicity

Diversity and unity

Pakistan is a work in progress, more so than many new nations. Undoubtedly, it inspires passionate loyalty from an overwhelming majority of its citizens. More than 90 percent of its population were born after the establishment of Pakistan, and their identity and destiny are bound up with it. Yet its peculiar political history has inhibited the emergence of a social consensus about its national purpose and identity as a society. The government-sponsored discourse about Pakistan's ideology has lurched from Muslim nationalism, Islamic socialism, and since 1977, vociferously toward a vision of an Islamic state and society organized according to Islamic laws. In the early 2000s, a vision of a liberal Islamic society based on "enlightened moderation" has been advocated by President Musharraf.

Yet on the ground, social life continues to advance toward modernity, adopting new technologies, contemporary consumption patterns, and production practices. What with the periodic military rules, failures of electoral democracy, bursts of ethnic, regional, and denominational strife, the breakaway of East Pakistan, social inequalities, inefficiencies of public institutions and wars, Pakistan has not been able to reconcile divergent interests and values. Pakistan means different things to people of different ethnicities, regions, and social classes.

It continues to be a society contested between two sets of sentiments and ideals, national-democratic versus puritanical Islamic. Each of the two themes accommodates a wide range of interpretations, models, and goals. Thus, Pakistan remains a country of divergent visions and commitments about its national identity and goals. The ground for this divergence was laid in the half-century struggle for independence from British colonialism and in the Indian Muslims' quest for community solidarity and identity.

The political history of Indian Muslims' search for self-rule, culminating in the demand for a separate homeland, has been extensively examined and analyzed.[1] How and why did the idea of Pakistan, as a separate homeland for Muslims, develop and what vision did Muslims entertain about it? These questions have engaged historians and ideologues for many years. I cannot add much to this discussion. The contending positions are well entrenched and each has its passionate advocates. Furthermore, the political history is of interest to me only to the extent that it affects Pakistan's social organization and culture. I will recount briefly the social forces, ideologies, and events that gave rise to divergent "ideas" of Pakistan.

Ideas of Pakistan

Pakistan has been imagined in many forms. Neither in the days when it was only a dream nor now when it is an established state and nation, has Pakistan been envisioned in terms of a singular idea or social order. Almost always there have been many models or interpretations of the purpose and structure of Pakistan as a society and nation, although at any one moment a particular viewpoint may temporarily sweep across for political reasons. Yet the debate resumes as the moment passes.

These divergent ideas have "competed" for people's commitments and ideologies. This historical fact is not unlike experiences of other modern nations and societies. Furthermore, the notions and ideals that define Pakistan continue to evolve in response to changing conditions, both external and internal. The notion of a multiplicity of ideas of Pakistan is, of course, contrary to the position subsumed under the slogan "the ideology of Pakistan" which has been appropriated by protagonists of Islam as the defining theme of Pakistan's culture. All one can briefly say in response to this position is that the history and sociology of Pakistan suggest that Islam itself invokes different models of social order for Muslims of different persuasions. There is more than one vision of the promised Islamic order. The following is a thumbnail sketch of the forces and processes that have germinated multiple visions of Pakistan.

- The British conquest culminated in the dethronement of the hapless Mughal emperor in 1857, bringing to an end almost a millennium of Muslim dynastic rule in India. With the defeat of the Mughals, the Muslims of India lost the status and power that come with belonging to the rulers' community. Defeatism and nostalgia for past glories preoccupied Indian Muslims. They retreated from public space and stood aloof from the political and social developments coming in the wake of the British rule, thereby remaining stuck on the lower rungs of colonial economy and polity.
- Muslims' reaction to their marginalization took two broad forms: first, the reformist advocating accommodation to British rule and the restructuring of social institutions in contemporary idioms while retaining Islamic identity and moral order as the basis of community life. Some examples of such initiatives were the Aligarh Movement, Anjuman Himayat Islam, Lahore, Islamia College, Peshawar, National Mohammadan Association, Calcutta, etc. These movements spawned ideas about a Muslim community as a socially and culturally distinct group. Second, Islamic revival movements such as Deoband, Firangi Mahal, and others, aimed at reforming religious practices and beliefs and thereby creating an Islamic "Millat" (solidarity) and fostering Islamic social institutions. The puritanical wing of Islamic movements sought to resist modern ways and recreate the imagined life patterns of the "glorious

era of Islamic society."[2] Even migration from British India to Afghanistan, Turkey, or Iran was advocated as an option by some, on the plea that Muslims could not live in the "house of infidels." Yet within each of these thematic categories, there were a great many discourses, which straddled accommodation and resistance strategies toward the modernist thrusts of colonial rule. The debates were passionate and arguments vigorous, not infrequently taking the tone of personal animosities.

- The political stirrings for representation in the colonial government, starting in 1892 with the Indian Councils Act establishing advisory councils for the governor general and provincial governors, precipitated what Ayesha Jalal has characterized as the conceptualization of Muslims as a legal and political category.[3] The prospects of self-rule and representative government in India brought to the fore a familiar conundrum of the electoral system. Many Muslims feared that if people voted on the basis of their community and caste interests, social identities, and religious solidarity, the Muslims would be permanently reduced to the status of a powerless minority. Although outnumbered by Hindus four to one, Muslims were numerically too large a group, forming majorities in territorially large regions, to accept this prospect with resignation. Their feelings of economic deprivation further sharpened their differences with the Hindu majority and added to their apprehensions. These sentiments fomented Muslims' quest for political and cultural rights and led to their demands for self-rule, job quotas, and social opportunities. Thus the movement for freedom and representative government spawned communal politics and adversarial relations between Hindus and Muslims. Undoubtedly, there were years of mutual cooperation and communal unity in the anticolonial struggles of the 1920s and early 1930s. Yet the project of building a singular Indian national polity broke down in the face of power enjoyed by Hindu majorities in the provincial elections of 1937. The provincial administrations formed by the Congress, for example, the Ministry in the United Provinces (UP) during 1937–9, neglected Muslims' needs and interests and created doubts in the Muslim minority about the workability of the electoral theory of representation.[4] British colonial policy certainly facilitated the sharpening of communal differences rather than building on the historical commonalities.[5]

- The Muslim League's argument of "community before individual" and its claim that only a Muslim can represent Muslims gradually evolved into the demand for representational parity between Hindus and Muslims. From these premises, the idea of Muslims as a separate nation and the demand for parity in negotiations for independence were just logical steps. Muslims' ideas about their place in Indian society evolved from viewing themselves as a community of identity and common interests to the consciousness of a nation of distinct culture and territoriality. Religious identity became the ethos of Muslims' cultural nationalism.

- Lest this description suggest that Muslims were all of one mind, it may be hastily added there was a wide divergence of opinions and feelings within the

Muslim community. A sizable segment of the Muslim public was opposed to the Muslim League's agenda and subscribed to the Nationalist project of Gandhi, Nehru, and Azad's Congress Party. Paradoxically, some of the most vociferous opponents of the idea of Muslim nationhood were the *ulemas* (Islamic scholars and leaders), and Islamists aligned with the Congress Party.[6] Such were the crosscurrents within the Muslim community.

- The idea of Pakistan as a political unit(s), where Muslims govern themselves and thrive as a cultural and economic community, was articulated as the Two Nations Theory. Its notion of Muslim nationhood was founded on viewing Hindus as the significant "other." This differentiation from Hindus has been built into the conception of Pakistan and it continues to define its national policies and outlook.

Four dimensions of the ideas of Pakistan

Muslim nationhood and Pakistan as a society and state are ideas that kept on changing in form and content as the Indian Independence Movement gathered momentum. These ideas had four dimensions: (1) political status, (2) social order and legal system, (3) individual and community rights, and (4) national culture. For each of these dimensions, a variety of concepts and values were advanced at different times, and are outlined below.

1   Politically, Pakistan was conceived both as a territorial grouping of the Muslim majority provinces in a federal India, and as an independent state(s) separated from Hindu-dominated India. Jinnah's acceptance of the Cabinet Mission Plan in 1946, only a year before the partition, underlines the fact that the former model was almost as acceptable as the latter, almost up to independence. Pakistan's break-up in 1971, the separation of East Pakistan, and the lingering discord about provincial autonomy in rump Pakistan, all point to the divergence of conceptions and interpretations about the form and structure of the nation.

2   Social and legal systems envisaged for Pakistan have turned out to be the most contentious aspects of its conceptions. These aspects are the battleground for ideologies. The proffered conceptions include: a *Sharia*-based Islamic order, a democratic Islamic state, a national-democratic state of Muslims, a society based on the moral order and ways of life of the righteous Khalifas in seventh century Arabia, a society of liberal Islamic mores and individual rights, a modern secular society of universal human rights, and even Islamic socialism. Most of these models had protagonists among the Muslim leaders even in the days of the political struggle for Pakistan.[7] Jinnah and the dominant faction in the Muslim League, by and large, held to the line of a national-democratic order of liberal and modern tenets and Muslim identity. Although, in the heat of political struggles, slogans such as *Pakistan ka mutlab kia .... La Illaha Il Lilha* (Pakistan means affirmation of one God and one Prophet) were raised, a theocratic state and collectivist social order enforcing Islamic mores were not

among the conceptions of the framers of Pakistan's ideals.[8] In practical terms Pakistan meant economic advancement for the Muslim salariat (salaried classes), the liberation of peasants from money lenders and feudal lords, and an opportunity to express liberal Muslim values. All in all, various Muslim interest groups projected their own ambitions and ideals in the idea(s) of Pakistan.

3   Individual and community rights were not given much attention in the run-up to the independent Pakistan. In the political struggle to promote Muslims as a community of distinct culture and national identity, the emphasis was on collective or community rights vis-à-vis other communities inhabiting India. How were individual liberties and rights to fare in the Muslim state and society? This question was seldom in the discourse about the structure of Muslims' projected homeland. All the various ideals of individual citizenhood were highly gendered. They centered almost exclusively on the man, conceived as an autonomous self of the poet laureate Mohammad Iqbal, Shaheen (literally meaning falcon, symbolizing strength, soaring height, and nimbleness), the novelist Nasim Hijazi, and Murd-e-Momin (righteous and God-fearing man) of popular culture. Woman was faithful, forbearing, submissive, a paragon of domesticity, and the bearer of family and community honor.[9] For Islamists, state power is the means to make the individual conform to Islamic norms and morality. Individual liberties and choices are constrained by the community norms based on the precepts of the Quran and Sunnah. Yet, there are divergent interpretations and meanings of these precepts. Jinnah and a majority of the Muslim League leadership inclined toward individual rights and liberties in personal matters, but these issues were seldom vigorously discussed. Pakistan came into existence with ambiguous notions of individual liberties and rights.

4   National culture has been the most controversial dimension of the notions of Pakistan. Muslim nationhood implies promoting Islamic mores, institutions, art, and aesthetics, but it recognizes citizens as the agency that gives form to these notions. The notion of Islamic order, on the other hand, has been a code word for the claim of the *ulemas* to be the sole "agency" to interpret and enforce divine laws. The former notion leaves room for pluralism whereas the latter envisages a centralized command structure for "managing culture." Islamic order, *per se*, is not enough to clinch the debate about national ideology and identity. Islamic laws and norms about marriage, family, personal liberties, social obligations, dress, music, femininity, customs, and symbolism vary by sect, country, and historical and anthropological conditions. The cultural universal laws that range across Muslim societies are few and particularities are more common. These debates simmered on within the Muslim leadership, but in the heat of political struggle for independence, these differences were glossed over.

In the popular mind, Muslim nationhood and Pakistan promised economic freedom and political liberation. Jinnah gathered in Pakistan's tent divergent viewpoints about its political and cultural make-up, yet tacking close to modern-liberal visions of the Muslim state. His detractors mocked his Islamic credentials.

Further complicating the idea of national culture are long-entrenched regional cultures, ethnic identities, and languages whose role remained unresolved in the discourse about national culture. What was to be the role of the customs, language, or temperament of Bengal, Sindh, Punjab, or the Delhi–Lucknow belt from the United Provinces (UP) in the national culture? It is not a surprise that within a few months of independence, the controversy about a national language (Urdu versus Bengali) surfaced, catching Jinnah by surprise. All these factors again underline the diversity of meanings that different groups give to the term "national culture."

To have multiple concepts of a nationalist project is not surprising. It is a part of the process of forging communities and building nations. The USA, France, or Russia were not full-blown ideas at their inception. They emerged as nations through debates, arguments, and even civil wars in the course of their historical evolution. For example, American ideals of individualism, the free market, or civil rights were not the values the founding fathers articulated, at least in their contemporary form and meaning. Yet they have found a place among American ideals with the rise of an urban ethos and the welfare state.

Thus, the existence of a multiplicity of ideas about Pakistan is not a symptom of its ideological weakness. It is the misguided attempt to silence divergent voices with state authority and political intimidation that has not allowed the ideological contradictions to be resolved and a dynamic consensus to be formed. The unresolved ideological conflicts have created a persistent identity crisis in Pakistan.[10] Yet it may be worth noting that various visions of Pakistan continue to be in play even when they are suppressed in the name of a singular ideology. Most of the above-described ideas have continued to resurface periodically in one form or the another. The social history of Pakistan is, partially, a reflection of the conflicting visions of its national society.

The imagined nation

The Pakistan that emerged at independence was territorially divided into two parts, separated by about 1,000 miles of India with which relations were embittered from the start. One condition that facilitates unifying a new nation, namely territorial contiguity and geographic unity, was absent. Independence led to the reopening of the debate about the purpose and structure of Pakistan's state and society. The provinces, particularly East Bengal (renamed as East Pakistan in 1956), demanded recognition of their cultural and linguistic distinctions and protection of their economic interests as well. Refugees coming from India asserted their claim to citizenship on the basis of Islamic bonds. The social and political elite proceeded to consolidate their powers and privileges. The flush of patriotism engendered by the war in Kashmir and the bloodbath of the partition wore out, and people's expectations about their economic welfare and civil rights bloomed. Right away, Pakistan began to be pulled in different directions by social groups of divergent interests and ideas with each significant interest group harking back to the ideals and promises of Pakistan in support of its claims. The raising of all these voices alarmed the ruling clique, driving it to perceive dissent as a threat to national unity. Jinnah's adage, "Unity, Faith and Discipline", became its rallying cry for demanding conformity.

National unity was often defined in the idioms of homogenization. It was seldom conceived as unity built on diversity. What is the basis of Pakistan's nationhood? This question resurfaced in the process of the making of the constitution. The *ulemas* and Islamists, even those who had opposed the formation of Pakistan, pressed for what Ishtiaq Ahmed calls "the sacred state excluding human will."[11] Sayyid Abul-A'la Moudoodi, the leader of Jamaat-e-Islami, for example, maintained: "The Sharia ... prescribes directives for the regulation of our individual as well as collective life ... (touching) such varied subjects as religious rituals, personal character, morals, habits, family relations ... laws of war and peace."[12] The *ulemas* are the agency through which the divine laws are interpreted.

The position of the *ulema* was self-serving and fundamentalist in conception, anticipating the Taliban and the Iranian *mullahs'* models of an Islamic state by about half a century. People in Pakistan were not prepared to give such wide powers over their personal life to *mullahs*. Yet any discourse about Islam was too sacred to be rejected altogether. There were more democratic versions of the Islamic order proposed during the constitutional debates, with wider space for individual freedom and choices of civic life. Istiaq Ahmed calls them, "The sacred State admitting human will."[13] The poet-philosopher Mohammad Iqbal, and the Islamic scholar Khalifa Abdul Hakim, among others, subscribed to this position, envisioning an elected assembly to be the agency for interpreting and enacting Islamic precepts. This notion of Islamic Pakistan came close to what was generally understood to be the essence of nationhood.

The Objectives Resolution passed by the Constituent Assembly in March 1949, as a statement of constitutional principles, sought to combine modern liberal ideas such as democracy, freedom, equality, tolerance, and social justice with the desire of Muslims "to order their lives in the individual and collective spheres in accord with ... teachings and requirements of ... Quran and Sunna."[14] The Objectives Resolution was meant to end the public discord about the goals and purposes of Pakistan. It represented a compromise between the Islamic promises of Pakistan and democratic liberal notions of individual freedom and social justice. Yet, as the subsequent history of Pakistan shows, it did not resolve the "identity crisis" of Pakistan.

A nondenominational liberal-democratic state based on the Muslim majority's moral order was another option feebly in play for the national identity of Pakistan. Jinnah, in his inaugural speech to the freshly formed Constituent Assembly of Pakistan on August 11, 1947, laid out such an ideal as the unifying principle of the state. He proclaimed: "every one of you ... is first and last a citizen of the state with equal rights ... you may belong to any religion or caste or creed that has nothing to do with the business of the state ..." This speech seemed to change the whole rationale of Pakistan.[15] The secularists have often relied on this speech in support of their vision of Pakistan, although their voices have been steadily marginalized.

These ideas about the ideology of Pakistan not only describe the different viewpoints about the national constitution and identity, but they also project particular social orders, each offering specific models and norms about all four dimensions discussed above. They come with particular prescriptions about the constitution of the state and the structure of society, national culture, individual and community rights, etc.

Yet, the practical matters arising from the attempts to organize systems of governance and social relations in a post-independence Pakistan brought up issues that were more pragmatic in scope, with greater impacts on the life of citizens. How will authority be divided between the national and provincial governments? How will an effective and fair system of governance be established? How will economic opportunities and jobs be distributed among provinces? What will be the national language and what will be the status of Bengali, and later on Sindhi, and Pushto, in relation to Urdu? What will be the role of ethnic heritage, customs, music, and art in the national culture? The ideological debate had a bearing on all these matters, and thus each model implicitly became associated not only with specific cultural and social groups, but also with particular political factions, parties, and power configurations. The politicization of the discourse about the ideas of Pakistan narrowed the scope for forging a stable consensus about the basis of nationhood.

Ideology and nation building

The reigning ideology of Pakistan's nationhood shifted in parallel with changing governments and ruling cliques. The basis of national solidarity was defined in the idiom of successive phases of Pakistan's political evolution.

During period 1 (1947–70), the idea of Muslim nationhood (as distinct from the Islamic religious order), bound by a common struggle for independence and a willing submergence of ethnic and provincial identities in a centrally organized state, prevailed over the competing ideologies. The first constitution that designated Pakistan as the Islamic Republic (1956) promised that "(it) would be a democratic state based on Islamic principles of social justice." It envisaged a federal state of autonomous provinces, guaranteeing fundamental rights of equality; freedoms of expression, belief, and faith; and political, social, and economic justice. Note the precedence of democracy over Islamic principles of social justice. The modernist thrust of the Ayub regime further consolidated territorial Muslim nationalism as the basis of Pakistan's national identity. The constitution of 1962 that this military government imposed on the country even dropped the Islamic appellation from the title initially, although it was re-enacted later.

Period 2 (1971–7) was a time of populism. Although a short span of six years, it was a period of radical realignment of Pakistan's identity, goals, and nationalism. East Pakistan's violent breakaway starkly revealed the fragility of Islamic identity and Muslim nationalism as the bases of nationhood. These bonds could not overcome ethnic and linguistic differences, geographic disconnect, and economic disparities.

The post-1971 Pakistan is a coherent geographic unit, territorially unified and historically linked. It had to reconstruct the bases of its nationalism anew. Social justice and the fulfillment of people's economic and political expectations came to be the bases of national solidarity. A new constitution (1973) and Bhutto's passionate advocacy of the rights of the masses injected new themes in Pakistan's national discourse. The constitution recapitulated the national goals laid down in the 1956 constitution, although with greater emphasis on social justice and "the resolve to protect our national and political unity and solidarity *by creating an egalitarian society through a new order*" (emphasis added). The bases of nationhood were redefined. Islamic themes were interpreted to mean the new national mandate for an egalitarian social order.

The third period of Pakistan's evolution as a nation began in 1977 and continues to unfold along the lines laid out by General Zia-ul-Haq's military regime. The 1971 rout of the army by the arch-rival India drove the military to embrace the defense of ideological frontiers as their mission. Bhutto's experiment in Islamic socialism was betrayed by his politics and authoritarian style. The opposition to him was mobilized by promising Prophet Mohammad's just order (Nizam-e-Mustafa). The goal of social justice was incorporated in to Islamic ideals.

General Zia seized on the aroused Islamic fervor as justification for his military coup. He instituted Islamic laws and punishments and patronized conservative Islamists in resurrecting notions of the Sharia (Islamic jurisprudence) based order. A number of constitutional amendments were introduced to transform the parliamentary form of government to the presidential system, reminiscent of the Islamic Khalifat under the leadership of a pious Muslim, the Amirul-Momineen. Pakistan's national mission was recast in the Islamic mold, an idea that had simmered all along but was not the primary claim to nationhood so far. Islamic bonds and beliefs were increasingly regarded as the cement that bound together the ethnic and provincial communities into a nation.

The post-Zia period has not witnessed a significant melding of different ideas of Pakistan's nationhood. On the ideological plane, Islamic ideals, conservatively interpreted, continue to be on an ascendant. Presently, Pakistan's nationalism is anchored to Islamic identity and has been linked to the electoral practices of democracy.[16] Pakistani discourse about national goals oscillates between aspirations for a modern economy and democratic society on the one hand, and the promise of a stable and predictable moral order associated with a historic Islamic one on the other. The five national elections of the period 1988–2002 have not resolved this conflict of national values. The conception of Pakistan's national identity continues to suffer the contradictory pulls of contending forces and ideas.[17] National society as a lived reality exists on one plane and the ideals of what it should be on another.

The lived nation

The nation is defined as a political community that binds together people of common heritage, language, religion, culture, race, ethnicity, or ideology into a unified body over a shared territory.[18] The idea of a nation is linked with the notion of an independent state free to fulfill its citizens' aspirations. A nation state has been the historical expression of a people's nationhood. Yet there is no one essential criterion for defining a nation. People of the same language, religion, or ethnicity are found making different nations, as often as people of different races, religions, or languages constitute one nation. Ultimately the theorists concede that a nation is what people living together come to regard themselves as. It is as much a matter of becoming as of being. Pakistan as a nation has also evolved through the experience of people living together although the seed of nationhood was planted in the struggle for independence.

As a lived nation, Pakistan began truly on faith in its destiny. It was territorially split; the majority of its population spoke Bengali, yet Urdu was the language of Muslim renaissance. Punjab and the Frontier Provinces had shared the west to east axis of population movements, historic invasions, and common rulers, but the desert insulated Sindh and Balochistan from northern influences. The economies of these provinces were at divergent stages of development, ranging from tribal pastoralism, feudal agrarianism to peasant cultivation. There were no common institutions among these disparate communities. Only the political will to live together as one nation state, free, democratic and Muslim in identity brought them together. This national sentiment has stood the test of time, even the trauma of break-up in 1971. Pakistan has survived and continues to command its citizens' loyalty and commitment. It has become a living nation despite the ideological confusion and political instability.

What processes, aspirations, and feelings constitute the lived nation as experienced by people? Or in other words, what bonds make Pakistan a lived nation? At the beginning, Pakistan was the promised land for Muslims fleeing from the communal bloodshed of the partition. "The train to Pakistan" is a symbol of the relief and joy millions felt on crossing Wagah and Khokhrapar border posts. Pakistan was the homeland where they could be free from fear forever and hopeful of making a new start.

For locals, Pakistan meant the promise of better opportunities of jobs and freedom from wants. Independence also meant entitlement to public services and the dignity of citizenship. These expectations occasionally resulted in comical situations such as ticketless travelers claiming the right to travel free on their national railways. Such sentiments were the first flush of nationhood for people.

Pakistan's birth was an act of separation from the predominantly Hindu India. The Kashmir dispute leading to a veritable war between the two young countries compounded the embitterment of partition. "Indian hostility" became a unifying sentiment for Pakistanis. Colleges and schools would periodically organize military training for the defense of the homeland; school textbooks were revised to include patriotic themes; periodic apprehensions of an Indian invasion stirred people to respond, in Prime Minister Liaquat Ali Khan's symbolic gesture, with a "fist in the face (*mucca*)." India became the foil for defining Pakistan.

People's nationalist feelings came out most vividly in the periodic armed confrontations with India, starting with the Runn of Kutch skirmish in 1964, and the full-scale wars in 1965 and 1971. As an expression of national unity, nothing surpasses the national fervor evoked by the 1965 war. Almost all parts of the country and all sections of the population fervently felt the cause of their nation.

Madam Noor Jehan's songs were the voices of every heart. Such valiant sons are not a common commodity, she crooned. It was the letdown from the aftermath of war that started President Ayub's slide from power. Later, confrontations with India may not have stirred all citizens as strongly, but they have always been moments affirming Pakistan's national coherence.

On the positive side, Pakistan has been stitched together by national institutions and infrastructure. Leaving aside physical infrastructure mentioned earlier, an extensive institutional framework of the press, laws, health, educational systems, political parties, and civil society organizations has evolved to touch everyone and link far-flung areas together. People expect Pakistan to be the provider of security, welfare, and prosperity.

Basant (Kite-flying festival) and the Independence Day annual celebrations as well as music, art, sports, film songs, and literature resonate in all parts of the country. Pakistan's cricket matches suspend business and glue people to television sets everywhere and wins are occasions of celebration in most homes. Imran Khan, Abida Parveen, Noor Jehan, or Sattar Edhi among others, are national icons.[19] These are the symbols of the national consciousness.

In the hierarchy of personal communities, Pakistan is now well embedded in the national psyche. It does not mean regional, ethnic, or local identities have been diminished. They exist at other planes of consciousness and command considerable loyalty. One litmus test of Pakistan's nationalism came in 1971 with its break-up; the rump Pakistan rallied round and reconstituted itself as a viable nation. Regrettably, there was no deep popular anguish about the separation of East Pakistan, as it was always such a distant and different presence. This event consolidated Pakistan territorially and socially.

Like any other nation, Pakistan also has internal dissensions, ethnic grievances, regional disparities, and even occasional armed insurrections. Its constitution promises provincial autonomy. Yet politically, Pakistan remains a centrally commanded country. There are deep divisions among provinces about public policies and distribution of resources. Its national destiny lies in being a multicultural society, yet its public discourse remains locked in arguments about the dominant ideology of state. Pakistan's nationalism is buffeted by the dissonance between its lived and imagined versions.

Layered ethnicity

Ethnicity is an attribute of groups, which is passed on to individuals as their identity and behavioral guide. It sets apart a group on the bases of its heritage, nationality, religion, language, cultural, and/or racial inheritance. Ethnicity is an objective reality reflected in the shared characteristics of a group, but it also has a subjective dimension in the consciousness of individuals.

Typically a Pakistani is raised in the mother tongue of his region, goes to school with children of her or his ethnic background, marries within the kinship circle, and relies on family and clan for security. Her or his daily life is defined by regional (sub)culture and community. Undoubtedly, the national institutions envelop regional societies and economies, but their influences largely affect economic conditions, laws, government, education, and other more formal aspects of social life.

In Pakistan, ethnicity is closely bound up with provincial societies, which may be further differentiated internally by tribes, clans, and regional and local communities of distinct dialects or languages and traditions. One may ethnically be a Punjabi, yet would be swayed by her or his identity as Riasati of Bahawalpur while voting in national elections. What level of ethnicity is triggered for an individual varies with the social context. A Pakistani in London is a Punjabi in Karachi, but a Saraiki-speaking Multani in Lahore. Yet each layer of identity is rooted in linguistic, cultural, and physiognomic distinctions. These distinctions are not fixed to begin with, but migration, travel, trade, and television are further scrambling them.

For example, Balochis are a segment of Pakistan's population distinguished by their tall and straight bearing, dark eyes, flowing black hair, tribal mores, and strong commitments to honor and freedom. As a group, Balochis display a discernible social solidarity. This group consciousness is imprinted in individuals as a self-image and sense of belonging. Yet among themselves, they are Marris, Bugti, Rind, or of other tribal identities.

Ethnic consciousness is heightened in contrast with others. A Baloch in his hometown is almost unaware of his ethnicity, but transplanted in Islamabad, he is very conscious of his Baloch identity. The point is that ethnicity comes to the surface when a group or an individual competes with others for economic resources, political power, and cultural or linguistic autonomy.

Social history of ethnicity

Pakistan is an ethnonational state. Its nationalism is based on the Muslims' claim of being a distinct religiocultural nation. Yet soon after independence, the provincial ethnicities started to surface. The Baloch Chief, Khan of Kalat, proclaimed independence; Pashtoon nationalism was rampant in NWFP; Bengali students rioted for their language rights; and Punjab was preoccupied with resettling refugees from the Indian Punjab. Refugees settled in Karachi became conscious of their ethnolinguistic identity.

Struggling for an appropriate share in economic development, maintaining cultural and linguistic identity, and preserving a modicum of self-rule were the motives that agitated ethnic interests. Pakistan has been periodically buffeted by upsurges in ethnic discontent, often coinciding with political turmoil and erosion of the legitimacy of the government of the time. Periods of ethnic agitation coincide with political disillusionment.

After the first flush of independence, the theme that stirred ethnic consciousness was the perceived disparity of opportunities for refugees and locals. Sindhi leaders protested resettlement of refugees on their lands. Punjabi and Bengali politicians resented domination of *UP walas* in the national power structure.

Urdu-speaking public officials migrating from India had an edge in positions of authority in the new state.[20] Stereotypically, they were assumed to be favoring their co-ethnics to the disadvantage of locals. These were the first stirrings of provincialism, which is the sentiment of solidarity with people from the province of one's origin and ethnicity.

The inequities of access to jobs have been the most potent force of ethnic discontent in Pakistan. Indian Muslims' demand for job quotas was interwoven in the struggle for Pakistan. Bengalis' main grievance against the state of Pakistan was the disparity in civil and military appointments. The anti-Ahmadi movement in Punjab in 1953 was inflamed with accusations of Ahmadis appropriating "high positions." Muhajirs in Karachi were aroused by the shift in the civil service quotas. All small provinces have long been aggrieved about Punjabis' domination in the military and civil administration. One could sum up the history of Pakistan's political crises and ethnic nationalism in terms of fights over job quotas.

The next major threshold in the rise of ethnic consciousness was the merger of four western provinces into the One-Unit in 1955. This obliteration of the historic provincial polities aroused regionalism and ignited distrust toward Punjabis. Restoration of the four provinces was a demand voiced in all parts of West Pakistan in the 1968 anti-Ayub protests. Paradoxically, ethnic identities grew sharper when they were attempted to be diffused.

The dissolution of the One-Unit in 1969 was an acknowledgment that ethnicity and language were the defining realities of Pakistani society. It was an appropriate prelude to the crowning of the folk traditions in the Bhutto era. Folk music, ethnic crafts, local attire, and country idioms were patronized. Sindhi *kurta*, Pashtoon vest, Swati cap, or Punjabi *shalwar* became the preferred wear in the halls of power. Mystical poetry, country tunes, and local crafts found a place in the pantheon of national arts. Ethnicity became chic, but only in cultural matters. Public authority continued to be concentrated in the federal government, although the 1973 constitution envisaged a high measure of provincial autonomy.

Not all ethnic groups gained equally from Bhutto's policies. Urdu speakers of Karachi were alienated by the reservation of jobs and educational opportunities for Sindhis. This alienation helped consolidate the Muhajir ethnicity both socially and politically. The suppression of the Frontier and Balochistan provincial governments sparked protests in these provinces. The "army action" suppressed the tribal revolt in Balochistan in 1973. Pashtoon leaders were persecuted to suppress demands for provincial autonomy.

From 1978 onward, the cultural pendulum has been swinging away from the folk traditions, which essentially reflect regional and local heritage. General Zia's Islamism was, in intent, a thrust to realign beliefs, practices, and habits in a predominant Islamic narrative, although it did not actively suppress the regional cultures. His regime selectively co-opted *mushaikhs* and *pirs* (mystical and spiritual guides) to bring folk traditions within the national narrative by proclaiming sufis (spiritualists) and *ulema* (priests and Islamic scholars) to be one and the same.

The process of constructing a unitary narrative continues through political Islam as well as through the globalization of the 1990s. Although mutually contradictory, these are forces of homogenization. Paradoxically, they simultaneously erode and reinforce regional cultures. Ethnic poetry, music, or crafts find wider markets and are thus enriched on the one hand, whereas the universalistic notions and beliefs displace local knowledge and languages on the other.

The Baloch tribal insurrection of the Bhutto era was defined by Mr Bizenjo, the deposed governor and a *sardar* of Balochistan, and some Leninist theorists as the struggle for "nationality rights," implying the rights of secession and self-determination for linguistic and cultural minorities.[21] This assertion alarmed the ruling elite in Islamabad, both political and military, and added to their distrust of ethnic autonomy. Bhutto reacted with force against such expressions. General Zia deployed Islam to override ethnic nationalism.

When Sindhis' disaffection with the Zia regime turned into a sustained agitation under the Movement for the Restoration of Democracy (MRD) protest movement, his government leaned toward Muhajir (later renamed Muthida) Qaumi Movement (MQM) to counterbalance it. Sociologically, these political maneuverings fostered interethnic strife, widening the gulf among ethnic communities living side by side in Karachi, Hyderabad, and other cities of Sindh. The mutual distrust between Sindhis and Muhajirs turned into endemic ethnic violence. Sindhi–Muhajir–Pashtoon riots flared repeatedly during the 1985–8 period. Since then, the social distance between these groups has widened so much that violence can erupt almost any time on a rumor or traffic accident.[22]

For Balochistan and the Frontier Provinces, the Soviet invasion of Afghanistan and its aftermath were the transforming events of the 1980s. These two border provinces were host to about three million Afghan refugees whose presence changed their demography and political culture. As a result, Balochistan become a Pashtoon majority province. The Frontier has been pulled into the Afghan imbroglio.

By the beginning of the twenty-first century, Pashtoon ethnicity has been overlaid with Islamic conservatism of the Taliban variety. Islamic ideology itself is being Pashtoonized with the incorporation of tribal traditions as the authentic elements of Islam. Even the leadership of Islamic movements in Pakistan has passed on to Pashtoon heads of *madrassahs* (seminaries) and political leaders. The tolerance and hospitality of Pashtoons and Baloch are yielding to the militancy of their faith. A sectarian fissure has appeared in Pakistan's ethnic mosaic.[23]

Social expressions of ethnicity

How does ethnicity affect group relations and daily life in Pakistan? Ethnicity is visibly woven into the politics of the country, but it also underlies social relations and affects economic and social organization. Ethnicity comes into play at three levels: (1) as moral communities and linguistic/cultural solidarities of primordial uniformities, such as Punjabis, Pashtoons, and Sindhis; (2) as tribes, clans, castes, and *biradari* (groups bounded by endogamy); (3) as kinship and family groups. Ethnicity represents "roots" for an individual. It is what one is born with.

Provincial ethnic communities are not organized as social structures, rather as solidarities that have a common heritage, language(s), values, beliefs, and myths but few, if any, institutions. They are moral communities. There are no province-wide institutions that link members together except some political and cultural associations. Common expectations and a sense of belonging tie members to each other, but these subterranean bonds come alive in the political arena.

Punjabis are the majority of Pakistan's population. They are well represented in political, bureaucratic, and military establishments. Like many majority communities, Punjabis serve as the political other for Sindhis, Balochis, etc. For Punjabis, ethnicity is not as much a matter of public discourse as it is for others. Ethnicity is a low-key affair in Punjab. Punjabi is largely a spoken language, while Urdu rules as the written medium. Punjabis are like Anglo-Saxons in the US, where Jews, Italians, or Latins are ethnics, but Anglo-Saxons are rarely so in public discourse.

Pashtoons, Balochis, Sindhis, and lately Muhajirs are relatively more conscious of their ethnicity as minority communities. They demand a fair share of political authority and economic development as well as the preservation of their cultural and linguistic heritage. Unsurprisingly, these are the common expressions of ethnicity, particularly those of minority communities, in a multiethnic society.

It is in second-level groups, namely tribes, clans, and *biradaris*, that ethnic values and mores are enacted in institutionalized ways. Such groups hone and elaborate ethnic identities and exercise social control for the observance of customs and traditions. Often these identities, indicating lineages, are reflected in the last names of individuals. Names such as Awan, Mazari, Jatoi, Khatak, or Rajput, are lineage or clan identities for millions of Pakistanis. These identities and norms also filter down to the third level of ethnicity, namely in families and kinship groups.

Socially, ethnicity in Pakistan works from inside out, beginning with family, clan, and kin and extending to tribe, *biradari,* or caste and through them merging into Pashtoon, Muhajir, or other cultural/territorial community. For example, a Punjabi is first a Qureshi, Chaudhry, or Sial, as is a Balochi first Brohi or a Bughti. *Biradaris* in Punjab and clans and tribes in NWFP, Sindh, and Balochistan are the groups whose identity, values, approval, or ostracism have direct bearing on an individual's status, heritage, and identity.

The prevailing provincial ethnicity is not the primary reference point for people's behavior. For example, marriages are not contracted freely among, say, Punjabis or Pashtoons, but within specific clans and *biradaris* and even within these groups with cousins or other blood relatives. Kinship networks and clan identities map the everyday life of a Pakistani. They are the channels through which the broader ethnic bonds are routed.

Ethnic bonds and identities in Pakistan do not prevail in all situations. Social movements and religious or sectarian loyalties and political ideologies can trump them. Even within a tribe or *biradari*, Sunnis would not normally marry Shias, although they may unite in disputes with other clans or tribes.

Jinnah, a Bohra from Bombay, Bhutto, a Sindhi, and even Nawaz Sharif, a Punjabi, could energize people across ethnic boundaries in support of their political programs. Ethnonationalist parties, such as Jeay Sindh or Baloch Liberation Front, have never fared well in elections. Ethnicity operates within the scope of Pakistan's nationalism and in tandem with other social forces and ideologies.

In everyday life, ethnicity defines an individual and circumscribes her or his social network and community. One largely lives among co-ethnics and depends on them for emotional and social support. Underneath the formal organizational structures of public or private agencies are informal networks of provincial, linguistic, or tribal and caste solidarities. A ministry may have a Punjabi or more refined Multani or Syed network for mutual support in postings and promotions.

Often the ethnic networks are based on finer identities of tribes, localities, or castes. For example, student organizations are initially based on political and/or linguistic/provincial affinities, but within these structures, there are fraternities of tribal, *biradari,* or locality origins. The Islamic Jamiat-i-Tulaba (IJT) may dominate a university students union, but leadership cliques and social clubs could be based on networks or *anjumans* (associations) of, say, Syeds of Narowal, Yousafzais from Mardan, or Muhajirs from Bihar, etc.

Such second-level ethnic bonds attain a primacy within provincial/linguistic communities. For example, the Agricultural University of Punjab is predominantly a Punjabi institution. Its faculty has long been divided into cliques of Jats versus Arians, affecting careers and defining their affiliations and professional loyalties. Even the civil service and military appointments are enveloped in "whispers" of ethnic, tribal, or *biradari* advantages. Why did Nawaz Sharif attempt to oust General Pervez Musharraf and appoint General Zia-ud-Din Khwaja as the chief of the army in 1999? Because he expected a Kashmiri-Punjabi to be more loyal, popular speculation suggests.[24] The point of these examples is not that all members of a tribe or caste are tightly bound together – in fact most of them do not know each other – but that such subprovincial–ethnic identities have a role in everyday life and are the basis of social organization. Yet, configurations of ethnicity are continually changing.

Fuzzy boundaries and changing identities

Ethnicity is not a fixed attribute either in time or over space. It is built on a set of beliefs by which a community defines itself. These beliefs are social constructs in the sense that they have been forged over a long period in the course of a group's historical evolution. They can change as the internal and external conditions alter. Seldom are sharp geographic and social boundaries of an ethnic community observed. Altogether, ethnic definitions and identities evolve and change. Even individuals opt in and out of particular ethnic identities as their social status and geographic locations change. Pakistan has witnessed considerable revisions and realignments in ethnic identities.

To begin with, the geographic boundaries between all pairs of ethnic communities overlap. Balochis live in Dera Ghazi Khan and Mianwali districts of Punjab and Dadu, Jacobabad, and Karachi districts of Sindh, as Sindhis and Punjabis have lived away from their ancestral provinces. Similar overlapping of ethnic groups occurs in NWFP.

In periods of political protests or unrest against the national government (1968, 1973–5, 1983–5), Balochi, Pashtoon, or Sindhi nationalists have laid claims to the bordering districts for ethnic unity. During the tribal insurrection (1973–6), Balochi unity resonated among the youth in Punjab and Sindh. However, such sentiments fade away after the heady days of political battles. My point is that the presumed geographical boundaries of ethnic communities expand and contract with evolving political agendas and ideologies.

The linguistic and cultural boundaries of an ethnic community are also malleable. Each of Pakistan's provincial ethnic communities is internally differentiated by dialects, customs, and social organization. These differences form the bases of subethnicities, which sometimes assert their distinctness and at other times submerge into the larger community. Saraiki-speaking areas of South Punjab were well integrated in Punjab's urbanizing economy, but during the nationwide agitation in 1968, the demand for a separate Saraiki province galvanized some regional leaders and sparked interest in the local heritage.

Sindhis' agitation for "Sindhu Desh" in 1983 was supported by pirs of Hala and Ranipur in the Southern and northern districts of Sindh, but Pir Pagara's followers in the upper Sindh remained aloof. The Balochi language has six dialects, speakers of which J. Elfenbein maintains militated against the formation of a standard literary language.[25] Apart from the politics of regionalism, these subethnic movements are indicative of shifting notions of cultural and linguistic communities. Who is Punjabi or Pashtoon has different answers on the social and territorial margins and at different historical moments.

The formation of Muhajir identity is an illustrative example of how ethnicity is socially constructed. Muslim migrants from the northern provinces of India started settling in Karachi and other cities of Pakistan after the partition. Some were refugees from communal riots and others were immigrants of choice. As the majority came from Urdu-speaking areas, all were lumped together as "Urdu speakers" in popular parlance even though many came from Gujarat and Bombay. Karachi became their base from where they spread out to Hyderabad, Sukkur, and other towns of Sindh, thereby turning urban Sindh into an immigrants' base.

Urdu speakers of Karachi in the 1950s and 1960s identified themselves as Pakistani nationalists, defining it as the marriage of Islam and Urdu. When Bengali was declared as the second national language in 1952, Raees Amrohvi, a popular poet, wrote a ditty proclaiming Urdu's death (*Urdu ka janaza hai zara dhoom say niklay* – Urdu's funeral, let it rise in style). Karachites started feeling alienated with the shift of the federal capital to Islamabad in 1959, but their feelings turned to anger on the Bhutto government's policies differentiating between rural and urban Sindhis. These political sentiments forged a new consciousness of a distinct community called Muhajirs. The Muhajir Qaumi Movement (MQM) emerged as the political voice of Muhajirs and it jettisoned Urdu speakers' identity as Pakistani nationalists and Islamists. Its slogan in 1986 encapsulates this transformation: *Ham nain Pakistan aur Islam ka theka nahin liya hai* (We have not contracted to uphold Pakistan and Islam).

Interestingly, Urdu speakers who settled in Punjab or the Frontier Province do not identify themselves as Muhajirs, but those in Sindh have chosen to acquire a distinct ethnicity. MQM is now in continual conflict with the Jamaat-i-Islami (JI) with which immigrants in Karachi had aligned at first.[26] From their identity as a linguistic group, immigrants in Sindh have evolved into a regional ethnic community.

Islam and ethnicity

About 96 percent of Pakistan's population is Muslim. This overwhelming uniformity of faith characterizes all regions of the country. Sindh is the province with the lowest proportion of Muslims, but even there they make up about 91 percent of the population. Given that Islam is a defining element of Pakistani nationalism, its religious uniformity overarches ethnic communities. The bond of common faith militates against ethnic segregation. Islam is a historical force of social convergence.

Yet the relationship between Islam and ethnicity is not one-directional. Ethnicity colors religious beliefs and practices and co-opts them to rationalize cultural mores and values. Furthermore, Islam as a religious doctrine admits a variety of interpretations and has accommodated a diversity of practices. As an institutionalized religion, the house of Islam is divided into sects, jurisprudential schools, and spiritual *tariqas* (circles). All these differences interact with "cultures" embedded in ethnicity. The result is that social organizations of Islamic institutions vary from region to region.

Pashtoons practise *vulver* (bride price) while Muhajirs and Punjabis give ruinously lavish dowries to their daughters, both tracing their practices to the Prophet's example. Pashtoon tribes' Islamic calendar is often out of sync with the rest of the country by a day or so, particularly on Ramadan and Eid, each region proclaiming the accuracy of their Islamic calendar.

Ethnic norms about marriage and divorce, women's rights, ritual washing and spiritualism, inheritance, and land tenure differ, despite the discourse of Islamic unity. Most strikingly, the custom of arranging marriages within one's family and tribe or *biradari* has withstood all the sermons about "Islam is free from caste and clan restrictions." Islamic brotherhood does not easily penetrate the bonds of family. Often economic change and mobility including diaspora have proven to be a more potent force of eroding clan ties than the Islamic brotherhood.

Shrines and spiritualism (sufism) are more unifying influences than government institutions, ecclesiastical doctrines, and religious discourses. Shrines of Shahbaz Qalander (Sindh), Baba Farid, and Dahta Gunj Baksh (Punjab), for example, draw devotees from all parts of Pakistan. Even sectarian differences do not matter at these shrines. Everyone is accepted for what he or she is. This is how ethnicity fits into Islamic practices. It negotiates its place in the house of Islam.

Convergence of ethnicities

Provincially based ethnic communities have diverged from one another in the political arena. The competition for economic resources and political powers divides smaller provinces in Punjab but their views too have differed from one another regarding the distribution of water, energy, finances, and national authority. The politics of ethnicity in Pakistan divides ethnic communities.

Although away from the political arena, there are social forces that are bringing the ethnic communities closer. A process of social convergence is also underway.

Economic development has changed the social relations of production in Pakistan. The nation has evolved from a predominantly agrarian-peasant to a semi-industrial economy. Cash has become the measure of most transactions. Capitalist order has filtered down into the remote parts of the country and brought about an interlinking of regional production and markets. This realignment of the productive forces has breached ethnic frontiers and linked provincial and regional communities. What are some of the manifestations of the convergence?

Paralleling other contemporary societies, the primary fault line in incomes and living conditions in Pakistan now runs along the urban–rural divide. Undoubtedly, there are provincial disparities. Balochistan really lags behind other provinces. But even here, the provincial capital city, Quetta, is closer to Lahore, Peshawar, or Hyderabad economically and socially than it is to Kalat or Zhob, predominantly rural districts of the province. Cities, in particular, interact with each other more than with their respective hinterlands.

Occupational and income differentiations have been laid over ethnic and clan or caste identities. Corporate executives, political leaders, the officer class, businessmen, and even clerks and industrial workers associate as much with one another across provincial and ethnic boundaries as with members of their clans or castes. They have similar lifestyles, ambitions, and interests although they still fall back on kin and clan for support.

Serena's "food fiesta" is as popular in Quetta as the Avari's is in Lahore. The newly affluent classes share many tastes in common. Even the "market" for pornographic clips interjected in movies operates in similar ways in Quetta, Peshawar, Faisalabad, or Karachi.

Trade and travel are also intertwining ethnic communities. Sindhi *ajraks* (printed cotton shawls) and bedspreads are now given in dowries in Lahore and Islamabad; Punjabi tubewell parts-makers explore Balochistan's towns for agents; Pashtoon dealers are suppliers for Lahore's carpet market. Grain, fruits, and cloth have long been traded across the provincial boundaries, but now cars, motorbikes, fans, and other manufactured goods flow freely across provinces. Even the bazaar economy of smuggled Russian refrigerators, Japanese TV sets, and English dinnerware is now a seamless web distributing such "imported stuff" from Quetta or Chaman and Peshawar or Landi Kotal to *baras* (smugglers' markets) in Lahore, Karachi, Islamabad, and other cities.

Families and youth groups from all parts of the country flock to hill stations in summer to escape the heat of the plains. Modish girls from Karachi and Islamabad stroll in bazaars of conservative Saidu Sharif and Kaghan in the Frontier province. Postings and transfers in military and civilian agencies bring persons of diverse ethnic backgrounds to the farthest corners of the country, although more strikingly in the urban centers and cantonments (military bases).

Popular television serials introduce Punjabi audiences to the tensions of Balochi or Sindhi landlords' households. Conversely, Punjabi vendettas are played for the amusement of Pashtoons, Sindhis, or Hunzas. The isolation of ethnic communities has become a memory of the past.

There is no part of the country that has been left untouched by the flow of people of diverse ethnicities. About eight percent of the total population had migrated to their place of residence from somewhere else in 1998, but migration into the cities like Karachi, Lahore, and Islamabad/Rawalpindi was as high as 25–30 percent of the population. Normally people of different ethnic backgrounds live side by side in harmony, except in times of politically charged violence as happened in Karachi (1968, 1985–6) and Hyderabad (1990).

The only area in which ethnicity, rather more precisely tribal or *biradari* ties, remains largely unbreached is in matters of marriage and family. Interethnic marriages are rare, except in districts of historically co-inhabiting ethnic communities of Balochis and Sindhis. Mixed marriages are beginning to become frequent in the thin slice of the professional class engaged in art and fashion industries or global businesses.

Social integration: national society and ethnic communities

How well do provincial ethnic communities fit into the national society? Or in other words, what is the level of social integration in Pakistan, which has been branded a "failed state" by some observers who believe that it may be on the verge of splitting apart.[27]

Social integration is a process and not a structure or (permanent) condition. Even in the unitary state of Britain, Northern Ireland and Scotland's identity and autonomy remain matters of national debate and occasional violence. Pakistan is undoubtedly figuring out a satisfactory way of balancing ethnic and national interests, particularly in political and economic realms. Yet there are forces and processes that are promoting the integration of civic society and social institutions in the manner of two steps forward and one backward. I would judge the national society fairly well integrated, despite political discontents about provincial rights. This judgment is based on the observations of the preceding sections.

Ethnic communities are anchored territorially (provinces) and historically. While Pakistani society has crystallized in the course of state formation, it is relatively new. But it has rapidly evolved as the embodiment of national values, institutions, and identity.

Ethnic identities and community bonds in Pakistan are hierarchically organized from kinship groups or clans at the core, extending to tribes or *biradaris* and merging into the broad provincial/linguistic communities.

Sociologically, kinship-tribal and *biradari* institutions are central to the identity and the status or role of an individual. These institutions are changing under the influence of economic development, national legislation, information explosion, urbanization, etc. Ethnicity embodied in these institutions is being integrated in the emerging national system.[28]

Broad ethnicity, Punjabi, Pashtoon, etc., is mainly triggered in the national discourse about provincial autonomy and economic disparities. It represents community solidarity to advance collective regional interests. The struggle for a fair share in the national resources and authority reinforces ethnic consciousness and promotes the commitment to ethnic, cultural and linguist heritage.

Pakistan's political instability, the basis of the "failed state" thesis, is largely the result of the inability of the ruling elite to forge a social contract that accommodates pluralism and balances traditions with modernity. Ethnic conflicts in Pakistan are largely the Pakistani state's inadequacies projected onto its society. Aside from the political arena, Pakistan is coming to terms with its social diversity. Parallel social norms and cultural values have emerged in all ethnic communities. People of diverse ethnic backgrounds live and work side by side in most urban areas, especially in major cities. Ethnicity is not diffusing, but is settling into the national society and politics as a structural component. Pakistan is a pluralistic society; its state has to be structured to reflect this fact. I will have more to say on these changes in subsequent chapters.

5 Urban transformations

Cities and society

Human progress has primarily been forged in cities. Name any significant religious or philosophical idea, technological invention, artistic production, or social movement; it will have originated in a city. Mohenjo Daro, Athens, Jerusalem, Medina, and London, to name a few, are familiar way-stations in the march of human civilizations. The role of cities as crucibles of social and cultural change is documented in history. It speaks of their contributions to the dynamics of social change. They are equally central to the structure of a society. They are hubs of economic, political, and social life. To observe a society and its culture, one turns to its cities for a quick read. Pakistan's cities also encapsulate its essential institutions, both as they exist, and as they are changing. We look at them for an understanding of both the structure and dynamics of a society.

Cities are an integral part of a society, but they are also different in some ways from its villages and countryside. The culture of cities is anchored in the values and norms of society at large, yet in a city these elements assume distinct forms arising from the concentration of population and interconnectedness of activities. For example, Pakistani society traditionally values segregation of women from men. This value in villages becomes a norm for women to shun interaction with nonkin males. In cities, the same norm takes different forms, for example, avoiding intimacy with strangers, putting on a *dupatta* (shawl), *burqa*, or separate seats for women in buses, and in situations where contact with unrelated males is unavoidable (a situation normally not common in villages) to maintain an unsmiling and expressionless visage. The norm grows out of the same value, yet in cities it carries more latitude for interpretation to suit varying situations; it almost becomes a different practice.

Such rural–urban differences have long been considered a defining characteristic of urbanism as a way of life. Modernization theories have seized on these differences by viewing rural areas as the bastions of traditions and by regarding cities as the vanguard of modernity. The theoretical roots of this proposition can be traced back to medieval times, but it was explicitly articulated in the nineteenth and twentieth centuries.

Long before the discovery of agglomeration economies and the beneficial effects of division of labor in cities, Ibn Khaldun (1370s) had observed that cities are places of luxury and civilization because of "the cooperation of a group of human beings."[1] The French Revolution and the end of monarchy/feudal order initiated the transformation of Europe from feudal/religious modes of living to constitutional rule and capitalist economy. Max Weber associated this transformation with urban life.[2] At the core of this argument is the notion that social relations in cities are based on self-interest more than blood or tribal obligations. In cities, people relate to one another in specified roles for particular purposes (secondary relations) as opposed to emotional bonds and person-to-person dealings (primary relations) in rural communthe ities.[3]

Culture of cities and modernization

Sociologists view the culture of cities in terms of the quality of social relations and community life. Usually urban ways of life are presented in contrast to those prevailing in the country. Emile Durkheim (1893) was among the pioneering theorists to focus on societal changes arising from urbanization and industrialization. He maintained that the "mechanical" (unity of the similar) solidarity of rural communities gives way to "organic" (interdependence of the diverse) cohesion in cities.[4] Georg Simmel (1902) pointed out that the money economy pervasive in a city fosters individualism, blasé attitudes, and secondary relations, thus linking urbanism with a particular social psychology.[5] Louis Wirth (1938) carried this line of reasoning to its logical conclusion: linking large size, high density, and heterogeneity of urban population to anonymity, impersonalization, and segmentation of social relations in the city.[6] These theories, starkly contrasting city and country cultures, have not fully withstood the empirical scrutiny of the late twentieth century. The differences do exist but they are variations along a common base.

From these formulations two diverse themes emerged: one, "loss of community" and "lonely crowd" in the city and two, the city as a metaphor of individual liberty and social change. These themes have promoted contradictory views of the role of the city, namely, it is a source of human misery versus an embodiment of human progress. The modernization theorists have embraced the latter viewpoint. Presently the question is: do cities modernize the Third World and, specifically for us, do Pakistani cities play this role?

The modernizing role of cities has been a controversial topic. Long before social change in the Third World emerged as a topic of interest, the experiences of an Italian neighborhood in Boston or Bethnel Green in London had refuted the notion that community solidarity does not exist in cities.[7] Cities seemed to be not of one uniform culture, but they seemingly supported a diversity of lifestyles and social organizations. From urban villagers to ethnic enclaves, a wide range of (sub)cultures and communities thrive in cities. Also, it has been observed that rural and urban communities converge toward a common culture with the emergence of a mass society. These observations revised the formulations of Louis Wirth and other urban sociologists and have given a new perspective on the role and culture of cities.

Cities have certain common physical requirements arising from large numbers of people living in high concentrations. The high density of population and activities necessitates the laying of proper streets, parceling of land and regulation of tenure, water supply and waste disposal arrangements, fire control and safety systems, parks and public health, etc. This hard infrastructure has to be complemented by soft services and institutions, such as municipal organizations, land use plans, sanitation practices and traffic laws. This is the public space of a city, which is similar across countries and over time.[8] The similarity is of structure and functions, although form and meanings may differ.

The notion of a common culture of cities is inspired by the universality of public space. It implies that a similar public space fosters similar norms and behaviors. Yet the private space of social relations and values in cities differs by nations, economies, and cultures. This is the source of the plurality of communities and diversity of local cultures in cities. Thus the culture of public space is functionally singular, but that of private space pluralistic. This dichotomy defines the role of cities.

Architecturally and organizationally, cities have some uniformity of forms and functions. Regardless of where a city is, it is likely to imbibe some modern forms in modern times. Every contemporary city has glass-encased office buildings, brightly lit shopping streets, traffic laws, universities, laboratories, and municipal governments, for example. In form, they are similar across countries although some may be more striking and efficient than others. A large population and multiplicity of activities in a city require bureaucracies and the rule of rules. Some impersonalization of dealings is also necessary. When one encounters crowds in a public space one cannot respond empathetically and warmly to everyone, unlike a village where primary relations are unavoidable because of the frequent contacts with one another. Urbanization changes the physical base and social institutions of an area. Such changes have been associated with the modernizing role of cities.

The private realm of personal and community life is influenced by class, ethnicity, and the culture of a society at large. A city's private space is anchored in its society and culture. In private space, a city has a dual role, to represent the high traditions of the national culture and to lead in changing those traditions. This balancing of continuity and change is the wedge of urbanism.

The private–public dichotomy is complemented by contradictions between material and nonmaterial sectors of culture. This is why, at one level, a Third World city appears to be a replica of London or Toronto, but at another it appears to be an overgrown native village. Both are realities, but at different planes of observation. This is the dialectic of change, different parts responding to different forces.

Pakistan's cities are the platform for its modernization, particularly in economic production and consumption. They are also steeped in history and swamped by traditions. They play multiple roles and are internally divided; some parts are emblems of modernity, while others are the base for reinvigorating and inventing traditions. How are they evolving and what are they contributing to the continuity and change of Pakistani society? To answer these questions, we have to begin by describing the system of cities and towns in Pakistan.

Urban system

Pakistan has become an urban society. This assertion may surprise many observers of Pakistani society who have long regarded it a rural country. Undoubtedly Pakistan has been a country of farmers' villages and herders' tribes since time immemorial. But it has changed in the past century, more rapidly in the last five decades. As I have pointed out in Chapter 3, by the density criterion, in 1998 a majority (56 percent) of the population lived in settlements that were either classified as urban or had urban-level densities.[9] Thus, a majority of Pakistanis live in a public space that requires piped water and drains, traffic regulations, housing policies, etc. They may not have these urban services, but since they are needed it has affected the quality of community life. Physically and institutionally, the social life of a majority of Pakistanis has crossed the threshold of urbanization. The rest of the population living in villages are also being swept along by urban influences. These facts lead me to apply Janet Abu-Lughod's apt phrase "urbanization of everybody" in referring to Pakistan.[10]

Cities and towns form a thick network over the plains of Punjab and Sindh, but they are few and far between in hills and deserts, primarily dotting the historic trade routes. The British established a hierarchy of administrative areas, *tehsils/ talukas* (subdivisions) covering the whole country. These basic administrative units dovetail to form districts, which in turn have been combined in divisions and provinces. The seats of *tehsils*, districts, and provinces emerged as administrative and service centers forming layers of towns and cities of varying sizes and functions. This hierarchy of towns and cities, now topped by megacities, forms the urban system of Pakistan. The population growth has swept through almost all towns and cities, but some have exploded with their transformation into major commercial/industrial centers.

The extent of Pakistan's urban system is indicated by the fact that there were 515 urban places in 1998, some very large but a majority in the 10,000–50,000 population range. In 1951, there were only 238 urban places. The number of urban places has been consistently increasing since independence. Punjab has almost half of the urban places, followed by Sindh with about a quarter. NWFP and Balochistan have comparatively fewer urban places.

Cities and megacities

The locus of urbanism lies in the 12 major cities with a population of about 500,000 or more. About 60 percent of the population classified as urban live in these cities. Karachi alone has more than 10 million people living in it, followed by Lahore with about six million. These two megacities are the growth poles of Pakistan's economic and social life. They produce new technologies, behaviors, beliefs, and fashions. Their economic opportunities draw workers from all parts of the country and abroad, Karachi more so than Lahore.

Below the two megacities are nine cities of a million or more population plus another three that had between one-half to one million inhabitants in 1998. Punjab led in the number of major cities – 8 out of 12 were in this province – followed by two in Sindh and one each in the Frontier (NWFP) and Balochistan.

Karachi

The growth of these cities in general, and Karachi/Lahore in particular, is a metaphor of social change in Pakistan. Karachi was a somnolent seaport, which served as the outlet for the export of wheat and cotton from the newly irrigated lands of Punjab and Sindh in the early part of the twentieth century. During World War II it was a naval base for the British fleet. Its population was only 386,000 in 1941, which almost tripled to more than a million in ten years (1951), largely with the influx of refugees from India at independence. Urdu-speaking refugees transformed Karachi from a Sindhi port town to the multicultural first capital of Pakistan. It has continued to grow exponentially ever since and has become the premier industrial and commercial center of the country. Between 25 and 40 percent of the value added to the national economy originates from Karachi.[11] This is an indication of its economic role in Pakistan.

Lahore

Lahore has almost the same story, fast take-off after independence and explosive growth since then. It is an ancient city, which was the second court of the Mughals. Historically, its economic base lay in administrative and commercial activities. It has been the capital of Punjab since the Middle Ages. During British rule, it became a cultural and educational center as well. The land settlement after the building of irrigation canals in Punjab in the 1920s created a rich class of newly minted landlords. Lahore became the place of second residence for the rural elite. Here they played politics and indulged in conspicuous consumption. Its leisurely pace, literary ferment, and political power turned the pre-independence Lahore into a place of fun and culture. In Pakistan, Lahore continued to be a major city, but unlike Karachi it was initially not impacted by industrial development.

Lahore's growth in the first period (1947–71) was essentially driven by the natural growth of population after the exchange of population in 1947–8. By the 1960s, large industrial establishments started to locate around its periphery, in commuting distance but outside local jurisdiction to avoid industrial controls and taxes. By the second period (1972–7), a ring of industries had emerged around the city, pulling in rural migrants and changing the social structure. The third period (1978–present) has turned Lahore into a sprawling and fast-paced metropolis of mercantile ethos. It is more oriented to its hinterland than Karachi, which has extensive links with Gulf countries in particular and internationally in general.

Karachi and Lahore attract attention for their dominance of Pakistan's economic and cultural life. Yet the relatively unheralded story of the secondary cities and district towns has a strong bearing on the social changes in Pakistan. Seven other million-plus cities have evolved largely since 1947. Faisalabad, a farm-market town, had a population of about 100,000 and ranked sixth in 1947. It has grown to be the third largest city, with a population topping two million, and an international

Table 5.1 Ranking of major cities*, 1951–98

	1951		1972		1998	
	Population	Rank	Population	Rank	Population	Rank
Karachi	1,068,459	1	3,515,402	1	9,339,023	1
Lahore	849,333	2	2,169,742	2	5,443,495	2
Faisalabad	179,127	6	823,343	3	2,008,861	3
Rawalpindi	236,877	4	614,809	5	1,409,768	4
Multan	190,122	5	538,949	6	1,197,384	5
Hyderabad	241,801	3	628,631	4	1,166.894	6
Gujranwala	120,852	9	323,880	7	1,132,509	7
Peshawar	151,435	8	272,697	8	982,816	8
Quetta	83,892	10	158,026	11	759,941	9
Islamabad	—	—	76,641	12	529,180	10
Sargodha	78,447	11	200,460	10	458,440	11
Sialkot	156,378	7	203,650	9	421,502	12

Source: 1998 Census of Pakistan, Publication 160, Table 2.5
*Cities include Cantonments and other contiguous urban localities.

center of textile trade and manufacturing. Multan, Peshawar and Hyderabad grew by five to six times in about 50 years (1951–98). Gujranwala and Quetta both expanded nine times in the same period. The parallel growth of these cities has resulted in their keeping their ranks in Pakistan's urban hierarchy almost unchanged (Table 5.1). Each one of them casts a long shadow on its surrounding region, spreading urbanism all around.

Islamabad's growth, the new but not-so-new-any-more capital, is another story of dramatic development. Starting from scratch (1959), its population passed the half a million mark by 1998 in about 40 years, and its proximity to Rawalpindi makes the twin-cities a major metropolitan area. It has been designed in the suburban idiom, sprawling, green, and lacking in focus. As a city of bureaucrats and politicians, it has an aura of power and affluence.

Secondary cities

Two different development thrusts have driven the growth of second-tier cities. Punjab's cities, Faisalabad, Gujranwala, and Multan grew by becoming industrial and service centers in the midst of farming regions, which have been transformed by the green revolution. The technological transformation of agriculture depends on urban services for farm production. These cities became centers of those services.

Peshawar and Quetta, two provincial capitals bordering Afghanistan, leapt to the million-size class during the period (1981–98) of the Afghan war, serving initially as the bases for the flow of US funds and arms in the war against Soviet Occupation but subsequently as the reception areas for Afghan refugees. This role has transformed these two cities economically, demographically, and culturally. They are now big centers for trade in smuggled goods and contraband. They have become predominantly Pashtoon cities, whereas historically Peshawar was a Hindku-speaking city and Quetta was a Baloch town. Both have become places of social conservatism and assertive Islam.

The third-tier cities, with 100,000–200,000 population, are usually district seats and market/service centers that have colleges, hospitals, public agencies, and small industries. They are usually the regional centers for the surrounding regions, but sometimes they excel in one or another industry or are centers of religious significance, for example, Wah as the defense industry town, Shikarpur as the historic market, or Kohat as the military base and gateway of smuggled goods from Afghanistan. Pakpattan's economy has grown on the shrine of Farid Shakargunj. These cities also act as links in the global chains connecting local areas to Karachi, Dubai, and even New York. In 1998, they numbered 30 and had 9.6 percent of the urban population. Still lower on the urban hierarchy are towns of 25,000–100,000 population, 197 in number and containing about 21 percent of the urban population in 1998. Such towns form the spine of urbanization in Pakistan. They are the transportation and commercial/service hubs for their surrounding countryside.

Even off-the-main-axis places, which are not on the Peshawar–Lahore–Karachi corridor, have grown rapidly in the half-century of Pakistan's history. Take the example of the seats of four such districts that I have selected as representative of social change, namely Sialkot, Mardan, Sukkur, and Kalat: three of these four towns have become veritable cities. Sialkot, a historic town experienced some stagnation in the first two decades after independence due to the loss of its role as the gateway to Kashmir, but then its sports goods industry boomed with exports, turning it into a thriving city of about half a million. Sukkur (1998 population 329,000) and Mardan (1998 population 245,000), also historical towns, essentially took off in the second period (1972–8) and gained further momentum in the third period with the development of commercial crops and fruit orchards around them. The sugar, cigarette, and textile industries have developed based on the produce of the surrounding farm areas. Kalat, the ancient seat of Balochistan's tribal confederacy, is a small town of 23,000 (1998) people perched on a sparsely populated dry and stony plateau. Even emigration has not affected the city and it continues to have a subsistence economy. The remoteness and aridity of the region reflects in the town. Small towns of Balochistan are the only exceptions to the urban boom that has swept Pakistan.

Three distinct patterns of urban growth can be discerned. One, Karachi and Lahore are driven by global and national growth impulses. Beginning with the advantage of being provincial capitals in an emerging state, they have the institutional base and the infrastructure to attract modern commercial and industrial activities. Both are transmission points of global influences, one more than the other, and national powerhouses of economic and social development. At the same time, they are also custodians of traditions.

Two, some cities have thrived on the increasing agricultural productivity in their surrounding regions. Their economic bases have expanded with the opportunities to process agricultural produce and provide services for the surrounding region.

Three, the international political events, such as the "Iranian revolution" and the Afghan *jehad*, have had a dramatic impact on the fortunes of some cities and towns in the western provinces of NWFP and Balochistan.

All in all, Pakistan's cities and towns have undergone unprecedented changes since independence. How are these changes reflected in their internal structures?

Historical urban structure

A city is an engraving of a social organization on land. It is a physical record of an area's society and economy. It can be thought of as a text, which yields its meanings to readers savvy about its history.[12] The internal structure of a city is a description of how its residential, commercial, and industrial areas are laid out and how they are related to each other socially and economically. It is as much a reflection of present functional relations as it is a record of past processes.

In Pakistani cities and towns, history is a living reality. Although sixteenth-seventeenth-century mosques and shrines, palace-forts, *havelis* (mansions of notables), and remnants of town-walls are living symbols of the past, the core of cities lies in the historic *mohallas* (residential quarters) and bazaars. Yet history is not frozen in these places. The historic fabric of cities and towns has been continually adapted, modified, and added upon to accommodate new functions and demands of the increasing population.

Many cities and villages in Pakistan originated in ancient times during the Indus and Gandhara civilizations and the brief period of Greek rule, for example, Mohenjo Daro, Harappa, and Taxila. There are many archeological remains of settlements founded by the Persian and Greek empires that extend to parts of present-day Pakistan, as well as ruins and stupas of the Mauryan period at the turn of the first millennium. The cities and towns inherited by Pakistan were largely shaped by the Mughals at the zenith of their empire (1483–1707), with Sammas, Kalhoras, and Ahmadzais imprinting their values on the urban landscape of Sindh and Balochistan respectively in the waning days (eighteenth/nineteenth centuries) of Mughal rule. The short rule of Sikhs in the nineteenth century made some mark on the Mughal inheritance in Punjab, but it was the British empire (1843–1947) that restructured cities and towns and transformed their landscape. Much has happened in cities and towns since the birth of Pakistan, but the British laid the framework of their contemporary internal structure on medieval foundations.

At independence, a typical city consisted of four distinct parts: (1) historic indigenous core area (walled old city) of narrow streets; caste/clan residential quarters; artisans' living-and-working quarters; bazaars and markets for grains, jewelry, or utensils bustling with activity in the shadow of medieval forts/palaces or mosques; (2) Civil Lines (suburb laid out by the British outside the historic core) of spacious bungalows, district courts, and secretariat laid out on a grid of wide streets; (3) Cantonment, satellite military base of parade grounds, barracks, residences, and commercial markets for army officers and Sadar Bazaar for native officers and ranks also laid in the modern idiom; and (4) New Indigenous Communities (NIC), residential subdivisions (new *mohallas*) of rectangular blocks, streets wider than those in the old city but narrow enough to be in scale with the courtyard houses of the emerging indigenous middle class.[13]

Initially, a wide open space formed a *cordon sanitaire* between the native and British parts of cities, but in time this space was filled up with colleges, hospitals, playgrounds, and NICs. The noteworthy part of this internal structure was that it segregated the ruling British and the native elite from the local middle and lower classes. Each part had its own focal point or "downtown," making the city a multinuclear settlement.[14] Pakistani cities do not have a central area or classical downtown. A daughter of Lahore comments on this absence of a city center thus, "one is always expecting to find Lahore without quite locating it."[15] Karachi, Lahore, Peshawar, Multan, and Rawalpindi and on a smaller scale Sialkot and Hyderabad conform to this pattern.

The British built railways, which skirted around cities and towns, spawning new developments near train stations and promoting intercity movements of passengers and goods. The water supply networks were built; sewers were installed in areas of officers' residences. Municipal governments were instituted and rudimentary transport services were introduced in the late nineteenth and early twentieth centuries. These measures introduced some modicum of modern infrastructure and laid the bases for the expansion of cities.

New towns were built in the irrigated districts, for example, Montgomery (renamed Sahiwal), Lyallpur (now Faisalabad), and small settlements were expanded and refurbished to form almost new towns, such as Abbotabad, Jacobabad, Rawalpindi, and Quetta.

In small towns such as Wazirabad, Lodhran, or Rohri, railway stations became the nucleus of modern life. Young men from towns gathered in railway stations in the evenings for tea and ogling at fashionable travelers from cities as mail trains made a short stop. Near railway stations, new bungalow estates were built to house civil officials and accommodate courts, police and revenue offices, high schools, and public works departments. Even at the lower levels of the urban hierarchy, the distinction between the modern and the traditional parts of a town was evident. The internal structure of Pakistani cities and towns evolved into a dualistic structure, differentiating the historic from the new.

Postcolonial developments

What has happened to Pakistani cities and towns since 1947 can be summed up by two terms: spilling out and filling up. Physically they have expanded, spreading out over green fields. Also within their inherited boundaries, open spaces have been built over and sparsely inhabited neighborhoods have been stuffed with houses, stores, and workshops. Two design idioms have come into play: (1) indigenous neighborhoods of narrow and twisting streets, lined with one or two storey structures and crisscrossed by commercial arteries; and (2) modern planned areas of geometrically laid-out streets, rectangular blocks, and ostensibly segregated land uses. The former idiom is a contemporary version of the traditional mode of development, built in incremental and informal ways (house by house and street by street) and largely in disregard of building bylaws in force. The latter is the much-honed mode of contemporary town planning.

Indigenous incremental developments are mostly for low- and moderate-income households, the majority of whom are rural migrants and refugees. Primarily they take the form of unauthorized *katchi abadis* (squatter or unapproved settlements) and informal housing subdivisions often tagged as "colonies." They may be carved house by house or organized and laid out in blocks by landgrabbers or real estate dealers in connivance with public officials and police on public or disputed lands. *Katchi abadis* may begin as hastily built huts and abodes, but in time, after long occupancy, huts are converted to houses, streets are paved, and utility services are installed or improvised. Years later, a *katchi abadi* is indistinguishable from a low-income NIC.

In Karachi, the enterprise of land invasion and development for squatter colonies has evolved into an organized industry under the patronage of the police and municipal officials.[16] Partially, it is the availability of vast tracts of public lands, relatively easy to grab, that has sustained organized businesses of unauthorized land development in Karachi.

The landgrabbing and incremental housing industries have developed gradually. In the first period, indigent refugees from India squatted on footpaths and in parks. This first wave of squatters were periodically resettled in hastily built one-room "quarters" (single-storey one-room courtyard houses). Korangi, a project with a target of 50,000 quarters, was inaugurated in Karachi in 1959. In other cities smaller but similar projects were undertaken in period 1, yet public housing could not keep up with the burgeoning demand.

Katchi abadis

Urban housing needs began to grow from a new source of demand in the 1960s. Industrial development in Karachi and other big cities started casting a pull on rural labor. The rural migrants replaced refugees as the primary source of demand for cheap housing in cities. They turned to squatter colonies for supply. By the second period, *katchi abadis* were so common that the Bhutto government (1972–7) adopted the policy of giving land titles to squatters. The policy has not been fully implemented, but *katchi abadis* have become an accepted part of the urban structure in Pakistan. The military governments of the third period had no choice but to continue regularizing *katchi abadis*.

The activity of developing *katchi abadis* in Punjab and NWFP provinces has not been as organized as in Karachi. It has been dominated by small and opportunistic operators who work with the protection of political leaders. Such networks of officials and landgrabbers are popularly called *qabza* (land invaders) groups.

How big a role *katchi abadis* have played in the growth of cities in the post-independence period can be judged from some scattered data. A World Bank team estimated in 1985 that there were 2,302 *katchi abadis* occupying 36,773 acres belonging to the state and 5,372 of private land, and housing about 18 percent of the urban population in the four provinces.[17] The *katchi abadis* or informal developments accommodated about 37 percent of Karachi's population in 1987, but by 1999 that proportion was estimated to have risen to 50 percent.[18] Lahore's *katchi abadis* housed about 23 percent of the population in 1980; increasing at the rate of 17 percent a year, their share of the city's population rose to about 38 percent by 1993.[19] Similar conditions prevailed in other major cities, and towns were only marginally behind.

Given the ambiguity of criteria to define *katchi abadis*, which include illicit, unregulated as well as incremental settlements, it is difficult to count them. Within these limitations, an idea of the scale of this form of development can be further gained by the estimates that Karachi had about 550 (1993) and Lahore 236 (1987) *katchi abadis*. They accommodate households of peons, clerks, hawkers, domestic workers, etc., and include many artisans and craftsmen working from their homes. *Katchi abadi* residents initially recreate the living patterns of their home villages contributing to the process dubbed the ruralization of cities. By the time the second generation grows up, a *katchi abadi* may even have doctors, military officers, and business owners among its residents. It evolves with the upgrading and rebuilding of houses into a low-income neighborhood.

Planned communities

Planned communities mostly serve the housing demands of middle- and upper-class households. Some planned public housing projects, such as Korangi in Karachi or Angori Bagh in Lahore were meant for low-income households. Planned developments have led the expansion of cities and towns by laying the axis of their growth. Look at maps of Karachi, Quetta, Peshawar, or any other major city and even towns; they are stamped with names such as Nazimabad, Housing Society, Gulberg, University Town, Nishat Colony, Defense Society, Baharia Society, Satellite Town, People's Colony for geometrically laid-out neighborhoods. These are areas of "good living" with provisions for water supply and sewers, wide streets, schools, parks, and commercial zones.

The indigenous incremental and planned communities are the two metaphors of post-independence urban development. Each metaphor is further differentiated into physical forms of distinct lifestyle, class, and location. For example, there are Defense Societies (cooperative housing societies of military officers) catering to the rich and influential classes and Gulbahar colonies or Gulshan parks for the moderate- or low-income households that fall within the metaphor of planned communities, but they are worlds apart in the density and size of houses, provisions of community services, and cultural orientations of residents. Similarly the indigenous incremental developments range from middle-class housing districts to *katchi abadis*. The two metaphors of development reflect class divisions. They have realigned the internal structure of cities.

Fragmented cities

Pakistani cities have evolved into places of sharp contrasts. There are upscale neighborhoods of air-conditioned shopping plazas, palatial bungalows, and neon-lit roads, rivalingWestern suburbs in modernity. Yet the same cities have communities where homes are mere shacks, streets are permanently layered with muck, and stray dogs tear through garbage piles. These are the two polar examples, but segregation by income and social status is a pervasive characteristic of post-independence urban development.

The physical separation by social classes is further fine-tuned by differences in the cultural ambience of neighborhoods. *Katchi abadis* and NICs are not only low-income areas, but also tend to be places of traditional modes of living. In these places, women usually go about covered with *chadors* (long cotton shawls) and children play in streets. Civil Lines, cantonments, and planned communities are the parts of a city with modern lifestyles and affluent living. Here fashionably dressed women drive around in cars and children chaperoned by servants have parks to play in and McDonald's to snack at.

The contrast between living in the Clifton Scheme and Orangi in Karachi, Model Town and Angori Bagh in Lahore, or University Town and Gul Mast Colony in Peshawar approximates to living in two different cultures or even eras. These are symptoms of fragmentation by class and lifestyles, laying the ground for the emergence of a multiplicity of territorial communities that are only loosely connected with each other. This is the structure of a fragmented city that has been described in these words: "physical environment, services, incomes, cultural values and institutional systems can vary from neighbourhood to neighbourhood, often from street to street."[20]

Internal structure: the dialectic of tradition and modernity

Historically, Pakistani cities were organized by neighborhoods of a particular clan or occupational groups whose rich and poor, tenants and owners lived in close proximity and mutual interdependence forming symbiotic communities. This social organization of the historic core areas (walled cities) is reflected in layouts and street names, such as storytellers' street in Peshawar or the neighborhood of arrow makers in Lahore. Even housing lots of different sizes are found in the same block, a practice that reflected the proximity of various classes.

To illustrate the point about how small and big houses being side by side and rich and poor living in close proximity produce an organic community, I will recount the social life of the street in the walled city of Lahore where l grew up. It had nine houses and fifteen households who were not related. Among the household heads were the owner of a furniture shop, a property dealer, a railway official, seven carpenters, a mechanical supervisor, a clerk, and two destitute widows. Widows were looked after by the three relatively affluent households primarily and by others on need. Wives and daughters of some poor households did domestic chores for neighbors to supplement their family incomes. There was frequent borrowing of flour, lentils, or money among neighbors. Children played in the street and their occasional fights could embroil adults. Poverty and affluence existed side by side, but honor and respectability was everybody's prerogative. Age and family standing were the markers of social status in the street. It was a microcosm of the old city social organization, a small but cohesive (micro) community where class differences dovetailed to form a system of mutual care, although not without tinges of malice, to make it all human. An account of an old city street in Peshawar at the same time indicates similar social relations.[21] This was the community organization of the cities of Pakistan. Towns were all the more organized along these lines.

Modern city development is based on the principle of segregation of activities, land uses, and lot sizes. Whole neighborhoods are laid out in standardized lots of one or two sizes, residences separated from commercial areas, and workplaces clustered in separate zones. Even in government officials' estates, company towns, and university campuses, housing is clustered by its size, which corresponds to the rank of occupants in the organizational hierarchy. Islamabad, the national capital, is laid out in blocks of uniform lot and housing sizes. If you know the sector and street address of a resident, you can almost guess the salary and rank of the occupant. Planned communities finely divide residents by income and class. They represent a break with urban Pakistan's historical social organization.

The idiom of segregating by house type, physical layout, and social class has permeated all forms of post-independence urban development. It even underlies *katchi abadis* where poverty and indigenous lifestyles blend with modern notions of subdividing land.

The sum total of these changes is a city that is a mosaic of divergent communities. Pakistani cities are expanding and splitting simultaneously. They are being divided into socially and physically distinct segments; each part is primarily identified with a particular "housing class" (households of similar means, lifestyles, and cultural orientations) complete with its own commercial focus and activity patterns.[22] The divisions are not just those of economic status and social class, but also of cultural practices and lifestyles. Muslim Town and Samanabad in Lahore, for example, are planned communities of comparable house prices, but they represent different slices of the city's culture in that the former is identified with a modern-executive outlook, while the latter is reflective of bazaar-indigenous values. Within the spectrum of the same class, local communities could differ in cultural orientations. The range of cultural distinctions among neighborhoods extends from the global, Western, modern, and indigenous to the traditional. Thus the internal structure of Pakistani cities is made up of territorial communities finely differentiated by cultural image, social reputation, and design. Social and economic linkages loosely tie territorial communities together.

Unlike Western cities, Pakistani cities do not have a central district that is the fulcrum of an urban structure. They have multiple and autonomous focal points, each representing a particular sociocultural stratum. Even the provision of infrastructure and community services differs from neighborhood to neighborhood.

Streaming of collective services and tracking of people

The fragmentation of the city is also reflected in differences of the type and quality of services such as water supply, parks, street maintenance, garbage collection, schools, and public transport from neighborhood to neighborhood. Undoubtedly, Pakistan as a whole is a poor country. It cannot fully meet its growing population's needs for utilities and services. Its cities and towns are deficient in urban services and what is available is distributed very inequitably.

The disparities of services run along the economic and cultural contours of cities. The rich and modern communities have better services than *katchi abadis*, historical areas, and even the NICs of middle classes. Anyone who has seen the Defense Society or Clifton in Karachi on the one hand and Lyari or Korangi on the other, for example, can testify that these neighborhoods could be from different eras and countries. The former areas have wide boulevards, water and sewer networks, schools, hospitals, and spacious parks; while the latter have pot-holed streets, dirt patches, overflowing drains, nonexistent sewers, and intermittent water supply. Such disparities have further widened with the expansion of cities and the straining of services.

The relatively different quality of community services in different parts of cities is not the result of just the inequitable allocation of resources, such disparities are rather built into their processes of production. Distinctly different types of services are produced and delivered for different parts of cities. This is the phenomenon of the streaming of services for the rich and the powerful on the one hand, and the ordinary citizens on the other. It is a symptom of the fragmented structure of a city. The streaming of services is often an explicit part of public policies but it is also ingrained in the community or market modes of production of collective goods.

The road and street design standards vary by the economic and social standings of neighborhoods. Water and sewer services are similarly targeted for different areas at varying capacities; one neighborhood may be planned with 40 gallons of water supply per capita and another may be designed for 80 or 100 gallons capacity. Further differences arise in the operations of these facilities. Citing again the example of Karachi, one of the cities about which more information is available, piped water was available to 84 percent of planned areas and only 50 percent of *katchi abadis*.[23] These figures refer only to the installed capacities. What flows out of pipes is all the more divergent in the two types of neighborhoods. How wide the differences are in the provision of delivered services can be gauged by the fact that garbage collection covered about 60 percent of the Planned Areas, but only 10 percent of the *katchi abadis*.[23]

The phenomenon of streaming is also a defining condition in soft services such as education, health, or safety. In period 2 (1971–7), schools were nationalized and a certain uniformity of services was promised for all. What happened is a different story. The nationalization resulted in two-tier education: English medium schools for the middle and upper classes, and Urdu and Sindhi curricula for the working class and the poor. This divide not only separated the well-off from the poor, but also differentiated people of modern outlook from those of traditional orientations. For the destitute and the orthodox, Islamic *madrassahs* (religious schools) served as the third educational tier, multiplying particularly in the third period (1977–present). Similarly, public hospitals for masses, but company clinics and private hospitals for the rich and influential emerged as the two distinct streams in health services.

The point being driven home is that the splitting of the public space in cities and towns, and even in rural areas, into distinct streams of community services has become a defining feature of urban development in Pakistan. It lays life-tracks for people and reinforces the fragmentation of cities. Millions live in the same physical city, but their living conditions and life circuits are far apart.

Economic sectors and circuits: foundations of fragmented cities

Pakistan's economy is organized in three parallel modes of operation: (1) the "modern" or what Clifford Geertz calls the "firm" sector and is now commonly described as the "formal" sector in the development literature; (2) the "informal" or in Geertz's terms "bazaar" sector; and (3) the "illicit" sector, commonly described as corruption but which in fact has become a distinct way of carrying out economic transactions in Pakistan and in many other countries.[24] The precolonial economic organization was predominantly based in the bazaar sector although foundations for the modern sectors had been laid during British rule. After independence, the modern sector expanded rapidly particularly through public enterprises; the bazaar sector also spread widely and the illicit sector came to acquire a more organized form.

I find Geertz's term, bazaar, more expressive of Pakistan's reality, which is rooted in the historical economic organization. The bazaar mode of operation is highly structured, based on small family enterprises, regulated by both economic and cultural/religious mores. It relies on social capital and cultural resources almost as much as on financial investments. It is not fluid or informal by any stretch of the imagination. This sector has a near monopoly on the grain, cloth, and staples trade. It prevails in small industries and artisan enterprises. Since independence, it has spawned carpet, agro-industries, tool, and construction industries. It is very extensive and employs almost the majority of the working population.[25]

The firm or the modern (formal) sector is organized in the corporate mode with occupational division of labor, presumably impersonal dealings, hierarchical organization, and operating essentially for defined objectives. Public and private corporations, sizable family enterprises, medical, educational and professional establishments, government departments and agencies, and the military are producers of goods and services in the modern mode. All of these have increased manifold since 1947.

The illicit sector has emerged with the institutionalization of previously contingent illegal practices. It is pervasive; by one estimate almost 40 percent of Pakistan's national income arises from the illicit sector which includes smuggling, drug trafficking, unlicensed manufacturing (commonly called "number two" goods), and, of course, bribery and crime.[26] The illicit activities congeal into institutional practice when they are ongoing and structured like businesses, and are pursued as a trade. When the engineering supervision of road construction, building of canals, dams, or other public works involves fixed rates of kickbacks for various ranks of engineers and accountants, it represents an organized illicit mode. In this situation, the illicit sector is embedded in the bureaucracy. The illicit sector also has autonomous existence in the form of *bara* (smuggled goods) markets in major cities, as workshops for manufacturing imitations of branded goods or networks of currency exchangers, quacks and unqualified practitioners of medicine as well as *qabza* (property grabber) gangs and promoters of land invasions.

Hierarchy of circuits

Each of these three sectors is vertically divided into circuits of higher and lower orders, according to size, economic and political power, and market areas. Each circuit is defined by its mode of operation and by the population that it caters to.[27] The national chain of preparatory schools for Senior Cambridge diplomas is in the upper circuit of the modern sector, while a Mission School in Sialkot or Shikarpur for poor minorities is an example of the corresponding lower circuit. Similarly, landlords are among the upper-circuit operators of the bazaar sector while landless labor is in the lower circuit.

Figure 5.2 presents a graphic model of the sectors and circuits forming the organizational structure of Pakistan's economy. Sectors and circuits differ not only in the mode of operations and organization, but also in the business culture and participants' lifestyles. The bazaar sector in general and the lower circuits of the other two sectors in particular operate in vernacular norms and languages. Those involved in these sectors and circuits tend to be guided by local knowledge and family/caste traditions and values. A bearded Haji who shrewdly pursues profits and riches shrouded in an aura of piety and modesty is the symbol of this business culture.

The upper circuits of the modern sector are more affected by capitalist ethos and Western values. English is in common use and participants imbibe cosmopolitan lifestyles. The point is that sectors and circuits differ not only in modes of operation, but also by institutional culture. They represent variant lifestyles and subcultures. This diversity of economic organizations and group cultures underlies the fragmentation of urban structure.

As the geographic anchors of Pakistan's developing economy, the fragmentation of cities affects both society and the state.

A few examples may illustrate the economic and cultural divide between sectors and circuits and their geographic bases in cities. Islamabad is basically a new city of the modernist bent. Its rank- and class-based neighborhoods, its clustered shopping

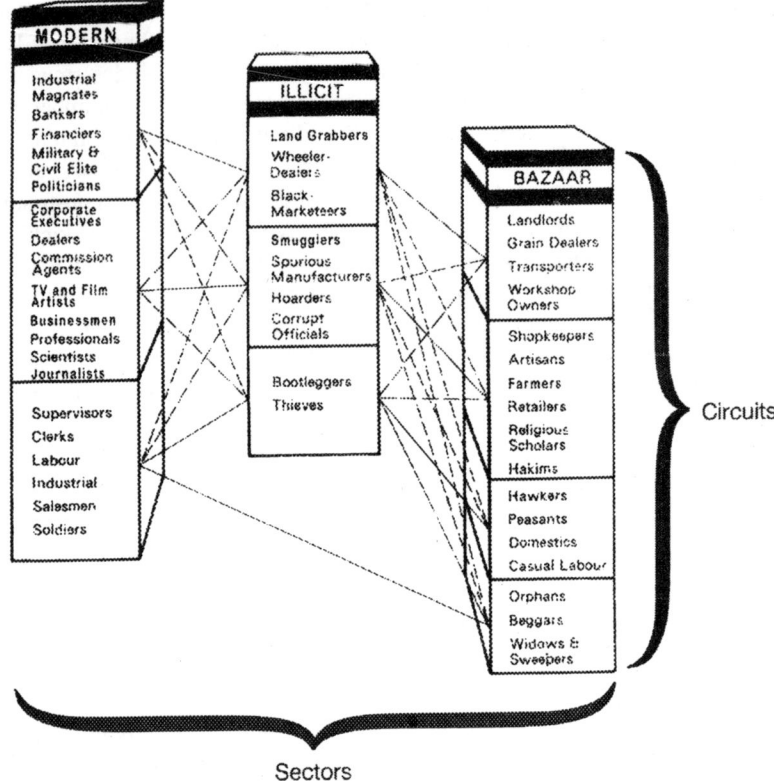

Figure 5.1 Economic sectors and circuits

markets, and tree-lined streets are emblems of modernity. Even the lower circuit, comprised of sweepers' *katchi abadis* and "servants' bazaars" in the back alleys of commercial markets, is a world of "English-speak" and "up-to-date" tastes. Its twin city, Rawalpindi, has a more divided structure, like Lahore, Karachi, or Peshawar. As the headquarters of Pakistan's military, its cantonment is suffused with a bureaucratic economy and the spit-and-polish bearings of the army. Yet the bazaar sector holds its ground in Banni Chowk, Telli Mohalla (oil pressers' district) and Sarafa Bazaar (goldsmiths' market) as well as in the old neighborhood of Tanch Bhata, for example. These are the areas where the Pothohari dialect of Punjabi is spoken, sermons from mosques mix with strains of Bollywood songs from tea stalls, and residential streets are identified by *biradaris* and religious sects.

As an example of the lower circuit of the illicit sector, encroachment of public lands for residential development is an illustrative case. Yakoobabad, Karachi, or Green Town in Lahore are documented examples of the process of incremental development of low-income neighborhoods[28] The "culture" of these neighborhoods is defined by poverty and the ethnic origins of residents as well as the political struggle against the threat of evictions. They are defined by language, extended families, ethnic solidarity, casual employment, and folk-religiosity. It is not just the economic class that differentiates these neighborhoods, but also the lifestyle, values, behaviors, and even dress.

Dynamics of sectors and circuits

Before concluding the discussion of the sectors and circuits that divide Pakistani cities, the following clarifications need to be registered.

- The sectors and circuits are not strictly compartmentalized but interweave and overlap. The modern sector has some indigenous norms and practices and the bazaar sector adopts technological innovations and new processes that enhance its business interests. For example, the power alliances in public bureaucracies or corporate organizations largely revolve around ethnic, clan, and linguistic bonds whereas the bazaar sector has shrewdly adjusted to the currency floats and bank finance.
- The bazaar sector in particular is opportunist in its approach despite its roots in traditions. Ethnic clans, such as Memons, Chinotis, and Sheikhs, have histori-cally dominated particular trades, occupational castes have specialized in specific skills, and some towns and localities are long known for their special-ized crafts and industries, such as Daska in Punjab, the home of tool-making *lohars* (blacksmiths).[29] Yet when markets have shifted and new opportunities have arisen, these clans, castes, and towns have been quick to branch out of their historic niches. It would be a mistake to look upon the bazaar sector as a precapitalist institution. It represents a form of indigenous but familistic capitalism.
- Circuits also have porous boundaries. There are discernible paths of upward and downward mobility for groups and individuals. The second period partic-ularly witnessed an upsurge in the expectations of the lower ranks. Van drivers wanted education with English as the medium of instruction for their children, and peasants' sons migrated to Denmark and Britain, for example. With development, new occupations have emerged that cut across the hier-archy of circuits, for example, highly paid earth-moving machinery operators may be occupationally in lower circuits but they outclass college professors or magistrates in salaries.
- Imprints of sectors and circuits on urban space as neighborhoods and markets also reflect the malleability of their boundaries. An upscale modern neighbor-hood has in its back lanes and "servants' quarters" a lower circuit of bazaar life. Similarly, a *katchi abadi* of the 1950s may be redeveloped as a fashion-able neighborhood as it comes to be at the center of a spreading city.

The question of social class

The tripartite social economy of cities and towns is also partially a reflection of class differentiations. Together they form a finely delineated system of social stratification in Pakistan. One's social status and earning potential depends upon which circuit and sector one is located in. A distinction of this stratification is that it has cultural dimensions. A hawker from the lower circuit of the bazaar sector could make more money than a clerk from the middle circuit of the modern sector, but he has lower social status, less economic security, and a more vernacular lifestyle than a modernist office worker. The two may fall in the same economic strata but they stand apart in social status and living patterns. The sociocultural factors combine with the economic criteria in the structuring of social class in Pakistan. Class in urban Pakistan is a multidimensional concept that goes beyond conventional Marxist notions.

The notion of social class is fundamental to sociological analysis. A class is primarily defined in economic terms, conceived as strata or categories of people having similar material conditions and chances in life. What determines the bunching together of people in layers of similar material status and opportunities is a question about which ideological and theoretical views differ.

Karl Marx based the standing of a class on how it relates to the means of production. Max Weber found class differences arising from resources that various strata bring to the market. The rise of corporate capitalism and the postindustrial mode of production has redefined the notion of means of production and consequently revised the bases on which people's access to them is determined. Thus the theories of the determinants of class status continue to evolve. The social structures and historical experiences of the Third World countries add another layer of difference from the European capitalism of the nineteenth century that was the social context of Marxian and Weberian formulations. All in all, there is a near-consensus about the notion of social class as a strata or layer of similar economic and social statuses, but the forces and processes that structure these strata remain matters of theoretical debates.[30]

Pakistan's class structure has been described both in Marxian as well as post-Marxian terms. Hamza Alavi, a leading theoretician of developing societies, links the status of urban classes to their respective standing in relation to the state, particularly singling out salaried functionaries as a distinct class. Feroz Ahmed in his later writings recognized that ethnicity and economic status operate in tandem to form class hierarchy in Pakistan.[31] Most widely used classifications of class are based on the combination of income/wealth and position in the social structure. Classes are variously described as upper, middle, and lower income; rich versus poor; managerial versus working; or in rural areas as landlord, owner farmer, tenant, and *kammi* (crafts and service worker). These are the commonly used categories of class in Pakistan.

The term "class" has two meanings in Pakistan. One, the social meaning refers to the hierarchical position in society and community. It is determined by one's position at the intersection of economic sector, social circuit, and clan/cultural roots. The fragmentation of Pakistan's urban structure follows social class lines. Social class is what people live with in everyday life. An individual is a Chaudhry or Junejo by birth, for example; added to it are his education, occupation, social power, economic mode of operation, and earnings as well as property, resulting in a composite notion of his class standing in community and locality.

Two, the political meaning refers to broad categories of economic status, namely upper, middle, and working classes or in Marxian categories, capitalist, bourgeoisie, and proletariat. Political categories are used for purposes of building broad alliances of social classes that fall in comparable economic strata. Bhutto's PPP employs the rhetoric of representing working and middle classes, whereas the various Muslim Leaguers talk of improving workers' and peasants' welfare while supporting businessmen and landlords. In the political discourse, class is a large tent under which groups of comparable life-chances, but diverse ethnic and cultural backgrounds are gathered.

The discourse of class in Pakistan largely refers to its political meanings. In period 1, progressive writers and socialist parties attempted to raise class consciousness among workers and peasants. Trade unions and students' organizations advocated workers' rights, youth employment, and land reforms. The public discourse about class was trumped by provincial and ethnic interests in the run-up to the first constitution of Pakistan (1956). Ayub's military rule initially attempted to sweep aside class and ethnic differentiations, but in the popular agitation of 1968 that led to its downfall, all social classes came out to press their respective interests. Interestingly, mass protests became the platform for articulating narrow class grievances, such as engineers protesting against the domination of administrative civil servants, textile workers protesting against cotton ginners, doctors differentiating themselves from health administrators, although all joined hands to agitate against Ayub's rule. This historical fact illustrates that below the overarching political class are classes of narrowly differentiated social bases.

The second period was the era of heightened class consciousness and populist class rhetoric. Bhutto's socialism was built on uniting workers, peasants, clerks, and residents of *katchi abadis* into a political class, conscious of its common interests. Bhutto's downfall six years later from the mass agitation indicates how brittle this political class was as a united front.

The third period has· subsumed political class consciousness into ethnic and sectarian discourse. Class interests exist essentially as a political theme, but social classes have flourished under the liberal–Islamist divide, ethnic differentiations, and clan (*biradari*) and sectarian identities. All in all, social class with its narrow but multidimensional social base is the enduring reality of Pakistan's social structure. Cities and towns have been the stage for the forging of sharply defined social classes. Such differentiated classes have spread into the countryside with the diffusion of urbanism. The fragmented social structure of cities has been enveloping society at large.

Symbiotic interdependence

The fragmentation of urban structure does not mean apartheid-like separation of social classes and communities in everyday life. Occupationally, people in upper and lower circuits are interlinked with one another. The three sectors are symbiotically related to each other. Clan and tribal solidarities, kinship bonds, and religious obligations also tie together persons of different circuits and classes. Both socially and economically, various segments of urban society are intertwined. Then the question is how can such an interlinked structure be labeled as fragmented?

It is the differences in physical environment, public services, and quality of life in different parts of the city that divide territorial neighborhoods from one another. In other words, it is the fragmentation of public space, which is meant to be the common ground for all, that is the defining characteristic of fragmented cities. The social and cultural distances among various sectors and circuits pull various neighborhoods apart, but these differences can be largely contained in private space with equitable and effective urban development policies. Pakistani cities have not had such policies. Western cities have their ghettos and upscale neighborhoods, but they also have common infrastructure and (public) institutions that tie them together.

The sociocultural and territorial divisions of Pakistani cities, paradoxically, coexist with wide ranging interdependencies and regular contacts among people from all across the social spectrum. The everyday life of a typical middle- or upper-class household depends on the services of domestics, cleaners, chauffeurs, or *chowkidars* (security guards). Frequently these helpers live with their employers. In offices and businesses, peons, delivery boys, and clerical assistants do personal chores for their bosses. Affluent and influential persons often have a needy relative staying or visiting them. On the backsides of glittering shopping centers are alleys lined with tea and food stalls, *tandoors* (bread bakeries), and makeshift accommodations for laborers and workers. The poor and the rich are seldom out of each other's sight.

The scale of this social intertwining is illustrated by a population count of a professors' residential colony at a university campus in Lahore.[32] On average a university teacher's household had 3–5 members, while in the servant quarters of the same residence lived 6–10 persons including visitors. The subordinate use in this "modern upper-class" residential area was that of a workers' neighborhood. My argument is that almost everyone in Pakistani cities has close encounters daily with persons of different social backgrounds, yet the physical proximity does not bridge the social distance.

Social divisions have sharpened with post-independence economic development and urban growth. What is different from the "moral economy" of the old city (described above) is the erosion of customary obligations and interdependencies. The present interdependence of different groups is contractual in nature and drained of moral obligations. An American journalist's observation about Karachi captures a common condition of Pakistani cities: "Most Third World cities manifest dramatic contrasts between rich and poor. But in no other place have I seen rich and poor live in such close and hostile proximity as Karachi. On one street a grimy warren of *Katchi Abadis* lay to my right, and a high wall guarding luxury villas and a Kentucky Fried Chicken outlet to my left."[33] One caveat that I may add to this conclusion is that it is not just economic status that separates the two side-by-side neighborhoods, but also their group cultures and civic entitlements.

One of the impacts of independence is the explosion of expectations and, with it, the uprooting of people from their social niches. Each period of Pakistan's social history has opened new paths for mobility. The first period witnessed the opening of commercial and industrial opportunities due to the exodus of Hindu traders from Pakistan. Historically enterprise-shy Muslims of Pakistan embraced new opportunities, particularly the artisan classes and traders' clans whose fortunes were not tied to the ownership of land. The second period, as mentioned above, stimulated the flocking of rural labor to cities and the beginning of emigration abroad. While the previous paths of mobility continued to expand, the third period expanded the military's participation in business, industry, and real estate. It also opened the opportunities for Islamic scholars. All in all, Pakistan's fragmented social structure, paradoxically, also lays the ground for functional interdependence.

Imperatives of urban life

City life is a piece of its societal fabric, yet different in many ways. Common social institutions and customary behaviors take different forms in cities to fulfill the functional requirements of fast-paced routines and a thick web of activities. Social patterns in cities represent a distinct configuration of national institutions.

What makes the city (and town) a distinct form of human community is the interconnectedness of activities and people. The division of labor and specialization of production, characteristic of urban economy, increase efficiency and multiply output. By linking activities and people, a city becomes a socioeconomic system that is more than the sum of its parts. Cities essentially thrive on what economists call external economies, namely unaccounted beneficial (positive) effects of one's activity on others and vice versa. External effects can also be negative, as is the case with auto emissions as a by-product of auto transport. The quality of city life depends on harnessing positive externalities and containing negative externalities.

Interconnections (externalities) are not only the foundations of urban economy, but also the defining condition of urban life. They link the fate of the rich with the poor. For example, rats in my ill-kept home could be a source of plague for my neighbors, or traffic gridlock strands executives as much as workers. In the city, the welfare of some is indivisible from the well-being of all. City life is founded on a common base of infrastructure, (public) institutions, and policies. This is the arena of public space described earlier. It is largely impersonal and institutional.

The public space of cities has the following four prerequisites or conditions that have to be fulfilled for it to be effective. These are the imperatives of urban life.[34]

1   *Collectivization (group-based production) of utilities and services.* What pass as private goods in low-density areas have to be collectivized and communally produced in cities. What are private goods in villages turn into public needs for common infrastructure and services by the concentration of population in cities. Be it water supply, garbage collection, schools, electric grid, traffic control, building regulations or housing supply, for example, these hard and soft services cannot be provided on individuals' initiatives. They

have to be produced as collective goods to ensure everybody health and welfare.

2   *Organizing space and using land for common good.* Land is the stage onwhich the drama of city life is played out. Its efficient and equitable use can result in a satisfying urban life and conversely its haphazard development can lead to chaotic traffic, long commutes, and a spoiled environment. Thus cities require a system of plans, rules, and practices that guide private actions to ensure an overall pattern of land and environmental use that is convenient and sustainable. Such a system doesn't arise from market processes. It has to be organized and enforced by public/community initiatives in the form of city plans, zoning bylaws and housing codes.

3   *Establishing civic order and culture.* A city is a corporate entity. Its viability as a community depends on responsive local government and effective institutions, in short a vigorous civic order. Such a civic order has to be deliberately developed and managed, particularly in modern times of growing cities and continual social change. Western cities went through numerous legislative reforms in the twentieth century to establish effective civic authorities to address Dickensian living conditions, periodic epidemics, and other urban crises. Pakistan and other Third World countries are now faced with similar challenges. The task of building an urban civic order also requires institutionalizing citizens' rights and obligations and norms of public behaviors, in short a civic culture.

4   *Institution building and cultural reforms.* City life demands punctuality, regularity, trust of strangers, and impersonal dealings, among others, to be observed as norms of everyday life. These norms have to be fostered through institutional reforms and civic education. In contemporary Third World cities, the influx of migrants from the country makes the deliberate fostering of urban norms an all the more urgent necessity.

Pakistan's transformation to an urban society is also to be assessed by the fulfillment of these imperatives. Obviously these imperatives have been fulfilled only partially and also for some segments of urban community life.

Urban development and institutional lag

The story of Pakistan's urban development can be summed up by the phrase, individual successes and collective failures. Pakistani cities pulsate with individuals' drive while simmering in collective inertia. The material or technological base of urban society is advancing and the nonmaterial institutions are lagging. The fragmentation of cities facilitates this cultural lag, by funneling scarce collective facilities and services (material resources) to neighborhoods and groups that are powerful and affluent.

Regarding the imperatives of urban life, Pakistani cities fall short, particularly in terms of building institutions for advancing the common good, providing basic services, and promoting civic order and culture. Pakistani society is urbanized but its social institutions and organizational cultures remain bound to the traditions forged in preindustrial times. Let us illustrate these points with some concrete examples.

Pakistani cities have not just expanded, they have also progressed materially. In 1998, there were 4.1 million houses in cities and towns, about 37 percent had been built in the last ten years. It is estimated that only about 0.6 million houses may have been of pre-independence vintage. Thus Pakistan's urban areas are largely built after independence. The quality of housing has also registered some notable improvements. By 1998, 87 percent of urban housing had an indoor water supply (pipe or pump) and 93 percent had electricity, for example.[35] These proportions had increased 4–6 times since 1947. Undoubtedly there was a big backlog of unmet housing needs, a shortage of about 6 million dwelling units in 1998; affordability as well as crowding were major problems, but the structural quality of most of the housing had improved.[36] These are largely the fruits of individuals' initiatives and energies.

Compare this private advancement with the public programs for urban development. Pakistan has not been lacking in public actions for urban development. It is the ineffectiveness of programs in building a common base for modern urban development that has been the major drag on people's initiatives. The Government of Pakistan took an early lead (1955) by including "Physical Planning and Housing" as a sector in its five-year plans. Over nine plans, spanning almost one-half century, billions of rupees have been invested in this sector. Urban utilities and government buildings, including the new capital, have been the top priority areas of investment, the two together drawing 50–70 percent of the national investment in this sector.[37] Public housing to resettle refugees in the first period and *katchi abadis* upgrading in the second and third periods have been the third priority in five-year plans.

On the surface, these programs are on target, but their implementation tilted them in favor of planned communities, where military and civil officers as well as political and business leaders live. Developing housing lots and distributing them at subsidized rates to political constituencies and public officials have been the main output of the five-year plans. Urban works projects also dovetailed into the "plots" production priorities.[38] Water and sewer development programs were repeatedly hijacked by the drive to produce "plots" for expanding middle and upper classes.[39] The outcome of urban programs has been, by and large, the division of cities into serviced and unserviced neighborhoods. Yet the fate of the rich cannot be entirely divided from that of the poor in cities. Many facilities and services are indivisible, for example, traffic control, public health, air quality, governance, etc.

Neglected collective goods

The indivisibility of common services and therefore citizens' welfare in urban areas can be illustrated by the example of sewers. Despite the investments of nine five-year plans, at the beginning of the twenty-first century, there is not even one city in Pakistan that had a fully functioning sewerage disposal system and storm drains. Only 40 percent of Karachi's area, that, furthermore, not contiguous but in patches here and there, had some form of sewers. Lahore did not fare any better nor even Quetta, a smaller city.[40] Everywhere upscale planned communities have been built with internal sewers, which have no citywide trunk lines to connect to. The result is that polluted groundwater and sewer backups plague even these salubrious neighborhoods. The inadequacies of storm drains affect everybody when heavy rains flood major roads and endanger people and property.

Karachi is not near any river, but periodic heavy monsoons flood its major streets and exact a toll in deaths. There are no citywide systems of run-off drains. In July or August of 1949, 1950, 1954, 1967, 1976, 1979, 1989, and 1997, for example, there were rain floods that caused so many deaths by drowning that they were major national news of the day. Over five decades, these predictable annual rains in Karachi, or anywhere else, have not been adequately dealt with. This is the state of common services that constitute the public space in Pakistan's urban areas.

The shortfalls in legislative, organizational, and policy realms are all the more striking, for example, a responsive local government, appropriate traffic rules, town planning and building bylaws. These "soft" collective goods lay the ground for social transformation. They promote new community goals, reorganize public institutions, and infuse public spirit. They have been the most neglected aspects of Pakistan's urban development. Again it is not that nothing has been done for institutional development, rather it is the ineffectiveness, compounded by corruption, of many measures taken in this regard that have contributed to the lag of normative and organizational structures. Many agencies, departments, and institutions have been established, but most of them are afflicted with organizational sclerosis from the start.

Hollow institutions and stillborn organizations

Institutions that imbibe modern forms without performing the associated functions, serving the self-interests of those involved instead, are mere shells and are drained of their proclaimed purposes. Such institutions are hollow in content and meaning. Often they are borrowed or imported from other societies, usually the West, without appropriate adaptation to local conditions. Many institutions promoted deliberately in the course of Pakistan's development, particularly in cities and towns, have turned out to be hollow. Particularly the organizational and normative parts of institutions turn out to be dysfunctional more often than the material/technological elements. This observation is the basis of my foregoing conclusion about the lag in institutional and organizational development. Let us examine the evidence for this observation. The story of the development of electricity supply and distribution network in urban areas is an illustrative example of how hollow institutions evolve and organizations are stillborn.

Case study: managing electric utilities

To begin on a positive note, power-generating capacity increased by 192 times since independence, from 60 megawatts in 1947 to 11,566 in 1998. Despite explosive population growth, per capita power consumption increased 22 times in five decades.[41] The evidence of national electrification is written all across the land in the illuminated skies over villages and cities from Peshawar to Karachi. In the 1950s, one could go for miles without seeing an electric light. The physical base of electric supply has undoubtedly developed since 1947 despite severe resource limitations.

The organizational structure for efficient management of this basic resource did not develop in parallel with its technological advancement. Some indicators of mismanagement are recounted ahead. Since the late 1970s, transmission and distribution losses have ranged between 25 and 40 per cent of the electricity supplied; influential consumers, with the connivance of officials and protection of politicians, have escaped paying electricity charges piling up huge revenue short-falls for the Water and Power Development Authority (WAPDA) in the 1990s and 2000s; power outages (called load-shedding) have been a daily affair; billing and collection of consumer charges have been in shambles; poor maintenance of the electric network has been compounded by the endemic corruption.[42] The two major public utility corporations, WAPDA and Karachi Electric Supply Company (KESC), have been on the brink of bankruptcy, running deficits of billions of rupees annually.

Local utility corporations ran the urban electric generation and distribution systems before 1947. These corporations were merged into the provincial depart-ments of electricity after independence. In 1959, WAPDA was established, on the model of the American TVA, as an integrated public corporation for irrigation development and power generation as well as distribution. It is a monopoly whose jurisdiction extends to almost the whole of Pakistan with Karachi being an excep-tion. Its operations touch everybody, be it to irrigate fields, run industries and busi-nesses, or illuminate homes and streets. Its engineering feats are evident in gigantic dams, tubewell networks, irrigation channels, and the national electric grid. Its organizational failures started emerging soon after its inception. By the 1990s, WAPDA's annual deficits were so large that they threatened to break the national budget. For example, in the four years, 1998–2002, about 300 billion rupees (Rs) of taxpayers' money was consumed by WAPDA and other public utility corporations (Railways, PIA, and KESC) to make up their revenue short-falls. The World Bank/IMF made their loans to Pakistan conditional on the straightening of WAPDA's finances and management. To illustrate how the poli-cies and management practices of WAPDA have resulted in colossal inefficien-cies, widespread corruption, and the exasperation of consumers, I will recount briefly only one aspect of its organizational performance, namely the system of billing and collecting electric charges.

From its inception, WAPDA gave little attention to consumers' needs and convenience. It is a public monopoly organized as an authoritarian bureaucracy protected by the government. The first step in consumer billing is to establish effi-cient procedures for monthly meter readings of consumers' draw of electricity. WAPDA has failed to organize this operation effectively and fairly. Its meter readers and linesmen, poorly paid and low-skill employees, through their omis-sions and commissions misread and tamper with electric meters, resulting in nominal bills for those who bribe them and exaggerated charges for others. Presumably they are not alone in this racket; bosses receive their share from the rake. Consumers are largely at the mercy of WAPDA officials. How persistent and widespread consumer dissatisfaction is can be vouched from "Letters to the editor" columns in newspapers, particularly in the Urdu press. For almost 40 years, "the exaggerated electricity bill" has been a regular topic of letter writers in all parts of the country.

A parallel illicit sector has also emerged to bypass paying electric charges. It is called the "*kunda*" system whereby households and businesses tap into power lines to get an unauthorized supply. In metropolitan Karachi, whole streets are serviced with *kundas*, visible to anyone. There are fixed rates of bribes for such connections and in some parts of the city, political parties actively run protection rackets. *Kundas* are not just a specialization of Karachi. They are in use in many other parts of the country. A bazaar sector cottage industry has emerged to manufacture *kundas* and service them. The illicit tapping of electric supplies and tampering of meter readings lead to revenue losses, which in turn precipitate rate hikes imposed by the World Bank and other international lenders. A vicious circle of rate hikes, consumer resistance, and lenders' pressures has buffeted WAPDA.

Collection of payments for electric bills is another link in the chain of poor management. Mailed out bills often arrive only a few days before the payment date. Up to one-third or more of bills may need corrections for unaccredited payments of previous periods or inflated charges, requiring hurried visits to the WAPDA accounting offices. For paying bills, consumers line up for hours in the winter rains or summer heat at the designated banks. Informal arrangements emerge to get around the long waits and the inconvenience of lining up to pay bills. Some cultivate bank officials for depositing through the back door; others bribe or hire someone to stand in line, while the poor and unconnected have no choice but to bear the pain. All in all, payment of electric bills is an exhausting job for a majority of citizens. A day or two are spent every month just to pay the bills. Similarly, telephone and gas billing and collection further compound people's exasperation.

The point illustrated by the above case study is that institutional development in Pakistan has lagged behind material and technological advances. Particularly the normative organizational changes have come about slowly and often not in correspondence with the intended functions of institutions.

Nongovernmental organizations

Pakistan has not lagged behind in developing new institutions. It had a quick start in establishing family reform commissions, Islamic law councils, industrial investment boards, science and industrial research councils, appropriate technology laboratories, press clubs, family planning associations, and many other bodies soon after independence. While driving in Pakistani cities, one is struck by the number and range of public organizations whose offices line the main roads, be it traffic management agencies, women development directorates, or environmental conservation corporations. There is hardly an international program or idea around which a public or voluntary body has not been formed, often parallel to or ahead of Western countries. On the evidence of the existence of modern institutions and organizations, one could conclude that Pakistan is a well-served society. Yet it is not! This is the cumulative outcome of the three periods of Pakistan's deliberate efforts to pursue development and modernization.

Most of the institutional development in the first and second periods was in the form of public agencies and semiautonomous corporations. In the third period, since the 1980s, international development paradigms shifted to privatization programs and nongovernmental organizations (NGOs). Pakistan was quick to take up this form of institution-building. NGOs mushroomed on public grants and foreign aid. Reliable data about the number and types of NGOs are nonexistent, but a fair idea of their sweep can be gained from some fragmentary numbers. From a few hundred in the early 1980s, the number of registered NGOs increased to 8,500 by 1991.[43] This number does include local community and charity organizations, but it is also a fact that globally linked developmental NGOs were formed in large numbers for human rights, urban community development, housing aid, advocacy of good governance, etc., during the 1980s and 1990s. The point is that both public and nongovernmental forms of institution building have coursed through Pakistan.

Undoubtedly there are some very effective NGO projects, such as the Aga Khan Rural Support Program (AKRSP) in Northern Areas, the Orangi Pilot Project (OPP), SHEHRI, Citizens Police Liaison Committees (CPLC) in Karachi, the Human Rights Commission of Pakistan and a few others. Yet the fact is that even the successful NGOs have been effective only in carrying out pilot projects, and have not been able to turn their projects into national programs or movements. Overall, NGOs are viewed with skepticism and their outcomes have not made a noticeable change in urban conditions. An opinion like that of a federal minister, reputed to be modern in outlook, reflects this sentiment: "Most of NGOs, with few exceptions, are busy minting money from donors."[44] Islamists have continually bashed NGOs as promoters of foreign culture and values and thus corruptors of Pakistani society. Whether public, private, or voluntary in origin, most of the institutions and organizations fostered by development have not lived up to their intended objectives. There is a lot of activity but no commensurate results. This is the phenomenon of hollow institutions.

Culture of cities

If Hindu or Sikh residents of a Pakistani city, who migrated to India in 1947, were to revisit their erstwhile hometown now, they would find the place bewilderingly unfamiliar. Their neighborhoods would have been built over and the quiet streets on which they had lived could be bustling bazaars. Outlying rivers or canals where they might have gone for a day's picnic would now be lost amidst housing colonies, truck stops, and garbage dumps. Even the spoken tongue and the sociological feel of the place may not be reminiscent of their past. Yet hidden below the surface would be some familiar sights and practices.

The urban culture of Pakistan is both new and old. Its precolonial and colonial heritage is reflected in its social structure and more visibly in the "walled cities," Civil Lines, as well as Mall roads. There are historical continuities in people's temperament, in the consciousness of their *nang* (family and clan honor), and the religious (largely Islamic, even sectarian) identity.[45] On these foundations, new configurations of social relations, interests, and values have emerged since 1947, wedging modern norms and behaviors into indigenous institutions. The outcome is a fragmented urban community where diverse ways and disparate quality of life coexist in a shared public space.

Public space has not evolved in parallel with the variety of private realms. Social institutions and collective services that form the common ground for interactions and transactions among persons of diverse expectations have not grown in parallel with cultural pluralism and economic disparities. It is no wonder that a Pakistani city appears to be a bundle of contradictions. Traffic in Pakistani cities is one manifestation of the contradiction between the lagging public arena of road maintenance and traffic management and the exploding private realm of motorbikes, cars, and camel carts.

Pakistani urbanism is not fully recapitulating the (presumed) universals of urban life. It blends the preindustrial city's modes of operation with the imperatives of modern urbanization.[46] Simply speaking, it is a hybrid of modernity and tradition. The following is a listing of its emerging characteristics.

- Social relations in Pakistani cities and towns continue to be based on kin ties, clan/ethnic networks, and religious affiliations. Friendships cross these boundaries, but they are invested with fraternal sentiments and family-like structures if they are enduring. Professional and occupational relations are interest-based on the surface, but underneath there is a substratum of ethnic, clan, or territorial networks. Student associations, for example, are ostensibly organized on politico-ideological bases, but they are suffused with territorial, ethnic, or sectarian interests. Groups as sharply defined as Sayyids of Narowals or Arian of Tobas or as broadly based as Balochs of Karachi, or Saraiki-speaking Punjabis band together to capture college students' unions. The point is that primordial ties permeate urban social organizations and interest-based, secondary relations have little traction in Pakistan.

- Impersonalization and anonymity are not the defining elements of urban culture in Pakistan. Of course, they are not as elemental as they were once thought to be even in Western cities. Yet in Pakistan most interactions proceed by personalizing the impersonal. On entering an office or store, one instinctively looks for someone to connect to; it could be a familiar face from the neighborhood, a sister-in-law's friend, someone with whom one prays in the mosque, or even a co-ethnic. Instinctually one looks to personalize dealings. Little trust is put in impersonal rules and procedures. And one is often looking for an "inside" track for one's transactions. This is the process of cultivating primary relations in interactions organized for secondary dealings. The need for personalizing the impersonal arises from the hollow public institutions, compounded by authoritarian bureaucracies and arbitrary rules. One's assurance of fair dealing lies in establishing personal bonds, transitory though they may be, a form of institutionalized nepotism.

- Particularistic arrangements permeate presumably universalistic urban institutions. Daily routines of Pakistani urban life are often carried out on the basis of negotiated and personalized arrangements. Market transactions, including prices, have to be generally negotiated and frequently bargained for, except in upscale stores and elite areas. Almost every transaction has an element of *ad hoc* arrangement. One's daily commute is often fraught with unpredictability. One day the bus breaks down, another day the bus leaves before time. Driving in one's car gives only marginally more certainty; one week the road may be blocked for a president or governor's travel and at another time it could be flooded from a broken waterline, and so on. The point is that so many uncertainties surround an activity that one's strategy has to be adjusted from day to day. There are so many variations of carrying out routine activities that individuals experience them as *ad hoc* operations that have to be particularly arranged every time. Punctuality is not valued. One may show up for an appointment with a doctor and find her/him an hour late or occupied in prayers. In Pakistani cities and towns, a lot of energy and time is taken up by activities that are meant to be done in cities as regular routine on the basis of universal principles and impersonal dealings. Pakistani urbanism is largely comprised of *ad hoc* and negotiated routines.

- The civic fabric of Pakistani cities and towns is thinly woven. The sense of community is rooted in one's social status and family/clan attachments. The evidence for the clannish bases of community identity can be seen in people's names. One is Laghari, Khan, Kasuri, or Bhutto at the core of one's being and it is reflected in one's name. Interestingly urbanization has increased rather than decreased the use of clan titles in names. This practice has resurged since the 1970s, after a brief diminution in the 1960s. Civic commitments are weak. Local governments are poorly organized. Citizen participation in community decisions is nonexistent. Neighborliness is strong in old mohallas (residential quarters) and in NICs, but decreases with the increasing size of houses and modernity of an area, as in upscale Planned Communities.

- Cities are sites where political power is exercised, protests organized and governments challenged, social movements germinated, and conspicuous consumption indulged in. Cinemas, cafes, parks, and the bright lights of shopping streets are to be found there. Pakistani cities have age-old traditions of poetry competitions, kite flying, itinerant theatre, and fairs. These practices thrive; some have been transformed into national cultural icons. The festival of Basant (spring heralded with flying kites) has spread beyond Lahore and neighboring cities to all parts of the country as a national day of celebrations. Modernity has brought literary clubs, art galleries, banquet halls, videos, television, and Internet. Air travel was unknown before independence; now it is a common mode of travel within the country and abroad. Persons who may not have climbed aboard a train for the initial 10–20 years of their life fly across continents for work and migration. Many such practices of modernity have been incorporated into Pakistan's urban culture. Globalization has also come to Pakistan through the cities, in the form of McDonald's, Kentucky Fried Chicken, and World Bank dictates.

- Since the 1980s, cities have also become centers of Islamic movements. Piety is on the rise. Mosques, shrines, and *madrassahs* (Islamic academies) dot the urban landscape. The sounds and sights of streets have a distinct Islamic flavor. *Azans* (prayer calls) and Koranic recitations broadcast from mosques reverberate across cities at almost all times of the day. Traditions are being reinvented and public space is being increasingly Islamized. For example, under the influence of Islamic revivalism (the 2000s), many women members of the national and provincial assemblies wear *niqabs* (face veils with slits to look through) in legislatures – a practice observed by almost no one for the initial 30–40 years of Pakistan's history. Secular pleasures and pursuits, such as music concerts, dances, and art shows are on the retreat from the public space into homes and clubs. Paradoxically private life is being secularized, but the public space is being Islamized. Witness the prayer recited at the start of every air flight and intercity bus journey.
- Pakistan's urban culture is being extensively infused with rural norms and values. Continual rural to urban migration brings in its wake rural values and practices into cities and towns. This migration is not limited to the laborers seeking work in cities, but it draws village "brains," that is, educated youth, as well as landlords who dominate national and provincial politics. At one level, urban society is being ruralized. *Katchi abadis* recreate a village-like environment as rural migrants from particular areas congregate together. Clan/tribal solidarities are recreated in planned communities. The process of ruralization reinforces the urban strains of conservatism and traditionalism.
- The local cultures of small cities and towns are primarily colored by a regional ethos, although national and global influences are filtering down, grafting modern practices and mores onto traditional institutions. Commercialization has been a particularly potent force in eroding customary transactions and realigning social structures. Development has promoted the growth of small industries and service establishments in these places. Regional towns function as way-stations in the chain of migration from villages to Karachi, even beyond to the Middle East and North America. They also play a significant role in national politics. Elected representatives from rural areas operate out of these places. During periodic national agitations, small towns become the venues for decentralized protests, difficult for the government to control, and the diffusion points of political movements.
- Social disparities between the rich and poor have been etched in urban land-scapes. They are evident physically, socially, and economically in everyday life.

Summing up: cities and social change

Are cities leading the modernization of Pakistan? The answer is a qualified "yes," but raises another question, namely what kind of modernization? Undoubtedly, cities have changed and they have also radiated out social change. Both within and around cities, modern technologies and institutions are being grafted onto traditional structures, producing diverse social forms and precipitating contradictions in values and practices. Pakistani cities have not followed the path of modernization postulated by theorists, at least not entirely in the idiom of Louis Wirth or Georg Simmel or even that of their critics. The theories are out of sync with reality in Pakistan and probably in many other non-Western countries.

Pakistani cities follow a hybrid form of modernization similar to other Third World societies. This form of modernization has been variously called adaptive, involutionary, or post-traditional.[47] It is often the modernization of forms and organizations without corresponding changes in functions, meanings, and attitudes. For example, many cities and towns in Pakistan have developed Master Plans but they have no legislative or administrative connection to public decisions about development. Plan-making has been adopted as a ritual of modern city governance, but the function of city development proceeds on *ad hoc* decisions of politicians and administrators.

New material and technological traits, mostly Western in origin, diffuse rapidly into Pakistan's urban culture. Similarly, modern consumer goods and preferences spread without much resistance except for their affordability. Television sets occupy pride of place in living rooms, merchants haggle with customers using electronic calculators, and farmers pay black market prices for miracle seeds, but family planning or mores for the disposal of household garbage seldom catch on. This fissure between the material and nonmaterial (values and norms) segments of culture is indicative of adaptive modernization.

The phrase culture of cities suggests a singular way of life. This singularity of urban culture exists at the plane of values and norms that are of universal scope, such as goals of personal advancement, formal mores and laws, corporate community, organized political activity, self-expression, etc. Within the bounds of such cultural norms, Pakistani cities are split into groups of distinct lifestyles and mores. The social fragmentation of cities extends beyond social class differences to customs, value-orientation, and even languages, making cities pluralistic at the level of community (sub)cultures. This pluralism is expressed in many forms, in the everyday life of neighborhoods and in the house design, street art and even signboards of stores. Shop signs in bazaars are in Urdu or Sindhi while those in the shopping malls are often in English. Also many poor neighborhoods have distinct ethnic identities, Pashtoons here and Punjabis there. Yet pluralism has not entered the discourse of Pakistani urbanism, except in Karachi.

Family, clan, and religion are the foundational social institutions of Pakistani urbanism. These institutions have been resilient. They have accommodated the functional demands of living under conditions of large populations in high densities. In families and clans, bonds among members have loosened, individuals' pursuit of personal fortunes is more acceptable, but both institutions retain the first call on a person's loyalty and identity. This is an important point in that the group, not the individual, is the building block of urban social structure. More about this phenomenon is discussed in later chapters.

Family and clan norms underlie the urban culture. The subterranean roots of Pakistan's urban culture lie in historic castes and tribes. These roots structure social order and people's attitudes and behaviors. On these scores, Pakistani urbanism differs from the individualistic and interest-oriented social organization of Western cities. Contrary to Western experiences, religion has not retreated to the private sphere of social life; rather, since the 1980s it has resurged with renewed vigor in the public arena.

The cohesiveness of norms and values has been cracked. Different institutions are changing at different rates and frequently in different directions, resulting in institutional lags. Material and nonmaterial divide is one form of lag, but there are others such as administrative norms and practices that remain traditional, while technological and organizational structures are being modernized, at least in form. Simply put, social and moral orders are not in sync with the demands of contemporary urban living. These institutional lags are the source of urban, nay national, problems.

For the smooth functioning of cities, a few conditions have to be met. These are the imperatives of urban life, namely collectivization of utilities, organizing space, building civic order, and instituting cultural reforms. Institutions for fulfilling these imperatives are not developing in parallel with emerging urban needs in Pakistan. Such institutions could be local in form but they have to fulfill functions that are common across cultures.

In cities, the welfare of one person is inseparable from the well-being of others. My garbage affects my neighbor's health and vice versa, for example. Therefore, some collective arrangements for the disposal of a whole neighborhood's garbage have to be made for everybody's good. Similarly, water supply, fire safety, and even burial practices have to be regulated in the collective interest. In this respect, the city is a democratic community. All residents are equal at some level. Paradoxically, in cities people are interconnected without interacting closely. This condition gives rise to urban imperatives.

Those imperatives call for certain universal urban institutions that were historically forged in Europe and North America, for example, traffic laws, environmental policies, or building controls. Such urban institutions may appear to be Western in origin, but their essence is universal. Thus, urban cultures cannot but have some universal (Western in form) facilities and practices. Pakistani cities are not an exception. They have replicated Western institutions, many of which are mere imitations without corresponding functions. I have called them hollow institutions. This is another form of institutional lag in Pakistani cities, namely the lag between form and functions. Pakistan needs institutional reforms to meet the requirements of urban imperatives. Some universal urban norms and technologies may have to be adopted, both in form and function, for the health and welfare of urban residents and society at large.

Finally, it is not right to view Third World urbanism only through the lens of Western theories and models. Its divergence from the old models of Louis Wirth and Georg Simmel or the recent formulations of Henri Lefebvre should not entirely be the basis of adjudging them.[48] These theories have been questioned even in Western contexts. The universality of some of their propositions is suspect. Despite glaring internal contradictions, Pakistani and other non-Western cities are forging new forms of modern urban cultures and institutions. The effectiveness of these institutions depends on their capacity to fulfill functions necessitated by large and concentrated populations, mass society, and a monetized economy. These functions are universal in that cities have to fulfill them for efficiency and equity. Yet they can be fulfilled through institutions that are local in form and meanings. New theories and models are needed to apprehend the diverse realities of urbanism in the Third World.

6 Development and the countryside

Villages and towns in Pakistani society

The village has been the soul of Pakistani society. Its hierarchical social order of *biradaris* (clans) and quasi castes underlies the traditional social structure.[1] Even urban Pakistanis have long subscribed to notions of honor, shame, or reputation, which originated in agrarian villages and tribal communities. Unsurprisingly, for example, in 2004, the National Assembly was sharply divided in attempting to legislate against *karo kari*, a tribal custom of killing female family members suspected of liaison with unrelated men to uphold the honor of clan and family. Yet this custom was rarely followed in the twentieth century. Many urban parliamentarians and Islamists joined landlords representing rural constituencies to defend the custom as "our culture" or Islamic justice, despite its contravention of Islamic laws.[2] Villages and towns are undoubtedly the home of traditions and customs, yet they are not unchanging.

Pakistan's countryside has many places that appear to be standing still in time, but below the surface even they are continuing to change with the advent of new technologies, shifting modes of production, evolving communication and transport services, or religious/political movements. It is the solidity of social organization and the entrenchment of the land tenure system that help maintain the appearance of timelessness in villages and towns. Incremental changes are absorbed into traditional ways of life by realignment of social relations and economic activities. Yet cumulatively these changes build up to transform local communities gradually over a long period. In recent times, the pace of change has picked up to the point that the timelessness of villages has become a tired cliché.

In distinction to incremental changes, catastrophic events, regime changes, or social revolutions precipitate sharp breaks with the past in villages and towns. These are the hinges of history. In the past two centuries, British colonization and Pakistan's independence were two such threshold events that changed the course of history in Pakistan's countryside.

The British conquered Punjab, NWFP, and Sindh in the 1840s, whereas Balochistan came under British influence in 1847 but its incorporation into imperial rule proceeded slowly, to be completed by the 1880s. British rule marked the end of the medieval era and the beginning of the modern phase of history. Land tenure was drastically revised from essentially collectivist ownership under feudal assignees to freeholds and hereditary tenancies. Landlordism displaced Mughal feudalism in large parts of the settled districts. Railways, canals, and roads opened new lands and breached the isolation of villages and towns. Cash dealings were injected into the rural economy of barter. The countryside was carved up in territorial districts, subdivided in *tehsils, talukas* (subdistricts), and municipal bodies, for the administration of law and order, tax collection, and the delivery of public services. Such measures changed the face of the land that Pakistan inherited.

Independence in 1947 was a veritable revolution. It triggered large-scale migrations, breaking open self-contained village communities, loosening local caste and clan bonds, and promoting entrepreneurship. People acquired new aspirations and entertained rising expectations of a free nation. Economic development was adopted as a national goal, and programs for land reform, modernization of agriculture (the green revolution), and industrialization were introduced under the successive five-year plans. Public and private schools and clinics multiplied in the countryside. Radio, television, and, lately, cellphones have spread into villages far from cities. All across the country, people began demanding good governance by periodically agitating for deliverance from official corruption and arbitrariness. These forces and processes continue in an uninterrupted march up to the present, transforming the landscape and reordering social life. The rest of this chapter describes in detail how villages and towns have changed socially and culturally and what forces are shaping their evolution. Before that, I will sketch the historical social organization and land systems of Pakistan's countryside, as it was, more or less, at the time of independence.

Traditional social organization

Despite linguistic, ethnic and geographic differences, families and clans of the four provinces have similar structures, partially rooted in the Islamic faith. These similarities also arose from the common heritage of the Indus Valley civilization, centered on settled agricultural communities and influenced by tribal migrations from central Asia and beyond. The conquest by Muslim dynasties of Persian and Afghan origins created a new elite class who were installed in local communities by successive rulers. Tribal identities of the local population were overlaid with the conquerors' privileged status as *Ashrafs* (noble born) to form Muslim castes such as Sayyids, Qureshis, Ghaznavis, and Mughals. Former Hindu high castes on conversion to Islam kept their lands and ancestral identities as Rajputs, Jats, Junejos, Dars, etc. Craftsmen continued with their hereditary occupations and identities, classified in occupational castes, such as weaver, carpenter, barber, or potter. The untouchables became *musallis* (cleaners and scavengers), even after changing their religion. Thus the caste and clan identities evolved into a social system based on *zats* (castes), which correlated with land ownership and occupational specialization of high or low status. Among Muslims a kind of caste-like system emerged on the foundations of ancient Indian castes.

Undoubtedly, *zats* among Muslims do not segregate various groups socially nor do they carry religious sanctions. Different castes share food and pray together.

Islam has a leveling effect. Yet Muslims' castes are endogamous and confer identity and status on individuals. This is how tribalism morphed into castes and clans in villages. Akbar Ahmed maintains that a tribal structure, active in some parts and residual in others, lies beneath the social organization of all four provinces.[3]

Of course, the tribe has been an overt social structure in Balochistan and the Frontier province. Tribes and clans have fused with feudal land tenure to form the social structure of Sindh's villages and towns and in parts of the southern Punjab, particularly in dry lands and deserts.

Out of these influences have emerged a typical village of *zat* and *biradari* hierarchies, which correspond to the hereditary occupations and corresponding social standings, layered hierarchically into landlords, tenants, farm workers, *maulvis* (priests) and *kammis* (serving castes such as cobblers, carpenters, matchmaker, and cleaners). Historically a village was a self-contained world. Landlords owned land and practically ruled over tenants and *kammis*, who provided the labor to produce goods and services including cloth, utensils, tools, matchmaking, cooking, etc. Everyone had customary shares from harvests in exchange for labor and services provided the year round. The basic contours of village organization emerged from the Indus Valley civilization but it evolved over two millennia, realigning land tenures and social relations with successive dynastic rules, periodic invasions, migrations, and changing economy and ecology.

Historical land tenure systems

There are common threads in the historical land tenures of the four provinces, briefly discussed in Chapter 3, but regional divergences in land rights are also striking. Typically a few large rent-receiving landowners, whose castes/clans usually dominate the surrounding regions, have headed villages. Below these elite strata is the middle layer of owner farmers, followed by a large number of occupancy tenants vested with varying rights to cultivate landlords' farms but standing a notch above the lowly landless workers. Village craftsmen and service workers, called *kammis* in Punjab and *kasbis* in Sindh are integrated into this agrarian order. They provide services the year round for stipulated but meager shares from the harvest.

An idea of the concentration of land ownership in the early days of the British rule (1890s) can be gleaned from two pieces of information: (1) 300 families owned over 80 percent of Sindh's total agricultural land (about 14 million acres)[4] and (2) in Punjab, about 36 percent of those supported by agriculture were actual cultivators, others being workers and a small number of rent-receivers.[5]

The divergences from the above-described patterns occur primarily in areas whose social organization is based on the tribal system, for example, Balochistan and NWFP. Historically, a Baloch or Brohi tribe has been a cluster of lineage groups, not of the same ancestry, collectively owning land and water resources. A tribe is a political unit divided broadly into three to four strata headed by *sardars* called *hakims* (rulers), with free tribesmen forming the cultivator/herdsmen class in the middle, and menial workers called *hizmatkar* (dependent) constituting the base.[6] Tribesmen have inheritable rights to particular pieces of land and water share for use and profit, with the obligation to contribute to *sardars'* levies. Of course, within Balochistan there are regional variations in tribal land tenures, such as Afghan and Makrani tribes who differ from Balochs.

In NWFP, the tribal land tenure has been a combination of collective–individual ownerships. A tribe as a body is the collective owner of a block of land, which is divided into *tappas* (lots) of clan joint shares, further subdivided into family shares called *kandis* and ultimately in individual entitlements called *wands*, comprised of fragmented slices (*bakhra*) of lands to ensure proportionate distribution of lands of different qualities among members of clans. The economic share of a family or individual within a tribe correlates with its political power and clan standing.

These historic land entitlements confer private rights for use and profit, but not for selling out a tribe's holdings. The communal ethos of this tenurial system is further reflected in the custom of *vesh* (redistribution), whereby a tribe periodically redistributes *bakhras* and *wands* to its component clans, and from thereon down to families and individuals to ensure fair distribution of good and poor quality lands.[7] Of course, this combination of collective–individual entitlements to land is a traditional tribal tenure, which in the settled districts has evolved into the landlord–tenant system and the peasant economy.

The British conferred individual proprietary and tenancy rights. Thus, they laid the foundations of landlordism. The settlement of newly irrigated lands in the Punjab and Sindh extended this tenurial system, fostering a class of yeomen farmers who brought their attached tenants and *kammis* to recreate self-contained village communities. The interests of landowners were protected by barring nonagricultural castes from owning farmland. All in all, under the British, the land tenure systems, with all their regional variations, became largely based on individual freeholds complemented by occupancy and at-will tenancies.[8] Landowners took a large share of harvests, leaving tenants often in penury. In Sindh, tenants had fewer rights than in Punjab; many known as *haris* were virtually indentured labor. This was the land economy of villages and towns at the time of independence. From this base began the post-independence journey of social change.

Rural communities

Despite being home to some of the world's oldest cities, Pakistan has been a rural society.[9] It is undoubtedly becoming more urban year by year, both demographically and culturally, but the rural population was still the majority at the beginning of the twenty-first century. Pakistan's rural population increased from 27.7 in 1951 to 89.3 million in 1998, although its share in the national population decreased from 82.2 percent to 67.5 percent. If one adds the population of high-density rural districts and areas near cities to the urban population, the rural–urban balance tilts toward an urban majority, an argument developed in Chapter 3. Rural communities have been central to Pakistani society although rural life itself is changing rapidly, as will become obvious later.

What does the term "rural communities" mean? The Pakistan census defines "urban" as localities that have some form of municipal government, be it metropolitan corporation or incorporated city or town committee, although the municipal designation is assigned on the basis of population size, existence of commercial and manufacturing or administrative activities and/or political standing. In the census, rural is a residual category. It includes villages, clusters of homesteads, encampments, towns supporting agriculture, and fishery or mining activities. The "village" as a clustered and compact settlement is the main group of rural settlements in Pakistan, followed by small towns.

Rural localities can be as small as villages of 200 persons to towns as large as 5,000 or more population. Balochistan has small villages with a median population of 340, and Sindh province on the other end of the scale had a median village population of 2,060, while Punjab and NWFP fall in between the two provinces with the average population of their villages being 1,300 and 840 respectively, in 1998. Historically, villages have been self-contained communities, growing food, producing household goods, building houses, and largely ruling themselves, all through the customary modes of bartering goods and services, rooted in the ancient *Jajmani* system.[10] That is one reason villages tended to be clustered settlements of sizable population, especially in farming areas.

Pakistan had about 48,400 villages and towns in 1998 with about 53 percent of these in Punjab followed by NWFP (15 percent), Balochistan (14 percent), Sindh (12 percent), and the Federal Areas (6 percent). Rural localities can graduate into the urban category on the establishment of municipal governments. Thus their number is affected by the loss to urban designations and by gains through the splitting away of satellite villages as independent settlements and by the development of new villages. The net effect of these changes is relatively small. The number of villages and towns has grown relatively little from census to census (Table 6.1).

The settlement pattern in rural areas is hierarchical by size and function. Small villages and hamlets are usually farming or fishing communities; a number of such settlements are linked with a large village/small town with both farming and

Table 6.1 Numbers of rural localities 1981–98

Area	No. of Villages and Towns	
	1981	*1998*
The Punjab	25,266	25,875
Sindh	5,848	5,871
Balochistan	6,111	6,554
The NWFP	7,809	7,335
Federal Areas*	133**	2,728
Total	45,167	48,363

Sources: Population census organization, Government of Pakistan, 1981 and 1998 censuses.

*Federal Areas include federally administered tribal areas and Islamabad

**Figures only for Islamabad

service activities such as schools and repair shops; and at the still higher level are central places that have high schools, clinics, or administrative offices serving a number of villages and towns. This hierarchy of rural settlements dovetails into urban places of progressively larger sizes and upper-order activities. What quality of life do these places provide and how has that been changing? This question leads us to the discussion of social indicators of rural life.

Rural quality of life

Rural living conditions in low-income countries are spartan to begin with. Over the years droughts, wars, famines, and epidemics have periodically devastated Pakistan's countryside to add to the misery of the people. For example, cholera killed 65,000 persons in Punjab in just one year, 1892. Famines ravaged Punjab seven times between 1830 and 1900.[11] Poverty was the destiny of almost everybody except landlords and *jagirdars* well into the twentieth century. Undoubtedly, economic conditions improved with peace, order, and irrigation works under the British but an overwhelming majority of the rural population lived at subsistence levels without health and educational facilities at the time of independence.

An analysis of rural living conditions is usually presented in the form of rural–urban comparisons to allow normative assessments. For example, it is not enough to say that poverty prevails in rural areas without comparing it to urban poverty rates to be able to make some judgment about its scope. Does rural living offer a good or poor quality of life? How is it changing in comparison with other parts of a society? These are the implicit normative questions that have to be addressed. That is why much of the sociological analysis of rural or urban life is couched in models of rural–urban comparisons.[12] Modernization theories also, partially, build on historical rural–urban continuum models, identifying modernism with urban ways of life.[13] No matter how we approach the examination of rural life, we have to view it in a comparative perspective, recognizing that both rural and urban social organizations are pieces of the same societal fabric.

Sex ratio, defined as the number of males per 100 females, is an indicator of the status of women, life expectancies by gender, differential migration of males and females, and even census variations in the enumeration of men and women. Biological sex ratio at birth is about 102 boys for 100 girls. So a variation of one or two points around 102 is the yardstick for a balanced sex ratio. Pakistan's sex ratios have been high, indicating proportionately more males surviving and/or living in an area. The sex ratios, contrary to Western trends, have been consistently higher in urban than in rural areas. Rural sex ratios consistently fell from a high of 114.6 in 1951 to 106.7 in 1998. Similarly, urban sex rations fell from 126.4 to 112.2 over the same period. Rural areas send young men to urban areas for work and schooling. Among the provinces, Balochistan had the highest sex ratios, urban (118.1) as well as rural (113.6) in 1998, while NWFP had the lowest ratios by a small margin, urban (113.2) and rural (103.4). What these trends suggest is that perhaps the care of the female child is improving and the inhibition to enumerate women in a census may also be waning. Despite the falling of sex ratios over time, there is still a disparity in the ratio of males to females in both rural and urban areas, suggesting greater survivability of males due to better care and nutrition.

Indicators of the quality of life of an area include life expectancy, infant mortality, literacy, and housing conditions. Pakistan's statistics on each of these indicators are not adequate to allow a consistent comparison over time. National censuses have been held sporadically. Definitions of various indicators as well as the areas covered have changed from census to census. National sample surveys report data to varying degrees of detail from one year to another. Thus I am reduced to using different time periods for different indicators, some spanning the 1961–98 period and others limited to 1981 and 1998, to trace temporal trends. With this caveat, let us examine how rural quality of life has evolved using urban indicators as comparators.

Despite the limitations of data, there is unmistakable evidence of improvement in the quality of life in both urban and rural areas since independence. Even the rural–urban gap has been narrowing. This is not to say that living conditions have become healthy and satisfying for everybody. Poverty, disease, or even illiteracy are endemic, particularly in rural areas. Yet in relative terms a substantial proportion of the burgeoning population has been climbing up the ladder of rudimentary modernism. Proportionally more of the expanding population in rural areas has become literate, healthy, and has electricity and water supply in homes (mostly hand pumps) than at the time of independence. The quality of such services, though, is very poor and the availability sporadic. Urban areas are only slightly better served in terms of the quality of services.

From the perspective of social change, rural areas have unmistakably changed since independence. The change is in the expected direction, toward modern ways of life. It is striking in absolute terms, but it appears unimpressive by comparisons with urban changes and with other countries of similar economic standing, such as Sri Lanka, Myanmar, or India.[14] After 50 years of independence, the social development of villages and towns is a matter of the proverbial half full or half empty glass, depending on how one views it.

Rural literacy

To start with, let us consider progress in literacy. Pakistan was largely an illiterate nation at the time of independence. Only about 15 percent of the national population was literate in 1951, obviously mostly concentrated in cities. The urban literacy rate was about 35 percent and the rural rate was 11 percent in 1961. By 1998, the urban and rural literacy gap was still large, 63 percent literate in urban and 34 percent in rural areas. Punjab and NWFP have progressed more than Sindh and Balochistan in rural literacy. Yet almost two-thirds of the rural population in the advancing provinces were still illiterate after 50 years of independence. A majority of the urban population was literate, but more than one-third remained illiterate. Balochistan stands out as lagging behind in both urban and rural literacy. On this indicator, considerable progress is evident but much remains to be achieved.

Female literacy is an indicator of gender equality and women's status in a society. Human development theorists take it to be essential for economic and social progress. On this indicator, Pakistani society shows some advancement since independence, but still lags behind comparable societies. Rural areas, especially, have been slow to progress in matters of female literacy. From an abysmally low level of rural female literacy in 1961, two percent of rural women being literate, Pakistan's rural areas advanced to about a 20 percent female literacy rate in 1998. In the same period, urban female literacy rose from 21 percent to 55 percent. Punjab charted the biggest gains and Balochistan the least. Despite the progress, an overwhelming majority of rural women and a little less than half of urban women were illiterate in 1998.Undoubtedly, the reluctance of parents to allow their daughters to commute long distances to attend schools inhibited female literacy as did the norm of female segregation at a young age. A girl child was about 24 percent less likely to be enrolled in a school than a boy in the 1990s.[15] Public educational programs could have countered these inhibitions with mobile schools for girls or female educational drives which were carried out but corruptly and ineffectively. The ineffectiveness of development planning on this score is incontrovertibly reflected in the data.

Health conditions

Life expectancy and infant mortality rates are two simple measures of the health of a population. On both these indicators, Pakistani society has registered substantial advances. Yet rural–urban differences have been persistent, and compared to other countries of similar economic standing Pakistan has been falling behind. The infant mortality rate for males was 137 and females 135 deaths per 1,000 live births in 1962–5.[16] Rural rates were significantly higher than urban rates. The infant mortality rate came down over the next two decades, falling to 116 in urban areas and 124 in rural areas by 1981. In the 1990s, there was a more precipitous drop, 83 deaths of children under one year of age per 1,000 live births. Yet this gain compares unfavorably with India's rate of 72 and Sri Lanka's 15.[17]

As pointed out in Chapter 1, life expectancy in Pakistan increased from 48 years for males and 45 years for females in the early 1960s to 63 years for males and 65 for females in 2001. One can see the impact of longer life spans all around. It was rare to find even an urban family with one or more members who were 60 years or more during my childhood (1940s), but in the 2000s, it is common to see persons living well into their sixties and seventies. It is particularly true for middle- and upper-class households in both urban and rural areas.

Housing

Finally, housing conditions, exemplified by the availability of indoor water supply for domestic use and electricity, have registered striking improvements in 50 years. The housing censuses of 1960 and1972 did not collect data about these indicators. Yet it would not be far off the mark to say that the majority of urban houses were without electricity and indoor piped water or a hand pump in the 1950s. Rural houses were one-room mud structures with one or two wells for a whole village. Women's daily chores included drawing and carrying water from a village well. Punjab's folklore situates many youthful romances at village wells where young girls congregated to draw water and exchange glances with young men. Electric lights were a rarity. By 1998, 89 percent of urban houses and 68 percent of rural houses in the whole country had indoor sources of water, mostly hand pumps in villages. Punjab and Sindh were more advanced than NWFP and Balochistan on this score. Electricity was available to 93 percent of city homes and 60 percent of rural homes. NWFP was ahead of other provinces on this indicator; 96 percent of urban and 68 percent of rural houses had electricity. Public programs for village electrification have had a salutary impact.

Mud houses in the villages of central Punjab and irrigated parts of NWFP and Sindh have been giving way to *pacca* (brick walls and concrete or brick-lined roofs) houses. In 1998, about 46 percent of rural houses in the whole of Pakistan had walls of stone and/or brick, while 88 percent of urban houses were similarly built. While about 80 percent of urban homes had *pacca* roofs, only 30 percent of rural housing had such roofs.[18] These proportions represent vast improvements over the housing conditions of the 1950s and 1960s but still almost one-half to two-thirds of rural houses are made of mud or thatch walls and/or roofs.

These improvements are evident to those old enough to have lived in the 1960s. In those days, rural homes visible from a train or bus were mostly mud houses of a one-room-and-courtyard style. By the 1990s, one saw houses of brick, often with water tanks standing atop like pinnacles, with few mud houses, all along the bus or train routes. A repeat survey of three villages in Punjab, for example, showed that over a 20-year period between 1962 and 1983, the proportion of *pacca* houses increased from about 15 to 40 percent.[19]

Change in living conditions

Underlying these indicators is a story of the process of social change. The salient features of this process are summed up below.

- Rural and urban living conditions have improved but unevenly. Housing conditions have improved relatively more than the educational and health levels. Cities and males have gained more than villages and females. The irrigated districts of Punjab, NWFP, and Sindh have progressed more than Balochistan and the peripheral and dry lands of the other three provinces. On the human development indices, Pakistan as a whole has lagged behind other countries of South Asia.
- Gradual but unbalanced development has been unfolding. The transformation from feudal-agrarianism to monetized economy has been underway. The middle and lower-middle strata have expanded with economic development, raising living conditions of those floating up into these classes. This process is more extensive in urban than rural areas although the latter are not entirely

bypassed. Some elementary facilities have partially filtered down to rural areas, for example, electricity, literacy, and rudimentary medical services.

• The process of social change can be described in a variation of the Galbraithian phrase, as a phenomenon of private progress and public squalor. Social indicators of private consumption show greater change than those of public goods. Medical care has spread more than public health; hand pumps are more common than drains and sewage disposal. Electricity is one exception but its supply is intermittent and inadequate (more about the delivery of the electric supply later). Quantitative expansion of services has progressed more than qualitative improvements.

• Rural–urban differences in the quality of life remain wide. Rural areas lag behind cities in the provision of services and facilities although the floor has been raised overall.

• A stubborn core of poverty persists in rural areas.

What are the forces that have brought about these changes? This question will be addressed in the following sections.

Evolution from the agrarian to the capitalist mode of production

Village economies in Pakistan have changed fundamentally in the post-independence period. Of course, the change has not swept all parts of the country uniformly; yet almost every village has been touched by it. The broad swath of the country along the Peshawar–Lahore–Karachi axis, which is also largely an irrigated plain, has been the most affected by the change. The dry plateaus of Balochistan, NWFP, the arid districts and deserts of Sindh and southwestern Punjab have not been affected so much.

How have village economies changed? The single most pervasive change is the progressive monetization of economic transactions. The traditional *seypi* (customary and obligatory barter of goods and services among landowners, farmers, tenants, workers, and *kammis*) system of economic dealings has given way to cash transactions and pricing mechanisms.[20] Paralleling the monetization of village economies, social relations of production have evolved from interlocking obligations to contractual dealings. Villages have largely ceased to be self-sufficient economies providing locally for the essential needs of consumers. They now produce cash crops, goods, and services for national and international markets. Communal and joint property ownership has been yielding to individual freeholds with the consequent erosion of the tenants' entitlements. These changes are the hallmarks of what Mahmood Khan called in 1983 "the burgeoning 'capitalist' system which had come to coexist with the feudal and peasant agrarian systems."[21] Of course, since the 1980s, the capitalist mode of production has penetrated more deeply and widely in the village economies. It has even touched the tribal communities of Balochistan and NWFP, even though feudal and peasant relations survive in modified forms in these areas and on the peripheries of Sindh and Punjab.

Demography of independence

The social and economic forces that have driven the transformation of village economies germinated in the demographic upheaval of Partition (1947), gathering momentum steadily since then. The caste hierarchy and power structure in villages were realigned by the resettlement of refugees from India on lands and houses vacated by the departing Hindus and Sikhs. Local communities were reorganized with the injection of new castes. Migrant landowners had to negotiate anew arrangements with resident tenants and *kammis*. Historic customs and traditions were not binding for settlers and locals had to adapt to the different ways of the migrants from India. Farmers coming from different regions introduced new farming practices. Arians (a garden-farmer caste), for example, brought their progressive farming practices to peasants' villages of subsistence agriculture, as did many other refugees, thus putting roots down in the new country. Altogether traditional relations of production were shaken, laying the ground for monetary dealings.

After the turmoil of independence, Pakistan's death rates started to decline and population growth took off, almost quadrupling the national population in fifty years.

Modernization of agriculture

National programs for economic growth laid the bases of agricultural development through irrigation works and technical assistance. A nationwide rural self-help program called Village Agricultural and Industrial Development (VAID) raised awareness of modern farming methods and built rudimentary infrastructure in villages during the period 1953–62. It was hurriedly wound up to make room for Ayub Khan's guided democracy, called the Basic Democracies system (1962). Basic Democracies were organized as the three tiers of local, *tehsil*, and district councils that were conveniently turned into the electoral college for the indirect election of the president in 1965. Winding up development programs for political purposes before they begin to bear fruit has been the Achilles heel of Pakistan's rural development.

Despite administrative inertia and corruption, public efforts of the first period "softened" the ground for the modernization of agriculture. The green revolution, based on promoting the use of miracle seeds and chemical fertilizers, started unfolding from 1966 to 1967. Its success can be attributed to farmers' awareness and their capacity to perceive the usefulness of new practices. The yields of wheat, cotton, and rice, and later on fruits and vegetables, tripled and quadrupled over the following 30 years. The green revolution accelerated the mechanization of farming. Farmers began to take stock of their costs and base their production decisions on returns and profits. They started planting orchards and vegetable crops which traditionally were looked upon as unbecoming of high-caste Jats and Chaudhris.

The *yamla jat* (naïve farmer) stereotype of the early 1950s gave way to the reality of a businessman cultivator by the late 1970s. Gilbert Etienne illustrates the new village economy in Punjab by highlighting the production decisions of middle-level farmers in a village in the district Gujranwala, Punjab, in 1979. Distributing his 14-acre land judiciously among rice, wheat, fodder fields, and mango orchards, an enterprising farmer managed with the help of daily wage labor, to earn enough income to support a family of eight in comfort, owning a brick home, bicycle, radio, and tubewell.[22] It may be added hastily that this was not the story of all farmers. The disparity between the large and middle farmers on the one hand and small landowners, tenants, and landless workers on the other widened with the green revolution.[23] Similarly regional disparities between irrigated districts and rain-fed areas increased.[24]

To bring the narrative of agricultural modernization to the end of the twentieth century, I will briefly recount the developments of the second and third periods. Period 2 witnessed a flurry of rural development programs aiming to improve access to schools, dispensaries, and agricultural credit; to build farm-to-market roads; and to distribute house lots among the landless in villages. Among such programs were the Integrated Rural Development Programme (IRDP); the United Nations/World Bank's flavor of the year, People's Works Programme; the Three Marla Rural Housing Programme; and the cooperative societies for village development.

It was the era of Bhutto's populist egalitarianism, in which the rhetoric of peasants' and laborers' rights was louder than actions. Although most of the second period programs had little impact, Bhutto's egalitarian ideology resonated among peasants and workers. For example, an evaluation of the IRDP concluded that the agricultural improvements and increasing provisions of education and health services had been proceeding at a steady pace under private and community initiatives before the program, which essentially complemented ongoing processes.[25] Whatever small benefits this program produced, they were largely appropriated by the middle and upper classes in villages, as is often the outcome of developmental initiatives. Despite their ineffectiveness, the programs of the second period further eroded peasants' and workers' fatalist acceptance of their status and raised their expectations. The change of the national regime resulted in the hasty abandonment of Bhutto's initiatives without any attempt to draw lessons from their experiences.

The third period has shifted the national discourse to the promotion of Islamic order and private enterprise. On both counts, property interests and conservative ideologies have been reinvigorated. The decade of General Zia's rule (1978–88) witnessed the imperatives of the green revolution unfolding in the form of demand for water and machinery. Landowners invested in tubewells and tractors. These technologies displaced tenants and accelerated their slide into wage labor. Owner-operated farms, employing labor, became the norm in the plains. The scale of such transformations is indicated by two sets of figures: (1) The number of tractors in Pakistan increased from 18,900 in 1968 to 178,700 by 1992–3,[26] (2) The number of tubewells increased more dramatically, from 86,000 in 1970 to 483,700 in 1995.[27]

The manufacturing and import of tractors was subsidized with favorable terms of credits and tax exemptions. Benazir Bhutto's government, for example, launched a rural program of tractor imports in 1993–6 for farmers, called the Green Tractor Scheme, as a counter to her predecessor's city-favoring scheme of

Yellow Cabs. Similarly, public tubewells were installed in areas where groundwater levels were rising from the seepage of canals but the trend to install private wells took off in many parts of the country. The spread of tractors and tubewells was largely a private initiative but it was stimulated and complemented by public programs. The third period has been, by and large, an era of privatization in agriculture. By the end of the twentieth century, natural resource constraints had started bearing down. Particularly, the canal water shortage and the depletion of groundwater supply for tubewells raised provincial conflicts about river water distribution. Farmers complained of the impending return of their lands to desert conditions.

Realignment of the land system

Land is the foundation of farming communities. One's access to land determines not only one's income but also one's social status. Historically, Pakistan's land system was a mixture of tenures, feudal and hereditary tenants, as outlined above. Independence came with expectations of land rights for tillers and tenants. The Pakistan Muslim League, the ruling party of those days, estimated that at the time of independence, tenants cultivated about 50 percent of the farm area in Punjab and NWFP, and over 70 percent in Sindh.[28] Of course, the promise of land reform was not fulfilled although the necessity of reducing iniquities of land tenure continued to be a theme in public policy discourse. Landlords, dominating the political parties, managed to block efforts to any meaningful land reforms.[29] The reform had limited impact; relatively little land (1.9 million acres only) of dubious quality was surrendered for distribution among tenants.

Another attempt to acquire land from large landowners was made in the second period by Bhutto through the Land Reform Ordinance (1972). It lowered the ownership ceiling to 150 acres, hoping to acquire more area for redistribution. But landowners had grown "wiser"; most of them had registered their lands in the names of their children and family members, and sometime even in the names of loyal domestic servants, in anticipation of Bhutto's policies. The second cycle of land reforms also had a negligible impact. By the third period, land reforms had slid off the national agenda. Many Islamists were opposed to it. General Zia explicitly declared that there would not be any more land reforms.

Land reform measures may have had little direct impact but the overpowering role of the landlords was dented by the threat of land distribution. New technologies have turned agriculture into an industry, revising parameters of costs and profits and redefining tenurial relations. Landlords are cultivating their farms with the help of labor. Owner farmers are planting orchards, specialty crops, and sometimes renting their land. *Kammis* are becoming tractor drivers, tubewell operators, factory workers, or migrating to cities. Except for a few, the labor on farms is becoming a seasonal activity and it has to be combined with casual work in nearby cities and towns to eke out a living. The population explosion has led to the fragmentation of lands into small holdings. All in all, rural land tenures have been realigned to the point that they represent a new land system. The social disparity between the propertied and the landless has widened, and the misery of the rural poor may have increased with the breakdown of the mutual obligations embedded in the historic *seypi* system.

Cumulatively, how are the technological changes in agriculture and the realignment of the land system affecting rural economies? This question can be answered at macro and micro levels – the macro level by an overview of the changes in land ownership patterns over the 50-year period, and at the micro level by the trends in local living conditions.

Land ownership

Small farms of less than 5 acres constituted 15.3 percent of the farm area in 1950, by 1976 their proportion had increased to 24.9 percent, but amazingly by 2000, their share had dropped to 16.2 percent. Farms of 5–25 acres increased in proportion from 31.7 percent in 1950 to 39.4 percent in 1976 and 47.4 percent in 2000. At the other end, large farms of 100 acres or more were 33.4 percent of the farm area in 1950, dropping in proportion to 9.2 percent in 1976 but surprisingly rising to 11.6 percent in 2000.[30] The middle range of large farms, 25–100 acres in size, also increased steadily in proportion over time, from 21.8 percent in 1950 to 24.9 percent in 2000.

What these figures suggest is that large estates broke up during the first and second periods (1960s and 1970s), but they have begun to be reconstituted in the third period of market-oriented policies. The small farms of five or fewer acres may be fragmenting to the point of being uneconomical, thus the drop in their proportion in recent times.

In the third period, corporate farming by the military, urban investors, and private corporations began in earnest.[31] These are new trends that are introducing a new form of land ownership. The land loot described in Chapter 3 also included the distribution of newly irrigated lands in the Barrage schemes of southern Punjab and upper Sindh among selected civil and military officers, influential politicians, and well-connected landlords. Many of them are running family corporate farms. Through these incremental steps, land-ownership patterns and tenurial relations have been transformed.

Before concluding the discussion of changes in land ownership, a brief mention of the tenurial changes in rural residential land should be made. Land for homes in villages was almost free for use until recent times. Land within the boundaries of a clustered settlement, village, or hamlet, was often common or state property with family/*khel* entitlements. Each family had a right to use them for homes and animal sheds but it could not be, or seldom was, bought or sold. Of course, landlords and clan leaders had the lion's share and control, but tenants and *kammis* had customary entitlements. There was no market for residential land.

Population pressure and changes in land tenure precipitated problems of homelessness and displacement of the poor from communal lands. These issues were acknowledged by the Bhutto government and it initiated a program to distribute five *marla* (125 sq yds) residential lots to the rural landless. As is often the case with public programs in Pakistan, the proclamations and promises are much larger than the achievements. During the 1970s, successive governments claimed big successes in distributing rural housing lots to the landless. For example, Punjab was claimed to have distributed 1.8 million rural lots under the Five Marla program between 1972 and 1976 and 5 million more were claimed to be ready for distribution.[32] Yet the actual achievements were far more modest.

Equally important is the fact that the need for a systematic supply of rural residential land surfaced in Pakistan in the 1970s. In the third period, General Zia's government felt constrained to follow Bhutto's policies. It gave the rural housing policy its own imprimatur by offering seven marla (150 sq yds) lots under the scheme called Jinnah Abadis. The achievements of this program were as much out of line with the objectives as they had been for Bhutto's policies. Between 1982 and 1987, for example, in the Punjab 1.3 million households applied, 300,000 lots were targeted to be distributed, but only 98,000 were actually produced.[33] Similar policies were periodically announced by Nawaz Sharif's and Benazir Bhutto's governments in the 1990s but little was delivered before they were successively ousted. All in all, the institutional arrangements for the provision of residential land in rural areas started shifting from communal/family to individual ownership and in many parts of the country the buying and selling of homes and lots in rural areas began to be a practice from the 1980s. A market has now emerged even for rural residential land.

Urban infusions

Apart from the gradual commercialization of agriculture and changing land system, the gradual spread of urbanism and the stitching together of urban and rural areas have also transformed villages and towns. Even remote regions such as the Northwestern tribal belt and the Makran coast of Balochistan, have been affected by urban influences through migrations, improved transportation and travel, and trade which have facilitated a diffusion of consumer goods, radio, television, telephone, and urban mores. Of course, the social organization maintains its historical forms and traditional values but even these structures have a new gloss on them. More about the structures of change later.

Extensive regions radiating out from cities have emerged, closely tying distant villages with urban centers. Factories, truck stops, gas stations, auto and tractor repair shops, and eateries march out along highways forming ribbons of urban development projecting deep into the countryside. The Karachi–Hyderabad megapolis, the Multan–Rahim Yar Khan–Sukkur corridor, most of central Punjab surrounding the urban triangle of Lahore–Faisalabad–Gujrat, and the Peshawar Valley are examples of such mega "rur-urban" or "ruralopolitan" regions. Villages in these areas are an integral part of regional economies, exporting vegetables, milk, meat, grains, and labor and importing consumer goods, machinery, educational, medical, and administrative services. Such linkages thin out but are not displaced beyond these mega regions. Manzur Ejaz, a newspaper correspondent and economist, in writing about the village where he grew up, recounts his memories of school days and compares them to the situation in 1999. He says visiting Sahiwal, the district capital, was a "once-in-a-while experience by a few lucky ones," but in 1999, several buses went back and forth to the city daily, "always full to their tops with college going students, shoppers, employees and even those who just want(ed) to kill time."[34] This is a typical situation.

The thickening of rural–urban linkages began gradually and gained momentum cumulatively. The green revolution made agriculture dependent on inputs – fertilizers, tractors, tubewells – produced or imported in urban areas breaking the age-old self-sufficiency of villages. Correspondingly increasing populations in cities consumed more and a greater variety of food, thereby extending farther and farther the circle of their suppliers. The web of these transactions promoted trade and travel between villages, towns, and cities. It also accelerated the monetization of village economies.

The gradual changes in the mode of production displaced rural workers. The erosion of their traditional roles combined with the population growth pushed rural labor to cities. Correspondingly, a city's imagined and real opportunities continued drawing rural workers who converged on cities in increasing numbers for work, education, and fun. They became the primary source of labor for manufacturing, construction, and transport activities in cities and towns. As domestics, watchmen, truck drivers, and construction workers, rural migrants have helped cities develop and provided for the comfort and security of urban middle and upper classes.

Karachi's Pashtoon bus and minivan operators/drivers have an ethnic/tribal monopoly of the local transport. They provided a necessary service at a time when it was almost nonexistent in the 1960s although over the years they coalesced into a strong-arm force and an economic monopoly, particularly with the arrival of Afghan transport mafias in the 1980s. Similar primordial structures, recapitulating rural clans and castes, underlie the social organization of construction or industrial labor and domestic workers in various cities. *Katchi abadis* (squatter settlements) in almost all cities are a stark reminder of how the cheap labor of rural migrants has subsidized the growth of cities.

Landlords, owner farmers, and craftsmen gradually imbibed an entrepreneurial spirit. Many began to branch out in renting tractors or selling tubewell water and gradually, in parts of Punjab, Sindh, and NWFP, started small industries such as carpet weaving, cotton ginning, and rice husking. By combining farming with agro-businesses, segments of middle and upper rural strata have incorporated urban activities in village and town economies. Children of prosperous peasants pursued education, some qualifying as doctors, engineers, lawyers, and public officials. Yet unlike Western experiences, most of them have kept their links with villages and have even invested in land and houses. The rural–urban migration in Pakistan does not result in uprooting people from villages, once and for all. It results in rural families planting branches in cities while retaining a strong base in villages for the next two or three generations.

The political elite of Pakistan have largely come from the ranks of the village aristocracy. From Ayub Khan's much trumpeted "decade of development"

(1958–68), the politically connected rural elite began to own factories, cashed in their influence by obtaining subsidized urban lots, import licenses, and industrial permits. By the second period, rural landlords were also involved in urban businesses, funneling their wealth into investments likely to be unaffected by land reforms. This trend has accelerated in the third period.

Noon, Daultana, Talpur, and Gurmani are names on the "who's who" list of leaders who ruled Pakistan in period 1. Almost all of them were educated in Britain or in elite colleges in India. They were landlords whose estate included many villages, yet each one of them had opulent city properties. They were among the early wave of industrialists/importers in Pakistan. Bhutto, Junejo, Laghari, Mazari, and even opposition leader Wali Khan were big landlords who also owned cinemas, factories, businesses, and/or urban properties. Many of them had two or more wives, one a cousin in a village and another a modern woman of the city.[35] The interweaving of rural and urban life has filtered down to the middle and even lower classes in villages. A farmer with 50 acres of orchards and cotton/wheat could also be an owner of a rice-husking mill in the town nearby and would indirectly own urban properties in the name of his children, one of whom may be a major in the army, while another could be a doctor in a city, for example.[36] These examples illustrate how urban influences have permeated into villages along many paths, trade, migration, family ties, and mobility.

Mobility

One of the explanations of the presumed "backwardness" of villages is that they are closed communities where one's social status is ascribed by birth and one's geographic sphere of activities is confined to a local area. Lack of mobility, both social and geographic, is assumed in the modernization theories to be a contributor to stagnation. Danial Lerner has particularly emphasized the role of mobility as an agent of modernization. His parable of the opening of a road leading to the passing of traditional society is a metaphor of modernization.[37] People can seek better opportunities and learn new skills, ideas, and attitudes by moving out of closed communities, he holds. This model's limitations are well recognized. Exposure to an unfamiliar social milieu can arouse the revival or re-enactment of traditions as much as it can bring out new institutions and social organizations. For us, the question is how has mobility for the rural population in Pakistan increased since 1947 and what changes has it brought to villages and towns?

Historically, Pakistan's villages were closed communities but they were not frozen in time. Social change was slow and often imperceptible, yet different regions were subjected to varying types of influences that affected the course of their evolution. In Punjab, colonization of newly irrigated land (1880s to 1920s) led to extensive migrations out of historical villages and settled districts. This migration involved the resettlement of whole families/clans, largely recreating traditional social patterns.[38] Similarly many pastoral Pushtoon and Baloch tribes settled down to a life of farmers and herders. British policies promoted these movements. The army and public services became another path for rural young men into the wider world of cities, other provinces, and during World War II, to foreign lands.

In Pakistan, rural mobility increased slowly and gained momentum in successive periods to reach levels of almost mass migration by the 1980s. We have already observed how the changing mode of agricultural production and increasing interdependencies between urban and rural sectors laid the ground for the movement of people out of villages and small towns. Population explosion built up the pressure for rural young men to seek whatever opportunities cities could offer, as did the mechanization of agriculture. Two other factors must also be noted – the spread of schools and transport facilities.

Despite the striking neglect of education by successive governments in Pakistan, schools, mostly of poor quality, were opened in villages and towns all over the country (see Chapter 1 for numbers). Paralleling public schools, Islamic *madarrasahs* and private schools have also been established in most towns and large villages, particularly during the third period. Cumulatively these facilities have been producing hundreds of thousands of educated and semi-educated rural youths every year. Education is a ticket out of villages. Almost anybody who gets a high school diploma wants to go to the city for further studies or a job. Much of the migration is circular in nature, migrants going back and forth between village and city while remaining attached to the family base in the village. Usually men migrate and after years of toil in the city, the women join them. Overall in 1998, about eight percent of Pakistan's population had migrated away from their places of birth and 63 percent of migrants lived in urban areas. These were permanent migrants, seasonal or those urban inhabitants maintaining village residences were not included. Obviously mobility has become a normal condition for villagers.

The push or pull factors impel people to move from one place to another and transport facilities make it possible. Probably minivans and small trucks (Toyotas, for example) have contributed more to break the isolation of villages than any other single factor. Plying ancient trails and footpaths, loaded to the rafters, these automobiles connect remote villages to district towns and regional cities. They carve routes along dirt roads, taking children to schools, commuters to work, and families to shops, clinics, or to visit relatives. The "minivan revolution" started in 1961 and has swept the country. There was one registered van and carrier per 20,000 persons in 1961; in 1997 the ratio was 1 to 790. These are ratios for vans registered with the vehicle authorities, probably an equal number were on the road with forged license plates and papers, mostly smuggled.

In the 1960s bicycles and in the 1970s motorbikes became new means of personal transportation, and were often ingeniously packed to carry families of 4–5 members. A new chapter in personal mobility opened with motorcycles for the middle classes in villages and cities. The bullock or camel carts that in the 1950s were the primary means of goods transport were reduced to supplementary roles by the 1980s, except in remote areas. Of course, the road networks, particularly local roads, were built under successive rural works programs to keep up with rapidly multiplying vans and buses.

Patterns of rural–urban migration

Mobility can be broadly divided into two categories: (1) movements in and out of a community on a daily basis, for example, commuting to/from work, going shopping or visiting and (2) long-term transplantation of individuals/families in other places which may even lead to permanent resettlement. The second type of mobility is called migration. In modern times almost all over the world, people have been migrating out of rural to urban areas in the hope of a better life despite many hardships and sufferings. Like the rest of the Third World, Pakistan has been in the midst of the tidal wave of rural–urban migration. The migration out of villages and small towns was just a trickle in the 1950s but it picked up momentum in the 1960s and has been accelerating since then.[39] Migration in Pakistan has some distinct characteristics.

First, the rural–urban migration in Pakistan is primarily a movement of males whose families join them years later. Second, unlike the historical Western experience, it does not result in the snapping of ties with villages. Third, much of the rural–urban migration is circulatory in scope, at least for the first generation, with migrants periodically going back to villages to look after land or homes, start a business, join brothers/relatives in farming, or take a breather from the city. These patterns, of course, vary by class, occupation, and ethnicity. Educated migrants with steady careers keep village bases for family ties, supplementary incomes (rent from family land), vacations, and retirement.[40] Landlords maintain a full establishment in villages for income, social power, and a political base. The lower classes return to villages for security, identity, and support. Family obligations and *biradari* connections keep rural migrants tied to villages even years after settling in cities.

The migration of the enterprising, young, and educated from villages is the biggest brain drain in Pakistan. Individuals and families are the direct beneficiaries of migration but villages as communities bear social costs. Particularly, the loss of the middle-class and educated youth results in socially truncated communities where the old and the poor remain behind under the domination of landlords and public officials. Villages have been polarized into two classes, the lower and the upper. The middle stratum that is the backbone of a modern community is drained away to cities. It is no wonder that a systematic process of rural development has been so hard to promote.

The geography of rural–urban migration is structured around ethnic and regional clusters. Pashtoons from the dry lands of NWFP and tribal areas started migrating from their villages directly into the biggest city, Karachi, to work in the new textile mills and the expanding transport and construction industries in the early 1960s. This migratory stream turned into a river drawing workers from remote areas, from Dera Ghazi Khan and Dera Ismail Khan districts and the northern region.[41] This long-distance link has grown stronger with the successive waves of migrants since then, resulting in the formation of the largest Pashtoon community outside Peshawar in Karachi. Similarly workers from Hazara and Swat, even young boys, have been converging on Lahore and Rawalpindi to work as domestics, peons, and security guards since the 1950s. There are sizable "colonies" (squatter settlements) reminiscent of Swati/Hazara villages in these cities. Faisalabad, Multan, Peshawar, and the second-tier cities have essentially drawn peasants and workers from surrounding regions, although even those from the same region segregate themselves at workplaces or in neighborhoods along caste or places-of-origin lines.[42] Middle-class professionals and public/corporate officials originating from rural areas do not manifest such clustering tendencies. These examples illustrate the point that rural migrants follow paths carved by their neighbors, friends, and relatives, clustering in different cities by ethnicity, *biradari/khel,* and places of origin, at least in the first instance. This clustering is as much for mutual support and familiarity as for political protection and security in an alien place.

International migration and rural life

Migrating abroad for work or resettlement is a different category of mobility because of its promised riches from earnings at international rates which, converted to Pakistani currency, bring family incomes to the cusp of affluence. International labor migration has a long history in Pakistan. In the early twentieth century, the British authorities periodically recruited craftsmen, clerks, and merchants, occasionally farmers, for work and resettlement in Kenya, Uganda, Trinidad, Fiji, etc. Most of these expatriates settled in those countries. After World War II, the demand for labor in the textile factories of Britain drew migrants from India and Pakistan in the 1950s. From Pakistan, these migrants largely came from the Mirpur district of Azad Kashmir, the Pothohar plateau, and the Sialkot district of the Punjab. It was a chain migration: once someone settled in Britain, he facilitated friends and relatives to follow, who in turn encouraged and assisted still others. Thus the cities of Bradford, Manchester, or Leeds came to have "little" Jhelums, Mirpurs, and Gujarats.[43] This was the beginning of organized migration abroad after independence.

The next wave of international migration was of Pakistani workers to the Gulf countries in the 1970s. The oil price boom of 1973 fueled massive construction projects in Dubai, Kuwait, Iran, Saudi Arabia, and Libya. Bhutto's government pursued a policy of "manpower export" and negotiated arrangements for the workers' recruitment with these "brother" Muslim countries. The government benefited from remittances in the form of foreign exchange earnings, reaching up to 3 billion dollars a year in the late 1970s.

A study of Pakistani workers in Kuwait (1975) estimated that about 60 percent were in manual occupations, needing little training or education, and another 20 percent were just laborers not requiring even literacy. Overall it was estimated that most of the unskilled workers came from rural areas, almost two-thirds of those working in the Gulf.[44]

"Dubai *chalo"* (let's go to Dubai) was the byword in many parts of the country in the 1970s. Village carpenters, blacksmiths, and tractor drivers were in demand and many poor farmers sought their fortunes as laborers, security guards, etc. The impact of this migration varied from region to region. Punjab's districts and Azad Kashmir that had sent young men to work in England were already organized to benefit immediately from the opportunities in the Gulf countries. Labor from NWFP's Peshawar, Swabi, and Kohat districts followed suit, as did Karachi's and central Punjab's. The Makran coast of Balochistan became the recruiting ground for the military and security services of Oman, the Emirates, and Iran. This wave of migration bypassed rural Sindh and the interior of Balochistan.

The labor migration to the Gulf countries was an organized activity recruiting and placing thousands of contract workers every year. It was almost exclusively a migration of men. Only doctors, engineers, accountants, and other professionals were allowed to bring their families. Almost everybody was a "guest worker" on renewable annual visas. This meant that their earnings were primarily spent or invested back home in villages and cities of their origins. The remittances became a major stimulus to social change in communities from where substantial number of migrants had gone abroad.

The 1970s migration to the Gulf spawned an emigration industry whose reach filtered down to the rural areas. Authorized recruiters, travel agents, visa facilitators, and fixers of all varieties, formal, informal, or illicit, emerged from this migration bonanza. The formal and informal sectors of this industry became the platform for the migrations of the 1980s and 1990s to Europe, the USA, and Canada. Many operators of the Gulf migration became immigration consultants and agents for emigration to the West. By the 1990s, more than a million Pakistanis were settled in the USA, Canada, Britain, Denmark, Australia, and even Japan, most as legitimate and approved immigrants, but many were illegal.[45]

By the 1990s, the Gulf's construction boom was over and skilled or unskilled labor was not needed in large numbers although migration still continued at a reduced scale, primarily of white-collar workers and professionals with a sprinkling of workers. The major migratory outlets in the 1990s were in Europe, North America, and select oil-exporting countries. Dubai by then had become a global business center. Many Pakistani businesses were based in Dubai, including some private television channels. Even Pakistani politicians escaping periodic military accountability proceedings settled in Dubai, making it a surrogate capital. These links continued to be the source of jobs and businesses for many migrants.

This brief history of emigration points out three facts. One, the strong desire to seek fortunes abroad, even to the point of desperation for many, and the erosion of commitments to local community. Two, expatriates and remittances became a significant element of local economies and social organization. Three, rural areas partook in this migratory boom. They were strung into the global economy through their sons' and daughters' labor. What social and cultural changes were promoted by the international and internal migrations in rural areas? This question leads us into the next section.

Social impacts of internal and international migrations

The scope of these migrations is illustrated by the following figures. The scale of internal migration can be observed from the census counts of persons living at the time of enumeration at places different from where they were born in Pakistan. In 1961, about 0.8 million persons, 1.7 percent of the population, were such internal migrants; by 1998, the number of internal migrants had swelled to 10.8 million, about 8 percent of the population. Obviously, internal migration had ballooned over the years.

Regarding international migration, accurate figures are hard to come by. No census has been taken of Pakistanis working abroad. Those settled abroad with rights to citizenship in the USA, Britain, or Canada merge with local populations, particularly their children born or raised in the adopted countries. To compound these difficulties, the illegal or undocumented migrants cannot be easily accounted for. Yet some idea of the scale of international migration can be obtained from the figures released by the Overseas Pakistanis Foundation. Between 1971 and 2001, three million Pakistanis were sent abroad by authorized employment agents, mostly as expatriates working in other countries.[46] These figures refer only to legal expatriates. Altogether, the above figures indicate that almost one in ten Pakistanis were migrants of one sort or the other by the end of the twentieth century. Even international migration was of such a scale that many areas would have been strongly affected by it.

Many anthropological studies have documented the impacts of international migration and remittances on village life and families, particularly on the women left behind.[47] They show three types of impacts. The first type are the impacts on individuals and families, namely the difficulties returning migrants have in reset-tling, the increase in households headed by females, and problems of keeping family farms running without young men. The second type of impact is on the social organization of villages, arising from the rise in incomes of the families of migrants and the consequent change in their economic status in relation to other social classes and castes/*khels*, some from a higher level in the hierarchy. The third type of effect is the changes in cultural values and consumption patterns.[48]

Migration, by and large, raises incomes although often it is only marginal. Even the rural poor and landless living miserably in *katchi abadis* in the cities vote with their feet for apparently a better life. International migration offers very high rewards. The major impact of the migrants' remittances is the immediate rise in consumption by their families and acquisition of presumably prestigious goods, such as radios, cycles, televisions, fancy clothes, and *pacca* homes. In the words of a mother whose son worked in the Gulf, "now we live in peace... don't have to think about food and money."[49] Lavish marriages, honor and status-affirming ceremonies follow better food, clothing, and household goods. "I built a house, married into a good family and got my sisters married with pomp and ceremony," said a young man who had worked in Saudi Arabia.[50] Such expenditures are seldom limited to an expatriate's personal consumption. Remittances also sparked off a real estate boom and raised prices of agricultural and urban land.[51] Their effects reverberate through the social organization and culture.

When a family of poor or modest means and/or lower caste becomes more affluent and lives better than those above it in social standing, notions of caste and *biradari* superiority are shaken. Initially it breeds social tensions although it is also a wedge that breaks open traditional structures of dominance and subordination. It scrambles notions of age and gender hierarchy.

Balochistan's Makran coast is an illustrative example of the social change that international migration brings. In the 1990s, Makrani *hizmathkers* (menial workers) went to work in the Gulf and Iran in large numbers. Their remittances sparked off local commerce and agriculture. They also raised their social status by buying land and water rights, a phenomenon not much different from the Sanskritization of Hindu lower classes. Balochs of high standing had to adjust to the new status of *hizmathkers* as landowners with better houses.[52] Such social restructuring does not happen without conflicts and not everywhere. Alain Lefebvre concludes from his village studies in the Rawalpindi and Sialkot districts that "foreign remittances do not lead to productive investment... although the consumption of local goods has stimulated some domestic sectors of economy, especially construction."[53] Remittances have often been blown up in conspicuous consumption and holding up family prestige and status yet they inspire others in villages to follow the footsteps of migrants.

Remittances have a direct bearing on family dynamics. A son's earnings may go to a patriarch but the migrant's wife has a sense of ownership and a claim to special status within a household. Overall, women left to manage a home on their own, men having gone away, become *de facto* heads of household. They have to learn about dealing with banks, schools, *patwaris* (land revenue officials) or *biradari.* This is a change in the roles of women and makes such families into what has been called matri-weighted households.[54]

Overall, the primary impact of migration is on material institutions. New goods such as radios, televisions, and telephones may arrive in an expatriate's family but they spread into the local community as well when others with means acquire them. Social organizational changes and the multiplier effects of expenditures by migrants vary according to local social structure and traditions.

Prosperity does not lead to the modernization conceived by theorists. Social conservatism increases as households with a lower status climb the social ladder. For example, women of migrant households start observing *purdah* (veil) and stop working in fields, as they become more "respectable." More money also means that those who could not have afforded them before could now follow religious and spiritual practices of the traditional rich. Holding *Khatam-e-Quran* (organized readings of the Quran) feasts, slaughtering goats at Eid-ul-Azha (annual festival of sacrifices), offering *nazrana* (ritual alms) at a shrine, or performing Haj (pilgrimage to Mecca) are practices that have become common among migrant households. What it means is that traditions and religious observances are reinvigorated with material advancement. Social change proceeds as much by reincorporating traditions and reviving religious practices as by adopting modern material ways. Migration is a driving force in this dialectical process.

Diffusion of radio, television, and telephone

Marshall McLuhan's adage "the medium is the message" heralded the communication revolution that transformed everyday life in the second half of the twentieth century. Radio, television, cinema, and now Internet and satellite dishes are undoubtedly bringing new ideas, images, and products from all over the world straight into people's homes. They have made it possible to maintain almost instant connections among friends and relatives, even strangers, across continents and oceans. The friction of space has been greatly reduced, if not eliminated.

Pakistani villages and towns have not remained untouched by these technologies. The question that arises from this observation is how widely have mass media spread and what routes have they followed into rural areas? This question has additional significance for Pakistan's rural areas that are assumed to be "backward" and slow to change.

Briefly, the history of mass communication in Pakistan is a story of a gradual build-up to a point that radio, television, and access to telephone are available to lower-middle-class households. Geographically, people in the remote parts of Balochistan, the Northern Areas, parts of the tribal belt, and the socially poor everywhere may be without access to these goods.

Like all other modern trends, the foundations of radio and telecommunication services were laid by the British colonial government. Pakistan inherited two radio stations, Lahore and Peshawar, and a countrywide network of telegraph services at the time of independence. Bombay, renamed Mumbai, leaped to fame in the 1940s as the movie capital of India, although Calcutta and Lahore also had a sizable movie industry. Independence was a stimulus for the expansion of radio services. New broadcasting stations were started in Karachi, Azad Kashmir, Rawalpindi, and in the 1960s Quetta and Hyderabad. The arrival of the transistor radio carried the diffusion of radio to new heights. The popular stereotype of the 1970s that "every farmer has a radio blaring from his plough" may have been a caricature but it pointed out the spread of transistors in villages.

Radio service used to have a popular "village hour" of humor and advice for farmers in the 1950s and 1960s.The populist second period gave prominence to folk culture and arts. Bhutto's government promoted regional literature and country music, romanticizing rural values. The third period brought FM stations, which in the 1990s led to partial privatization and decentralization of radio broadcasting. However by then the radio had lost its appeal, having been overtaken by television and videos.

Pakistan television started broadcasting with three hours of daily service in 1964 from Lahore, gradually extending it to about 8–12 hours of programs daily. Karachi station began telecasting in 1967, Islamabad in 1971, and Peshawar and Quetta in 1976. By the 1980s with a network of relay stations, Pakistan television could reach 90 percent of Pakistan's territory.[55] By 1998 about three million registered television sets were owned by Pakistanis, each set accessible to 10 viewers on average.[56] There could have been another million or more unregistered sets. Thus almost 30–40 percent of Pakistan's population had access to television in the late 1990s and it was increasing year by year. Television sets had come to so many homes that they ceased to be an admirable possession.

Television dramas were the most popular programs. The themes that had great resonance among viewers in cities as well as villages were the obscurantism of feudal traditions and the rural–urban or intergenerational value conflicts.

Television serial dramas such as *Waaris* (The Heir 1979), *Deewarain* (Walls 1983), *Tanhaiyan* (Loneliness 1985), *Ghardish* (Going in Circles 1988), and *Chand Grahan* (Eclipsed Moon 1992) revolved around the themes of exploitative intents and the violent consequences of feudal traditions. Exploration of the dynamics of rural social change has been a theme of unending interest in television and movies.

No account of television's history is complete without mention of the draw that the Bombay movies telecast from India had on the Pakistani audience. Markets would be deserted in areas within reach of a television broadcasting Indian stations on the evenings when a popular Indian movie was telecast. Indian television has been a symbol of "the invasion of alien values and culture" for Islamists. They have always focused their ire on television for disseminating "vulgarity and immorality." Yet their admonishments and protests have had little effect, except in the Taliban-like raids by *mullahs* in Dir, Chitral, and some Pashtoon areas. The satellite dish and cable television, combined with the emergence of private channels beamed from Dubai and Hong Kong in the 1990s, blew away even the possibility of censoring what people could view.

The telephone was a rarity up to the 1960s. Only public officials, influential businessmen, and eminent professionals had telephones, and those too only in major cities. Villages and towns were generally beyond the reach of the telephone. Toward the end of the first period, the telephone network began to expand. By the 1970s, telephone exchanges had multiplied connecting towns and central villages to the national grid. The use of the telephone became common in villages also, where private call offices ran messaging services for families without telephones. By the third period, one could drive along the back roads and come across the "international call" outlets in most crossroad towns, particularly within the Peshawar–Lahore–Karachi axis. The introduction of wireless cell technology has further extended access to telephones in the 1990s. Cellphones have rapidly spread across social structures. By the end of the twentieth century, most of the rural areas were physically plugged into the telephone network.

By the early 2000s, video players and/or televisions could be found in the middle-class homes of villages and towns. Internet cafes were sprinkled among off-the-beaten-track towns such as Panjgur, Balochistan, and Bhuttal, NWFP.[57] Pakistani rural areas have been incrementally swept by the communication revolution over the 50-year period. How have these "mediums" affected people's beliefs, practices, and everyday life; do social and cultural changes in Pakistan recapitulate Western experiences? Is there a universal model of sociocultural changes induced by communication technologies, or in other words is the medium so powerful that the messages cease to be differentiable? These questions will be addressed in the next section.

Mass communication and cultural change

The cultural changes induced by the spread of radio, television, videos, and telephone follow a dualistic path, reinforcing and reinventing some beliefs and practices while displacing others. It may be said right away that Pakistani society's response to the new "mediums" is demonstrably affected by the "messages" they bear. In the consumption and adoption of new products, Pakistanis respond opportunely, but in family values, gender relations, and political and religious beliefs they tack close to traditions in meaning and function, even if not in form. Let us illustrate this interplay of continuity and change with some examples from rural areas.

Village people were long presumed to be resistant to change in their ways of life. They were overwhelmingly illiterate, wedded to the security that the old and tried ways offered. They were particularly skeptical of modern city ways which appeared to them to be immoral. One such case was of tea as a drink. Up to the 1930s, tea was used essentially as a medicine. When Lipton attempted to market tea, it met with strong resistance in Punjab and Sindh, in the cities as well as villages.

I vividly remember the 1940s of my childhood when big cauldrons of steaming tea were hawked in the streets of Lahore, offering piping hot tea free to sample. The talk in my street was that it was a British attempt to dampen the virility of martial Punjabis. It took years for tea to become the morning drink in Punjabi households, initially finding acceptance among clerks and soldiers. It began to be a symbol of modernity and *babu*ism (officialdom). With this prestigious "educated middle class" identity, tea bore a message of progress, spreading up and down the social structure. By the end of the twentieth century, tea was the daily drink in almost every household in villages. It had displaced *lassi* (yogurt shake) as the breakfast drink.

The example of tea's diffusion illustrates two points: (1) new products carry social symbolism and meanings and (2) those symbols and (social) meanings become the message that trickles along the pathways of class, ideology, and geography. These lessons also apply to mass communication technologies.

Radio was largely shunned in villages as a voice of sin but its value as a source of news during World War II and the partition of India gave it a foothold in the men's quarters of the homes of the rural elite. After independence, it gradually became a source of entertainment and music (film songs) for village youth. Rural migrants to cities were often pioneers in the adoption of radio and, later, television. Transistors individualized radio ownership. Highway teashops and town eateries began to play radios, and in the 1970s music tapes, to entertain customers. Videos of movies sparked businesses of mini theatres run by enterprising shopkeepers in their backrooms. The television set became the prestigious possession of affluent households, filtering down gradually to lower income groups. Even *mullahs* found taped recitations of the Quran and sermons convenient for broadcasting from mosques. Of course, these products spread in parallel with the electrification of villages.

Migrants, particularly those working abroad, primarily popularized the use of telephones in rural areas. Their need and affordability to keep in touch with their families back home fostered the business of "international call" outlets. By the 1990s, many families of migrants and affluent farmers had telephones.

From the above account, it is obvious that new technologies spread along socially defined pathways. They follow class and clan lines, from upper and middle to working classes; from urban and expatriate migrants to their families and clans; from young to old; and from men to women. Shops and teahouses, places of gatherings, and mosques, also function selectively as the nodes for the spread of new products.

Radio, television, and other modern products widen social disparities between the poor and the well-off in villages where proximity sharpens contrasts in living conditions and heightens feelings of deprivation for the poor.

The primary impact of radio, television, and videos is in the changing modes of information dissemination. Villagers used to gather in a landlord's or *numberdar's* (headman) *baithak* or *hujra* (guest/gathering room) in the evenings for news passed by public officials, visitors from cities, or readers of newspapers. This communal information exchange was further promoted in the early days of radio, when people gathered around a landlord's or some other influential person's radio set for news and entertainment.

As radio, and later on television, spread, households began to have personal access to information and news. The practice of communal narration of the newspaper or sharing of information declined. Similarly, village entertainment and leisure activities broke up into individual and family pursuits, television-watching in private quarters displaced communal poetry recitation; listening to music of drums, flute, or tambura (a bow instrument); or watching traveling theatre in the village *choupal* (square). The individualization of entertainment has displaced communal leisure activities.

Radio, television, and videos have undoubtedly made people more aware of politics, personalities of their leaders, international events, and the latest fashions in clothes, food, and furniture. A villager now is more informed compared to the days of oral dissemination of information. National events and notable persons become instantly known across the country. For example, Imran Khan, Wasim Akram and other cricket heroes of the 1990s were as popular in Karimabad, Hunza, as they were in Lahore and Karachi. Pakistan's devotion to cricket has been cultivated by television.[58] The inspirations of young villagers are not landlords or local *pirs* (spirtualists), but television or film actors, national cricketers, and other public figures. The easy access to information has also made villagers skeptical of public announcements and self-serving politicians.

Mass media have come to play a leading role in the marketing of new products. From cakes to new hairstyles, all kinds of new products filter down to villages with promotions and suggestions by the television and movies. Yet the adoption of new products is mediated through local notions of honor, respectability, and social status. For example, pirated Indian movie videos spread rapidly but family planning messages have had a relatively feeble effect. The material goods of pleasure and convenience find ready acceptance, new ideas about women's status, religious beliefs, or family values seep through the national consciousness very slowly. This filtering of message by individuals themselves is well illustrated by the case study of women's viewing of television in a Pashtoon village in NWFP.[59]

Pashtoon households traditionally practice strict *purdah* (seclusion of women) within a house as a matter of family honor and basic values.[60] A case study of a

Pashtoon village observes that men and women did not watch television together so that men may not be seen to be watching other women and women other men on the television in each other's presence. Women did not understand the Urdu spoken on television, although they inferred from gestures the drift of a drama's plot. They observed dresses or gestures of actresses and hesitantly experimented with some of those new fashions. Yet they discussed among themselves the "shamelessness" of actresses and their sinful behavior.[61] The reactions of Pashtoon women to television were filtered through their culturally defined roles.

Similar moral judgments about gender relations and women's behavior characterize responses of the Pakistani and Indian public to Western and Bollywood movies. One enjoys screen romances vicariously, but retreats behind the "they versus us" dichotomy in banishing thoughts of pursuing similar pleasures. These examples suggest that the cultural change resulting from exposure to mass media is mediated through the values and (social) structures of a society. The medium is not everything.[62] New products may end up serving traditional functions and reinforcing established behaviors.

The case in point is the deployment of television, radio, and tapes for broadcasting Islamic precepts and prayers. The rise of conservative and puritanical Islam in Pakistan is partially explained by the strategic use of radio, television, and loudspeakers by priests and Islamists.

Rural development programs

The above-discussed processes of rural change are neither centrally planned nor controlled. Yet successive Pakistani governments have also made deliberate attempts to foster planned social change in the countryside through the rural development programs. Rural development has been a permanent item on the national agenda since independence. What it has achieved is a story of big promises and modest results. Presently the fact to be noted is that repeated attempts have been made to stimulate modern changes in village economies and social organizations. A starting point for discussing the scope and directions of the envisaged changes is to recount briefly the history of the rural development programs.

Whether villages, small towns, or homesteads, rural communities of all types have long been regarded as steeped in hidebound traditions and raked by superstitions and ignorance. Their pervasive poverty and illiteracy combined with caste/ *biradari* or *khel* rigidities categorize them as backward communities. However this image is simplistic at best. Even in the nineteenth century, there were social movements for *dehat sudhar* (village reformation), mostly to banish ruinous customs and superstitious practices. The British sporadically experimented with "rural reconstruction" and the *punchayat* (village council) system for self-rule and arbitration of disputes in villages.[63] Independence made rural development a national priority. After all, the overwhelming majority of the population lived in villages and that was where the development efforts had to begin.

The VAID program (1953–62) was the first and the most comprehensive attempt at rural development in Pakistan. Its strategy was to promote aided self-help in villages, following the community development approach. An appointed VAID worker, covering 4–5 villages, was to motivate villagers into forming local committees to identify community needs and to mobilize voluntary labor and materials for meeting those needs. A village's self-help efforts were to be supplemented by technical and financial assistance from public agencies. The VAID department was organized in five tiers, namely the village, development area, district, divisional, and provincial level. It was generously supported by American aid and technical assistance and thus got identified as the American "import." It covered most of the country.

The program ignited some initial enthusiasm and aroused consciousness among villagers about social development, apart from initiating many local projects of building drains, paving streets, organizing literacy circles, etc. However it soon got mired in bureaucratic inertia and political interests. The assumption that villagers' labor can be mobilized free of cost was paternalistic at best and exploitative at worst. In practice the landless laborers and *kammis* bore the burden of the voluntary self-help. The social structure of villages ensured that the middle- and upperclass households benefited from the program while avoiding volunteering for work efforts. The program was rolled into Ayub Khan's Basic Democracies and disappeared with the discrediting of that system.[64]

The public works part of the VAID became the Rural Works Programme (RWP) in 1963, administered by the Union Councils (village level councils) of Basic Democracies. About 60,000 infrastructural projects were undertaken under the RWP. The corruption associated with these projects was the lightening rod that sparked off agitation against the Ayub regime in small towns and the countryside. Thus the rural development programs of the first period had the unintended effect of promoting factionalism and politicizing local leadership.

Bhutto's government in the second period could not have been more enthusiastic about rural development despite the disappointments of the VAID and RWP. It had been voted into power largely by peasants and workers in defiance of landlords and village notables. A flurry of rural development schemes unfolded in the early 1970s; some were stillborn such as Agrovilles and *Sipha-Khidmat* (volunteers corp for eradicating illiteracy), while others took off with good prospects such as the People's Works Programme and the Integrated Rural Development Programme (IRDP), 1972–7.

The IRDP was the jewel in the crown of rural development programs of the second period. Defining rural development as a strategy to improve the social and economic life of rural residents, particularly of the rural poor, the IRDP was conceived in an idiom thought to be relevant to Pakistan. Its core idea was the concentration and integration of agricultural, health, educational, and other public services at *markazes* (small towns as central places) for easy access and ready extension to linked villages. A *markaz* was both a geographic center for the provision of services and a program for promoting village cooperative societies and people's participation. The IRDP incorporated many features of the VAID but it differed in strategy in that it was more of an extension arm of public agencies than a village self-help effort. The IRDP was the international flavor of the decade. The

United Nations and the World Bank actively promoted IRDPs in many countries of the Third World. Pakistan, of course, enthusiastically embraced international advice and aid. Each province implemented the IRDP with some minor variations of the strategy and established a network of *markazes*, staffed with managers, engineers, cooperative society supervisors, and village workers. The district and divisional commissioners were given the supervisory responsibilities for their respective jurisdictions. Ironically, public servants were the pivotal points of the IRDP.

Within five years, the IRDP had run its course and turned into another ritualistic exercise of fashionable ideas. An evaluation of the program in Punjab and NWFP concluded that the IRDP did not improve people's access to services any more than what they had without it. Village entrepreneurs, well-connected farmers, and officials living in villages, namely "the same class of rural bourgeoisie, Sofad Posh, who normally appropriate any public development programme," captured its cooperative societies.[65] The mortal blow to the IRDP came from the downfall of Bhutto's government.

By the time General Zia's regime of the third period settled down, the international development paradigm had shifted to the ideology of privatization and the reduction of the public role in national development. Nongovernmental organizations (NGOs) emerged as the new vehicles of social development. Rural development in Pakistan was adjusted to this new ideology.

Self-help and NGOs

The new model of rural development was inspired by Akhtar Hameed Khan's approach of grassroots development, forged in the famous Comilla project in the erstwhile East Pakistan and adapted to the new conditions of the 1980s in the Daudzai experiment in NWFP and the Orangi Pilot Project in Karachi.[66] From these roots emerged the Aga Khan Rural Support Programme (AKRSP) in the Northern Areas in 1982. It became the template of rural development in the third period.

The AKRSP approach is based on organizing farmers into a village organization around sustainable activities, training members in new skills, and generating equity capital from members' savings.[67] The program itself is "supportive," and not managerial in conception. Its support takes the form of providing the services of community organizers, technical experts, financial grants as well as acting as a channel between the public agencies and village organizations. Another point of distinction of the approach is that it is based on villagers being organized as interest groups of prospective beneficiaries, instead of attempting to mobilize a whole village as a single body. The AKSRP has had success in Northern Areas. It has been internationally acclaimed as an example of the NGO effort in rural development and poverty alleviation although it has also aroused the hostility of the orthodox Islamic elements in the area. The international agencies and the Canadian and European aid missions have lavishly funded the AKRSP. It also suffers from the developmental paradox of a successful pilot project but a disappointing program.

The AKRSP approach, in modified forms, has been applied to other parts of the country. Sarhad Rural Support Corporation (1989) and the Balochistan Rural Support Programme (1991), both registered as NGOs, followed the AKRSP approach in NWFP and Balochistan. The respective provincial governments with public officials serving as the chairmen and senior managers, have sponsored both programs. In 1991, the Government of Pakistan established the National Rural Support Programme (NRSP) as another NGO for the purpose of implementing the rural component of its Social Action Programme (SAP), which was meant to improve the quality of life of the poor through investments in health, education, and infrastructure. About 500 million rupees were given to the NRSP to establish community organizations, initially in eight districts. Yet the NRSP became a victim of the revenge politics of Nawaz Sharif and Benazir Bhutto.[68] The military government of General Musharraf that followed them included rural development in the responsibilities of the reorganized local governments in the year 2001.

The 2001 Local Government Ordinance of General Musharraf, popularly known as the Devolution Plan, created three-tiered elected *nazims* (local executives) and legislative bodies at the Union Council (cluster of villages), *tehsil*, and district level. This system brought rural and urban areas into an integrated local government structure. *Nazims* and the Councils became responsible for local development, both rural and urban. In all, 6,455 local self-governments were established, including 6,022 largely rural Union Councils, under 307 tehsil and 92 District Councils. In this set-up, rural development has been largely trumped by the administrative preoccupations of *nazims*. The elected provincial and national parliamentarians have pressed hard to keep their control of the development funds allocated for their constituencies. These political/administrative issues have drained the promise of the local governments as vehicles of development. Although the World Bank and other aid agencies have praised the local government reforms, on the ground the promise of the Devolution Plan has been swallowed by patronage politics and administrative ineffectiveness.[69] Thus the cycle of high hopes and quick disillusionment once again has been the fate of the latest round of rural development.

A critical evaluation of these programs is not of immediate interest to us. Many good accounts of such evaluations are available.[70] What is central to our narrative is the role the rural development programs have played in promoting social change. On this score, some general observations are presented from the experiences of the successive programs.

- The primary focus of public programs for rural development is mainly local works such as projects of drains, roads, and schools in rural areas. These projects have contributed in keeping some semblance of balance between community needs and minimal public infrastructure. At the same time, these public works are also a fertile ground for political patronage and corruption.
- Pakistan's successive rural development programs have raised awareness of community needs but have not been very successful in promoting collective action to fulfill those needs. In sum, they have increased the demand for public goods without entrenching the promised community-based mode of supply.

- Perhaps the most significant impact of the rural development programs is in their opening up of opportunities for rural middle-class individuals to local leadership. The local power structure expanded beyond the traditional landlords and patriarchs of the dominant *biradaris*. Rural development programs spawned positions of village councillors or committee members who became middlemen between public officials and local communities. Often they would enrich themselves or favor their *biradari*/tribe by bringing schools, drains, or roads to their areas. They have access to commissioners, agriculture officers, or irrigation engineers, for example, which enable them to intercede on behalf of their relatives, friends, and sometimes, villages. This capacity to intercede with public authorities is the ladder to power and leadership in rural communities and the rural development programs laid out these ladders.
- Overall, an informal division of power has taken place in rural communities. Rural elites and big landlords concentrate on national and provincial assembly and district councils/boards, whereas middle-class farmers, *biradari* heads, or merchants and imams compete for positions in union councils, cooperative societies, or village committees. Rural development programs have contributed to the emergence of middle strata of leaders in rural areas.[71]
- Rural development programs have had the unintended effect of promoting factionalism. *Biradaris*, *khels*, or tribes compete for influence and access to resources resulting in political and social divisions in local communities.
- Rural development programs have not succeeded in promoting people's participation because they are based on unrealistic assumptions. There cannot be a participatory decision making in a village when an authoritarian order prevails nationally and provincially. Also the burden of participation, if it involves voluntary labor, falls on the poor who neither have the time nor the energy to spare from eking out their living.
- These programs have been repeatedly co-opted to advance the political interests of the ruling regimes. None of the programs have lasted more than a few years. They modulate with shifting development paradigms and international aid fads.

Before concluding the discussion of rural development, it should be pointed out that public programs have not been the only organized efforts for improving rural quality of life. There are thousands of charitable and community initiatives to build schools, clinics, orphanages or wells, pave streets, provide dowries for poor girls, etc. Similarly, there are innumerable local reform campaigns advocating sectarian harmony, Islamic piety, or simplicity of marriage customs, for example. Unsung heroes of rural reforms are young female teachers or doctors who travel long distances to serve in villages, often beyond the call of duty. Many expatriate Pakistanis sponsor schemes for improvements in their home villages as do other rural migrants who have prospered in cities. Since the 1980s, NGOs have sprung up in hundreds in all parts of the country aiming to improve sanitation or water supply, introduce new domestic practices, or income-generating activities, etc. These private efforts, although diffused, are a source of succor and support in rural areas.

Undoubtedly they contribute to improving the quality of life of some segments of local populations, if not whole villages. Altogether, both public and private rural development initiatives are resulting in incremental, not comprehensive, changes in local communities. They are the raindrops that could turn into rivers of change. Rural development so far has worked along the general trend of social change, namely one step ahead, two sideways.

The state and village power structure

The state influences all social institutions in Pakistan. Its role as the framer of laws, enforcer of order, and the provider of public services structures other institutions. The evolution of the state in Pakistan has directly impacted the social structure in rural areas. How this has happened is a question that needs some exploration.

Historically, rural areas were ruled according to local customs by tribal *sardars* (leaders) and feudal lords. The Mughal State "rented out" local rule to its vassals for annual tribute and obedience. The colonial Indian state, founded by the British, was centrally organized but, to control the vast rural population, it cultivated local landlords/tribal *maliks* and *sardars*. It dispensed justice and enforced law and order through provincially organized police and courts but patronized the local elite to keep rural populations subservient.

The power structure in villages and small towns was centered around prominent landlords on the one hand, who were often caste/*biradari* heads, and public officials on the other. Even landlords sustained their power by their access to officers of the police, land revenue, and civil administration departments. A village *numberdar mukhtar* (headman) was an intermediary between farmers and the government. Usually an influential landlord residing in a village was appointed to this position. A *patwari* (an official of the land records and revenues department) and *thanedar* (police inspector) were the public functionaries who, for all practical purposes, were "the government" for villagers. In irrigated areas, the irrigation department's officials also became part of the official troika in villages. All in all, a symbiotic relationship between local landlords and public officials undergirded the village power structure. This power structure has continued to dominate even after independence; its authority, though, has diffused with the emergence of elected local councillors and parliamentarians. The monetization and diversification of village economies have brought new claimants to power and prestige in the village social structure.

The British administration of the areas that now form Pakistan was based on the model forged in Punjab of creating landed aristocracy, lording over occupancy tenants who as sharecroppers farmed their estates. These landlords (called *Choudhris*, *Zamindars*, or *Khans*) remained the power elite in rural areas even after independence. They have continued to maintain their economic domination by taking advantage of commercial and industrial opportunities. Thus the power base of the landlord families now incorporates both, the traditional and the modern, bases of the elite status. Many of them join political parties and promote administrative and military careers for their brothers, sons, or daughters. These families form the top echelon of the power structure in villages and beyond.

Villages seldom have any local governments to sweep streets, provide drinking water, or regulate building construction. Local governments have been basically organized at the district level, with towns and cities having town committees and municipalities. In Pakistan, local government has remained a neglected institution despite successive legislations to reorganize it in 1959, 1973, 1979, and 2001.

At the village level, the introduction of union councils (1959) as the lowest-tier local authority has turned out to be the most enduring change in local administration since independence. Union councils and the upper-tier *tehsil* and district councils have created opportunities for a second-level leadership in villages.[72]

Also, a number of new public functionaries have become crucial for the provision of modern services in village life. Officials of the Agricultural Development Bank are a source of credit for farmers. Electric linemen, meter readers, and WAPDA's tubewell operators are lowly but, for villagers, they are important functionaries on whom they depend for the supply of electricity and water. Rural development officers hold the promise of building roads, arranging vaccination for livestock, or providing grants for youth or literacy clubs, for example. These officials have become a part of the local power structure. They can "get things done" and thus connections with them are a source of power. In these ways, the power structure has expanded to include new actors and to become less monolithic although it is still dominated by the rich and influential landlords. The repressive edge of the power structure has been blunted but its exploitative role remains intact. The poor remain powerless and dependent.

The dialectic of power structure is illustrated by the local council elections of 2002. About a third of the members of these councils were stipulated to be women's representatives. In Balochistan, parts of Sindh and Punjab, leading landlords nominated and supported the wives and daughters of their tenants or servants for election as members of union councils. Even some Islamists took advantage of the opportunity to grab political power by making their wives and daughters stand for elections. Presumably the lure of political influence trumps Islamists reservations about women's participation in public life. Even these manipulative attempts added new ladders for upwardly mobile tenants and women. The power structure has been pried opened, although not realigned. The state remains the defining element in rural life and the "connections" to its functionaries continue to be a source of local power. Of course, there are other forces that are eroding the authority of the state including its general inefficiency and corruption.

The responsibilities of the state have expanded with the economic and social development of the past 50 years. Yet its structure has been steeped in agrarian values and an authoritarian ethos. It operates as a personal fief of whosoever, the military or politicians, happens to hold power. It is characterized by person-based rule, reminiscent of feudal ways, behind the facade of impersonal institutions. This "real culture," in contrast to the legislated culture of the state makes it incapable of efficient, just, and responsive governance. It is buffeted by political and ideological factions and threatened by ethnic insurrections.[73] Rural areas have particularly suffered from the failures of the state. Law and order have steadily deteriorated and basic services, such as public health and water, remain lacking.[74]

Cattle hustlers and dacoits (bandits) with colourful aliases such as Malango, Khumeni, and Moto plagued villages periodically, allegedly under the patronage of the police and landlords.[75] The feudal lord's exploitation is a popular theme of movies (for example, Maula Jat and Jugga Dacoit) and TV dramas (for example, Chand Grahan and Waaris). These narratives are indicative of the disrepute in which the traditional power structure is held. Other forces that have eroded the power structure are the ability of many to escape the landlords' domination and the officials' oppression by migrating to cities and, even within villages, by following commercial activities. For a majority of villagers, landlords cannot provide economic or personal security any more. The traditional social structure is not functional; its *seypi* system has broken down. A sort of social vacuum has developed: old norms and values are increasingly irrelevant and new institutions appropriate for contemporary social relations have not emerged.

Cultural change and community life

The preceding narrative points out that towns and villages in Pakistan have changed physically, socially, and culturally since independence. The physical changes are self-evident. The social and cultural changes are topics of daily conversations among successive generations, elders extolling the old ways, and the youth talking about new possibilities. They can also be observed in the attitudes and behavior of people.

Physically, villages are large and crowded with almost as many brick homes as mud houses. Music from videos, television, or radios, or the call for prayers from mosques, pierced by backfiring motorbikes or bus horns, create a cacophony. Fumes from tractors and water pumps drift across the dusty sky producing a stinging brew of smog. People have more possessions; they are better dressed and proportionately more literate than in the 1950s or even the 1960s. This is especially true of the populous but irrigated plains of the central and northern Punjab, the lower Sindh and Peshawar Valley of NWFP. Even in the dry lands of Kalat district, about 39 percent of rural houses had electricity in 1998, up from almost 0 percent in 1961. For the Sukkur district, in 1998 a majority (59 percent) of rural houses had electricity, as did those in Mardan district (81 percent). These are indicators of improving housing conditions in off-the-main-road rural districts of three provinces. Of course, this material progress has so far bypassed Cholistan, south-western Punjab, and the vast but sparsely populated Balochistan's plateau and tribal areas. In the 2000s, few adults walk about shoeless whereas in the 1950s, barefoot villagers could be seen even on their visits to cities. The material and technological base of rural areas has changed and has led to the usual ills of lopsided modernization.

Hand pumps and electricity have improved the domestic water supply, but the absence of drains has turned village streets into open sewers and drowned them in muck.[76] Industrial and road accidents have become a major cause of deaths and injuries in villages.[77]

Social changes are equally remarkable. The self-contained life, wherein most daily needs were met within the village, has almost disappeared. Shah Nawaz Khar says that "self-sufficiency is a thing of the past," even in the flood plains of Muzaffargarh district. "The Bait people sell their milk ...and no longer make their own butter but buy Dalda (hydrogenated cooking oil)" for consumption.[78] It represents the decline of the village as a closed community. *Biradari* and *khel* rivalries frame political development, opposing groups affiliating with competing parties. Income and profession have come to be significant determinants of social status thereby injecting class into the caste hierarchy. Yet primordial ties continue to be strong. *Biradari* and family remain strong institutions, rather strengthened, for the purposes of dealing with the world beyond.

Islamic spiritualism and the faith in *pirs* (holy persons) and shrines are being overlaid with scriptural Islam originating from the puritanical and revivalist movements in cities. Tableeghi Jamaat, a proselytizing Islamic movement, sends volunteers to villages to teach *kalima* (profession of the faith), ironically to Muslims of many generations but who are presumably ignorant of this elementary Islamic obligation. This example shows how the juridical Islam of cities is replacing the laid-back rural Islam.

All in all, rural social organization is being gradually urbanized while migrants are ruralizing cities. Social transformation is following a circular path. It entails the interpenetration of rural and urban modes of living, instead of the presumed supplanting of the rural ethos with urbanism. The traditions arise in new forms to fulfill needs arising from changing roles. They serve as the base for changing family values and community norms.

Defined as the codebook and the driving force of behaviors and attitudes, culture also changes, sometimes slowly and at others times quickly. Pakistani culture has been changing at a fast pace. New values and norms are supplanting traditional rules and many conventional practices are assuming new meanings and purposes. Again the process of cultural change is not that of sweeping out the old and installing the new. It is a movement of a pendulum from the traditional to modern and back. A few striking examples of the change in values and norms as well as their meanings will illustrate this point.

Izzat (honour and respectability) is a value that is common in all provincial and ethnic cultures. It is one of Pashtoon's three defining values, the other two being *malmasta* (hospitality and protection according to defined expectations) and *purdah* (seclusion of women).[79] For Balochis, honor is above everything else. Punjabis and Sindhis also treasure honor and "keeping face" as the bases of their social relations. What acts hold or take away somebody's *izzat* are significant from the perspective of cultural change. The ideal of *izzat* remains intact but its meanings change from region to region and over time. Among all ethnic groups, *izzat* is tied to women's sexuality, although not exclusively. The groups differ slightly in their interpretation of what acts are considered honorable or dishonorable. From being seen by unrelated males, talking with them to being in their company is a range of acts variously regarded as transgressing the honor of women and through them of the family and tribe. [80]

The norms that enforce *izzat* have been changing even in villages. Women from rural elite families, such as Benazir Bhutto, Nasim Wali Khan, and Abida Hussein, have contested elections, held appointments, were imprisoned, or feted nationally and internationally without bringing any dishonor to their families. Instead they have been held to be models for advancing the family's or community's power and reputation. They may not shake hands with men or be found in the company of a lone male but in their villages they enjoy power and prestige and in some cases even dispense blessings as *pirs*.[81] Even for women from the middle or lower classes, norms of honor have changed in response to economic and physical imperative. They travel alone in buses daily, taking up remunerative occupations, thereby stretching the norms of *izzat* and *purdah*. These changes have come gradually but have built up to a major cultural change.

Paradoxically, incidents of *karo kari* in Sindh (male relatives killing a woman for romantic liaison, often alleged), honor-killing, or wife-burning in other provinces have increased in parallel with the relaxation of norms of *izzat* for women.[82] The uncertainties and conflicts engendered by the changing norms also arouse extreme reactions. Many a time the material interests of a father, brother, or clan intertwine with "honor" leading to the victimization of women. The dialectic of the continuity and change of culture is reflected in this example. Similar processes are unfolding for the norms of respect for elders, arranged marriage, friendship obligations, individual entrepreneurship, and family bonds, for example. The lived or real culture has been changing but the ideal or believed culture lags, leading to a state of imbalance between different social institutions. Divergence between the ideal and the real culture is so wide that social cohesion and the moral order are threatened in both rural and urban communities. The real culture is in a state of flux and changing rapidly but the ideal culture remains static. The lag between the two underlies the political and religious behaviors that appear to be contradictory.

The moral order of social change

What are the bases of the moral order that is emerging in the wake of social change? In other words, what social glue holds rural community life together in contemporary times? Rural social life has long been regulated by folkways and customs rooted in caste, *biradari* or tribe, and an agrarian ethos. Many of these folkways carry an aura of Islamic edicts but have changed gradually from generation to generation. The moral order embodied in these folkways is increasingly inapplicable to the urbanizing and commercializing villages and towns. Historically, in other societies this trajectory of social change has led to contractual and legalistic moral codes. The state assumes the role of laying out laws for social relations and cultural mores. Often the intelligentsia, as a social class, articulate and communicate new mores and values. But in Pakistan, the state has not been able to provide the lead in forging a coherent moral order.[83] It is permeated with ideological confusion, the legacy of feudal/agrarian values, and corruption. The inadequacies of the state have impeded the implementation of social reforms necessary for changing times. The intelligentsia has been suppressed and restrained by the state. Only *mullahs* are at liberty to propagate their viewpoints through sermons. The result is a wide-ranging divergence between beliefs and practices. These contradictions are evident in rural life.

Taboorwali (code of agnatic rivalry) is an ancient Pashtoon code of competition among cousins for land and power. The code of bravery, honor, and protection, called *pakhtoonwali*, neutralizes some of the excesses of *taboorwali* for tribal peace and solidarity.[84] Migration and occupational changes of rural Pashtoons have affected both these codes. Now power and affluence do not come from land and water resources shared with cousins, but from jobs and businesses. Thus new mores are needed to regulate relations among cousins and tribesmen. Those are emerging sporadically, while the state's ineffectiveness leaves a vacuum filled by *jirgas* (tribal councils) and *mullahs'* rule such as in Swat, Dir, and other parts of NWFP and Balochistan. The point of this example is that traditional rural/tribal moral order is being eroded by the changing economy and social organization but appropriate norms and institutions to regulate new behaviors are lagging. Revivalist norms and institutions are, meanwhile, filling the vacuum.

Family and kinship bonds have been further strengthened, reviving traditional values (more about family and kinship in a later chapter). These social structures function as power blocks and social networks for their members in negotiating their way through economic and administrative institutions. The solidarity of family and kin is now also sustained by the power and influence exchanges among members. One brother moves to a city and provides the base for younger brothers/ cousins attending college, learning a trade, or looking for jobs. The latter's success in turn becomes a source of power and pride for the one who promoted them. The more highly placed one is, the more is the demand for using one's influence to help in-laws, nephews, or nieces in getting jobs and fixing medical or legal problems. It is not surprising that rural tribal and biradari titles (Khurul, Niazi, Maher, etc.) are now common as last names of doctors, lawyers, engineers, and politicians of national prominence.[85] These identities are a source of pride and mutual support among those bearing similar names. They also underline the "arrival" of such groups in positions of prestige and authority. Such primordial ties of rural origins have been wedged into urban power networks. Often successful professionals and businessmen of rural backgrounds are more resourceful, even in cities, because of their tight-knit networks and group solidarities.

The impersonal modern institutions arise from the rule of law and effective government, but these conditions have not been fulfilled in Pakistan. This lack has reinforced personalized moral codes and primordial ties. The moral order of villages as communities has been breached but family and kin group norms and revived Islamic revivalism are filling the void.

Gainers and losers

Is social change like a tide that lifts all boats? Undoubtedly social change sweeps everybody but it does produce a rich crop of gainers and losers. Different categories of people are affected differently. Presently I will examine who are the gainers and losers in Pakistan's rural areas.

To begin with, we must keep in perspective that Pakistan is a poor country, even poorer on measures of human development. So gainers and losers coexist within a framework of scarce resources and limited opportunities. Paradoxically, such inadequacies sharpen even small differences between the gainers and losers.

Poverty has declined in Pakistan a little, even though differences in living conditions are sharper. Sohail Malik after reviewing most of the poverty estimates spanning about 40 years concludes, "growth of incomes in Pakistan has translated into declining level of poverty especially since the 1970s";[86] a conclusion that has been borne out by World Bank's Pakistan Poverty Assessment for the 1990s although the decline was vulnerable to variations in the level of monsoon rains and other natural and man-made events.[87] There has been a stubborn level of poverty hovering in the 25–35 percent range nationally; variations occur within this range. Poverty is defined by the yardsticks of minimum income necessary for meeting basic needs or allowing consumption of a given level of food.

Urban poverty rates have always been lower than the rural rates. In 1998–9, 24 percent of the urban population fell below the poverty line compared to 36 percent of the rural population.[88] Rural poverty fell periodically, in the late 1960s, mid-1970s, and 1980s, and then between 1990–1 and 1993–4 although it rose between these periods.[89] These fluctuations of rural poverty underline the factors that contribute to changes in the fortunes of the rural poor.

The periods of declining poverty coincide with bursts of industrial development and agricultural growth, which lift the marginal poor. Another set of factors determining numbers of losers and gainers lie in regional and provincial economies. Balochistan tends to have the highest levels of rural poverty, followed by Sindh, Punjab and NWFP, although in short terms their relative positions shift.[90] Interestingly rural poverty is high in agricultural areas of conventional crops, wheat and cotton, while the Pothohar region of dry lands has a low rate of poverty on account of its proximity to urban centers and military job opportunities. Those with access to urban jobs and diversified agriculture have a greater probability of being gainers. Yet it must be stressed that such gains are only relative in comparison to others. Poor villagers migrating to cities or laboring for urban wages may be better off but they still struggle at the margins of misery. Urban poverty stalks them in cities, where all transactions require money.

The gainers have some assets to capitalize on. They tend to have access to land, kin support, and powerful *biradaris*/clans, education, or occupational skills. Leaving aside landlords and village influentials, gainers are often the cream of the village peasantry and craftsmen who have some personal and family assets to build on. Achievements and enterprise have helped many individuals to climb out of poverty. Particularly, successive generations of young villagers who pursue education in colleges and universities find ladders to prosperity and status. Rural workers, who branch out into crafts and trade, migrate to cities or abroad thereby increasing their incomes. Generally speaking, men have gained more than women.

An illustrative case is that of Dogar truckers in the Faisalabad district of the Punjab.[91] One member of the Dogar clan, a farmer caste, started carting village produce to market towns in a horse carriage (*rehra*). From this opening, he found a job as a trucker's agent that led to a share in a truck and finally expanded into the ownership of a fleet of trucks. He brought his kin into the trucking business, contributing to a strong Dogar presence in Faisalabad's transport industry. This is not an isolated case. There are numerous similar examples all across the country. It illustrates the social resources that become ladders for a clan or community.

Losers are without assets, often belonging to low castes, minorities, or poor *biradaris*. Widows, the landless and displaced, the sick and victims of disasters, and persons coming from powerless clans predominate among losers. They tend to live in isolated and economically backward regions but their numbers add up to almost one-third of the population.

Internal dynamics of villages and towns

To conclude this chapter, I will draw upon its main findings and interpret their meanings. The starting point of this interpretation is the acknowledgement that the roots of Pakistani society lie in its rural communities and agrarian ethos. Rural communities are the bases of its social organization. The word "feudalism" is bandied about in Pakistani media to variously describe a mentality, domination of landlords, the village social structure, or rural values. Its common use itself is recognition of the centrality of rural norms and customs in Pakistan's social life. This chapter points out that these norms and institutions are not fixed but responsive to external and internal forces of change.

The chapter's findings do not fall into a neat pattern. Social change does not follow a linear path moving from tradition to modernization. Rather, the findings suggest a hopscotch pattern of change, one institution or component of an institution incorporates modern norms and practices, while another lags behind or, more often, realigns its norms and practices. This pattern can be described as the internal dynamics of social life in villages and towns. It refers to how various institutions and values respond to the forces of change. Deduced from the findings, seven propositions that sum up the process of internal dynamics have been summarized below.

First, villages and towns have changed in all aspects, socially, economically, culturally, and physically. Of course, the change is not spread uniformly everywhere although it has touched all parts of the country. Material culture has changed more rapidly than beliefs, values, and social relations. Wide-ranging institutional lags have developed between technology, economy, and consumption on the one hand, and family, kinship, and caste as well as political organizations on the other.

Second, social change is driven by forces such as the shift in the mode of production from peasant-agrarian to capitalist farming, the introduction of new technologies, demographic developments, the transportation revolution, the spread of urbanism and radio and television, rising expectations and increasing personal drive, and the loosening of geographic bonds and mobility . These forces of change have worked largely within the grooves of traditions, by modifying, reinterpreting and, not infrequently, reinventing them. Traditions are not static but have turned out to be resilient. Structural continuities of family, kinship, Islamic faith, and local power relations have maintained rural social organization. Institutional forms change but functions remain the same; functions change but meanings are unaffected. This pattern of "incorporating and reinventing" is how traditions have facilitated change while maintaining a moral and cultural continuity. Tradition and modernity should not be looked upon as polar opposites but as strands that interweave and interact. Pakistan's rural areas bear testimony to the dynamism of tradition and functionality of modernization. The adage that the more things change, the more they remain the same applies to rural communities in some ways.

Third, social life in rural areas has become more open, less bound by customs and conventions. Achievement-orientation is eroding ascribed caste roles and the rigidity of social structure is showing a tilt toward urban mores. Landlords and the rural elite have led in taking advantage of new economic opportunities. Their power has been sustained by their links to the emerging industrial/commercial economy. Owner farmers and enterprising craftsmen too have used education and commerce as routes to branch out in professions and businesses. *Kammis* and the landless remain tied to villages, although their younger generations migrate to cities, living in *katchi abadis* and providing cheap labor to urban formal and informal sectors. One way or another, people of almost all social classes have imbibed drive and mobility, breaking out of the fatalism for which they were long known. Yet often this drive is not rewarded by a decent living standard. Of course, there are regional variations in these patterns; some areas have been more extensively swept by the entrepreneurial spirit and social mobility than others.

Fourth, social institutions have fractionated and their structural coherence has given way to contradictions of enacted practices (lived culture) and believed intents (imagined culture). For example, economic rewards have come to largely determine occupational choices but social prestige and the rank of different occupations continue to be based on notions of caste stereotypes. The imbalance between social and economic roles has eroded bonds that underlie the territorial community. The loss of community in villages and towns has reinforced tendencies toward factionalism and subverted the collective welfare. Solidarities of family, kin group, and Islamic brotherhood (*pirbhais* and Islamic associations) have been filling up the community space. The traditional basis of social cohesion has weakened whereas the common ground of shared interests and legal institutions has not emerged.[92] This normative uncertainty has come to rule rural as well as urban areas.

Fifth, without romanticizing the social cohesion of historical village community, it can be said that social changes of the post-independence period have reduced the tranquility and harmony in rural areas. The customary social controls, based on the authority derived from age and status of caste, have loosened and mutual obligations that gave minimal security to the poor and the disadvantaged have weakened. Social disparities of income, lifestyle, and beliefs have increased to the point that households in the same village may appear to be living in different centuries.[93] Social polarization has intensified; although the national poverty level has fallen slightly, about one-third of the rural population remains bound in the stubborn poverty that has been made more striking by the cash economy and competitive ethos. Life for the poor has evolved from the oppression of landlords and caste hierarchies to the exploitation of commercialism and governmental corruption.

Sixth, the moral order of tribal/agrarian communities based on customary beliefs and spiritual-Islamic norms has eroded. The impersonal legal and adminis-trative order necessary for an emerging commercial/urban society has not been fostered, resulting in wide-ranging moral and social contradictions. This moral void is being filled by resurgent Islamic orthodoxy. Juridical and intellectualized Islam emanating from cities is displacing the folk traditions and syncretic–spiritual beliefs of villages. Sectarianism is on the rise, as is the power of the *mullahs*.[94]

Seventh, urban ways of life, such as interest-based social relations, rising expec-tations, and some degree of individualism are permeating rural communities. Villages and towns are being urbanized. Conversely, with mass migration to cities, particularly those of the upper- and middle-class ruralites, village/tribal mores are diffusing in urban areas. The "feudal" values and behaviors of the urban elite testify to the ruralization of cities; the parallel diffusion of respective norms and customs is resulting in the convergence of rural and urban mores.[95]

Eighth, urban traits diffusing into rural areas are not laying the bases for anonymity, impersonalization, or individualism often associated with Western urbanism. Urban functional requirements and values are shrinking the circle of groups that affect individuals' identity and behaviors. The tribe or caste is losing influence over everyday life and social relations. Yet individuals remain deeply embedded in family and kin groups and sentiments nurtured in these relations are carried into friendships, social networks, and associations. A Pakistani, a rural Pakistani all the more, takes her/his social bearings from a primary group and seldom functions as an autonomous individual.

Ninth, the evolving social organization is based on narrow differentiations of class, family, power, and lifestyle, moving away from ascribed statuses of caste, tribe, or clan. Modernization in Pakistan is selective in scope and mediated through regional and national cultures.

7   Islam and social life

Foundational institutions

Three societal institutions, religion (Islam), family, and occupation, are the anchors of Pakistan's social life. From a sociological perspective, family and work are the primary social institutions but religion is a particularly defining influence in Pakistani society.

In this chapter, I will explore Islam as one of the three foundational social institutions in Pakistan. I will examine how Islam affects social life and how social life in turn restructures Islamic discourse, which includes both conceptions and actions. I am not focusing on the doctrines of Islam. My analysis will trace the evolution of the Islamic discourse in Pakistan and the social patterns to which it has given rise.

Before discussing the role of Islam as an institution in Pakistani society, the term "social institution" needs to be explained. Social institution refers to society-wide structures such as family, religion, and government on the one hand, and to functional organizations on local or community scales such as a school, mosque, or shrine on the other. This differentiation of institutions in local versus societal or micro versus macro needs to be borne in mind, although my focus is on the macro or societal scale of Islam as an institution.

It should also be noted that small and single-function institutions nest within society-wide institutions. In that sense, a societal institution is a composite of multiple structures although by convention it is described in a singular noun.

A social institution consists of recurring patterns of behavior, based on interrelated norms regulating a significant aspect of social life.[1] Social institutions are clusters of rules and procedures, regulating a significant social activity. According to one famous historian, "an institution encompasses at once an activity, a pattern of social relations, and a set of mental constructs."[2] An institution is essentially a "manual of operations" of organization. It is imprinted in the human psyche as habits, norms, and values. For example, common norms and rules that define relations among family members in a society make up the institution of family, but not John's or Khan's family as such.

Religion, family, and occupation are the institutions whose norms and patterns permeate other elements of Pakistan's social organization. They structure the roles of everyday life and determine individuals' behavior. Other social institutions, such as education or politics, largely regulate their respective spheres, but these three have a more pervasive influence extending beyond their functional domains.

As a macro-social institution, religion cuts across communities, classes, and ethnicities. Yet within these broad categories, practices vary by sect, tribe, and region. I do not mean to suggest that Islamic precepts and practices are all the same among various sects. Of course, there are variations in these matters but what is uniform is ideology, values, and identities, although their meanings may be interpreted differently.

Social institutions shed norms, adopt new ones, and assign new meanings to long established practices. They are not immune to change, although some historic continuity is often maintained even in revolutionary times. Thus, the interplay of continuity and change is built into social institutions.

Bearing in mind this introduction to social institutions in general, let us turn to analyzing religion as a social institution in Pakistan.

Islam as an institution of Pakistani society

Pakistanis embrace many faiths: Islam, Christianity, Hinduism, and there are tiny minorities of Sikhs and Zoroastrians. Yet Islam, although divided into many sects, is overwhelmingly the predominant religion. About 97 percent of the country's population is Muslim and this proportion has not changed since independence. Islam's influence on Pakistan's social life goes beyond being the religion of such a large majority. It is the basis of Muslim nationalism on which the Pakistani state has been constituted. As discussed in Chapter 4, the meaning of the notion "Islamic versus Muslim nation" is contested, but Islam is accepted as the core institution almost consensually. The centrality of Islam in social life gives religion a special role in national society.

Two questions arise from the acknowledgement of Islam's role: (1) how Islam affects areas of social life that are outside the sphere of the "sacred," namely other than spiritual beliefs, practices, experiences, and solidarities and (2) how social life affects Islam as an institution, in terms of its ideology, patterned behavior, and practices. Addressing these questions will uncover both the structure and the dynamics of Islam as a social institution.

Before answering the two questions, a clarification is in order. I am analyzing the social ideologies and behaviorial practices emerging from Islamic discourses. The divine elements of Islam, its faith, and beliefs are not the object of my study. I consider those to be ordained for the spiritual and moral guidance of individuals and groups.

Historical roots of Islam in the subcontinent

Although the Arab conquest of Sindh (AD 713) introduced Islam in areas now constituting Pakistan, Muslim dynastic rule began in earnest with the annexation of Lahore by Mahmud of Ghazni (AD 1020). For almost 800 years, until Maharaja

Ranjit Singh's capture of Lahore in 1799, successive Muslim invaders from Afghanistan and Iran and the Turko/Persian dynasties they founded, ruled the territories that make up Pakistan. The millennium of Muslim rule infused Islamic social norms and legal precepts in the historic social order of these areas. The fusion of Persian/Afghan beliefs and practices inspired by Islamic ideas along with the Indus Valley modes of living, produced regional societies where folk cultures of villages and tribes were largely vernacular, and the high culture of courts and capitals was Turko-Persian with an Islamic imprint. Yet it should be pointed out that a majority of the population in India continued to be non-Muslim (Hindus) even under Muslim rule.

The subcontinental caste system assumed new forms in Muslim communities. The untouchables remained socially segregated in Muslim communities for their "unclean" occupations, such as cleaning latrines or disposing of dead bodies, even if they had accepted the Islamic faith. The progeny of settlers who came from Arabia, Iran, or Afghanistan became respectable Sayyids, Qureshis, or Mughuls, based on their claims of connection to early Muslims. They formed the upper strata. Muslim converts from the indigenous population, carried their tribal/caste differentiations into the new social organization, and renamed themselves in hereditary occupational classes identified by clan titles such as Khans, Sheikhs, and Gujjars. They dominated local social structures in villages and regions far away from Delhi, Lahore, or Multan. The social hierarchy of Muslim communities, though, was more malleable than the Hindu caste system.

Islam realigned historic social structures in Sindhi, Punjabi, Pashtoon, and Baloch communities, making ancestral identities and hereditary occupations the bases of social differentiation. Overall, medieval Muslim societies were based on the fusion of indigenous and Islamic norms and their Islam absorbed many local beliefs and practices. The social fabric of these societies was woven out of four strands: indigenousm Indian, Islamic/Arabian, Turkish, and Persian.[3]

The British period (1846–1947) witnessed a radical transformation of the historic society in Pakistan. Muslims in British India lost political power and cultural privileges. They invested a lot of energy and thought in ruing their lost power and glory. The British instituted social reforms and realigned the economy, for example, banning slavery; legislating property rights; promoting merit in public appointments; building railways, roads, and new cities. These measures reduced the influence of Islam and other religions in social life, although Muslims could follow "Mohammadan law" for family affairs and inheritance. Even local customary laws were applicable in these matters of individual choice.[4]

The ethos of the British era was secular. Civil and criminal codes were instituted to regulate civic life and promote peace and order. The state was effectively separated from religion, confining the latter to matters of personal faith and conduct. Islamic priests and jurists lost their juridical and legislative authority. The *mullah* (Islamic priest) became an ordinary functionary in Muslim communities, respected but dependent on the local elite for his livelihood.[5]

British rule and the Western influences it brought triggered opposing trends, reform movements on the one hand and revivalist efforts on the other. Many traditional practices and notions were turning out to be untenable. Triggered by these challenges, a wave of Islamic reform movements, both puritanical and modernist, rose among the Muslims of British India.

Deoband's Dar-ul-Uloom (Islamic college started in 1867) systematized the education of Muslim priests and promoted the purification of Islamic practices and beliefs, shedding saint worship and magical/cultist practices. The Ahl-i-Hadith (Wahabis) offered a still more puritanical doctrine of Islam. The Brelvi school defended experiential forms of worship and the intercession of saints and shrines for personal salvation. The Ahmadia sect, now legislated to be non-Muslim, also arose as a part of the ongoing struggle to reconcile Islam with modern paradigms. I am citing these late-nineteenth- and early-twentieth-century movements essentially to point out the trend of restructuring Islamic institutions in response to changing social conditions. Their history and outcome are not my immediate interest.

Sayyid Ahmed Khan's casting of Islam in the contemporary idiom, the poet Hali's laments of Muslims' backwardness, and Allama Muhammad Iqbal's attempt to reconstruct religious thought in Islam by his lectures and stirring poems are examples of intellectual efforts to reexamine Islamic doctrines and practices. Of course, there were also strident reactions to these movements from orthodox Islamists. Yet this vigorous and at times contentious debate among Muslims, extending over 70–80 years and spread by the "colonial gift of the print medium,"[6] spawned new interpretations of Islamic beliefs and practices. They also raised Muslim consciousness about their political and social interests. Out of these movements arose the Muslim nationalism that culminated in the birth of Pakistan.

Social history of the Islamic narrative in Pakistan

Pakistan was born in a paroxysm of communal riots which intensified the religious feelings of Muslims and Hindus/Sikhs alike. Millions had to abandon their ancestral homes and communities to escape murder and mayhem, primarily because of their religious identity. Almost all Muslims from Indian Punjab migrated to Pakistan at the time of independence. Similarly, many Muslims from Uttar Pradesh, Bihar, Gujarat, Hyderabad State, and other provinces sought refuge in Pakistan. The refugees initially felt a strong attachment to the Islamic faith and identity. After all, Islam was the basis of their claim to citizenship in Pakistan.

The early advocates of Islamic order were disproportionately of Muhajir (Muslim refugees from India) background. They conflated the Urdu language with Islam as the "ideology of Pakistan."[7] From the early days, Islamic political parties, *ulema* (Islamic scholars) and *mullahs* have claimed ownership of the ideology.

Despite a surge in religious sentiments, resulting from the partition's bloodbath and uprooting, the primary tenor of the time was secular. Not only were British laws and system of government maintained after independence, the colonial practice of separating state and religion also continued during the early period of independent Pakistan. There was a spike in mosque attendance and other religious observances but Islam largely remained a matter of personal faith. It was introduced into public life in the symbols of the state, for example, the national anthem,

Quranic verses emblazoned on state buildings, constitutional debates about the Islamic state, etc. How has Islamic discourse evolved since then? What combination of ideas and actions surfaced in the Islamic narrative? What effects has it had on social life and vice versa? To answer these questions historically, I will recount both the ideological themes and the political actions that Islamists promoted in the three periods of Pakistan's postcolonial history.

Political Islam in the secular era (1947–71)

Inherent in the demand for a separate homeland for Muslims was the question of Islam's role in such a state and society. This question persisted through the struggle for Pakistan but it became more pressing as the new nation started to chart its social course and frame its constitution. The leadership of the movement for Pakistan, particularly the Muslim League's executive, was "secular, Western-oriented and steeped in English Common Law."[8] They leaned toward a liberal modern society that embraces Islamic universal principles and symbolism, whereas *ulema*, the leaders of Islamic political parties such as Ahrar, Jamiat-ul-Ulema, and Jamaat-i-Islami, and some members of the Muslim League argued for a state where Islamic laws (*Sharia*) would rule.

After independence, the Islamists started to demand an Islamic constitution. Maulana Shabbir Ahmed Usmani, designated *Sheikh-ul-Islam* (Grand Islamic scholar), led the effort that culminated in the adoption of the Objectives Resolution (1949) by the first Constituent Assembly. It declared Pakistan to be the sacred trust of Allah Almighty who is the sovereign of the entire universe. What it meant in practice was not clear. It was a symbolic acknowledgment of the Islamic identity of Pakistan but for Islamists it became a justification for demands for an Islamic constitution.

However, Islamic discourse was unified only in broad generalities. What would an Islamic constitution look like? The Munir Inquiry Report on the Anti-Ahmadia Disturbances in Punjab (1953) concludes in dismay that leading *ulemas*, who appeared before the court of inquiry, could not agree on the criteria of defining a Muslim. The report observed, "if considerable confusion exists in the minds of *ulemas* on such a simple matter, one can imagine what the differences on more complicated matters will be."[9] This report is a seminal document in the national discourse about an Islamic state. It brought out the contradictions between the ideals of the promised liberal-democratic order and the conceptions of an Islamic state on the one hand, and widely divergent notions of the authority and responsibilities of an Islamic state among Islamists of various schools on the other. These contradictions underlie the ideological logjam that has plagued Pakistan since its birth.

The Jamaat

To put a face on the Islamic narrative, I will track the ideology and activities of the Jamaat-i-Islami (JI), founded in 1941 by Maulana Abul Ala Maudoodi, a distinguished Islamic scholar who interpreted Islamic creed in contemporary idiom. As a political party, the Jamaat is the most organized and active promoter of Islamic order in Pakistan, although before the partition it opposed Jinnah's claim to leadership of Muslims.

It envisions a radical transformation of society to bring about Islamic moral and social order. Its proposed order has been a work in progress, evolving with changing economic and political conditions. At its core is a mode of life in which individuals are required to follow religious observances in everyday life and mold their behavior in accordance with *Sharia* laws.

The Jamaat's program includes reform of the life and minds of individuals to turn them into *salih* (virtuous) men and women, thus building an Islamic community. At the national level, it aims at bringing all laws in conformity with the Quran and Sunnah.[10] It regards the state as the instrument of bringing about this social and political revolution.

The Jamaat-i-Islami aimed at restructuring the state through political means to fulfill its social agenda. It followed the constitutional route in the first period, arguing and politicking for an Islamic constitution, taking part in elections, and aligning with other opposition parties against governments not of its liking. Through all these maneuverings, it kept its sights on restructuring the state and capturing the government. Politics has been its tool for bringing about an Islamic society. Other Islamic parties have followed, more or less, a similar strategy but they were seldom as disciplined and organized as the Jamaat-i-Islami.

The Jamaat has had considerable influence on social thought but it had relatively limited impact on political developments until the 1970s. What positions it has promoted at various times and how its politicosocial stances have changed over time are reflections of evolving Islamic ideology in Pakistan.

Defining events

In period 1 (1947–71), the role of Islam in Pakistani society became a topic of daily conversation and a matter of public discussion. It has continued to be a central theme of public discussions in Pakistan ever since. Four events in the first period are threshold points in the evolution of Islamic ideas and politics: (1) Anti-Ahmadi agitation in Punjab in 1953; (2) framing Pakistan's constitution in 1956; (3) Ayub's constitution (1962) and social reforms; and (4) civil war and separation of Bangladesh in 1971.

1 Anti-Ahmadi agitation in Punjab

The Ahmadis are a sect that grew in the early twentieth century within the Indian Islamic discourse. Its founder, Mirza Ghulam Ahmed (d.1908) claimed divine revelation and offered new interpretations of Islamic beliefs and practices for the emerging Muslim middle class. His claim of divine revelation contravened the belief that Mohammad was the last and the final prophet. The mainstream *ulemas* rejected his claim and disputed the Ahmadis' credentials as Muslims. The British treated it as a doctrinal dispute and kept it contained in arenas of religious debate within the Muslim community.

The idea of making Pakistan an Islamic state soon morphed into the question about what school of Islamic jurisprudence will prevail and what will the status of other schools and sects be. This debate stirred sectarian feelings and provided an opportunity to Ahrars and other political parties, which had been outvoted in the 1946 elections, to whip up anti-Ahmadi sentiments. They demanded that Ahmadis be declared non-Muslims and a minority. Other political and social factors combined with the aroused religious passions, including personal intrigues among the Muslim League leaders, to build up an anti-Ahmadia movement in Punjab. It sparked protests that escalated into riots and mayhem in February–March 1953, largely in Lahore. Eventually the army had to be called, and Pakistan's first martial law was imposed on Lahore city. Leaders of the anti-Ahmadi agitation, including Maulana Maudoodi, were arrested and convicted. The Munir Court of Inquiry Commission investigated the causes and lessons of this civil disturbance.

This event marks a critical point in the history of the Islamization of Pakistan. It was the initial expression of the themes that have come to characterize the Islamic narrative. First, the authority of state is mobilized to settle religious arguments and to define Islamic identity, namely who is or is not a Muslim. Second, non-Muslims are to be excluded from high public office, implying full citizenship be based on religion and not nationality. One of the demands in the anti-Ahmadia movement was that Zafarulla Khan be fired from the foreign minister's position and Ahmadis be debarred from positions of authority. Third, the anti-Ahmadi agitation set the precedent for settling sectarian differences by violence. These patterns have recurred with renewed energy in each successive cycle of Islamization. The anti-Ahmadia movement was suppressed by force. The state maintained its neutrality in religious affairs but its secular outlook did not last long.

2 Pakistan's first constitution

The next strategic moment in the push toward the Islamization of state and society in the first period was the framing of Pakistan's first constitution. The Jamaat and other Islamic parties lobbied for a centralized state that enforces Islamic laws and regulates personal conduct. For example, Maulana Maudoodi's constitutional proposals included legislating *Sharia* as the law of the land, abrogation of all existing laws which were contrary to *Sharia*, making government explicitly responsible for promoting Islamic morals, and eliminating prohibited practices; these provisions were combined with some basic (liberal-democratic) rights of citizens.[11] Other Islamic parties and *ulemas* also pressed for the supremacy of *Sharia* but the consensus was only at the plane of symbols. When it came to meanings and practice of *Sharia*, protagonists differed among themselves.

The liberal-modern perspective on Pakistan's constitution was not devoid of Islamic commitments. Legislators and administrators to whom Islamists pressed their demands were Muslims too. They were not averse to an Islamic constitution but they viewed that to be based on liberal interpretations of Islamic edicts allowing individual freedoms and legislative sovereignty. They particularly resisted yielding legislative and judicial authority to *ulemas*, who presented themselves as the agency for interpreting Islamic laws. They had to balance regional interests, Bengali versus Punjabi, etc., which would not admit a highly centralized and socially commanding state.[12] These two viewpoints were passionately debated in the National Assembly and fought over publicly.

The constitution (1956) that was finally adopted named the state as The Islamic Republic of Pakistan and adopted the provision that no law shall be repugnant to the teachings of Quran and Hadith (the Prophet's sayings). The "repugnancy" clause is a negative canon, leaving greater leeway to the legislature in interpreting Islamic laws. Its preamble promised observance of principles of democracy, freedom, equality, tolerance, and social justice. It also called for Muslims to order their lives "in accordance with the teachings and requirements of Islam," but left it largely to an individual's conscience. The constitution laid the baseline, albeit fuzzy, for entrenching Islamic provisions in the state. It offered a liberal version of Islam but it had the potential of being used by Islamists to enact their social agenda if they could gain authority. The Jamaat and other proponents of Islamic order recast themselves into active political parties and geared up for elections.

Islamists had been unsuccessful in elections both before and after the birth of Pakistan. The Jamaat gradually built a political base in urban areas, particularly among Muhajirs. Its success in winning 19 out of the 23 seats of Karachi municipality in April 1958 gave it hope for electoral success. It formed an alliance with the Nizam-i-Islam party for the promised national elections of 1958 but these elections never materialized. General Ayub Khan's military coup (October 1958) upstaged democracy, setting back Islamists' hopes of advancing their ideology through electoral politics. Yet, they had a relatively free hand to proselytize their political aims, as they had a platform in mosques that could not be muzzled by the military government's censors. Their views found resonance among students and newly prosperous bazaar merchants.

3 Ayub's constitution and social reforms

Ayub's era was a period of secular nationalism.[13] He saw it as his mission to persuade Pakistanis to "respond to the challenges of modern age instead of…(believing)…that all problems…(have been) resolved for them in the light of Quran and Sunnah."[14] There was an attempt to drop the adjective "Islamic" from the new constitution (1962), but it was retained to quell the controversy engendered by this move. Ayub's Family Laws Ordinance regulated polygamy and prescribed the minimum age for marriage. He openly espoused family planning and promoted the distribution of contraceptives. The Ayub government accelerated economic development and introduced modernist social policies, embracing international, particularly American, aid and advice. Overall, the period 1958–69 witnessed the displacement of democratic politics and the Islamists' influence.

The Jamaat was banned (1964), but subsequently the Supreme Court deemed the ban illegal. Islamists, particularly the Jamaat, started identifying the Islamic social order with democracy. For example, it supported Fatima Jinnah in 1965's indirect presidential election against Ayub. Accepting a woman to be the candidate for the head of a Muslim nation represented a change in the *ulemas'* long-held contrary position. They revised their ideology to advance their political agenda. Curiously, religious modernism was tied with martial rule and Islamic revivalism became intertwined with democracy.[15]

On many other Islamic prescriptions, the *ulemas* changed their mind in this period. For example, Maulana Maudoodi and other *ulemas* had long refused to be photographed and held pictures to be *shirk* (contrary to Islamic norms), but by the mid-1960s, they had quietly dropped their objections to photographing humans. Their pictures began to appear regularly in newspapers and magazines. Political imperatives helped revise Islamic norms.

The 1965 war with India brought out Islamic fervor. The postwar disappointments and the increasing discontent with Ayub's rule channeled these feelings into the anti-Ayub protest movement. Islamic parties and *ulemas* joined hands with other politicians to agitate for the restoration of democracy and undoing many of Ayub's authoritarian but modernist policies. Ultimately this agitation brought Bhutto to the forefront along with his Islamic socialism as the progressive version of Islamic order.

Ayub's and his successor General Yahya's period was essentially secular although Islamic symbols were regularly employed. His minister of information, General Sher Ali, became the official advocate of "ideology of Pakistan" as a code word for Islamic order. Social life continued to evolve in modern modes and this period infused democratic and progressive ideas in Islamic ideologies in the course of the 1970 elections.

4 Civil war and the separation of Bangladesh

The culminating events of period 1 had a bearing on the Islamic narrative. The national election of 1970, followed by the civil war in East Pakistan, and the defeat of the Pakistani army by India in December 1971 were seminal events in Pakistan's history. Islamic parties were soundly beaten in the 1970 elections, a reaffirmation of the people's distrust of *mullahs* to rule the country. Their appeal for Islamic order did not sway the electorate, except in 18 constituencies out of the total 300. People felt confident about their Islamic identity, but the bread-and-butter issues as well as regional/ethnic bonds proved to be decisive factors in their electoral choices.

The civil war and the war with India brought out, for the first time, the resort to force for Islam in Pakistan. What came to be called "terrorism" in 2001 made its ugly appearance in East Pakistan (Bangladesh) in 1971. The Jamaat-sponsored youth groups, called Al-Badr and Al-Shams, were blamed for the cold-blooded murders of Bengali intellectuals and professionals for their purported support of an independent East Pakistan. This was a new turn in the Islamists' activism. It also marked the first systematic collaboration between the army and Islamists in general and the Jamaat in particular.

Reprise of the first period

As the religion of a nation of Muslims, Islam is a pivotal institution in Pakistani society. To what extent it has or should influence other social institutions has remained a contested issue in Pakistan's social history. Broadly, two ideologies have competed in public forums about the role of Islam, namely, literalist-revivalism versus a liberal-interpretative Islamic order.[16] The controversy centers on the meaning of Islam as an ideology and how it is to be interpreted, literally or metaphorically, in contemporary times. It is not so much about Islam *per se.*

The first period of Pakistan's history witnessed the drawing of the political battle lines between the two ideologies and their supporters. Islamic revivalists of the conservative cast appropriated the role of defenders and promoters of Islam. They assumed the mantle of Islamists, identifying the liberal interpreters of Islam as secularist and westernized.

The governments of the first period were organized around secular values, a British legacy, and the ruling Muslim League party and its successors espoused a society based on Islamic moral precepts, but of liberal-modern ethos. Islamists were outside the power structure and they aimed at capturing the state to remold it in their ideology. Politics and proselytizing were the main instruments of their strategy.

Islamic movements in the first period chose democracy as the path toward the Islamic state. They formed political parties, participated in elections, propagated their views, and organized demonstrations. Apart from the usual political activities, Islamists had the special advantage of access to mosques as a platform for advancing their objectives. Yet the people remained indifferent to the political aims of Islamists, particularly those of the revivalist strain.

Social life continued to be driven by material interests and cultural mores. Islamists were consistently voted down. They had to content themselves with remaining the second fiddle in the nationwide agitation against the Ayub government. Their demands for Islamic laws and practices were swamped by claims for the redress of social inequities arising from the much-touted Decade of Development and regional disparities. Undoubtedly, in times of wars and crises, Islamic fervor came to the forefront, but such spikes in Islamic sentiment could not be converted into political capital.

The social and political events of the first period politicized Islam and infused it with democratic values. Thus political Islam was the legacy handed down from the first period to the next.

Islam as an oppositional force (1972–7)

Islamists diverged from the path of constitutionalism and took a turn toward oppositional politics in the second period of Pakistan's history. With the traumatic breakup of the old Pakistan (of 1947 vintage), the challenge in the second period was to reconstruct the ideological bases of the truncated country. Islam *per se* could not keep the erstwhile East and West Pakistan together. What ideology would bind the remaining Pakistan? Two different responses emerged to this question.

One took the form of Bhutto's populism. He blended socialism and democracy with Islam, proclaiming "Islam is our faith, democracy is our polity, socialism is our economy." When Islamists accused him of drinking alcohol, he carried the day by defiant statements like, "Yes, I drink but I do not drink people's blood." This appeal to people's rights and interests under the Islamic umbrella was one type of response. By stitching together social egalitarianism and Islam, Bhutto fashioned a new model of a Muslim nation. People in Punjab and Sindh responded to this formulation by voting his party (PPP) in by a majority in the 1970 elections. The PPP also had sizable followings in NWFP and Balochistan.

The second ideological response took the form of blaming failures on the flouting of Islamic principles. Pakistan has suffered because it has betrayed Islamic values, the Islamists argued. Maudoodi blamed Yahya Khan's drinking and womanizing for the breakup of Pakistan.[17] The Islamists maintained that only by following pristine Islamic principles could Pakistan be saved and sustained. The Jamaat was the flywheel of this ideology. Its disappointment in the 1970 elections soured it on the subject of electoral democracy that it had espoused in the first period. Now it took to opposing Bhutto's government for its "un-Islamic" policies.

The second period was Bhutto's era. He essentially attempted to organize the state and society in modern modes while promoting Islamic symbolism and identity. Even some Islamic parties initially collaborated with Bhutto's government. Mufti Mahmood's Jamait ul-Ulema-e-Islam (JUI), for example, formed coalition governments in NWFP and Balochistan provinces under Bhutto's federal rule. All Islamic parties voted for the 1973 constitution in the National Assembly but Bhutto had to yield to the incorporation of Islamic provisions to get a consensus. This harmony did not last very long. The confrontational stance of Islamic and regional parties and Bhutto's authoritarian ways, compounded by the "army action" in Balochistan, turned their political differences into an ideological war.

Colleges and universities, labor unions, lawyers' associations, media and literature, as well as mosques became the arenas for ideological battles. Each forum was fought over by Islamists of various persuasions among themselves, but more strikingly together against the secularists and socialists. Each party recruited students and youth to advance its ideology. The Jamaat had a head start in organizing a disciplined student body countrywide.

Agitating students

The Jamaat established a strong presence among students through its nominally independent student organization, Islami Jamiat-i-Tulabah (IJT). Beginning with a nucleus of 25 members, mostly sons of the Jamaat members (December 1947), the IJT grew into the fighting arm of the Jamaat's puritanical Islam. It had been modeled after the Muslim Brotherhood of Egypt, providing material and academic support to students at college campuses, particularly to those coming from villages for studies, and organizing them for pursuing its political and religious objectives.

The IJT's initial base was among the Muhajir students of Karachi but it steadily spread to campuses in major cities in the 1960s. Students have always been the vanguard of political movements in Pakistan. They imbibed national political currents, having a particular affinity with left-liberal causes. The IJT was the Jamaat's answer to the spread of liberal-modernism.[18] From the early 1960s, the IJT started forming *danda* (stick-carrying) brigades at campuses.

In 1971, the army recruited IJT to fight Bengali nationalists in East Pakistan. This collaboration legitimized the IJT's use of strong-arm tactics to defend Islam. By the second period, IJT had become a fearsome force on campuses. It confronted nationalist and socialist student associations in colleges and universities. It contested elections for student unions and did not hold back from beating up rival students, teachers, or administrators to gain ascendancy. It particularly challenged Bhutto's policies on almost every occasion. From opposing the Simla Agreement with India and the recognition of Bangladesh to the second round of anti-Ahmadi riots (1974), the IJT continually agitated against Bhutto's government. Often these agitations would turn violent, pitching student factions against each other and fostering Muhajir, Sindhi, and Pashtoon confrontations on campuses.[19]

The Islamists' opposition compelled Bhutto to highlight his commitment to Islam. The 1973 constitution stipulated the president to be a Muslim, and strengthened the Islamic Ideology Council as the body that vetted legislation for conformity with the Quran and Sunnah.[20] For Islamists, there was always another issue to raise after one was settled. A local dispute in Rabwah (a new town founded by the Ahmadis) was blown into anti-Ahmadi marches in major cities, particularly at college campuses. Bhutto's pragmatism overrode his socialist rhetoric. In 1974, the PPP cosponsored, with the Jamaat and JUI/JUP, the second amendment to the constitution branding Ahmadis as non-Muslims.

In the waning days of Bhutto's government (1977), laws prohibiting alcohol, banning gambling, nightclubs, bars, and other un-Islamic activities were proclaimed to mollify the *mullahs* and quell political protests.[21] Even the weekend holiday was switched from Sunday to Friday. Such measures proved to be too little too late.

Social bases of protests

The nationalization policies of the second period alienated many groups and drove them into the Islamist camp. Those policies affected not only the big industrialists and bankers but also appropriated the properties and businesses of the bazaar merchants, small-town entrepreneurs, and urban professionals, for example, flour and rice mill owners, private schools, and colleges. Their frustrations were tapped by the Jamaat and other Islamists on the one hand, and by the ethnic parties on the other. In January 1977, all disaffected politicians joined hands to form a grand coalition called the Pakistan National Alliance (PNA) to mount countrywide protests. It had the Islamic imprimatur of *nizam-e-Mustafa* (The Prophet's system) and *musawat-i-Mohammadi* (Mohammad's social justice). This alliance anticipated the Iranian revolution by two years in the joining of forces by bazaar merchants, students, and Islamists. The manipulated elections of 1977, later abrogated, ignited popular protests and riots. The PNA shook Bhutto's government, but the army chief, General Zia-ul-Haq, brought it down with a coup.

The PNA's protest movement swung the pendulum toward Islamic revivalism. Its manifesto promised to "fully enforce the Holy Quran ... and to enable every Muslim to lead life in accordance with the tenets of Islam," at the same time guaranteeing "provision of food, dress, accommodation, education, and medical care to each and every citizen."[22] Its success in knocking down Bhutto's government was a seminal event in the history of the Islamic movement in Pakistan. For the first time in Pakistan's 30-year history, Islam became the launching pad for a mass political movement.[23] However, this success also came with the change in the Islamic narrative. This restructuring of Islamic ideals was Bhutto's legacy.

Reprise of the second period

New conceptions of Islamic order were forged in the second period, incorporating egalitarian values. In response to the rising expectations for equality and welfare, Islamists recast their ideology in terms of social justice. Yet the change was dialectical, one step forward, the next backwards. Egalitarian tenets waxed, while democratic commitments waned. The electoral disappointments of the first period drove Islamic parties, particularly the Jamaat, toward the politics of protests and the cultivation of street power.

The acceptance of violence by Islamists as a means for achieving their political goals germinated toward the end of the first period, but it became an accepted tactic with Islamic students' organizations. The precedent of collaboration between the army and Islamists (1970–1) was revived in the last days of Bhutto's rule and blossomed in the third period.

Islamization of institutions and culture (1978–present)

The third period, inaugurated by General Zia's military coup of July 1977, falls into two phases. The first phase was the era of Zia's military rule (1978–88), and the second phase was the decade (1989–99) of the elected governments of Benazir Bhutto and Nawaz Sharif, continuing with General Musharraf's coup and its controlled democracy. On the whole, the third period is defined by the leap into the Islamization of society. It is a period in which social life has been imprinted with Islamic ideology. A veritable cultural revolution has taken place, although like many revolutions it has bred both transformations and contradictions.

Institutionalization of Islam

General Zia was a conservative Muslim who shrewdly used Islam to legitimize his military rule. Both from personal convictions and for political expediency, he co-opted the PNA, particularly the Jamaat-i-Islami, in his regime. It was an unexpected but happy turn of events for Islamists. At long last they had found a back route to state power and patronage, landing two-thirds of the ministerial positions in Zia's appointed cabinet (1978). Maudoodi, for example, hailed Zia's policies as "the renewal of covenant between the government and Islam."[24] Islamists had their opportunity to utilize the state's authority to push their social and cultural agenda.

In the third period, the drive for an Islamic order came to mean changing culture and reorganizing society.

General Zia instituted three types of measures under the Islamization program: (1) legal reforms to introduce (1979) *Hudood* (Islamic punishments) for behavior prohibited by *Sharia*, for example, flogging, amputations, and stoning for drinking, theft, and fornication respectively as well as instituting the law of *qisas* (compensation and restitution) and *diyat* (blood money) for crimes against persons; (2) economic regulations to promote an interest-free economy and the introduction of *zakat* (Islamic wealth tax) and *usher* (public share from agricultural produce) for Muslims; (3) the establishment of Islamic boards and organizations to promote changes in morals and behaviors, for example, Islamic (*Shariat*) Courts, the International Islamic University, and the Council of Islamic Ideology. Also compulsory Islamic and Quranic learnings were added to the educational curricula. *Namaz* (prayer) was promoted in schools and offices and Islamic symbols and themes were patronized in literature, media, art, and popular culture.[25]

Islamic laws and practices

Altogether these laws and policies established parallel Islamic institutions in judiciary, education, and economy on the one hand, and injected Islamic mores and practices in everyday life on the other. It was an ambitious attempt for cultural and institutional reforms. On paper, the social and cultural agenda of the Islamic revivalists was largely implemented. Islamization sharpened cultural cleavages and precipitated institutional dissonance, that is, the divergence of values and norms within institutions. It created a new social category of the "Islam-inclined" among intellectuals, professionals, and students.

What have been the outcomes of the Islamization program? The answer to this question can be read in the social conditions and political situation of the third period. Three parallel systems of laws emerged, each harsher than the other, that is, civil and criminal codes, *Hudood* ordinance, and martial law regulations. Paralleling the three systems of law were three types of courts administering common law, the *Shariat* code, and military regulations, respectively. Prosecutors could slap on a case any of the three sets of laws, with very different requirements of evidence and varying prospects of conviction and punishment.[26]

Political opponents of the regime, particularly PPP workers, were lashed and imprisoned under martial law or *Hudood* ordinances. Criminals could be tried in *Shariat* or common law courts, depending on the inclination of prosecutors. An environment of repression and arbitrariness was fostered by public lashings and the threat of *Hudood* punishments. Yet they did not reduce crime or improve public morals as they were meant to do. A retired chief judge of the Lahore High Court, Javed Iqbal, observes that Islamization had no discernible impact on the spiritual and moral life of the people, rather it gave rise to new forms of exploitation and blackmailing, particularly of women.[27] *Hudood* punishments were so much out of tune with twentieth-century notions of criminal justice that the high and supreme courts invariably ruled out their enforcement in all appeals. The result was that no amputations of thieves' limbs or stoning of adulterers have been carried out in Pakistan despite such punishments being on the books.

Islamic amendments introduced (1986) by Zia's regime to the penal code (section 295-c) made blasphemy of the Prophets and the Quran a capital crime, and the revision (1984) of the Law of Evidence reduced a woman's evidence to half that of a man's in financial disputes, as per literalist interpretations of Islamic edicts.[28] The blasphemy provisions of 1986 allowed individuals (previously only district magistrates were empowered to initiate blasphemy proceedings) to file accusations, which, in the religiously charged climate of the 1980s and 1990s, effectively became an instrument of personal vendetta used largely against Ahmadis, Christians, and sometimes Muslims of unorthodox views. How the blasphemy provisions promoted a spate of charges is evident from the following data: the number of blasphemy cases registered was 11 in 1948–79, 3 in 1979–86 and 96 in 1987–2000.[29] Anyone accused of insulting the Prophet or the Quran, such accusations often prompted by personal vendettas or political motives, was doomed to spend life in prison or could be hanged under the blasphemy law.[30] It became a tool for Sipah-e-Sahaba (soldiers of the Prophet's companions – an extremist and violent Sunni outfit) to strike at Shias.[31]

Similarly the evidence (of women) and *zina* (fornication) ordinances led to anomalous situations, such as the sentencing to 15 lashes of a blind but pregnant girl, Safia Bibi, while the men who raped her were acquitted, because the required four eyewitnesses of the crime did not exist.[32] The Islamic laws have compromised women's and minorities' rights, and produced contradictions and uncertainties about the rules and regulations by which everyday life was regulated.

Fostering an Islamic economy

Promoting an Islamic economy was another major thrust of the Islamization program. It also resulted in many institutional changes, although they remained changes in form only, not in substance. The *zakat* tax became a compulsory annual deduction from bank accounts. The Shias agitated and got exemption from the tax because of the different requirements under the *fiqh jaffaria* (Shia juridical school). This exemption became a loophole through which large numbers of bank account holders avoided *zakat* deductions by filing false affidavits that they were Shias. Village and town *zakat* distribution committees, notoriously corrupt, did little good but served as the political base of Zia's regime. Similar dualities emerged in interest-free banking and *modabara* (profit-sharing investments) operations. The symbolism and nomenclature changed but functionally the financial institutions continued to operate on the basis of fixed interest rates, the only differences being that "interest" was renamed "profit." Corruption was rife and clever managers of the Islamic funds gobbled up people's savings.[33]

Islamic norms

Behavioral and cultural reforms were the third component of the Islamization program. The Zia government fully adopted the cultural agenda of the Jamaat-i-Islami and other orthodox Islamists. It reiterated the prohibitions on drinking, betting, and dancing, and upped the punishments for violations. President Zia set a personal example of "pious behavior" by praying and fasting.[34] Offices, schools, and factories were required to provide facilities to workers for prayers. During the month of Ramadan, everybody was expected to refrain from eating and drinking in public; deviations meant humiliation and punishment at the hands of enthusiastic police and fervent citizens. These pieties were promoted through governmental edicts and implemented by Islamic institutions and organizations. Islamization only succeeded in creating an aura of religiosity in everyday life.

Islamic themes and Quranic studies were introduced in school and college curricula. Textbooks were revised to indoctrinate children in the "ideology of Pakistan," a code word for the Islamists' version of history. Mosque schools and Islamic seminaries (*madrassahs*) multiplied under public patronage and funds. Women appearing on television were required to cover their heads. Bearded men "seized" the television, as the popular joke maintained. Conservative Islamic scholars became fixtures on television and radio holding forth on the virtues of Islam.[35] These practices have become features of Pakistani society.

In many ways, the Islamization program transformed society. It implemented much of what Islamic revivalists had been demanding since 1947. Yet the *Hudood*, interest-free economy, or mandated Islamic observances did not even begin to produce the moral and social order promised by the Islamists. Pakistani society was dualized into a public life of Islamic pieties and symbols and a private life characterized by the unabashed pursuit of personal gain and consumerism. Abdul Karim Abid, an erstwhile editor of the Jamaat's daily newspaper observes "Bhutto corrupted socialists but Zia did the same for Islamic scholars and *mullahs*."[36] In Pakistan, there is a chasm between politically expressed beliefs and private behavior. This dichotomy between the public and private sphere has become a structural feature of the Pakistani society, the one legacy of Zia's Islamization.

External influences

Just as an international wave of popular protests (1968) found an echo in anti-Ayub agitation and Bhutto's populism, the Iranian revolution of Ayotullah Khomeini (1979) and the Afghan *jehad* against the Soviet Union's occupation of Afghanistan (1980) accelerated the Islamization process in Pakistan. The Iranian revolution initially captured the people's imagination as the answer to the corruption and crime in Pakistan but its descent into harsh repression and economic decline eroded its early romance. Within Pakistan, it accentuated the Sunni–Shia schism and fueled a proxy war between Saudi Arabia and Iran through their Wahabi–Shia proxies in Pakistan. There will be more about the rise of sectarianism later.

The Afghan *jehad* spilled over into Pakistan in the form of bomb blasts, the gun and drug trade, and battling militants.[37] General Zia aligned Pakistan with the US to oust the Soviet Union from Afghanistan. Pakistan's intelligence services and the army were the conduits for the supply of armaments and aid to Afghan Mujahideen. The border provinces of NWFP and Balochistan became home to about three million Afghan refugees, whose camps were the recruiting grounds for Afghan fighters. All these measures had a blow-back effect on Pakistan.

Pakistan's involvement in the Afghan resistance was ostensibly unofficial, routed through the Jamaat and other Islamic groups. They marshaled public opinion and ran hospitals, schools, and base camps for Afghan fighters. The Jamaat, in particular, played the role of the army's auxiliary. Its new leaders, Qazi Hussain Ahmed as the Amir and Liaqat Baloch the chief of party in Punjab, for example, were veterans of the IJT, whose strong-arm tactics morphed into the freelance *jehad* of the 1980s.[38]

Battle-hardened *jehadi* fighters became the defenders of Islam in the 1990s. They returned to their home countries to bring about Islamic revolutions. Many Arab *jehadis* stayed behind in Pakistan to support the Islamic liberation movements in Kashmir, Uzbekistan, Chechnya, etc.[39] Their presence brought the US war on terrorism Pakistan's doorstep after the September 11, 2001 attacks on New York and Washington.

The Soviet Union's retreat from Afghanistan bolstered the Islamists' prestige and confidence.[40] The Afghan experience emboldened the local *mullahs* to proclaim *Sharia* rule, in defiance of the Pakistan government, in Dir, Swat, Waziristan, and even in localities of South Punjab. Sufi Mohammad's Tehrik-i-Nifaz-i-Shariat (TNSM – Movement for the enforcement of *Sharia* law) in Malakand and Swat mounted an insurrectionary challenge to Benazir Bhutto's government in 1994. Similarly Tanzeem-i-Ittehad-i-Ulema-i-Qabail (Association of Tribal *Ulemas*) attempted to enforce *Sharia* rule in the Khyber Agency in 1995.[41] The history of these movements is not of direct interest to us. These challenges to the authority of the state are significant as indicators of the Islamization process taking a turn toward freelancing.

Mullah power

Assertion of power by the *mullahs* indicates a new direction in Islamic revivalism. So far the route to Islamization primarily lay in influencing the state to adopt *Sharia* laws and install Islamists as rulers. Islamic revivalism had to control the center and then spread to the rest of the body politic. A combination of Zia's Islamization and the Afghan experience created conditions for Islamic challenges to be mounted from the periphery in the form of local initiatives for *Sharia* enforcement.

Local *mullahs* proclaimed Islamic goals to advance their political interests, combining Islamic revivalism with personal pursuits of power.[42] *Mullahs* and *ulemas* began declaring *jehad* and proclaiming *Sharia* rule on their own. Nonstate *jehadists* and self-proclaimed enforcers of Islamic order emerged as the purveyors of a privatized Islamic revolution.

General Zia's success in instituting orthodox Islamic laws and mores became the justification for his dictatorial rule. The Islamists took credit for these policies and enjoyed the fruits of martial law rule for a few years. Yet as the military regime began to seek legitimacy through managed elections, the Islamists distanced themselves from General Zia to enhance their electoral appeal. Also, the doctrinal differences among Islamic parties eroded the unity that they had forged in opposing the Bhutto government. General Zia played one party against another to keep them dependent on him. For example, he courted JUI and JUP as well as the custodians of shrines to the annoyance of the Jamaat.[43] After Bhutto's execution (1979), General Zia was even less dependent on Islamic parties.

The parting of ways between the military government and the Islamic parties was hastened, as popular discontent with Zia's regime began to bubble up. Despite Islamization, crime, unemployment, corruption, particularly of military officers, and social oppression continued to rack the country. The manipulative intent of the 1984 referendum further alienated the public and ignited popular protests under the banner of the Movement for the Restoration of Democracy (MRD). Islamization had "lost much of its luster and appeal."[44]

The second phase of period 3

General Zia's death (August 1988) ushered in the second phase of the third period. Pakistan's cyclical democracy came back although the military still pulled the strings. The Islamists found themselves again on the "out" vis-à-vis the power structure. People consistently voted for the mainstream political parties, such as the PPP, PML, or MQM, bypassing the Islamic parties. Three national elections respectively yielded only 17 (1988), 17 (1990), and 9 (1993) parliamentary seats for the Jamaat, JUI, and JUP put together in the National Assembly of 207 members.[45] The Islamization of the 1980s did not increase the electoral popularity of the Islamists. Each of the three main Islamic parties remained largely confined to their historical pockets in NWFP, Balochistan, and Karachi. So disillusioned were the Islamists with the electoral process that the Jamaat and some other Islamic parties did not participate in the 1997 elections.[46]

To bring this discussion to the present, a brief reference to General Musharraf's military rule is in order. Interestingly, the Islamists' biggest electoral success came in the 2002 elections. A coalition of Islamic parties, Muttahida Majlis-e-Amal (MMA – United Action Forum) succeeded in winning majorities in NWFP and Balochistan assemblies and forming provincial governments. At the federal level, they captured 60 seats in the expanded National Assembly of 341 members. For the first time in Pakistan's history, the Islamists have a sizable presence in assemblies and are ruling in two provinces.

However this success was not a clean victory. It came, partially, because, Nawaz Sharif (PML), Benazir Bhutto (PPP), and Altaf Hussain (MQM), respective heads of the three leading parties, were exiled abroad. Thus the military government tilted the scales by keeping away the leading claimants of the voters' trust. The MMA's success is attributed to the military's help, direct and indirect. The military–Islamists alliance, firmed up in the Afghan *jehad*, bore fruit for the Islamists in the 2002 elections. The process of Islamization has swung back and forth between the electoral and agitational/*jehadist* tracks in the 1990s.

The restoration of democracy (1988) did not affect the laws and policies introduced under the Islamization program. Although repeatedly condemned by national and international human rights and women's organizations, even the blasphemy law and the women's evidence or *zina* provisions could not be amended. The Islamists mounted loud protests even at a hint that any element of the Islamization program was going to be touched. It is another matter that with time the Islamic provisions seem worn out, compromised by corruption and contradictions.

The enforcement of the Islamic provisions, like all other policies and regulations, has been episodic and prone to manipulation. Often they were observed in form and symbols rather than in substance and meaning. The Jamaat would organize marches to protest women newscasters appearing on TV without headscarves but was not moved by the epidemic of bride-burning by husbands and in-laws. "Shariatization" (bringing laws in conformity with Islamic jurispudence, that is, *Shariat*) of laws brought to the surface the "old juristic and doctrinal differences not only between the Shias and Sunnis but also among the four Sunni schools themselves."[47] The *qisas* and *diyat* laws allowed murderers to be set free if they paid blood money to the victims' families. These laws promised a reduction of crime through community mediation in murder vendettas. Yet the incidence of murders increased rather than fell after the enactment of these laws: the total number of murders in 1984 was 5,104, in 1989 7,928, in 1994 8,303, and in 1999 9,332. Rich and influential persons could escape punishment by paying off victims' families under the *qisas* provision.[48] This is an illustration of how Islamization could not break the mold of the soft state that Pakistan has become.

The decade of 1988–99 had two distinct types of public sentiments: first, the conservative-centrism of Nawaz Sharif's PML; and second, the liberal-pragmatism of Benazir Bhutto's PPP. Bhutto's rule offered greater freedom of expression and it had a more liberal outlook than the Nawaz Sharif government. Within the Islamic discourse, the Bhutto years were slightly more tolerant of liberal interpretations of Islam. Yet after Zia's Islamization, the democratic era as a whole did little to open up the Islamic discourse. Puritanical doctrines and hard-edged views remained ascendant. For example, Masood Khuderposh led the *namaz* (prayers) in Urdu/Punjabi, an isolated experiment in the 1960s, but such a viewpoint was almost inconceivable in the 1990s.[49] Islamic revivalism had such a forceful presence that liberal Islam could not even be broached systematically, except in the English language media catering to the modern segments of the urban middle class. The widely disseminating Urdu media essentially remained wedded to doctrinal orthodoxy.

Jehadis and violence

In the second phase of the third period, militant Islamists, sectarian fundamentalists, and nonstate *jehadis* assumed the mantle of defenders of Islam. By the 1990s, they had come to form a fearsome group in Pakistani society. Splintered into small groups, Islamic militants and *jehadis* operated from different platforms outside the political arena. They preached *jehad* and resorted to marches and agitation to press their demands, while keeping away from elections. They projected themselves as fighters for Islam and were not reluctant to use violence for suppressing so called un-Islamic activities. For example, there were annual attacks, orchestrated by Shabab-i-Milli (youth wing of the Jamaat), on New Year parties in clubs and hotels.

Among the more notable *jehadi* organizations were Lashkar-e-Toyba, Jaish-e-Mohammad, Harkat-ul-Ansar, Hezb-ul-Mujahideen, and a few others.[50] These organizations recruited young men, ran training camps, carried out *jehadist* operations in Kashmir and propagated armed struggle for Islam through sermons and publications. By combining extremist doctrines with the warrior posture, these organizations became the "default" option of Islamization in Pakistan. They operated independently of the Islamic political parties but had their sympathies and support.

I am using the past tense in describing the *jehadi* organizations, although most of them remain active, because they have changed names and reincarnated themselves as *dawah* (disseminators of the message of Islam) organizations after being branded terrorists by the USA and being ostensibly banned by General Musharraf's government in 2002.[51] Whether any of the *jehadi* organizations were involved in the murder of French engineers or bomb blasts at the Sheraton Hotel and the US consulate in Karachi (2004) may not be provable, but they contributed to a climate of religious intolerance and extremism.

International terrorism has found fertile ground in Pakistan. On being driven out of Afghanistan (2002), members of Al-Qaeda (Osama Bin Laden's *jehadi* network founded in Afghanistan) dispersed among Afghan refugees living in Pakistan. They also found sympathizers among Pakistani supporters of Afghans' anti-Soviet *jehad*. Their presence drew the attention of the USA and prompted Pakistan's government to crack down on them, much to Islamic militants' anger. Thus international and local Islamic militancy have linked together to further fan sectarian violence and perpetrate mayhem in Pakistan.

The Ahmadis had long been the victims of the Islamists. Their plight did not register noticeably on the public conscience because of their small number and their helplessness. When the Sunni extremists targeted Shias, a wave of attacks and counterattacks was ignited, resulting in the bombing of mosques and murder of religious leaders and prominent individuals. Inflammatory writings and sermons were traded between Sunni Sipah-e-Sahaba and Shia Tehrik-i-Nifaz-I-Fiqh-I-Jaafria.[52] From sermons to guns and bombs was a short distance. Sectarian organizations of both groups sponsored armed bands, Lashkar-e-Jhangvi (Sunni) and Sipah-e-Mohammad (Shia), which murdered local leaders and the professionals of the other sect in Karachi and towns of southern districts in Punjab.[53] An environment of disorder and insecurity prevailed across the land in the 1990s and the early 2000s.

From newspaper headlines, I have estimated that there were 85 major incidents of bomb blasts, resulting in 714 deaths initially although many more were injured during the decade of Afghan *jehad* (1981–90). The legacy of those times has morphed into regular attacks on sectarian, Western, and public institutions in Pakistan. In the decade 1991–2000, there were 60 incidents of bomb blasts that made newspaper headlines resulting in 312 deaths. This level of violence has become "normal" in Pakistan. In 2004, for example, there were 12 bomb attacks killing and maiming hundreds of persons.

Although not all, most of these bombs blasts were attributable to the sectarian strife.[54] So widespread was religious militancy that in February 2004, the Punjab police identified 377 persons as sectarian terrorists in the province.[55] Sectarian violence has ironically turned mosques into some of the most dangerous places; Friday congregations now routinely need to be guarded by armed guards. Sectarianism has turned out to be the unintended outcome of Islamic revival in Pakistan and a spillover of Afghan *jehad*.

A discredited leader often falls back on the idea of reviving Islam as his/her mission. Bhutto found Islam at the hour of his unpopularity. Zia legitimized his long rule through Islamization. Faced with challenges from the Supreme Court, the military and the opposition parties, Nawaz Sharif introduced the Shariat Bill in the National Assembly (1998) to enforce Islamic practices and morals and for "promoting virtue and suppressing vice." Pakistan narrowly escaped this attempt at the further curtailment of individual freedom. The Bill was still awaiting the Senate's vote when Sharif's government was overthrown by General Musharraf (1999). The provisions of this bill have resurfaced in the Hasba Act of the MMA provincial government in the NWFP (2005).[56] It appears that there is always another road to cross in the march toward an Islamic order: It is a utopia, built upon the reinvention of traditions.

Social impacts of Islamization

In the third period, Pakistani society has almost undergone a cultural revolution. Religious observances and pieties have been embedded into everyday life. *Sharia* laws and Islamic juridical doctrines have been grafted onto the legal system. Banking and finance have been given an Islamic face. Murders can be settled by blood money. *Mullahs* and orthodox Islamists proclaim *jehad* and pronounce judgments about people's beliefs and behavior, claiming authority as the guardians of Islam. The rights of women and minorities have been whittled down. Islamic networks have been woven into the social structure. These changes have fulfilled many of the demands of the Islamists. Yet these measures have fragmented society and fomented the following social changes.

- Islamization has laid the ideological baseline. The laws, policies, and institutions created under the Islamization program of the 1980s have become the sociological baseline for Pakistani society. Any public move to fine-tune or amend them is strongly protested until it is withdrawn.
- Religious beliefs and practices, economic mores, and everyday behavior glaringly contradict each other. Family life as lived is widely different from the accepted mores of family relations. Economic behavior diverges from professed moral standards. Islamic tolerance is preached while sectarian violence rages.

- In the third period, the process of promoting Islamic ideology has split into two tracks: the electoral/legislative track, followed opportunistically by the Islamic political parties; and the agitational/*jehadist* track pursued by militant organizations.
- The privatization of *jehad* has led to a breakdown of law and order. The authority of the state has been severely strained.
- Islamization has sharpened the sectarian divide and highlighted denominational differences.
- The collaboration of the military and Islamists has been the primary force advancing Islamic ideology in the third period. Islamic parties have persistently failed to gain authority through open elections but their successes have come from street protests and the military's patronage.

Islamic discourse and social life

At this juncture, the questions raised at the beginning of the chapter need to be revisited, to tease answers out of the foregoing historical account. First, I will examine how Islamic conceptions and related sociopolitical actions have affected social life in Pakistan. The converse of this question will be addressed later.

Religious observances

The story of the impact of Islamic discourse on social life can be characterized as transformative, almost revolutionary, in public behavior. A very visible impact is in the increased observance of religious pieties in everyday life. Up to the late 1970s, a sizable minority of the population, predominantly elderly, performed obligatory *namaz* (prayers) on a daily basis. Perhaps in the only social survey of religious attitudes and practices of a sample of Muslims in Pakistan (college lecturers in Lahore) in 1959, I found that the largest group (52 percent) performed *namaz* irregularly, not daily, and the next category was those praying once a day, and less than a quarter (22 percent) fulfilled the obligatory five times a day requirement.[57] I expect that now the proportion of those who pray regularly would be much higher. There is no comparable survey, but other indicators of the incidence of religious observances, newspaper accounts, and general observations stand behind my estimate.

The Islamization of the 1980s fostered a culture of public observance of prayers and pieties. It does not surprise anyone now if during a flight someone starts praying in the aisles. Pakistan's cricket team was photographed lining up to pray on the grounds at a match with India in March 2004, a practice almost unthinkable in the 1970s and even the 1980s. In meetings, conferences, or weddings, the call to *namaz* suspends proceedings and even the not-very-observant Muslims feel compelled to line up for prayers. In earlier times, religiously inclined persons prayed mostly in private and refrained from public demonstration.

Women's *dars* (sermons) have become a popular occasion for gatherings of family and friends in middle-class urbanites' homes. Doctors, engineers, and civilian and military officers, among others, seek *murshads* (spiritual guides).

Young men sporting green, black, or white turbans, emblems of different evangelical persuasions, throng city streets.[58] Only a rare individual would observe *aitkaff* (the practice of intensive and exclusive devotional week-long prayers in the month of Ramadan) up to the 1970s but by the late 1990s and 2000s thousands were filling up mosques for this optional religious exercise every year.[59] Islamic observances have swept large sections of the middle and upper classes in the cities. In comparison to them, the poor and the illiterate have not become more visibly religious than they were in the past. The weekly *Economist*'s correspondent observes, "cities seem to have more fundamentalists than the countryside, and the north is certainly more religious than the south."[60] These observations point toward the social bases of Islamic revivalism.

Urban–rural differences in Islamic devotions

Islamic revivalism has been primarily an urban phenomenon. Cities are the centers of the Islamic discourse. It is there that the ideas and actions of Islamization are essentially formulated, discussed, and enacted. Islamic parties and their student/ youth wings are primarily based in cities, although there are pockets of rural/tribal revivalists in NWFP's tribal and northern belt.

Urban Islam tends to be relatively puritanical and textual compared to the spiritual/folk thrust of beliefs and practices in rural/tribal areas.[61] One way of highlighting the differences is to describe urban Islam as *ulema*-led and rural Islam as inspired by sufis and saints.

Rural Islam is easy-going and tolerant. It is syncretic in content and centered on *pirs* and shrines. Manzur Ejaz observes that while *ulemas* are "struck at the Islamic ideology of airwaves…at the grassroots (in villages) society has become more liberal."[62]

Akbar Ahmed identifies three archetypes of Islamic leaders, *mullah, mian* (sufis), and *sayyed*. The Islam of *mullahs* is exegetic, strict, and legalist[63] and thrives in urban areas. Sufis promise personal salvation by the divine grace. Sufism's roots are in rural shrines. The *sayyeds* are venerated for being descendants of the Prophet and inheritors of his temporal legacy. They are the upper castes in both urban and rural communities, although in rural Sindh they have large followings.

Overlaying rural–urban variations in the institutional practice of Islam are class and educational differences. Islamic revivalism is rooted in newly educated and prospering groups. They are urban by outlook and lifestyle, even those who live in villages and country. The upwardly mobile village families, who are educated and switch to industrial and service occupations, are drawn to relatively more exegeses-driven Islamic discourse. The saints-and-shrines infused Islam of personal salvation yields to *Sharia* norms and denominationally defined practices. This transformation follows the movement from lower to middle classes and from rural to urban ethos. A few examples will help illustrate this point.

Farm women work in fields and go about with uncovered faces. When sons become clerks or overseers, the young women of the family begin to observe *purdah* and don a *burqa* (body and face veil). When a family becomes rich and rises into the upper strata, its women may discard *burqa* and go about without a veil. The new custom of wearing a *hijab* among female students and professionals in cities is a modern form of the *burqa*, that is, covering the head but leaving the face open.[64] Veiling has been essentially a lower-middle-class custom, but in the late 1990s it has morphed into *niqab* (face wrapped but eyes visible) among conservative Muslim women, many of whom fully participate in public life. This example underlines differences in norms of women's modesty across the social and geographic spectrum as well as over time. Rural–urban differences overlap with social-class divergences of norms.

Rural boys and girls, on joining colleges in towns and cities, are swept into the folds of the IJT and other Islamic student bodies. They fervently vote for Islamists in college/university elections, while back home in national or local elections they vote for the Muslim League or the People's Party.[65] It appears that social context has a strong bearing on commitment to Islam.

Finally, the popularity of the Tablighi Jamaat (Missionary society) from the 1980s on is another example of the social dynamics of Islamic revivalism in Pakistan.[66] The Tablighis commit themselves to conform to Islamic edicts, lead devotional livese, and "periodically withdraw from worldly engagements and go on missionary expeditions."[67] They profess to be nonpolitical and nonmilitant, committed only to following the simple and devoted Islamic way of life, with emphasis on prayers and pieties, and to bringing this message to other Muslims. The Tablighi Jamaat had a small following until the late 1970s but it flourished in the era of Islamization. Groups of Tablighis could be seen saying prayers or chanting the *kalima* (profession of faith) at airports, bus stops, or other places of public gathering. They have been the pioneers of public pieties.

The Tablighi Jamaat has become very popular in the third period. Its annual gatherings in Raiwind draw hundreds of thousands of devotees for three days of collective prayers and "purging one's sins."[68] It is also an urban movement. It has little presence in villages and tribal areas. Again bazaar merchants, urban professionals, white-collar workers, and retired officers predominate in the ranks of the Tablighis. Yet it might be noted that these social classes are also the primary purveyors of corruption, black market, and public malfeasance. The Tablighis are not known to be more conscientious in commercial dealings or more public spirited than non-Tablighis of comparable occupations and social standing.[69] Their religiosity has not fostered public morality.

Sectarianism

The sharpening of denominational identities and increasing sectarian violence have been another impact of Islamic revivalism. Like any other religion, Islam admits a wide range of interpretations and includes numerous sects. The history of Islamic sects in Pakistan goes back almost to the beginning of Islam in the subcontinent. Different sects have lived side by side in relative peace and interdependence for centuries, although occasionally a zealous ruler or local strap would persecute minorities or Muslims of other sects to enforce "authentic" Islam.

In the early years of Pakistan, specifically in the initial two periods, sectarian violence was a rare and highly localized event, often driven by a clash of economic or political interests and exploited by extremist *mullahs*. There were periodic incidents of Sunni–Shia tensions about Muharram (annual commemoration of Imam Hussain's martyrdom) processions, or occasional wars of pamphlets and sermons between Ahl-i-Hadith and Ahl-i-Sunna over fine theological points, yet they seldom escalated into persistent violence. By the 1990s, the situation had entirely changed.

Sectarianism as a process of marginalizing people of other sects and challenging their identity as Muslims began with the anti-Ahmadia movement (1953). Getting the Ahmadis declared non-Muslims (1974) laid a legislative path for turning rival sects into minorities. This precedent has encouraged extremists to agitate for the state's help in restricting other sects' religious and social freedoms. Sunni–Shia agitations for the recognition of their respective *fiqhs* (juridical interpretations) under Islamic laws (1980) was the first confrontation between these two major sects at the national level.[70]

Sunni–Shia differences were not the only ones to come to the surface. Within Sunni traditions, Deobandi–Brelvi and Ahl-i-Hadith disputations also flared up with the Islamization of society in the 1980s.[71] The Islamization process transformed denominational differences into political interests and sharpened sectarian consciousness. Extremists exploited sectarian consciousness to scapegoat other sects and justify violent confrontations. The result was a spate of targeted murders and bomb attacks on mosques and Imambarahs (Shia places of assembly).

Sectarian violence became a regular feature of social life from the 1980s on. Systematic data about sectarian violence are nonexistent. Punjab police reported that between 1989 and 1994, there were 862 incidents of sectarian targeting of persons and institutions, resulting in 208 persons killed and 1,629 injured.[72] These figures refer to all major and minor cases reported to the police. Regarding major incidents involving organized murders or bomb blasts, I have estimated from newspaper headlines that up to 1977, there were less than 10 incidents of sectarian riots/violence; but in the period 1978–2000, there were 76 such incidents.[73] Most of these incidents were perpetrated by Lashkar-i-Jhangvi (Sunni band) or Sipah-I-Mohammad (Shia outfit) in tit-for-tat killings and bombings.[74]

After the American invasion of Afghanistan (2002), sectarianism and anti-American terrorism were intertwined, making shootings and bombings of one kind indistinguishable from the other. The Pakistan of the early 2000s was a place without internal security and peace. A bomb blast in a seminary (2003), an attack on Hazara refugees in Quetta (2004), and the cold-blooded murder of a family in their home in Lahore (2004) are examples of incidents that spread anxiety and fear. Everybody felt vulnerable to violence but the Shias felt particularly unsafe in their homes and workplaces.[75]

Sectarian violence came largely in the form of attacks on individuals or gathering places. Its most common manifestation was as an act of terror against a specific target. It did not normally escalate into communal riots or pitched battles between rival groups, except on the day of some extraordinary incident. Sectarian differences did not affect everyday life. People of all sects have continued to live and work side-by-side in harmony.

Islamization has been the necessary condition for sectarianism but for sectarian differences to morph into violence, the sufficient condition is competition for economic or political power at the local level. A case in point is the Jhang district. It has become the wellspring of Sunni extremism, as the home of Sipah-I-Sahaba and its strike arm, the Lashkar-i-Jangvi. The rival feudal factions have played on Sunni–Shia identities to win elections and patronize firebrand *mullahs* to mobilize votes. The Arian clans, which had settled in the district after independence, challenged the historic economic dominance of Shia merchants and landlords. Thus the confluence of feudal rivalries and Arian–Shia competition created conditions that allowed extremism to flourish.[76] The point of this example is that sectarianism is not just a religious argument and dispute; it is also a social and economic power struggle played in the religious arena.

To sum up this discussion of sectarianism in Pakistan, its salient points are recapitulated below.

- Sectarianism grew in parallel with the Islamization process. From occasional local disputes about religious beliefs and customs in the 1960s and the 1970s, sectarian differences have evolved into attacks on individuals and institutions of other sects by the 1990s and 2000s.
- The precedent of pressing the state's powers into the service of sectarian objectives, first applied to expel the Ahmadis from Islam, has embroiled the state in denominational disputes.
- Sectarianism has become a source of endemic violence, largely through acts of terrorism. However sectarian violence has not turned into communal riots.
- Sectarian violence tends to be concentrated in a few cities and regions, such as Karachi, Lahore, and southern Punjab's towns. In these areas denominational differences have been woven into local economic and political feuds and turned into sectarian incidents.
- Sectarianism is largely an urban phenomenon. Its social base is in the lower middle strata of, primarily, the "bazaar sector." Religious seminaries and *madrassahs* are the nurseries of sectarian soldiers.[77]
- The Iranian revolution and the Afghan Resistance have spilled into Pakistan, fostering sympathetic groups and fueling sectarian militancy. They have also been a source of arms and money for sectarian organizations.
- Zealous *mullahs* have used blasphemy and *Hudood* laws to harass rivals and to foment sectarian hostilities.
- Despite sectarian violence and the insecurity that it engenders, different sects have continued to live in mixed neighborhoods without much tension. However, increasing religiosity promotes sectarian consciousness even in urban middle classes.[78]

Islamic civil society

The Islamic discourse has also inspired social service organizations, universities, schools, clubs, associations, labor unions, student bodies, professional societies, and community organizations. These "intermediary" organizations that mediate between the state and citizens qualify as elements of civil society, which has been defined as the terrain for "private pursuit of public purpose."[79] Islamic organizations and associations have multiplied to the point that they constitute a distinct sector within civil society.

The trend of forming Islamic associations can be traced back to the early days of British colonialism. Here I am speaking about the voluntary or self-help associations of modern vintage and not the traditional Islamic institutions such as mosques, shrines, and *madrassahs*. Those traditional institutions have always been anchors of Muslim/community life. They have continued to thrive and multiply in Pakistan. The modern Islamic sector in civil society is relatively recent in origins.

From the founding of the Mohammadan Anglo-Oriental College at Aligarh (1875), to the organization of the Anjuman Himayat-i-Islam (Islamic promotion society) in 1884 in Lahore and the establishment of Islamia Colleges in Lahore (1892) and Peshawar (1914) are series of initiatives that marked the beginning of a Muslim movement for civic engagement and institution-building. From these beginnings, the Islamic sector in civil society has grown steadily; yet it blossomed from the 1980s onwards.

In the first two periods of Pakistan's history, Islamic political parties, particularly the Jamaat, spun off student organizations, lawyers' circles, Islamic labor unions and literary clubs, etc. These organizations were part of the modern segment of civil society, which also included Islamic charities for hospitals, women's homes, schools, and orphanages. Both the traditional and modern elements of civil society continued to develop with explicit Islamic imprimaturs. The Edhi Foundation and the Ansar Burney Trust are two well-known examples of such post-Pakistan civic organizations that cut across ethnic and community lines.

Coinciding with the Islamization process and the availability of *zakat* funds in the third period, conventional Islamic organizations flourished. The *madrassahs* multiplied exponentially. Although accurate figures about *madrassahs* are hard to come by, some idea of their growth can be gained from the example of the four southern Punjab divisions (Bahawalpur, Multan, Dera Ghazi Khan, and Sargodha): the number of *madrassahs* in these divisions was 551 in 1975, but it more than tripled to 1768 in 1994.[80] The Federal Ministry of Education reported a total of 3,807 *madrassahs* in the whole of Pakistan in 1999, the Punjab province leading with 1,800, followed by NWFP with 700, Sindh with 550, and Balochistan with 450.[81]

Regardless of data limitations, it is a fact that *madrassahs* and seminaries have increased manifold since 1980. Teaching opportunities opened for graduates of seminaries with the introduction of Islamic studies at all educational levels, even in engineering and medical study programs. *Madrassahs* and seminaries issue juridical opinions on people's behavior, social trends, and public policies. General Musharraf's government accepted seminary diplomas as equivalent to college degrees for eligibility to contest the 2002 Assembly elections. These measures undoubtedly enhanced the influence of theological schools.

Almost every social institution and professional association has developed an Islamic stream, organized formally or informally as clubs, circles, and networks. A fissure runs through civil society dividing Islamic from secular organizations.

Erosion of the state

Islamic organizations operate almost like estates within the state. *Ulemas* issue *fatwas* (binding opinions) about national policies, be it Kashmir, trading with India, or the decision to send a women's hockey team to the Olympics. General Musharraf's government denies sending *jehadis* into Indian-held Kashmir, but Hafiz Saeed, leader of Lashkar-e-Tayyba proclaims that the Kashmir *jehad* will continue.[82] Maualana Abdul Hadi of Tanzeem-e-Itthad Ulema of Khyber declares that registering female voters is against Islamic traditions. His *fatwa* scuttles voter registration and the government does not react.[83] Such incidents became common in the third period and the Islamic discourse turned into a parallel political process.

Islamic legal provisions have been used by zealous Islamists to implement their personal views. The session (district) judge of Gujranwala effectively banished music concerts and theater from the district by threatening to prosecute famous singers and musicians for "obscenity and immorality."[84] The *mullahs* rail against women's pictures displayed on billboards and whip up crowds to deface them. A divine of Chakwal gathers his followers to lay siege on Islamabad to demand Quranic rule and the government sends emissaries to negotiate with him. In remote regions, such as Northern Areas, Dir, and Dera Ghazi Khan districts, *mullahs* run private courts, collect *zakat* and intimidate state functionaries. The state ignores these challenges to its authority. These trends have gained momentum with the privatization of *jehad*. The conclusion is that the state's authority has steadily diffused since the 1980s.

Compartmentalization of social life

Despite the pervasiveness of Islamic observances and public religiosity, the Islamic discourse remains compartmentalized on the rhetorical plane of social life.[85] Islamization has affected people's images and beliefs about how they live. This is the imagined culture, which is suffused with Islamic imagery. Yet the lived culture, namely how people actually live, continues to be driven by secular socio-economic forces.

Undoubtedly, imagined and lived cultures are always at some variance from each other. Anthropologists have long recognized the difference between ideal and real cultures.[86] Yet in Pakistan the imagined culture has been Islamized, whereas the lived culture continues to be effectively secular except in symbols. This thematic distance between imagined and lived cultures reflects the compartmentalization of social life. Some examples will illustrate this phenomenon.

If one were to pick up a newspaper or better still watch Pakistani television, one would conclude that Islam is the preeminent and perhaps the only preoccupation of people: they think about it, talk about it, and give it precedence over all other considerations. A similar impression comes from listening to people's everyday talk. Even in mundane matters Allah's grace is sought, the Prophet's blessings are invoked, and Islamic rituals are observed. Yet the same persons in their economic dealings, work habits, and lifestyles are, by and large, unmindful of what they profess. Acquisitive interests and material considerations with strong inclinations to disregard laws and public obligations drive everyday life.

A case in point is the traffic situation on Pakistan's roads and streets.[87] Almost every trip is begun with *Bismillah* (in the name of God the compassionate, the merciful), yet on roads the traffic rules are habitually flouted and little regard is given to safety of either oneself or others. The moral principles of Islam are not reflected in road behavior. Pakistan's chaotic road traffic is the best illustration of professed piety and personal irresponsibility.

Ulemas and Islamic parties have been railing for decades against the obscenity of Bollywood movies and the immorality of New Year's parties and Basant (spring kite-flying festival) celebrations. They have organized demonstrations, put forth legislative motions, and provoked attacks on people indulging in such pleasures. Yet their pronouncements have had no effect; rather Basant has become a national day of kite-flying and partying even in areas where it was almost unknown. Bollywood videos have become the staple of home entertainment even in conservative households and in remote villages.

Similarly, ethnic and regional interests invariably trump Islamic brotherhood. The Jamaat's hold over Karachi's voters broke down with the rise of Muhajir consciousness. Pashtoon or Balochi solidarity has repeatedly swept aside appeals to Islamic unity in elections. In universities and colleges, the IJT faces stiff competition from ethnic or caste/clan organizations.

In brief, the evolving social life in Pakistan exemplifies the phrase, the Islamization of the imagination and the secularization of actions.

How has social life affected the Islamic discourse?

So far I have focused on how the Islamic discourse has affected social life in Pakistan. There is another side to this story, namely how changing social patterns have affected the Islamic discourse, that is, what conceptions and beliefs underlie the idea of Islamic order in the various periods? This question will be addressed below.

Over the three periods of Pakistan's social history, conceptions of Islamic order and the ideologies of their advocates changed in parallel with the evolving social and political situation. In the early years of independent Pakistan, the Islamic narrative emphasized the fostering of righteous behavior among individuals and creating an Islamic constitution for the state. The Islamic order was conceived in moral as well as legislative terms. It was envisaged to be built from the bottom up by reforming and reeducating individuals. The Islamists were confident that righteous Muslims would vote them to power, hence their faith in democracy. In the first period, the Islamic discourse was anticommunist (said to be Godless) and steered a middle course between capitalism and socialism.[88]

The national mood of populist socialism in the second period had a profound impact on the Islamic discourse. The Islamic welfare state and *musawat-i-Mohammadi* (Mohammad's social justice) became the lodestars of the Islamic order. It was a notable reformulation of earlier conceptions and goals.

The third period witnessed a series of further shifts in the Islamic narrative. The first shift was to view cultural transformation as the path to Islamic order. The Islamization program attempted to reorder social relations and cultural norms through *Hudood* and other laws. The second shift was the downplaying of democracy as an element of the Islamic order. The support that Zia's military government got from Islamic parties had a feedback effect on the Islamic narrative. Authoritarianism was acceptable if exercised to advance Islamic goals, it was argued. The third shift was toward conservatism in the Islamic discourse. Liberal Islamic viewpoints were effectively driven off the public platform. Segregation of women was idealized. Sectarian differences were highlighted. Militancy for Islam was justified as a necessary means for bringing about Islamic order. Cultural traditions were often invested with Islamic legitimacy.

Invention of traditions

Eric Hobsbawm's concept of the invention of tradition refers to the phenomenon of formalizing and ritualizing practices and rules by legitimizing them as historic norms.[89] The Islamic discourse in Pakistan has been continually inventing traditions. It holds the sayings and practices of the early days of Islam in Arabia as guides for present times. It legitimizes its political objectives on the sacred traditions of those times, and reinforces practices that emerged in medieval India or Iran. The patriarchal family, the arranged marriage, or landlordism are examples of social practices legitimized as elements of Islamic traditions by a majority of *ulemas* although these customs have been questioned by the liberal-reformist interpreters of Islam.

A common form of invented tradition is to read into the past modern ideas and practices. The Islamists have argued that human rights or women's equality, for example, were practiced in Islam long before the West adopted them. Such assertions are meant to rationalize, and sometimes to defend against, modern ideas by locating them in traditions.

The rise of the Taliban in Afghanistan (1996) reverberated in Pakistani society. The Taliban elevated Afghan tribal customs as the Islamic creed. Their austere and authoritarian measures appealed to orthodox Islamists in Pakistan. In the tribal areas of NWFP and Balochistan, many Taliban measures were upheld as models of Islamic traditions by zealous *mullahs*. Even some urban Islamists were romanced by the "purity" of the Taliban traditions. The Taliban's anti-westernism made them all the more popular among conservative sections of the population. The Taliban's Islam was certainly an invented tradition for Pakistan.

For a long time, green has been the Islamic color. Holy persons don green turbans or scarves as a mark of their devotion. The Taliban wore black turbans which became emblems of resurgent Islam. Soon the black turban was held by some to be the tradition of the Prophet. Thus even in the choice of color, a new tradition was invented. Such currents of inventing and reinventing traditions have coursed through the Islamic narrative in Pakistan.

Social organization of the Islamic discourse

The Islamic discourse has flourished largely during periods of military rule when Islamic parties aligned with the military. During periods of electoral democracy, Islamic symbols and rhetoric thrived but the influence of Islamists declined.

The Islamic ideology has been expressed through student activism, particularly in science and engineering faculties. Islamic student organizations and youth groups have been in the forefront of revivalist movements. Many have carried Islamic ideologies with them to their occupations and professions on graduation, thereby giving rise to Islamic factions within urban middle and upper classes.

Mullahs and their disciples in *madrassahs* have been the historic advocates of Islamic order. Their social status has improved in the third period. Thus the confluence of mosque-affiliated social groups and sections of the emerging urban middle class has created a sizable social base for the Islamic ideology.

The Islamic discourse has been advanced by the activism of small and close-knit groups, like the IJT, the Tablighis, and the Jamaat. The bonding in such groups nourishes the commitment of members to the Islamic ideology. Doctors, engineers, merchants, and other members of the middle class become the purveyors of Islamic ideas. *Madrassahs* provide foot soldiers for street power (for agitations and intimidations), but the Islamic segments of the emerging middle classes act as the vanguard of Islamic movements.

The Islamization program raised the status of the *ulemas* and *mullahs* and opened new opportunities for them in public affairs. A large number of *ulemas* became rich and powerful. While historically the *ulemas* lived simply with little income and continual dependence on charity, after the Islamization program new and lucrative opportunities have opened for them. Many have become very rich; leaders live in luxury.[90] They reside in posh bungalows, are chauffeured around in fancy cars, and employ security guards for their protection. Occupational affiliation with Islamic institutions has become economically rewarding.

In the 1990s, militants and *jehadis* introduced a violent streak to the Islamic discourse. These small and marginal groups have had a disproportionate public presence in the Islamic discourse. They have reinforced orthodoxy and discouraged public discussion of Islamic ideas.

Islamic revivalism and modernization

At this juncture, the question arises as to how Islamization has been affecting the process of modernization in Pakistan. The two processes are largely compartmentalized in their respective spheres, namely material and legal/cultural. Yet they clash as well as complement each other in myriad ways. The net result is a state of moral uncertainty and social cleavages. These points are elucidated below.

The Islamic discourse lays claim to its own form of modernity. It locates the origins of human rights, social justice, and even scientific progress in Islam and the civilization it spawned. It espouses these values and ideals in abstract and maintains that they have been appropriated by the West. Yet in translating them into institutions and practices, the Islamic discourse diverges significantly from modernity. It rejects Western individualism, sexual mores, gender relations, personal liberties, and consumerism but accepts individual enterprise and a form of capitalism restrained by "interest-free" transactions. It offers a morally guided social order that turns out to be a re-enactment of many agrarian/tribal practices packaged in a collectivist polity. The net result is an imbalance between what is said and what is practiced. Islamic measures enacted in Pakistan have not fulfilled their social objectives even partially.

The conflation of westernization and modernization in Islamic critiques of modernity allows Islamists to play on Pakistani nationalism and cultural pride. Yet many ideals and values of modernization, as discussed in Chapter 2, are universal. The Islamization process in Pakistan has shown no promise of realizing increases in productivity, socioeconomic equalization, efficiency, rationality, orderliness, punctuality, gender equality, individual rights, freedom, and other ideals of modernity. A certain degree of commonality of institutions and norms across cultures is inevitable if modern production and values are to be realized.

There cannot be an efficient factory without a regime of punctuality, secondary relations, fair wages, and impersonal rules for example, in sum a modern industrial organization. The material and cultural/moral aspects cannot be separated, one guided by technology and the other by orthodox Islamic norms. They have to dovetail into each other functionally. Similarly, as discussed in Chapter 6, modern urban life precipitates some imperatives whose fulfillment is a prerequisite for livability and productivity. All in all, modernization has some universal values and institutional forms. Pakistan's Islamization has, by and large, not realized both these in ideals and in practice. Instead it has fostered social divisions by giving rise to Islamic segments in schools, colleges, professions, politics, and social classes.

Overview: Islam and social transformation

Islam has flourished in Pakistan. From a religious institution, it has evolved into a social movement that has transformed Pakistan's culture and society in 55 years of independence. Its influence has not spread linearly but in a sequence of explosive leaps and quiet retreats. Its means have grown from sermons and proselytizing to political campaigns, electioneering, and agitation to capturing state authority for extending its influence. Lately, a violent streak has emerged with rising militancy among Islamists.

In Pakistan, Islamic revivalist mores and practices have spread from the spiritual/sacred sphere to the political, social, and economic domains of life. This permeation of religious values and themes in other social institutions is a measure of Islam's spreading influence in society.

Islamic norms and values were observed for long by ardent Muslims in their private life, but they were institutionalized as public practices largely in one fell swoop by General Zia's Islamization program. Through a series of ordinances, Islamic laws and punishments were enacted, religious observances were encouraged, school curricula were revised, the economy was realigned, and Islamists were installed in positions of power. These measures constituted a near-cultural revolution. Public life was transformed, inducing religious observances in everyday life, promoting pieties in verbal/symbolic behavior, layering Islamic rules and punishments over common law institutions, and realigning community relations.

Islamization also fostered the formation of Islamic networks within institutions and organizations. It strengthened the power base of Islamists in military and civil bureaucracies as well as in business and education. Altogether Islamization has realigned Pakistan's social and cultural systems. The spread of Islam as a political ideology has produced many intended as well as unintended effects.

The intended effects were aimed at two levels, symbolic and normative. Symbolically Islamic practices have swept through much of public life. Pakistani television announces prayer timings; devotes many hours to recitations and sermons; and even its entertainment programs, plays, and discussions in particular are built around Islamic themes. Mosques regularly broadcast the *azan* (call to prayers), Quranic recitations, and sermons on loudspeakers. Almost everywhere in Pakistani cities, *azans* and recitations fill the air. Despite many petitions, successive governments have shied away from applying noise control regulations on mosques. Architecture and art increasingly adopt Islamic motifs. The point is that Islamic symbols, sayings, and practices have gained prominence in public space. These developments have come in full force since the 1980s. Before that, such symbols and practices were largely private and not so prominent in public life.

Normative impacts of Islamic revivalism appear in many forms. The most visible is the increase in religious observances by people. Women's rights and personal freedom regarding marriage, inheritance, and public participation are another set of rules and norms that have been drastically redefined. Along the same lines non-Muslim minorities and even Islamic sects of small followings have been marginalized. Educational curricula have been packed with conservative Islamic learning said to be historically inaccurate and socially divisive.[91] Banks offer "profit" and not interest on savings. *Zakat* and *usher* taxes have been levied. All in all, the infusion of Islam in social institutions has introduced systematic changes in the normative order.

The ultimate aim of these intended normative and symbolic changes was the promotion of a virtuous, moral, and orderly Islamic society. After about two decades of the implementation of these measures and five decades of the Islamic discourse, that social aim remains elusive.

Pakistani society continues to be racked by corruption, inefficiency, black marketing, and indiscipline. Sectarian violence and *jehadist* terrorism have become a condition of life in Pakistan, so much so that Pakistan has been branded a failed state by some Western observers. The material and moral interests that underlie an individual's everyday behavior are untouched by values and norms subscribed to verbally and symbolically. A fissure has appeared between the verbal/symbolic values and the moral economy of behavior. Pakistani society is stuck between conservative Islamism and the imperatives of a semi-industrialized economy and nationalist polity.

The unintended effects of Islamic measures include the rise of sectarianism and militancy, the reinforcement of traditionalism, and mutually contradictory norms and values. With the state's backing, the Islamic discourse in Pakistan has privileged the Sunni–Deobandi–Wahabi discourse. Other sects and minorities have been marginalized, thereby sharpening denominational differences and fostering sectarian strife. The Islamic narrative itself has changed from the reformist-democratic orientations of the 1960s to the agitational politics of the 1970s and the authoritarian transformation of culture and society in the 1980s. Within Islam, the conservative-literalist school has swept aside the liberal-interpretative tradition.

External influences, such as the Iranian revolution, the Afghan *jehad,* and Saudi Arabia's oil-wealth-driven Wahabism, have complemented the Islamization program to spawn *jehadist* organizations and extremist ideologies. The US has also contributed to the rise of Islamic extremism by its massive support of Afghan resistance to the Soviet Union in the 1980s and even earlier in the 1960s by aiding Islamic institutions to contain the spread of atheistic communism. Cumulatively these factors have privatized *jehad.* Islamic extremism is their unintended consequence. Overall social life in Pakistan at the beginning of the twenty-first century is deficient in peace, security, and harmony.

Islamic ideology has also gained ground with the collapse of international socialism and within Pakistan by the discrediting of Bhutto's socialist rhetoric. Islam has emerged as an idealistic vision for the youth who hunger for purposeful social change. The market economy, free trade, elections, or other contemporary ideologies do not satisfy people's hunger for ideals. The ideological vacuum of the globalization era is a fertile ground for the rise of Islamic or other millennial movements, as is evident from the rise of Jewish, Christian, or Hindu fundamentalism. Islamic revivalism fills this vacuum in Pakistan where mainstream political parties have no vision or ideological commitment and offer only a choice of personalities.

To conclude, I will summarize below the structural features of Pakistani society as they have evolved under the influence of the Islamic discourse.

- Urban Islam has tilted toward puritanical creeds and ritualistic observances. In contrast, rural Islam remains open and experiential. One is mosque- and sermon-based, while the other is centered on shrines and *pirs.*
- Sections of the urban middle class, both of the modern and bazaar sectors, constitute the social base of the revivalist Islam. Islamic revivalism has driven a wedge in social classes and institutions along ideological lines.
- The Islamic political parties and Islamic segments of civil society are the promoters and organizers of revivalism. *Mullahs* and *madrassahs* are the muscular arm of Islamic movements.
- While the Islamic discourse began to be modernized in the 1960s and the 1970s, from the 1980s onwards the process of locating modernity in Islamic traditions gained momentum.

- Despite the extensive visibility of Islam in the public space, the web of daily actions is increasingly driven by nonreligious motives. A paradox of symbolic religiosity and secular actions defines everyday life.
- The Islamic revival has a stock set of measures that have been enacted again and again. Banning alcohol, gambling, and obscenity is one such measure, for example, which is the signature policy of Islamic revival. These practices were banned by public orders in 1948, 1966, 1977, 1980, and 1998, and again in 2003.[92] None of these successive bans was rescinded and legally they did not have to be re-enacted. Similarly many other Islamic measures, such as restricting coeducation, promoting interest-free banking, or mandating *namaz* (prayers) during business hours, have also been enacted repeatedly by provincial or federal governments seeking to promote Islamic values. The circularity of Islamic measures suggests that the revivalist project has a narrow range of options. Its choices are limited by its social conservatism.
- Islam has touched almost all social institutions, yet it has not engendered a moral order for the contemporary challenges of economy and society. Islamists have focused on reforming outward behavior, but not the functions and meaning of actions. The result is a wide chasm between how people believe they live and how they actually live, a divergence between imagined and lived cultures.
- The centrist and totalizing narrative of the Islamic project runs counter to people's commitment to regional culture and ethnic identity. The Islamic political discourse has met strong resistance from the ethnic movements of Muhajirs, Sindhis, and Balochs.[93]
- On the intellectual and verbal plane, Islamic ideology promises a millennial moral order, yet it has not fostered a morality that helps promote efficiency, fairness, and justice in society. The increasing corruption and intensifying social problems bear evidence of moral crises in Pakistan. This has become the dilemma of Pakistan's social change. Its resolution lies in a liberal and pluralist social order, while Islam could be the source of ethical and spiritual guidance.
- The social order promised by Islamists is collectivist, centrist, and conservative in conception. It envisages promotion of virtues and suppression of vices through the application of state powers. It is not inimical to material progress and favors individual enterprise within a rigidly controlled fiscal regime.
- Islamic revivalism is a process of reinventing traditions and clothing them in modern garb. It is a program of social change that is to be implemented by "righteous" men under the tutelage of the state. It is not a project to maintain the status quo.
- Islamic ideology has thrived in the "vacuum of idealism" after the collapse of international socialism. Islamization policies of the third period have been the instruments of promoting revivalism. External events and forces, such as Afghani *jehad*, the Iranian revolution, and oil money have also facilitated the surge in Islamic ideology.

8 Family, kinship, community, and civil society

Building blocks of society

Family, kinship, clan, community, and class are the social institutions that form a bridge between individual and national society. They are the building blocks of social organization and anchors of the cultural system. How are they structured and how do they change? This question is critical for understanding both historical and emerging social patterns in a society. Of course, these institutions do not stand alone. They are interwoven with political parties, economic organizations, and religious bodies and (social) classes. Changes in these institutions course through other social structures and vice versa. These interrelations underline the systematic nature of social organization, a fact to be borne in mind. In this chapter, I aim to examine the patterns of change in the above-listed institutions and illuminate their contributions to evolving Pakistani society.

Pakistani society is rooted in primordial ties. Family, *biradari*, tribe, and ethnicity are structures that define an individual's place in society and inform her/his beliefs and behaviors, although in the postcolonial period, class too has come to have a significant bearing. These institutions also modulate social change in Pakistani society.

Family, kinship, or community may appear to be constant, but they do change, sometimes imperceptibly and at other times drastically. The family, in composition, functions, and values, was not the same in the twentieth century as it was in the nineteenth and eighteenth century, for example; it had changed from generation to generation although the change may have been glacial and not very perceptible. In the modern era, the pace of change has quickened, more so since independence.

All these institutions are loosening up, their structures are becoming more malleable, and functions are being realigned and reinterpreted. Crudely, they may be said to be modernizing, but it is a modernization within the grooves of invented traditions. They are certainly not adopting Western trends entirely, although some are being incorporated. The empirical reality of the changes in institutions in Pakistan is not fully explained by modernization theories. Later on, I will elaborate on these observations. Presently for a start, it is enough to point out that change is the order of these institutions.

The change in family or community is seamless and not divisible into distinct phases. The three periods of Pakistan's social history are not differentiable in the evolution of these middle-range institutions. Our analysis will track patterns of change in these institutions, identifying significant phases of their evolution.

In examining these institutions, I have found that it is not enough to distinguish between their "ideal" and "real" forms, namely between what they ought to be as envisioned by values and ideologies, and what they are in actual practice. The fast pace of social change induces another distinction within the real form. It widens the chasm between the imagined or the believed reality and the lived reality of a situation. For example, the "imagined" idea of a Pakistani family is that it is a harmonious and united social unit, but the observed or "lived" reality is that there are entrenched internal divisions, such as the historical strife between daughter-in-law and mother-in-law. For example, the imagined reality is not the ideal culture, but what people believe or perceive to be which may be different from what actually is. This distinction between self-perceptions of one's behavior and the actual practice is an illuminative tool in the analysis of these institutions. I have discussed "imagined" and "lived" cultures in previous chapters. In this chapter, this distinction has been applied to the internal structure of institutions.

The imagined and lived family

Almost every historical description of a Pakistani family places it squarely in the category of joint family,[1] where a patriarch or the oldest male heads not only his own conjugal family, consisting of wife and unmarried sons/daughters, but also those of his married sons'/younger brothers' households.[2] This social unit purportedly functions as one family with a single kitchen, living in the same house, sharing incomes and properties, and raising children together. The joint family is the imagined as well as the ideal (desired) household of the traditional narrative. Yet the lived family even in bygone days included many variations of this image.

Undoubtedly, the family among all ethnic groups – Punjabis, Pashtoons, Baluchis, etc. – has been and continues to be male-centered. It is patriarchal, patrilocal, and patrilineal. There is both a structural unity and temporal continuity of these qualities across Pakistan. Even traditionally, the joint ownership of land and property, living under the same roof and sharing a kitchen between three to four generations was largely a characteristic of the landowning classes. Peasants, *kammis,* and the poor had to strike out on their own early. They formed autonomous households on becoming adults and marrying. In addition, life expectancy was short and patriarchs seldom lived to be granddads for long or in vigor. Interrelated households often lived in one compound, but maintained separate kitchens, worked on their own, yet depended on each other for mutual care and support, and called themselves a family. Such an overarching family, composed of conjugal households, is better described as an extended family, although it has been often branded as a joint family (*kunba*). The Imperial Gazetteer of Punjab notes that "the joint family system of Hindu law is almost unknown to the peasantry of the province."[3] This observation is about family life in villages of the late nineteenth century.

Of course, the traditional family was not an independent conjugal unit of husband, wife and children in the modern sense. A conjugal household was closely attached to the husband's parental families, but the norms of attachment differed by regional customs, rural/urban traditions, class, and occupational caste affiliations. Some families had joint residency, others lived independently, some pooled incomes and properties, and others established a newly married couple as a separate household on the birth of a child. Families in tribal communities blended with clans or kin groups for many purposes. Yet the interlinked households united, even merged, for mutual support and in adversity. The "jointness" was more the function of need, activity, and ceremony than a condition. This was the nature of a family historically.[4]

To illustrate the variety of arrangements by which families maintain ceremonial and functional unity, the following is a revealing example of how the symbolic unity of command is maintained in some extended families. Among some clans in the old city of Lahore, it was a custom up to the 1950s that married sons ritually handed over their monthly pay packets to their fathers, who after keeping a token amount gave back most of the pay for the sons' households. Patriarchs made major family decisions ceremonially but practically these were taken by each household for itself.

Persistent forms and changing functions

The family is shrinking in size, because of both fewer births and the erosion of extended families. Sociological theories hold that modern societies tend to have nuclear families, consisting of a couple and their dependent children. This notion has arisen from the proposition that industrialization and economic development require that social status be based on an individual's achievements and knowledge, rather than on the characteristics ascribed to them on the basis of family, clan, or gender identities.[5] Individuals develop the ambition for occupational advancement and are willing to follow opportunities near or farther away from home. Such new values loosen kin ties and restructure family around the conjugal nucleus. These ideas have found a place in theories of modernization. They are affirmed by the history of change in family structure in Western societies, particularly among the middle classes whose ranks swelled with industrialization.[6]

The question is whether Asian societies are showing similar trends as they traverse the path of development. A long-running controversy among sociologists, called the "Indian joint family debate," has brought up contradictory evidence about the presumed decline of the joint family.[7] Yet from the debate, it is obvious that a family can be "joint" in many ways and under different norms, such as living under one roof, living near each other, or even in far-off places but maintaining a single ceremonial head or common property. Alternatively, the jointness could be only for specific functions or rituals, such as taking care of the elderly and widowed, or religious worship. Studies of the Indian family point out that family is an evolving institution, whose level of unity is changing as the social order changes. That is why the term extended family is more apt to describe this multifaceted phenomenon than the notion of a single joint household, which was rare even traditionally. The Pakistani family also shows a similar variety of forms historically as well as contemporaneously.

A great variety of functional jointness has been practiced in different parts of the country. Henry Korson observes about the Pakistani family that the "great majority of families were, strictly speaking, of the nuclear type, (though) many extended and joint families live in close proximity to each other, so that constant visiting of family members is evident."[8] Obviously, there has not been one type of family, but many diverse forms that continue to be rooted in values of kin solidarity and mutual care. By and large, family structures have not changed much in form, but their functions and meanings have been changing. It is these attributes that have to be tracked to observe changing functions and practices of family. I will discuss in some detail the emerging practices of marriage and the functions they serve. This detailed examination is necessary because family and marriage encapsulate almost all processes of institutional change and thus are illustrative metaphors of social change in Pakistan.

Marriage

Marriage is a practice that is fundamental to the formation of a family for producing and raising children. In Pakistan, elders from time immemorial have arranged marriages for the young. Marriage among Pakistani Muslims is predominantly endogamous, arranged within *biradari*, *kor*, or *quom*, largely with cousins. Marriage between cousins is a norm, in the sense that almost a majority of marriages have been conventionally between first or second cousins. Several studies of rural as well as urban communities suggest that overall more than 50 percent of marriages have been between cousins.[9] Such marriages have been relatively more common in villages and tribal territories than in urban areas, among Pashtoons and Balochis than among Punjabis and Sindhis. Karachi may be the only place in Pakistan where marriages between cousins may not be the norm for a majority primarily because its Muhajir population, originating from India, may not have cousins nearby to marry.

Marriage between cousins assures a degree of marital stability and familiarity with prospective partners even within a strictly sex-segregated society. It also keeps property within the family and maintains clan solidarity. However, it has adverse implications for the genetic inheritance of children. Studies of children's health and mortality, few as those are, indicate higher rates of mortality and disease among children of married cousins.[10] Historically, the Pashtoon custom of *sar paisa* or *vulver* (bride wealth) was a barrier to the marriage of poor young men. Marriage between cousins, especially the exchange of daughters in marriage between brothers' sons (*badal*), helped poor young men to find brides. In Punjab and Sindh, dowry is given to a girl on her marriage. This custom has been a source of indebtedness for the poor and even middle-class families. It is not uncommon for fathers and brothers to seek work in the oil countries of the Middle East to buy a dowry and to bear the marriage expenses of their daughters or sisters.

Marriage between cousins keeps property and wealth within a family for the middle and upper classes, but it also alleviates the burden of the poor, as relatives are restrained in their demands for dowry. Thus, such marriages are intertwined with the institutions of property, inheritance, and caste/clan, but are essentially rooted in a society of limited social and geographic mobility. As kin begin to diverge educationally, occupationally, and geographically, the matching of relatives for marriage becomes difficult. With increasing mobility, both social and geographical, marriage practices have been changing and incrementally restructuring the family.

Matchmaking: stretching traditions

Traditionally parents or guardians of boys and girls selected partners for them, while those eligible for marriage were consulted either perfunctorily or not at all. In *purdah* (custom of veiling and segregating women) observing middle and upper classes, the boy and girl did not even see each other before their marriage. Marriages were arranged to keep an extended family bonded, to settle rivalries between feuding relatives, and to maintain family harmony by bringing in pliant daughters-in-law. Compatibility or liking of partners was a secondary consideration. These were the values that sustained endogamy.

Education and industrial/professional occupations fostered new expectations of marriage, particularly among boys. Little by little, boys began to be consulted (in middle-class families girls too), in the choice of their partners, although elders had the veto. These were the norms of matchmaking at the time of independence.

The spread of bourgeois or modern middle-class values, with the post-independence economic development and urbanization, introduced notions of personal choice and love for marriage among youth of the newly affluent families. In the 1960s, the relative merits of love versus arranged marriages were a popular topic of school and college debates. Films idealized romance as a challenge to traditions, in which heroes/heroines were torn between their love and family honor.[11] Yet the tradition proved to be resilient.

Since the 1960s, love marriage has gained acceptance in a small segment of university students, urban professionals, and film and television artistes. Islamists rail against the "love matches," even though Islamic youth groups and student organizations have been serving as the stage for match-shopping among the "pious."[12] The norms of arranged marriages have perceptibly changed. They have been stretched to include chaperoned meetings or "looking and greeting" visits of prospective partners. Liberal Islamists find support for these practices in Islam. Some modern families permit an engaged couple to "go out," a practice that would have been shameful and dishonorable in the past, and is still so for many families.

Even conservative parents are adopting new modes of finding mates for their children, such as resorting to the services of marriage brokers and matchmakers. In modish circles, matchmaking websites and personal advertisements are gaining acceptance.[13] Professional matchmakers have filtered down to small towns and rural areas near cities. Thus, the traditional practices have incorporated modern means of matchmaking to fulfill demands of a mobile and burgeoning population.

Expanding the circle for mate selection

Two contradictory trends are observable in the practice of mate selection. One, proportionately more marriages are being contracted outside extended family and *biradari* than before. Two, the practice of marriage between cousins is being rein- vigorated, sometimes in families where it was not common. The former practice expands, while the latter tendency pulls back the circle of persons eligible to be mates.

Mobility has necessitated a search for mates beyond the traditional boundaries of blood relations, caste, and *biradari*. Even within the same city, suburbanization has stretched distances between members of extended families. Boys and girls grow up without knowing their relatives. Disparities of income, education, or life- style distance relatives from each other. For those who move to other cities, regions, and even countries, contacts with relatives are all the more few and far between. Such social and geographic distances erode the norm of marriage with kin.

Increasingly, marriages are being arranged on the basis of class and lifestyle compatibilities, rather than caste or family ties. Sometimes mobility leads to painful choices. The case in point is that of small sects and persecuted minorities such as Ahmadis. Ahmadi men are migrating out of Pakistan to escape discrimina- tion, leaving behind women without eligible mates. Highly educated Ahmadi women are marrying men who are taxi drivers and laborers, sometimes even as second wives.[14]

The reinvigoration of marriage between cousins is, paradoxically, also a social impact of economic development and social mobility. As individuals and families find themselves in new places and among strangers, they are excluded from sources of mates. They do not know people around them intimately. In a segre- gated society, opportunities for meeting the opposite sex are very limited. Rela- tively few young men and women have the courage and emotional skills needed for a love marriage. Marrying cousins is one of the few viable alternatives.

Women are particularly disadvantaged by the difficulties of finding suitable mates. A pervasive social problem in Pakistan has been unmarried young women "waiting for proposals" to the desperation of their parents. The conventional modes of arranged marriages are not working smoothly and the new means of matching mates have not taken hold fully. A whole generation has been caught in changing norms, an uncertainty alleviated by reverting back to the practice of cousin marriage. Difficulties in finding suitable mates have also contributed to the new customs of elaborate marriage ceremonies, feasts, and expensive dowries.

Weddings: simplicity to extravagance

Conventionally, weddings were a prime occasion for family and *biradari* gather- ings and a pleasant break from everyday life. After independence, there was a social movement for simplifying marriages and reducing the burden of dowries. The Ayub government's Commission for Eradication of Social Evils (1965) identified many social problems such as the custom among Pashtoons and Northern tribes of a large *mehr* (bridegroom's gift to bride) and *vulver*, and the practice among Punjabis and Sindhis of demanding and giving a big *dahej* (dowry) and expensive feasts. These customs were driving families into huge debts.[15] The commission recommended public education campaigns and community mobilization for eradicating the excesses of such customs.

A trend toward simplicity did begin. Bridegrooms gave up riding on a horse to the bride's home, customs of *mehndi* (putting henna on bride's hand) and *mayun* (bride and bridegroom wearing tattered clothes for a few days before the wedding to contrast with their resplendent wedding dresses) were tempered down, even abandoned by sections of urban middle classes. However, modernity and a little affluence in middle and upper classes reversed these trends in the 1970s. Weddings and dowries have become increasingly extravagant almost year by year since then.

By the 2000s, weddings had been elaborated to become a many-day affair. They have become occasions for affirming the family's social status and demonstrating its connections to the rich and powerful. How sumptuous were the meals, how famous and influential were the guests, how sparkling were the receptions, what entertainment was provided and how big was the dowry, where the newly wed honeymooned! These are becoming the defining criteria of good weddings. *Mehndi* and *mayun* ceremonies have come back with elaborate feasts, music, and dancing. Modern props have turned weddings into unending celebrations. Loudspeakers blare film songs, videos are made of marriage ceremonies, and the bride/bridegroom's homes are brightly illuminated, even by families of modest means. The rich have theme decorations and feasts, entertainment by television and film stars, honeymoons abroad, and event managers to coordinate a wedding. A veritable industry has sprung up all across Pakistan for weddings, including banquet halls, caterers, dressmakers, decorators, jewelers, etc. Pakistani cities and towns may have one of the highest ratios of jewelry and fabric/clothing stores to population, based on the demand generated by dowry and weddings; probably, only India may come close to it on this score.

The title of an article in a Pakistani weekly captures the transformation of marriage ceremonies in the words, "Weddings: from dreams to themes."[16] Weddings and especially dowry/bride price have always been a strain on families' resources. As the article notes, "it has always been like this but the trend in conspicuous consumption and statement-making is recent happening." The wedding dress of a senator's daughter was encrusted with rubies; a helicopter showered rose petals at the marriage reception of a Karachi business tycoon's son.[17] Such are the extravaganzas of the rich, which raise the bar for everybody.

There have been periodic attempts to discourage extravagances of marriage. In 1956 the Justice Rashid Commission recommended curbing large dowries. Similar policy advisory was issued in 1961, 1976, and 1984. In 1997, Nawaz Sharif's government enacted an ordinance to limit food to be served at wedding receptions, allowing only tea and cold drinks to be served to the guests. It began to have some effect, but then his government was ousted. In 2004, the Supreme Court revalidated the ordinance on an appeal. Similarly, there have been periodic marriage reform initiatives among Kashmiri, Sheikh, and Memon *biradaris*. All such initiatives wither after some time. Such are the functional imperatives of the institutions of marriage and family.

Realignment of family

Outwardly, the structure of family has changed only slightly, but internally relations and expectations have been realigned considerably. The notion that modernity means the rise of the nuclear family to the detriment of the joint family is a static representation of family structure even in Western societies. Family structure varies over the lifecycle of a generation. The Pakistani family goes through phases, growing from a nuclear family, when a recently married couple establishes a separate household, into an extended family, when its sons and sometimes daughters continue to live with parents after marriage for a few years, although eventually separating to start the cycle again. This lifecycle continues, but the time period for living together has shortened. In addition, the norms of extended living have changed. Increasingly, adult children maintain financial and personal autonomy while living under the same roof. There is relatively more "freedom" for members of an extended family. The patriarch is increasingly a reduced figure and a mother-in-law does not have the same authority over a daughter-in-law.

The change is striking in urban areas and among urbanizing families of villages. It is palpable in central Punjab, urban Sindh, and Peshawar Valley. Rural Sindh, southern Punjab, and Balochistan lag behind.

Pakistan's extended family is taking a new form. It is becoming a polycentric family with a nucleus of parental family and satellites of grown-up children's households. The classical nuclear family, husband, wife and dependent children, is closely bound to parental households, sharing some financial burdens, taking part in child and senior care and acting as a single unit in dealings with *biradari* and community. Constituent households may live separately, frequently in other cities, and even Dubai, Manchester, or Toronto, but they feel and act in many ways as one family. Many Pakistanis who live abroad remain attached to parental homes. Correspondingly, parents feel they have another home somewhere else. Similar are the feelings among migrants to cities.

Circulation between two locales and split "family homes" is the reality for a large number of households. In sickness, unemployment, or for elder care, families return to patriarchal homes almost as a right or obligation. An urban family often has living with it, brothers, sisters, or other close relatives who may be studying, working, or just escaping dreary life in the village. These various arrangements are fully in conformity with family norms. A multinuclear household is the emerging form of the family.

That the family has not shrunk to its nuclear core is reflected in the statistics of household size. The average number of persons per household and those who eat from the same kitchen has puzzlingly increased over the past half century, rising from 5.5 persons per household in 1960 to 6.8 in 1998 and reaching up to 8.0 in

NWFP. Of course, there can be many contributing factors, such as housing deficit, and high fertility, but the fact that extended families include boarding relatives also explains the persistently large household size.

Functionally, the extended family has become an arena for "power pooling," in addition to the usual functions, for example, procreation and childcare, and emotional and physical support. It has become an informal corporate body that mobilizes members' connections to negotiate for basic services, such as getting a child admitted to school, fixing a traffic ticket, fending off criminals, or care of someone who is hospitalized.[18] This function has reinforced family solidarity through the pooling of individuals' influences, rendered necessary by institutional change and the inefficiencies of the state. However, this solidarity comes with social costs.

The underside of family

The thick bonds of the Pakistani family provide security, comfort, and social capital for its members, but they also exact many social and personal costs. By these costs, I refer to institutionalized conditions that almost everybody experiences, not some exceptional situations.[19] Conventionally, these costs have included, among others, curbing of an individual's autonomy, initiatives, and even ambitions, the historic tussle between mother-in-law and daughter-in-law lasting life spans, whose painful effects have been documented by generations of writers, and burdensome expectations. Family mores and customs were forged for an agrarian society and small population. With economic development, burgeoning population, and the spread of urbanism, social and cultural bases of family mores and customs have eroded. They are coming into conflict with the values and needs of the emerging society. A few examples will illustrate this point.

Traditionally, the family comes before the individual in matters of social relations, marriage, and personal feelings. Although practices have been slowly changing, beliefs and values lag behind. A sample survey of urban population, conducted in 1997 at Pakistan's fiftieth anniversary, showed that 87 percent had the opinion that "arranged marriages are better" than love marriage, indicating the primacy of the family's choice.[20] The literature and folklore of all languages and ethnic areas has a common theme of an individual's sacrifice for family and submission to community mores. Unrequited love is the destiny of those adventurous enough to fall in love; this is the abiding theme of songs and stories. As discussed above, the meaning of arranged marriage has been expanded to include the consent of prospective partners. Love marriage and "going out" have been accepted in small circles of Karachi, Lahore, and Islamabad. This is the extent of social change.

Family bonds and obligations have fostered a culture of nepotism in public affairs. Perhaps this is the most pervasive social cost of family loyalty. It has become almost a moral obligation to bend rules and procedures for one's family, kin, and co-ethnics, in this order. These mores have spread and gained acceptance cumulatively over the three periods of Pakistan's history. It was not always so. In the early days of independence, favoring relatives and friends was considered unethical and illegal. Not any more.

Women bear the burden of the family's *izzat* (honor) and reputation, enforced through the custom of *purdah* (female segregation), which is expressed in *burqa* (veil and coverall) worn by middle- and upper-class women. They are protected from out-of-home responsibilities but in the bargain are expected to have no dealings with men who are not kin. *Purdah* began to be redefined as "modest behavior" and *burqa* gradually disappeared, after morphing through various fashions, in the 1960s and 1970s, except in some pockets of conservative Islamists.[21] However, the tide turned again with the Islamization of the 1980s.

Hijab (head covering) and *niqab* (face covered with only eyes visible) came to represent the new forms of *purdah*. By 2000, well-educated *niqab*-wearing women could be seen daily on TV discoursing on Islamic feminism. An Islamic flank of women members of the National and Provincial Assemblies in the 1990s broke new ground by wearing *niqab* in legislative assemblies and public meetings. Women were increasingly taking up jobs and professions, redefining norms of *purdah* to accommodate emerging needs for contributing to family incomes and taking part in out-of-home responsibilities. Changing norms also had a backwash effect.

Incidents of violence against women have been much more noticeable, if not increased, in the 1990s and 2000s. The Human Rights Commission of Pakistan's (HRCP) annual reports point out high numbers of honor killing, bride burning (for not bringing the expected dowry), and *karo kari* (Sindhi tribal custom of family murdering a woman suspected of "illicit" sex). Of course, the killing and burning of women by their own families is not a common occurrence, but limited to some parts of Sindh, southern Punjab, Balochistan, and NWFP. They are more noticeable and equally more strongly condemned by the liberal modern segments of society.

HRCP's estimates, one of the few sources of information, report that in the years 2001–3, reported dowry deaths averaged about 400 per year, although an equal number may have gone unreported. About 800 women a year were killed for dishonoring family. Attiya Dawood narrates incidents in Sindh, when a man after murdering a rival kills his sister or brother's wife in cold blood to make the alibi of *karo kari* for his crime.[22] In the Mianwali district in Punjab, a tribal council composed of members of the National and Provincial Assemblies, clan elders, a school teacher, and a police inspector, arbitrated a long-running feud involving murders between two families by working out the deal that the murderers' families should give eight minor girls in marriage to the men of the victims' families, apart from some cash.[23] Extreme though these examples are, they illustrate a social streak that may have had traditional roots, but which has been revived in reaction to the changing role of women and shifting mores. The family becomes the mirror of moral and cultural contradictions. The state and orthodox Islamists have unwittingly acted as the agency for sustaining such tribal customs.

Gender relations, the state and Islam: three models of femininity

Family is the fort that protects women by herding them inside. It is true of many societies, but it particularly describes women's situation in Pakistan. Patriarchy rules women's lives, controlled by fathers when young and dominated by husbands as married adults. This is the imagined status of women, descriptive of traditional gender relations. Closer examination reveals a more nuanced reality. No doubt women are subordinated to men, but they have been carving out personal space in two ways.

First, over the lifecycle, a woman's status and authority changes. She is controlled almost completely by the family as an adolescent and marriageable young woman. The family's honor is tied to her sexuality and that has to be protected. Yet as a mature woman, particularly with grown-up children, she has more leeway in making decisions and exercising her will. She grows up from a suppressed daughter and daughter-in-law to a domineering mother and mother-in-law. The gender relations are often reversed in later age, men becoming dependent on women for care and support.[24] This is the lived pattern of women's social status.

Second, women of middle- and upper-class families and those living in urban areas have relatively more freedom than those in poor, peasant, or tribal households. The city requires that women share in family responsibilities as men's workplaces are separated from home, keeping them away most of the day.[25] Similarly a family's class-induced respectability rubs off on women, elevating their status.

Gender relations in public versus private space have to be differentiated. Women have more authority and freedom in the private realm of a household but are restricted in the public space. Patriarchy suppresses women relatively more in public than private space. State, religion, and social order regulate public space, making legal and moral codes the prime instruments of regulating gender relations. In Pakistan, the state has failed to fulfill the promise of equal rights for women, particularly in public space. Instead, the change in family and gender relations has been driven by economic imperatives, urbanization, and the Islamic discourse.

The question of women's role in social life began to surface with the colonization of India, particularly as the British started to codify laws and promote modern education to produce a skilled labor force. Muslims initially resisted both modern education and economic participation. Muslim women were all the more denied access to these opportunities because of their strict observance of *purdah*. Even Sayyed Ahmed Khan, a crusader for Muslim education, did not advocate the schooling of women. Yet consciousness about women's education began to grow little by little. Anjuman-e-Himayat-e-Islam (1885) started schools for Muslims in Lahore, including some for girls. At the same time the Sindh Branch of the National Mohammedan Association started advocating education for Muslims, laying the groundwork for the formation of the Sindh Madrassah Board (1885) to start a modern school in Karachi.[26] From these meager beginnings, a movement for

Muslim women's educational and political rights emerged among liberal sections of the community.

Women's participation in the struggle for independence and eventually in the Pakistan Movement further broke some of the barriers faced by Muslim women. Women's magazines began to be published raising questions about the restrictive practices of *purdah*. Conferences were organized and demands for Muslim women's rights voiced.[27] Muslim women played a significant role in political agitations and electoral politics for independence. Out of these movements emerged new role models for Muslim women, which combined family responsibilities with public life. Of course, these ideas remained confined largely to cities, but whiffs of change started blowing even in villages.

Since independence, the long-term social trend is toward liberalization of gender relations and increasing women's responsibilities, not rights, both in private and public spaces. This statement should be immediately qualified with the observation that this secular social trend has not moved forward in a straight line, but along a zigzagging course, two steps forward, one backward and one sideways.

In the course of Pakistan's social history, three models of femininity have emerged. The first is a woman of customary beliefs and ways, largely homebound but aspiring to modern material goods, even if such desires remain distant dreams. She represents a traditional Muslim woman. Second is a modern woman of liberal values whose domesticity is combined with a job and/or engagement in public space. She symbolizes a liberated Muslim woman. The third is an Islamic feminist who imbibes religious piety, puritanical values, and demands a share in public life, be it a job or political participation. Wrapping herself in a bubble of *purdah* (*hijab*, *niqab*, or *burqa*), she negotiates public space on her terms. She symbolizes a born-again Islamic woman. She has emerged in the 1980s. It must be mentioned that all three types are, by and large, believing and often observing Muslims, who are also attached to cultural traditions.

Phase 1

Of course, the traditional Muslim woman has been the norm in Pakistan, but in the 1960s and 1970s, the first and second periods, state-led modernization promoted the modern Muslim woman. Begum Liaqat Ali Khan, wife of the first prime minister of Pakistan, was among the founders of the All Pakistan Women's Association (APWA) whose goal was to promote women's rights and encourage their participation in public life. The monthly *Mirror* became the chronicle of the lifestyle of liberated women in the 1950s and 1960s. It highlighted gala evenings in military officers' messes, New Year's dances at Karachi's Sindh club and Lahore Gymkhana, and fashion shows to raise funds for refugees and displaced families. Girls were free to ride bicycles to colleges and a small section of women began to give up *purdah*. They were the trendsetters in the early years.

The 1956 constitution of Pakistan recognized the equality of women in fundamental rights. President Ayub Khan's Muslim Family Laws Ordinance (1961) introduced compulsory registration of marriages, restricted polygamy, and instituted women's right to divorce. These were progressive measures for those times. Though opposed by *mullahs* and Jamaat-i-Islami, these measures were enforced. However, Islamists had their day when General Zia in the third period canceled many provisions of that ordinance.

Phase 2

The second phase was the time of Bhutto's rule. Women's rights and public participation were promised as a part of the agenda of social equality. The 1973 constitution provided equality of all citizens before the law and their equal protection under Article 25-1. It laid down that, "there will be no discrimination on the basis of sex alone" (Article 25-3) and barred discrimination for public service jobs on the basis of religion, caste, sex, residence, and place of birth.[28] Prime Minister Bhutto passionately advocated women's participation in public affairs. His dramatic gestures of inviting women hidden behind screens to come out and sit in front of *sardars*, during his public meetings in Balochistan, enthralled people.[29] The federal civil services were opened to women. All in all, in the second period, women's rights were part of the national discourse despite the opposition of conservative circles. Although the rhetoric was not fully matched by actions, the discourse legitimized the modern Muslim woman.

Phase 3

The third phase has witnessed the reversal of the feeble movement toward women's equality and a drastic recasting of gender relations in forms that are nontraditional, although they reinforce traditional values and norms. This reversal and recasting began with General Zia's policies of Islamization but it has become a cultural force of its own. The *zina* (adultery or fornication) provision of *Hudood* ordinance (1979) requires four male witnesses, female witnesses are unacceptable, for conviction. A woman victim could be punished for adultery or illicit sex, if she is pregnant, or of false accusation if she brought the charge but could not produce four witnesses. Practically, the rape may have to be committed by the roadside to have four eyewitnesses – an anachronism, of course. This law produced anomalies whereby a blind raped but pregnant girl was convicted of illicit sex.[30] This devaluing of women's evidence was Islamic only under the conservative Hanafi school's interpretations but it was certainly contrary to customary norms. In the same vein of reducing women's legal status, the *Qanoon-e-Shahadat* (law of evidence) ordinance of 1984 almost debarred women's evidence in financial transactions.[31] These ordinances have produced a rich harvest of contradictions and anomalies. They have spawned voluminous law cases and have proven to be hard to implement. From a social and cultural point of view, they have resulted in legislating women's inequality and legitimizing gender relations of feudal/tribal origins. Obviously, they are contrary to the needs of an industrializing society.

The orthodoxy promoted by General Zia affected all spheres of life. His pronouncements about the sanctity of "*chador* and *chardevari*" (*purdah* and home) gave a new twist to the traditional beliefs about the desirability of women's confinement at home.

The economic and material bases of social life have continued to change, producing paradoxical situations. One of the striking paradoxes is that clerical jobs in the federal government were opened to women in Zia's era, essentially under the pressure of poor young girls' need for jobs.[32] Before those times, women could be found mostly in officers' positions and professions, for example, doctors, teachers, architects, and civil servants. In the 1980s, women in office jobs increased 12 times, including banks where women were recruited in considerable numbers.[33]

General Zia's wife stayed out of the public limelight but she did not observe *purdah*, as did the wives and daughters of most other members of the ruling junta. Female news anchors wore *dupattas* (scarves) to cover their heads, required as a symbol of Islamic modesty, while song and dance programs flourished on television despite Islamists' protests about their alleged vulgarity. Newscasters' *dupattas* have become a barometer of the cultural tenor of the times. They slipped back on the shoulders during Benazir Bhutto's government but went again over the heads in the days of Nawaz Sharif's zeal for *Shariat* (Islamic laws) rule, to come down again in General Musharraf's military rule.

The Islamic discourse captured center stage in the third period. Sustained organizational work of the Islamic student organizations Islami, Jamiat-e-Tulba, and Tablighi Jamaat began to yield results by the third period. After Bhutto's fall and the betrayal of his egalitarian promises, ideological space on the university and college campuses was almost completely occupied by the Islamic narrative. A large number of doctors, engineers, and managers of Islamist persuasions graduated into professions. Among them also were women graduates who had grown up combining student activism with *purdah*. Thus, a new woman came on the scene, clad in *hijab, niqab* or *burqa* but ambitiously pursuing a career and actively participating in public life. This is the third model of Pakistani femininity, the born-again Islamic woman.

After the interlude of the musical chair democracy of Benazir Bhutto and Nawaz Sharif in the 1990s, the return of military rule under General Musharraf, the "moderate Muslim" has become the official icon. Women are relatively freer in public space. *Mullahs* keep protesting at the vulgarity and indecency of modern femininity, sometimes harassing women "not properly attired." In NWFP, orthodox *mullahs* have organized campaigns to discourage women from voting. Yet, all in all, this is a period of relative openness for women.

Counterposing the liberal-modern models of gender relations is the demonstrable example of *purdah*-clad women, who are members of the National and Provincial Assemblies, local councils, and district councils. General Musharraf reserved 30 percent of the seats for women representatives at all levels of the elected bodies. Islamic political parties seized enthusiastically the opportunity to get their share of women seats proportionate to their electoral votes. Qazi Hussain Ahmed's daughter, Maulana Fazlur Rehman's sisters-in-law are members of the National and NWFP Assemblies, respectively, on the women's quota.[34] These are the two leaders of the main Islamic parties in Pakistan. They have not missed the opportunity to take their share of political opportunities.

Women's participation in public life

Unlike the customary norms of women's role, the reinvented Islamic tradition envisages women's full participation in economic pursuits and political institutions. Public space is splitting into two tracks: one, where women and men are segregated visually and physically but integrated functionally; two, where they are integrated both visually and functionally. Islamic traditions are accommodating modern material interests in religious beliefs. Overall, modernity and reinvented tradition are coalescing and colliding simultaneously.

Before concluding this analysis of gender relations and women's rights, it may be mentioned that in the modern sector a vibrant women's rights movement, albeit led by upper- and middle-class women, has evolved in reaction to General Zia's restrictive legislations. Woman's Action Forum (WAF) was founded in 1983 to protest *Hudood* and *zina* ordinances. Numerous NGOs and community agencies have emerged in the third period advocating women's rights and promoting women's development. The government of Pakistan has also established a federal division (ministry) for women's development. These are the voices of the modern Muslim women. Thus, the struggle for redefining women's status and gender relations is moving along numerous tracks. Modernization in the Islamic idiom is as much a trend as the drive toward global women's rights. Family is encased in kinship and the changes in the latter structure are also reflecting back on gender relations.

Kinship: *biradari, khel* or clan

Kinship means social relations based on blood ties and sometimes marriage bonds. All societies have kinship institutions of one form or another. In Western societies, kinship is a small part of the total social relations of an individual, but in Third World societies it looms large in a person's social network.

Historically, Pakistani society, including its regional and ethnic components, has had strong kinship structures. Kinship is the larger group surrounding a family with which its members are tied in bonds of mutual support, obligations, common identity, and endogamy. It is called *biradari* (literal meaning brotherhood) in Punjab and parts of Sindh, *khel* (clan) or *kaliwal* (community fellow) among Pashtoons, *quom* or *zat* by Balochs. The basic structures of these groups bear strong similarities.

These are essentially groups of relatives who can trace their lineage to identifiable male ancestors, whereas a tribe's common ancestor is only notional and frequently mythical. Thus, *biradari, khel* or *zat* is primarily a patrilineage although in Punjab and Sindh close blood relatives by marriage are often included.[35] Each of these groups is smaller than a tribe and keeps shedding relations with whom blood ties become too distant, many generations removed. Population explosion has further necessitated that the *biradari* or *khel* ties may not extend back to relatives more than three to four generations. Typically, such a group should be large enough to be able to assemble at marriages, funerals, religious, and political gatherings.

Biradari, khel or *zat*, traditionally, has been the group for marrying in. Its members also have customary relations for gift exchanges at marriages, births, or other passages of life; obligations of coming to each other's help in adversity or solidarity; and protecting collective identity and honor. In cities, these obligations have weakened, even worn out in many cases, but in villages they hold sway, although with mobility and changing local economies, their intensity is diminishing.

By and large, kinship is a force of conservatism. It upholds traditions and sustains customs. Yet functionally, kinship ties have shifted in emphasis from focusing on internal relations to pooling of social power for external dealings with other groups and smoothing transactions. This shift has largely occurred in the last 50 years.

Kinship ties began to loosen as a consequence of the mass movements of population at independence. Yet they have remained a significant force in electoral politics, particularly in the rural areas. Ian Talbot observes that *biradari*, along with *sajjadah nashins* (custodians of shrines), were used by the Muslim League to mobilize votes in the 1946 elections that led to independence. This pattern has continued in one form or another.[36] Landlords with strong *biradaris* manage to get elected in rural constituencies. Only the 1970 elections broke this pattern, but then in 1977 Bhutto's PPP reverted to nominating resourceful *biradari* leaders for elections.

Biradaris or clans strike an internal bargain of expectations – support *biradari* members with your connections and in return they will use their influence on your behalf, particularly in dealing with public officials. This power exchange has become a significant function of kinship. The need for a patron to mediate with the state apparatus has increased in direct relation with the expansion in the role of Pakistan's state and its increasing inefficiency and corruption. The state's softness indirectly promotes kinship solidarity. The *biradari* or clan's role as the pooling of social capital has grown in recent times.

In small business communities or clans, primordial ties, including ethnic bonds, are a source of financial resources for businesses. Gujratis, Bohras, Chinotis, Memons, and Sheikhs are known kin groups who have oligopolies over textile, leather, and other consumer goods industries as well as some import–export businesses.[37] Similar kinship dominations are observable in regional and local economies, such as Pirachas in Sargodha, Hotis in Mardan, or even minority Hindus in the towns of the Kacchi plain.

The workings of kinship ties are illustrated by a murder in Faisalabad, a case that inspired a novel.[38] Sehgals, a *biradari* of Chinoti Sheikhs, built the largest textile mill in Faisalabad in the 1950s.The Sehgal family acquired 48 acres of land to start a model farm near the city. Some dispute over the land led to the murder of Dildar Rana, a member of the local Rajput *biradari*; a scion of the Sehgal family was accused of masterminding it. The police tried to hush up the affair on Sehgal's behalf. General Bukhtiar Rana, a kin of Rana's, was the martial law administrator of the province at the time. He ordered the arrest of the accused Sehgal a day before he was to dine with President Ayub.[39] This is how the power of a *biradari* neutralized the influence and wealth of a big industrialist.

The failures of the state have contributed to the functional realignment of kinship ties, but there is also a feedback loop in this relationship. Kinship nepotism subverts rules and laws and erodes the state's authority. The culture of patron–client in public affairs is sustained by kinship obligations. This is one illustration of the Pakistani state and society mutually locking each other in a cycle of personalized dealings and arbitrary modes of operation that conflict with the imperatives of an urbanizing and modernizing society.

Two more points need to be made about kinship. One, a kinship is not an egalitarian structure; not all members and families are treated equally. There are class differentiations in status and influence. A Chaudhry landlord may not even sit on the same cot with a poor kin who is a tenant. Pashtoons tend to accord greater mutual respect to poor kin than to members of Punjabi or Sindhi *biradaris*. The overlaying kinship solidarity militates against the class differences. However, it must be borne in mind that these relations are changing with the changing class structure.

Second, kinship is not a completely harmonious group internally. There are disputes and feuds running over life spans. I have mentioned in an earlier chapter the Pashtoon custom of *tarboorwali*, competition among cousins for land and status. Anthropologists characterize such a structure as a segmentary lineage, wherein alliances and antagonisms coexist among patrilineal kin.[40] Cousins and brothers compete for land, yet join together to fight outsiders. Punjabi *biradari* may not have such an institutionalized competition, but nonetheless its internal feuds over land and women are a common cause of murders. There are patterned behaviors of recrimination and suspicions among relatives. A common saying is that with kin "one may not share the bread but one shares the blame."[41]

To sum up, kinship is weakening in cities and villages of high mobility and changing modes of production. Functionally its economic and symbolic functions are shrinking, but political and patronage bonds remain strong. Kinship dovetails into ethnicity and community. Changes in these structures also impact kinship ties.

Community in Pakistani society

Community is a weak social institution in Pakistan and it is getting weaker. I begin with this observation to highlight the community's role in society, although it will be validated in the following discussion. This observation should be qualified by making a distinction between a community as a sentiment and political symbol, and community as a structure or process. The former form is thriving while the latter is languishing. Maybe the point to begin the discussion with is to examine various meanings of the term "community."

Community is a term with multiple meanings. A sociologist collected 94 different definitions of the term in 1955.[42] How many would be there today is almost impossible to count. Newspapers continually refer to international or regional bodies as communities, such as the European or Islamic Community, in one column; in another they talk about the Muhajir or Ismaili community alluding to the ethnic or religious identities of societal components. Yet another reference may be to the Lyari or Chahiwal community, for example, a neighborhood or village; yet another usage of the term may be in the sense of a moral order or social process such as community solidarity or community development. In the academic literature, the term is used in as many ways as in the media. The myriad uses of the term have arisen from references to its different dimensions.

As a social structure, community refers to groups that have four characteristics: (1) a territorial base, usually a locality; (2) share common interests; (3) some level of interaction or awareness among members; and (4) a sense of belonging. Typically, it is a local group such as a village, neighborhood or even an ethnically distinct region.[43] My focus in this discussion is primarily on various types of territorial groups that have common interests, some level of awareness and shared identity and who function as a unit for social, political, and /or religious purposes. Thus defined, community is viewed as one of the middle-range institutions.

Of course, community is also a process in the sense that it exists as a subterranean awareness most of the time but surfaces when common interests have to be expressed or protected. It is as much in the making as in the being. In the same vein, community comes in various degrees of communal ties and sentiments. Once one begins to look at community as a process, the diversity of meanings and usages of the term is understandable.

Community is not a nation on the one hand, or family or any other intimate group on the other. An individual is enmeshed in various social networks, such as those of relatives, friends, and co-workers. Such networks could be a community, provided they come to have an independent existence over and above an individual's relationships. With these clarifications of the term, let us turn to analyzing community in Pakistan.

Loss of community

Historically, a village has been a community bound by territorial interests, economic and social interdependencies, and a sense of belonging. Despite its divisions of castes and *biradaris*/clans, it acted as one close-knit social organization, especially in matters relating to a locality's order and welfare. Since independence, the village's agrarian economy has weakened and self-contained social life is lost. A process of the "loss of community" is underway, as the population of villages increases and people move in and out. Intimacy and wholeness of social relations are giving way to purposive dealings and segmented roles. In other words, the village is losing the primacy of relations and stability of defined statuses, undoubtedly in some areas faster than the others.

Manzur Ejaz narrates the scene at Eid prayers in his village in Sahiwal. This annual communal prayer that includes a meet-and-greet gathering was, in 2002, largely attended by young men in "crisp city dresses." Older men, who conventionally would not miss such a gathering, were surprisingly scarce. They had stayed home to look after the cattle. To attend this important communal gathering was not as compelling as it used to be.[44] This may be the situation in one village, but it illustrates how the development is weakening territorial community. There are other indications of the weakening of community ties in villages.

There have been perennial feuds within villages about the distribution of water, land rights, or family honor that pitch *quoms/biradaris* or tribes against each other.[45] Such feuds were always a part of village life leading to litigation and heavy indebtedness, even in the early twentieth century, Malcolm Darling found in his inquiry about the economic conditions of Punjabi peasants.[46] Currently in addition to family feuds, the prospects of material gains and public investments fan the formation of political factions. Sometimes, the new riches divide villages along denominational lines, as was the case in Budhopur, Punjab, where the prosperity of an Arian working in Kuwait led to his building a separate mosque that effectively divided the village's congregation along caste lines.[47]

The ineffectiveness of successive rural development programs, discussed in Chapter 6, has been partially the result of factions that used to emerge in villages with the prospect of a new road, school, or investment loans. The delicate communal balance breaks down with prospects of public involvement and political power. The interests of *biradaris* and castes trump the collective welfare. The AKRSP approach, held to be more promising, is based on not attempting to mobilize a whole village for community development. It emphasizes forming cooperative groups of interested persons or clans for promoting improvements in their living conditions. Community thus becomes a coalition of converging interests.

Indigenization of communities of interest

A village or neighborhood may not be a strong social organization, but it is a symbolic community of some level of shared interests. Those interests come into play in interactions with others. Furthermore, the political and symbolic interests are so organized that they give rise to a hierarchy of community identities. For example, I may say that I am from Korangi if talking to another Karachite, but I would call myself a Karachite among a group of Peshawaris; yet if I was speaking about my political identity, I may say I am Sindhi or Muhajir, but place me among Americans and I am a Pakistani. Thus, it is the context of a discourse (and interests) that defines my community of identity. On the objective plane, each of these is a symbolic community commanding sentiments and a sense of belonging, but they are not organized groups. They are processes and not structures.

Community as a process and sentiment is strong in Pakistan. Its foundation lies in primordial ties. *Biradari, khel, quom,* or caste are the primary source of a sense of belonging for individuals. The sentiments and processes of such groups even permeate bureaucracies and professions. Military officers or members of the Federal Police or Tax services, for example, imbibe a sense of belonging, mutual obligations, and group identity reminiscent of a tribe or *biradari*. These organizations present a community-like face to the world outside, but internally they are divided along ethnic, sectarian, and caste lines.[48] For example, an army colonel would show regard for any other officer even to the point of doing favors for him in relation to outsiders, but he would form cliques with those from his own ethnic, sectarian, or tribal background for promotions, postings, and perks. The point I am making is that even modern organizations in Pakistan have an underside of primordial ties and community sentiments. This tendency has increased since independence.

An interest group is the weakest form of community, be it a professional body or citizens' organization, such as the Family Planning Association or a neighborhood welfare society, etc. Shared social or professional interests are not a good glue for community solidarity. They have to be complemented with ties of common identity and shared sentiments to constitute a strong community in Pakistan. The development paradoxically has reinforced communities of primary relations, formal or informal, and not promoted the interest-based communities expected in urbanizing societies. The post-1980s wave of NGOs is a phenomenon that is thriving essentially on public funds and foreign aid. They are viewed with great skepticism in Pakistan.[49] Whether they will take hold as interest communities remains an open question.

Ethnic community and identity

Finally, ethnic community of regional or provincial scope is one form of identity community that has grown strong since independence. I am here referring to the rise of community consciousness and political identity among Muhajirs, Punjabis, Sindhis, Balochis, Kashmiris, and Pashtoons. Within these broad categories, there are further subdivisions along ethnolinguistic lines into Sariaki, Hindku, Makranis, Brohis or Balti, and Hunza communities, claiming distinct identities and demanding political and cultural recognition. Such ethnoterritorial consciousness has grown in reaction to Pakistan's simmering political crisis about regional/ provincial autonomy, and economic disparity. These unresolved questions led to the break-up of the old Pakistan in 1971, namely the separation of Bangladesh. It continues to fan regional discontent and arouse ethnonationalism, such as Sindhu Desh or Balochistan liberation movements.

Feroz Ahmed has traced the evolution of political discourse about nationalities in Pakistan and its transformation into the process of ethnoterritorial community formation.[50] Hamza Alavi holds the salaried class (his term "salariat") to be the driving force in the formation of ethnonationalism after independence.[51] The point is that no matter how one views it, ethnic consciousness and its associated political demands have come to be a fact of social and political discourse in Pakistan. Ethnic identities are the bases of extended communities.

Community and Islam

A discussion of community in Pakistan is not complete without mentioning the role of Islam in community formation. The imagined Islam, one of discourses and ideology, overrules territory, ethnicity, or tribe/clan as the basis of a community. It posits a universal community of believers, *umma*, which may extend beyond national boundaries. However, the lived Islam is different. It includes *pirbhais* (spiritual brotherhood), denominational groups, Tablighi circles, congregational networks or (Silselas) followers of a Sufi saint. Many of these groups take on the character of a community. Overarching these small communities are sectarian alignments, such as Sunnis, Deobandis, or Shias, which generate identities and sentiments of solidarity. They foster a sense of belonging and community feelings among large blocks of population. Sectarian communities have multiplied since the 1980s at two levels, one as an extended community of shared faith, and two, as primary groups of face-to-face relations in denominationally divided localities.

Take the example of developments in the social life of university and college campuses. In the third period, student groups began to be organized on campuses combining sectarian identities and common territorial origins, such as Ahl-Hadith of Faisalabad or Imamia Students of Kohat, for mutual support and political solidarity. These groups are associations, precursors of communities, based on shared religious identities and common cultural interests. The national Islamic political parties, which have denominational roots, have established respective student groups at campuses serving both the political and sociocultural interests of their members. These groups are often close-knit and members' ties take on the character of a clan. Many of them grow into communities.

To sum up the discussion of this section, it can be said that primordial ties and identities, forged in *biradaris* and clans, are the bases of community organization in Pakistan. Wherever there is a strong community, it recapitulates the norms and ethos of those social structures. In addition, interests, territory, ethnicity, and spiritual or religious identities engender a sense of belonging and social solidarity, sentiments that bond people for purposes of competing with others. These processes lead to community formation. Thus, community as a process and sentiment is wide ranging, whereas community as a structure is largely limited to groups growing out of an extended family.

Class and community

At this juncture, the question arises as to how class and community are interrelated. After all, class is one of the basic organizing principles of social structure and community is an institution that clusters people in cohesive sociospatial groups. The two work in tandem to constitute the social organization of a society. What is the nature of the relationship between these two organizing institutions and how has it evolved in this period of social change in Pakistan? This is a significant question.

Social class is a concept simple to describe but complicated to define. Every day we categorize people as upper or lower class, landlords or tenants, owners and workers, etc. These are all references to some classification of class. However, what makes these categories classes, or, in other words, what are the criteria by which classes are defined? The answer is complicated. Obviously, class is a multidimensional concept. I have briefly discussed the meaning of the term in Chapter 5. Presently, it is enough to recall that a class is a stratum of social statuses with relatively similar material conditions, social standing, and life-chances. In Pakistan economic conditions; clan/caste identity; and affiliation with the modern, bazaar, or illicit sector together make up the bases of class statuses.

Class in Pakistan does not entirely conform to Marxist or functionalist conceptions. It is a social category of similar living conditions and life chances. Yet it is internally divided into segments of comparable economic statuses aligned with lifestyle and ethnic uniformities. Traditionally, class has been layered into a community. A *biradari,* clan, or village is stratified in layers of rich, middle, and poor, patrons and clients or landlords and *kammis*. The poor have depended on the rich and the influential for sustenance; in return they serve and support them. Symbiotic relations link various classes in a community. Obligations and charity have kept alive those in dire circumstances.

A somewhat similar structure characterized old cities. Rich and poor lived in close proximity. Even the layout of streets and neighborhoods mixed small and large houses, making a widow or craftsman, for example, neighbors of rich merchants and high public officials, living side by side. Thus, the social distance among classes was abridged by neighborliness.[52]

The division of labor and occupational specialization has changed the interclass relations to contractual dealings, weakening communal ties, and widening social distances. These processes began during British rule and have accelerated with post-independence economic development and modernization. New neighborhoods in cities and towns are laid out in blocks of same size lots, separating households by income and lifestyle. In villages, the affluent are building *kothis* (detached houses surrounded by gates and high walls) at the edges of settlements. Such houses discourage relatives from dropping by, as observed by Naveed-i-Rahat, in a study of a village near Islamabad.[53] The physical and economic bases of integration of different classes within a community are eroding.

Social differentiation within communities is increasing. Many fissures have appeared in community structure. The economic class differences of the rich and poor are visibly reflected in consumption patterns and lifestyles. Alongside income and wealth differentiations are small cultural differences between those adopting modern Western ways and others who remain attached to the vernacular modes of living. Persons of similar incomes may be worlds apart in their living conditions and lifestyle. Take the example of a rich bazaar merchant or landlord versus a corporate executive or doctor of comparable incomes; the former is likely to be dressed in *kurta-shalwar*, live in a joint family home, and conduct his business in Punjabi or Pashto; whereas the latter may wear pants and shirt, live with his wife and children only, and speak English or Urdu at work. The lifestyle differences follow the salience of the modern versus vernacular divide, respectively, represented in the English and Urdu newspapers and magazines.

Upper- and lower-class distances have become a sociological gulf. What a middle-class urbanite spends in a fancy restaurant on one meal may be more than the monthly food bill of a street sweeper or even a junior clerk. These differences have gradually increased over the three periods of Pakistan's social history.

Yet kinship ties and ethnic or religious bonds continue to reconfigure class relations. Poor relatives have customary claims on social and/or financial support from the rich and influential members of communities. Expectations of the patron–client network undergird social relations among different classes of a community, be it a *biradari*, clan, or even extended ethnic/denominational group.

Class consciousness was sparked during the second period by Bhutto's political program. It has simmered down with the opening of the safety valve of migration abroad from the 1970s, the tempering of socialist ideals, and the religious and ethnic resurgence in the third period. To some extent, community bonds have diffused class consciousness. Yet community and class are continually restructuring each other. They dovetail into the broad network of civil society.

Civil society

Civil society is not a conventional social institution normally included in descriptions of societies. It is a collection of groups, communities, associations, and organizations that function as the intermediary institutions between state, market, and society. Some conceptions of civil society reduce it to a moral order and customary rights and responsibilities defining citizenship. The intermediate structure is the more widely accepted notion of civil society. It is a component of society but not the society itself. It has been called the third sector between government and business. It does not include institutions of face-to-face relations and personal dealings, such as family, recreation, or religious congregations. Civil society refers to institutions and organizations that regulate and express collective interests of communities and groups. As a concept, civil society has a long history.

Traceable to Aristotle, the notion of civil society has evolved through Hegel's formulation as "legal sphere to govern civil life" to Gramsci's divergent ideas of "counterpart to the state" or "the realm of public opinion and culture."[54] Presently, civil society is regarded as "the sphere of associations (especially voluntary associations), social movements, and forms of public communications."[55] Civil society has become a popular term in international development literature, embraced by the World Bank and other aid agencies as an instrument of reforming an overstretched state and democratizing public decision making. The concept has been harnessed to the promotion of Western modes of involving people in governance. In practice, civil society has come to mean fostering NGOs as the medium of social and political development, paralleling the promotion of markets for economic growth.

If one judges Pakistan by the capacity of NGOs and other civic organizations, modeled in Western idioms, to influence civic life and the state, one cannot help concluding that civil society is very weak. Whereas if one takes a functional view of civil society in Pakistan and looks for organizations and institutions, including social movements that regulate civic life, initiate community action, and counterbalance the excesses of state, one finds a robust civil society of the traditional mold. In other words, NGOs or professional associations may not constitute a vigorous civil society, but other indigenous institutions and movements do provide civic infrastructure and collective action reflective of a vibrant civil society. This is the sociological view of civil society referring to social organizations that "are separate and enjoy some degree of autonomy from the state and are formed voluntarily by members of society to protect or extend their values."[56] Thus viewed, the picture of civil society in Pakistan appears to be quite complex. Like most other social institutions, it has two distinct tracks, traditional versus modern and some hybrid forms in between.

Historically, there have been middle-level regulatory institutions between the precolonial state and citizens, such as *panchayats, jirgas,* Friday congregations, tribes, *biradaris,* craft guilds, and bazaar associations. These institutions had considerable autonomy within their spheres, providing services to their members and regulating their behavior. British rule introduced European practices including the formation of educational, political, and religious and charitable associations with elected office bearers. Muslim communities formed educational *anjumans* (associations), women's welfare bodies, and charitable trusts to run orphanages, manage mosques, protect shrines, build clinics, run schools, and promote social reforms, etc.[57] Such organizations were voluntary bodies and thus had a modern form but they were indigenous in spirit and functions. The movement for independence mobilized these organizations and institutions to press political rights for Muslims. Thus, a tradition of civil society's activism was established in the years leading up to independence.

Evolving structure of civil society in Pakistan

Civil society at the time of independence was already dualistic in structure, consisting of an extensive network of indigenous institutions and organizations on the one hand, and a small but influential group of modern associations, newspapers and magazines, lawyers' bar councils, educational institutions, students' and women's organizations, political and social clubs on the other. The defining characteristic of the indigenous wing has been the manifest intertwining of organizational interests and goals with norms of personalized relations and kinship-like sentiments. It resembles the bazaar sector of the economy. Its ideology is based on customary ideas blended with pragmatic interests.

Modern institutions and organizations are manifestly corporate in structure, formally based on impersonal dealings and functional relations. Their formal structure is organized around shared interests, although latently they may have informal networks and caste or ethnic cliques. By and large, the modern wing of civil society is Western in orientation and liberal in ideology. With these distinctions in mind, let us briefly review how the two wings have coalesced and diverged in the course of civil society's evolution.

Pakistan's civil society has gone through three phases paralleling the three periods of the country's social and political history. In each phase, it has had a distinct ethos. The three phases can be represented by their dominant processes, namely:

1   Modernist thrust in institutions and organizations, 1947–68.
2   Ideological state and sharpening dualism, 1969–77.
3   Rise of denominationalism and fracturing of civil society, 1978 onward.

Expansion of the modern wing

Immediately after independence, the need to provide food and shelter to the refugees from India prompted a spontaneous response from charitable organizations and local communities. The indigenous organizations, such as welfare associations and neighborhood as well as mosque-based groups, were at the forefront of this effort. This challenge drew local organizations and institutions into the national arena and accelerated the formation of voluntary national bodies.

A national network of civil society organizations began to emerge soon after independence. This national network had a modernist thrust. The new organizations were largely bodies of volunteers with formal constitutions and elected executives: unlike the traditional trusts and associations that followed customary models of organization reflecting age, caste, and loyalty ties. Gradually, modern organizational practices, such as elected executives, also spread into the indigenous sector of civil society, despite maintaining its commitment to traditional values and customary goals.

A major expansion of civil society occurred in modern sectors of the economy and polity. Bar councils; labor unions; engineers', doctors', and civil servants' associations; chambers of commerce; literary circles; Rotary and Lions clubs; and student bodies with national scope came to be formed. Many of these bodies periodically would become active politically by organizing meetings, expressing opinions, and launching protests. When the government chose to join the American-sponsored regional defense pacts, such as the Baghdad Pact (1955) and Southeast Asia Treaty Organization (1954), students, journalists, writers, and lawyers organized countrywide protests.

When political activities were suppressed under the military rule of Ayub Khan, professionals' and lawyers' associations and students' unions served as platforms to express dissent. For example, Justice M. R. Kayani, the chief justice of the high court, used the occasion of annual dinners at the High Court Bar and the Civil Service of Pakistan (elite cadre of CSP) to humorously criticize national policies in the 1960s, when public criticism was suppressed.[58] These examples point out the emerging structure and influence of civil society in the first phase. Its role as the counterweight to the government and as an intermediary institution came to be consolidated, while its internal structure though continuing to be dualistic tilted toward modern practices and organizational models.

Civil society's influence had a tremendous boost in 1969, when it morphed into a political protest movement that brought down Ayub Khan's military-backed regime. When the labor unions as well as students, engineers, doctors, and lawyers joined the protests as organized groups, the Ayub government fell like a house of cards.[59] Civil society's ultimate power came to be determined by its capacity to mount street protests. This is how it has come to be a counterweight to the state in Pakistan.

Dualization of civil society

The social and political forces unleashed by Ayub Khan's downfall through street protests transformed Pakistan. Islamists who had been defeated in the 1970s elections turned to civil society for checkmating Bhutto. Jamaat-i-Islami in partic-ular worked at the grassroots by assiduously fostering Islamic groups in labor unions, Bar councils and, especially, student bodies. Civil society's unity forged during the anti-Ayub protests was broken. The dual tracks of civil society were revived with the indigenous sector becoming the base for Islamists. The modern components of various organizations and institutions came to be identified with either the People's Party or Baloch, Pashtoon, and Muhajir ethnic movements. All this led to the fragmentation of civil society. Yet as the disaffection with Bhutto's government began to build up, the Islamic-indigenous track of civil society gained strength. It demonstrated a remarkable street power by mobilizing students, merchants, and mosque-affiliated groups for the protest movement organized by the opposition parties' alliance, known as the PNA.

Indigenization of civil rights

The PNA movement shook Bhutto's government, but the final push was given by the military coup of General Zia. The military rule of General Zia ushered in an era of Islamization, strengthening Islamic organizations. With the introduction of *zakat* tax, ample funds became available to the government for distribution among *madrassahs* and Islamic seminaries. Within a few years of General Zia's rule, a network of new Islamic academies and mosques emerged in the country. By the mid-1980s, traveling along any major road, one would come across newly built mosques, *madrassahs* or shrines every ten or twenty miles. An accurate count of the number of Islamic seminaries and *madrassahs* is unavailable, but estimates range from about 4,000 to 20,000 for the late 1990s.[60] The fact that their number tripled or quadrupled from 1980 to 2000 is indisputable.

These institutions have served as the reserve force of Islamic parties for demon-strations and agitations. They also tend to defend customary practices that deny autonomy to women and discourage personal liberties.[61] The "Afghan revolution" and the rise of the Taliban regime in Afghanistan supported by the Pakistani, American, and Saudi governments, injected new resources into the Islamic wing of civil society in Pakistan. Out of these developments emerged militant Islamic organizations. Thus, in the third phase, Pakistan's social dynamics have been fundamentally affected and its civil society has been functionally Islamized.

Originally conceived in Western liberal milieu, current notions of civil society fail to acknowledge the role of the indigenous or religious organizations and insti-tutions. The indigenous wing of civil society in Pakistan has been streamlined and invigorated by Islamic movements.

Modern civic organizations and associations lost their ideological compass after Bhutto's fall. Later American triumphalism in the 1990s and the rise of the ethos of privatization have further drained modern associations and institutions of ideolog-ical contents. The discourse about individual rights, freedoms, and markets do not have as much traction in the public mind as the ideals of social justice and equality. The Islamic discourse at least offers a higher purpose than the prosaic goals of individual liberties and market efficiency in a poor society.

Paradoxically, the ethos of privatization has given rise to the global NGO movement, which has also swept Pakistan. NGOs have become, by and large, the flag bearers of the modern wing of Pakistan's civil society, essentially funded by international aid agencies. Those who could be the advocates of social justice and socialism, in the tradition of the 1970s, have become NGO entrepreneurs.

In the third phase, NGOs have mushroomed. From a few hundred in the 1970s, the number of NGOs increased to estimated 4,833 by 1991 and 8,547 by 1994.[62] About half were religious and professional organizations; the rest were involved in community service and social development. The Chambers of Commerce, Bar Councils, or other long-standing modern organizations have either split into Islamic and liberal wings, or are divided into factions.

Overall the modern wing has little street power and its influence is limited to public advocacy or what has been jeeringly called "holding seminars in five star hotels" and organizing marches in Islamabad. As a social and political force, NGOs have poor credibility.[63] As a default option, mobilizing people for social or political causes has fallen to the Islamic-indigenous organizations.

Yet regarding the provision of community services, another function of civil society, the modern wing and particularly NGOs have been quite effective. Take the example of the Pakistan Human Rights Commission, the Citizens Police Liaison Commission (CPLC) of Karachi, Edhi Foundation, or a community-based organization (CBO) such as the Society for Torghar Environment Protection in Balochistan, they are defending individuals from police harassment, providing ambulance services, or conserving wildlife in a tribal territory. The modern wing's community service has expanded the scope of voluntary action. Of course, innumerable schools, clinics, and orphanages have long been run by local charities, but the NGOs are branching out into the fields of legal rights, environmental protection or area development, etc., on a regional scale. They are taking up some of the slack in community services left by the shrinking of the public sector. Despite their increasing contributions to the provision of community services, NGOs are not capable of effectively igniting social movements or political mobilization. Civil society as a mediating institution between the state and society has come to largely depend on its Islamic-indigenous organizations.

The following points sum up my conclusions about the evolving structure of civil society in Pakistan.

- Civil society has always been divided into two distinct tracks, indigenous and modern. Since independence, both have taken on corporate organizational forms, but they have diverged in values and ideologies. The organizations and institutions that constitute the indigenous track are increasingly oriented toward Islamic ideals and values, particularly in the third period. The modern track's ideological underpinnings of liberalism, welfarism, or socialism have been compromised by national and global events. The resurgent indigenous-Islamic movements have filled the political vacuum thus created.
- In Pakistan, the state and civil society have evolved in tandem. The state has influenced the structure of civil society, which in turn has periodically

brought down the entrenched governments and thus functioned as the ultimate check on the state's power. The capacity of civil society to mount agitations is its "power" vis-à-vis the state. On this score, the modern track was effective until the early 1970s, but since then the indigenous-Islamic track has emerged as the font of street power. My conclusion from an earlier article still holds: "within the civil society, the power balance has tilted, with acts of omission and commission of the state, toward ethnic and denominational organizations to the disadvantage of the modern secular institutions."[64]

- Pakistan's civil society has a long history of community service and political activism. The balance between the state and civil society has swung back and forth, from the "strong state, weak society" to the "weak state, strong society" as Yahya Sadowski has observed about Muslim societies.[65] Pakistan's experience contradicts the Western view that Muslim societies have a feeble civic culture and weak social institutions that express citizens' rights.[66] An effective and responsive state is necessary for building a sustainable and modern civil society. Without it, denominational, ethnic, and tribal institutions come to dominate civil society. Pakistan has been undergoing this process since the 1980s.

- The term civil society also has another meaning, namely the domain of public morality and trust that regulate everyday life. This is the unspoken civil society that is seldom talked about in the current international discourse.[67] I will have more to say in the next chapter about the moral order of Pakistani society. Presently, it needs iterating that the corruption-driven and person-based, rather than rules-guided, dealings in the public realm subvert civic trust and erode citizenship. This is what has happened in Pakistan. A society of large and growing population, such as Pakistan, requires the rule of rules, that is a modern civic order. Yet in Pakistan the "soft state" has contributed to the resurgence of primordial institutions, marginalizing the liberal-modern wing of civil society.

Patterns of institutional change

At the conclusion of this chapter, an overview of its main findings and their meanings is needed. This section recapitulates the secular trends in the evolution of middle-range institutions and identifies the patterns of their change.

It is a common refrain in Pakistan that affection has seeped out of the family and "the blood of kin is losing color," the Urdu phrase is *khoon safed ho gaya*. This saying expresses people's feelings about changing family and kinship. These sentiments may not be fully borne out by the findings of this chapter, but the fact that family and kinship have changed is incontrovertible.

The family continues to retain the form of an extended unit, but its structure has been realigned. Members often live independently, sometimes not in close proximity, but they continue to be tethered to the family home, as branches to a trunk. Elders, including patriarchs, are increasingly nominal and symbolic heads, while nuclear households are becoming functionally autonomous. Filial ties remain strong and obligations of mutual support compelling. The family is evolving from an extended unit of common residence to a polycentric structure of multiple homes. It remains the defining element of Pakistan's social structure. Sentiments cultivated in the family are often transferred to friendships, office networks, and other face-to-face groups. Your good friend is "like a brother." Close male colleagues are fictive brothers to women in workplaces.

Marriage as an institution is an instrument of forming new families, but in Pakistan it also is an occasion to affirm kin and clan solidarity, to forge new alliances, to express social status and, traditionally, for all to take a merry break from the routines of life. All these functions have expanded over the 50-year period. Even the ceremonies, which were becoming defunct in the 1950s and 1960s, have been revived on a bigger scale. Marriages have evolved from gatherings of kin to lavish feasts and networking occasions. They are largely endogamous and arranged, though with an expanded scope for choice and involvement of the prospective groom and bride. Al¹ in all, marriage has become elaborate in form and diverse in functions, yet remains strongly anchored to traditions. Of course, many variations within these parameters have emerged, including love marriage in small liberal sections of the society.

Biradari, kinship or clan is an institution that envelops a family. Generally, its form has diffused in the post-independence period due to mobility, urbanization, and changes in the economy. In the urbanizing parts of the country, *biradari* or clan is not a cohesive group, although it continues to serve as the primary source of marriage mates. Paradoxically, for some functions it has grown strong. It increasingly acts as a body for political bargaining, particularly in rural areas. Internally, class and life differentiations have sharpened, although patron–client networks and power-pooling cliques of kin have increased. These trends have thrived with the increase in the corruption and nepotism of the state. Opposite tendencies characteristic of the dialectics of modernization have surfaced in kinship institutions. Norms and customs have become less binding, yet incidences of honor killings and intercaste/clan rivalries, particularly in rural areas, are higher. Primordial ties and their associated emotions seep into business, bureaucracy, and politics.

Territorial community is on the decline, although communities of identity, ethnicity, primordial, and denominational ties are flourishing. Community of interest, characteristic of modern urban social organization, is the weakest. Social differentiation by lifestyle is increasing. The lived culture is diverging from the imagined culture, namely the gulf between actions and beliefs is widening.

Civil society is divided into two main tracks, indigenous and modern. Rooted in customs and traditions, the indigenous organizations and institutions have been Islamized. Islamic formalism is absorbing oral traditions embedded in customary norms. Modern institutions and interest-based associations surged in the first and second periods, but their effectiveness to forge social movements and act as the counterweight to the government has declined in the third period. Civil society has fractured as an intermediate institution.

What social patterns are suggested by the changes in these institutions? The following points sum up my answer.

- Taken all together, these middle-range institutions are a metaphor for social change in Pakistani society. They show a pattern of continuity combined with change. The outward forms of social institutions persist but their internal structures and functions change. The architecture remains intact but the interior design changes.
- Traditions and customs are resilient. They provide a guidebook for individuals to apprehend and absorb new situations. They change and adapt incrementally and in the process are reorganized. Thus tradition does not invariably resist change but responds creatively by adopting religious and conservative ideologies and modifying practices. Scriptural Islam is merging with the customary institutions, forging norms and mores for contemporary living. This process is vividly exemplified by the emergence of Islamic femininity, in contrast to the "modern woman." Women parliamentarians covered in colorful *hijab* or *niqab* are at the forefront of the Islamic flank in elected assemblies. *Hijab/niqab*-clad women fully participate in public life, debating on television, organizing *dars* (the Quran-reading circles), working in offices, or leading political demonstrations. This is the new look of the segregated woman.
- Modern norms and practices, inspired by Western modes of living and liberal ideologies, exist as a sector separate from the indigenous. Social institutions are dualistic in structure. The phenomenon of institutional lag discussed in previous chapters is partially the result of this division. The two sectors have distinct lifestyles and values, resulting in sharpened social differentiation and fractured moral order.
- The lived social institutions are at variance with what are imagined to be norms and values. This divide between behaviors and beliefs has widened, giving rise to pervasive contradictions in Pakistani society.

Theorizing about social change in middle-range institutions

To round off the conclusions of this chapter, I would like to briefly trace their theoretical implications. What theoretical models either explain these findings or alternatively can be deduced from them? This question motivates my exploration.

These institutions have evolved not along a linear track, namely from tradition to modernity, from joint to nuclear family, or from communities of primary relations to interest-based associations. Social change is an evolutionary but dialectical process. It is not just an interplay of traditions and modernity, rather a process of anchoring modern norms and technologies to reinvented traditions and indigenous ideologies. In Pakistan, revivalist Islam has opened another path to social change.

Modernization is driven by changes in economic organization, modes of production, population explosion, urbanization, mobility, etc. The point is that the modernization of institutions is necessitated by the subterranean changes in the technological, economic, and social systems. It is not determined by any iron laws of social evolution or historical materialism.

Norms and practices do not completely recapitulate Western forms and even less so the meanings, but the functional imperatives of new technologies and changing living conditions create an institutional and moral vacuum that has to be filled in new ways. Historically, in modern times, this vacuum has been filled by the state through legislation (such as family reforms, old age pensions, and labor laws) and ideology, particularly in periods of rapid social change. A new institutional framework was consciously designed and not predetermined.

The Pakistani state, like other Third World countries, has not adequately played the role of a builder of modern but indigenous institutions. In this vacuum has emerged revivalist Islam, a form of reinvented tradition. In addition, it has been partially filled by borrowed Western and even global practices and mores. Traditions are being grafted onto modernity, often westernization, and modernity is being indigenized. It is a multitrack process.

In observing the changes in these middle-range institutions, known theories of social change namely linear, dialectical, diffusion, or conflict models, do not have a "good fit," although in parts nearly all have some bearing. An eclectic approach is the only way of explaining the patterns of social change in Pakistan. Ideals of modernization are embodiments of functional imperatives but they can be realized in different institutional forms. Pakistan's institutional change is following a path that is explosive, unbalanced, and full of contradictions, heading toward a modernity of its own brand.

9 Everyday life

Introduction

So far I have examined Pakistani society and culture largely at the institutional and structural planes, focusing on social trends and cultural patterns. In this chapter, I aim to describe the experiences of individuals living in Pakistani society in successive periods. The universe of discourse is a kaleidoscope of personal behaviors, daily routines, beliefs, and modes of thought observable among different groups and classes at various times. In other words, it is the universe of everyday life.

Everyday life is the arena of people's experiences of living in a community, described in concrete terms rather than in abstract and generalized theories.[1] It draws our attention to "the ways people actually live ordinary day to day lives."[2] Everyday life both reflects as well as constructs social structure and culture. In discussing everyday life, one does not need to focus on unique behaviors or singular feelings. One can and should remain at the plane of behaviors and beliefs common to groups but reflected in individuals' behaviors. It is necessary to follow the common threads that both bind groups and distinguish them from others, yet keep them tied together as communities and society. This approach guides my probe into everyday life.

Another procedural point to be reiterated is acknowledgment of the social diversity that characterizes Pakistani society. Undoubtedly, there are common values and themes that permeate through all segments of society, but the forms in which they are expressed vary by ethnicity, caste, class, and geography. I will concentrate on everyday behaviors and beliefs that are illustrative of these common elements. With this introduction to my approach, let us examine everyday life as it has been evolving in Pakistan.

Through my eyes

To give an insider's view on how the life patterns of a Pakistani middle-class person have changed over time, I will describe my experiences as an illustrative example. As a Lahori of many generations, I grew up in the Walled City, a place that embodies the historical urban culture of Punjab, but whose many norms and values had rural roots. As a child, I witnessed the communal harmony and tolerance for which this multifaith city was known across British India. I also saw these feelings melt away with the prospects of independence and the intense political conflicts that the impending partition of the subcontinent engendered, culminating in the horror of communal riots accompanying the partition of India.

As a state and society, Pakistan began deep in an economic crisis with jobless men, abandoned factories, and closed businesses. My father's job in the railways spared us from this fate, but poverty was palpable all around. Yet people coped with these hard times with the support of kin and neighbors until the economy picked up and Karachi, the capital of the new Pakistan, started pulling workers from all across the country for its new industries. Many men from my neighborhood went to Karachi. That was the first wave of mobility, which has grown into a flood tide of sojourning and migrating, both within and outside the country, in the last 50 years.

As a young man in the 1950s, I had a life of many cares, keeping up the appearances of our respectability and attempting to pursue my youthful dreams. I was the first graduate in my extended family but that was not enough for me. My friends aspired to be magistrates, police, and customs officers. Ambitions unknown to our elders drove many of my generation. For me too, dreams of a successful career and higher studies were a part of my inner life. This widening of horizons was the first fruit of independence.

In the 1950s and 1960s, Lahore was a city known for its tea houses, literary gatherings, fashions, gardens, and political activism. One could drop in the Pak Tea House or Shezan restaurant and join freewheeling political arguments, poetry recitations, or literary repartee. In the evenings, young men converged on the Mall both to watch girls, who came to shop at fashionable stores with English names, and to gossip about their dreamed-up romances, studies, and politics.

The city took the edge off young men's pecuniary difficulties. Its leisurely pace, human scale, and fun-loving ways compensated for the pervasive poverty. My day was spent in studies and work, followed by evenings of hanging out with friends in impassioned discussions, strolls on the Mall, and drinking tea. Concerns about personal safety or the fear of crime were almost unknown emotions. Lahore was special, but life in other cities too had a similar feel.

A government scholarship took me to Athens for graduate studies, returning home to an appointment as a university lecturer. Most of my friends had found promising careers in the civil services, banks, teaching, and the military. Education and business were the keys to new opportunities for many, although family connections gave some a head start. My contemporaries entertained desires for romance but readily settled for marriages arranged by parents. Marrying into rich and influential families was not an uncommon consideration.

After a few years of teaching and stung by university politics, I went to the USA for advanced studies. Supporting myself by part-time teaching, I got a doctoral degree in 1971, which launched me into a professorial career in Canada. I became a periodic sojourner in Pakistan, teaching, consulting, and writing to keep myself involved in the homeland and tied to my parental family. This life script of a migrant has been followed by thousands of others.

While political freedom liberated individuals and fired ambitions, family and kinship preserved the traditional order. Submission to elders and conformity to family values, by and large, underpinned the life of all, including youth. Girls were more restricted than boys in their personal life, but boys were far from being free to make their own choices of studies, jobs, and marriage.

In the 1960s and 1970s, there were stirrings of liberalism. Individuals began to break out of the caste and kin bonds. Women started shedding the *burqa* and competing for jobs. Marriage ceremonies began to be tasteful but simple. Despite the restrictions of military rule, one was uninhibited in private opinions and free to indulge in unconventional tastes. Hotels had bars and held floor shows. In Lahore during the 1960s, Princess Amina periodically thrilled striptease fans in a local restaurant.[3] Movies were the passion of the masses. Couples with infants in their laps sat alongside students and laborers in cinemas. Watching an English movie in the air-conditioned Plaza cinema on a searing June afternoon was the badge of modernity.

My kin started moving out of the congested Walled City and the grooves of traditional life. Living in one of the modern suburbs and owning a bungalow became the goals of the emerging middle class. By the 1980s, except for a cousin who had a store in the old neighborhood, all my relatives had moved out of the Walled City. An uncle built a house in Gulberg, the most fashionable neighborhood in those days, for his growing family. His son graduated to become an engineer, his daughters qualified as biologist and historian, respectively. Yet soon after he realized his life dreams, his children started migrating to the USA, leaving him watching over an empty nest. Eventually, he also joined them. The dream was realized but its social value dissipated.

Another cousin passed through a series of rented houses in the suburbs, before affording his own home after a long career as a public relations executive. Even my "Islamist" cousin prospering as a journalist and editor found the neighborhood suited to his preferences.[4] By the 1990s, I had almost no relatives left in the old city, a story repeated by many families in the old neighborhood. The Walled City has sprung a series of wholesale bazaars for cloth, toiletries, and smuggled goods. Merchants and workers in these bazaars are rebuilding homes with modern facilities, such as flush toilets and concrete roofs. The city has changed from the home of cultural traditions and close-knit neighborhoods to the commercial center of the bazaar sector and a smuggler's market.

I often review the situations of my relatives and friends who are poor. What held them back? The poor are of two distinct types: (1) the working poor; and (2) those afflicted with misfortunes, be it the death of a breadwinner, debilitating disease, or a flood and house collapse. Relatives and friends who have not fared well often followed the occupational footsteps of their fathers and grandfathers. An illustrative example is the life trajectory of two brothers. One followed the conventional family route of joining the railways' workshops in the city and rising to be a mechanical foreman. He lives modestly, barely keeping his head above water. The other brother went away to a small town in Sindh to work as a process engineer in the factory of an international corporation. He prospered and his children have gone on to become engineers, accountants, and teachers, further raising the family's fortunes. Dropping out of school and drifting into manual jobs is normally an economic dead end. Inheriting a neighborhood carpentry shop or becoming a clerk, for example, are also the paths taken up by the working poor. Of course, graduating with a degree by itself is not a guarantee of the good life as graduate unemployment is rampant.

There is no safety net such as unemployment insurance or old-age security in Pakistan. Poverty also lurks behind misfortunes. The consequent insecurity has contributed to greed and acquisitiveness. One attempts to grab as much as one can. This tendency has increased over time. By the 1990s, Lahore, in fact the whole of Pakistan, had become a place of unbridled competition, wide social disparities, and sharp contrasts in living conditions.

From the late 1970s, Islamization began to affect public life in Lahore. Gangs of IJT (student wing of Jamaat-I-Islami) zealots harassed women for not covering up or for wearing make-up, disrupted New Year's parties, and railed against music concerts and art exhibitions in colleges and universities. The likes of Princess Amina were banished and bars closed by a public ordinance. One pastime that thrived was eating. Fun in Lahore came to be eating out. *Kebab* and *tikka* shops and Chinese restaurants multiplied. Pizza Hut and McDonald's brought new tastes to Lahore's rich repertoire of cuisines. Afghanistan's *jehad* turned Pakistan into the route for smuggling cocaine and hashish to Europe and the USA. The flow of drugs created demand among the youth. Drug addiction, almost unknown before, became a national epidemic. By the late 1990s, estimates of drug addicts in Pakistan ranged between 2 and 5 million. These were the unintended consequences of the Islamization of the 1980s.

In the 1990s, cinemas were turned into shopping plazas as video shops started doing roaring business. While the role of cinema as a gathering place declined, watching movies became a private entertainment at home or in tea shops and *baithaks* (private party rooms). A gathering of family or friends often became a session for venting frustrations about pervasive corruption, crime, or immorality, while almost everybody's daily routines included skirting around some rule and indulging in questionable practices. Beliefs began to diverge from actions.

Home invasions, motorbike thefts, carjackings, and street hold-ups raised the level of anxiety in the city and spawned a new industry, namely security companies. Going out in the evenings, particularly for women, meant watching out for any sign of trouble, such as crime and rowdiness. Houses in Gulberg, Model Town, and other high-priced areas were turned into fortresses with high walls and armed guards. Kalashnikovs became a popular possession, meant for protection but displayed for status and image. Teahouses and the Mall of my youth had long fallen victim to the relentless traffic and the real estate boom. Coffee shops and bistros of the five-star hotels, such as Intercontinental and Avari, were the venues for literary and political discussions as well as organized seminars. Those activities became the preserve of the well-off. Unlike the teahouses of earlier times, persons of modest means could not afford to enter these premises. Public life shrank, but private pleasures boomed.

In this narrative, seven evolving themes are discernible. First, independence ignited the revolution of rising expectations and fired the ambitions of individuals. Second, enterprise as a personal quality, said to be lacking among Muslims, became a national trait. Third, new occupations arising from the industrial and commercial growth opened avenues of advancement for individuals. Fourth, social mobility has been the vehicle of personal advancement. Those who freed themselves from the traditional milieu were relatively more successful. Fifth, economic and material progress coexisted with an essentially conventional family system and traditional moral order. Sixth, social change also came with increased crime and a heightened sense of insecurity. Seventh, social disparities and divergences of lifestyles sharpened.

Class and lifestyles

What separates Defense Society, Clifton (Karachi), F-6 (Islamabad), University Town (Peshawar) or Model Town (Lahore) from Punghur (Balochistan), Gori (Sindh), or Sinawan (Punjab)? Is it just that the former are upper-class neighborhoods of capital cities and the latter are poor towns and villages? No, these two sets of places represent not only differences between rich and poor, but also communities of divergent lifestyles bordering on almost separate (sub)cultures. The former places are almost indistinguishable from the suburbs of Washington, London, or Athens, not only in physical layout, but also in social ambience. Here the spoken language is a concoction of regional dialects and Urdu liberally mixed with English, dress has a Western flair, home life and family relations are modern in form and, of course, affluence is written all over. Even mosques in these areas are grandiose.

The latter places are almost the opposite; here, vernacular languages and native dress rule, and joint families and kin compounds are the focal points of daily life. Mud or brick houses line dusty streets soaked with stagnant pools of water and sewerage. Mosques alternate with shrines as the nodes of community life. As Chapters 5 and 6 point out, there are many communities in between these two extremes, representing the spectrum of global and vernacular cultural idioms in a variety of combinations.

Travelers' accounts of Pakistan often point out that different sections of society live in seemingly different centuries, some in the twenty-first and others in the eighteenth century or earlier. Richard Reeves, for example, observes, "the division that struck me again and again traveling through Pakistan [in the 1980s] had to do with time…The question I mentally asked each man and women I saw was, 'What century are you living in'."[5] The material contrast points out class differences, but it also symbolizes cultural diversity. On Pakistan's roads and streets, for example, cars and camel carts reflect as much the differences of the modern and the traditional modes of transport as they highlight the new versus old ways of life.

Pakistan's class pyramid has a vertical fissure dividing the indigenous from the modern hierarchies, paralleling the division between the bazaar and the firm sectors. Mix ethnicity in this bipartite structure of upper, middle, and lower social layers and one gets a very complex system of social stratification, where every cluster has a distinct lifestyle – "Sindhi indigenous" here, "Baloch modern," or "Karachi global" there.

An *arhati* (commodity dealer) could be a millionaire, but he is not averse to carrying bags on his back to unload a truck of wheat if another pair of hands is needed. His soiled clothes and humble bearings may not suggest his high income and extensive properties, but cultivating this modesty is part of his values. Such a bazaar merchant is an archetype of the traditional rich. A person of similar financial standing in the firm or modern sector would be the head of a corporation, a medical specialist, or a reputable lawyer. He would be dressed in a tailored suit or a custom-made *Shalwar–Kameez*, working out of an air-conditioned office, attended by an assistant and maintaining an air of authority and status. Both fall in the same income strata, but have very different lifestyles and class status. Similar contrasts can be pointed out between a prosperous farmer and his middle-class counterpart, an engineer or university teacher. Only the bottom rungs of the modern and indigenous sectors have similar lifestyles brought on by shared poverty. These class and lifestyle differentiations are further sharpened by ethnic and regional cultures. It is this contrast in lifestyles and modes of living that strikes foreigners as centuries apart.

As discussed in Chapter 5, social class in Pakistan has to be seen in its historical context. It has the broad contours of upper, middle, and lower strata, arising from property relations and a commercial economy. These strata are regional in scope and suffused with ethnicity. Independence has interlinked, to some extent integrated, regional strata especially the urban segments and middle and upper segments. Yet each stratum is further divided into sociocultural groups differentiated by lifestyle and value orientations. Within the same social class, there are lifestyle or sociocultural segments defined equally by economic status, cultural values (traditional versus modern in broad terms), lifestyle, and consumption patterns.

Class segments include globally connected groups of executives, bankers, designers, and artists in Karachi, Lahore, and Islamabad. The monthly *Mirror* (1960s), *Dahanak* (Urdu social gossip magazine of the 1970s), and the "Scene and Events" columns of *The Friday Times* (1990s and 2000s) have been purveyors of the fast-paced life of this segment. The dance parties, obsessions with body weight, and dashes to Dubai or New York are the hallmarks of this striking lifestyle.

At the opposite end of the spectrum are *mullahs*, those who teach and study in *madrassahs*, run mosques, write and publish Islamic literature, and form the rank and file of Islamic political parties. They have been always a part of Pakistan's social mosaic, but their ranks have grown exponentially in period 3. This segment is very visible in the public space since the 1980s. Men of this group wear color-coded turbans, green, white, black, etc., indicative of their denominational affiliations. Women don varying types of *niqab* or *hijab* signaling their beliefs about *purdah*.

There are numerous class segments in between these two extremes such as Baloch tribes, Thar nomads, Muhajir urban workers, or Punjabi bazaar merchants.

Table 9.1 Opinion survey at the fiftieth year of independence

Question	Percentage of Respondents		
	Favourable Response (Yes)	Unfavourable Response (No)	Undecided (Don't Know)
1 Are you better off than your parents?	72	27	1
2 Will your children have better quality of life than yourself?	67	30	3
3 Given the choice to emigrate, would you stay in Pakistan?	82	18	—
4 Should imams give political sermons?	18	81	1
5 Have religious parties done more harm than good?	72	25	3
6 Are love marriages better than arranged marriages?	12	87	1

Source: Selected questions from the *Herald Annual*, 'What do Pakistani really want?", January 1997.

Yet a large majority of Pakistanis tack close to class segments that subscribe to liberal and pragmatic beliefs and values. They are modernist materially and open to change, although their family life and social relations tend to be traditional. Although the religion is central to the life of Pakistanis, most of them do not support Islamic political parties. *The Herald Monthly* conducted an opinion poll of a representative sample of adults in seven major cities in 1997, at the fiftieth anniversary of independence. Table 9.1 summarizes the findings about opinions on key sociopolitical topics. From this table, two indicators can be cited as evidence of urban Pakistanis' attitudes toward religion's role in social life. When asked whether imams (clerics) should give political sermons, 81 percent of respondents said "no." Similarly, a sizable majority of respondents, 72 percent, believed that the religious parties did more harm than good, women holding this opinion more strongly than men. Manzur Ejaz, a columnist for a leading English daily, supports this conclusion. He observes that Pakistani society is more liberal at the grass roots than all the talk of Islam suggests.[6] The intertwining of modernity and tradition is the thematic core of Pakistan's culture.

Elite and power structure

The elite are a small social segment that exercise a large influence in a society and are recognized to be at the top of the social hierarchy. Sociological literature differentiates between various types of elite groups, such as the economic and cultural elite. They may overlap, but the group that commands authority over others, namely the ruling elite, stands apart. It is this group that occupies commanding positions in the power structure of a society. Pareto, Marx, Mosca, and Mills are the leading theorists of the phenomenon of ruling elite and power structure.[7]

Both Marxist and structural theorists suggest that the ruling elite's power largely lies in their control of economic resources, such as land, industry, or finance. The power itself is the consequence of the structure of economic relations and control of the means of production, classical Marxism suggests. Antonio Gramsci's concept of hegemony explains how the ruling elite imposes an ideology and a worldview on subordinate classes through media and institutions to win their submission. Examining Pakistani society through this lens reveals a more complex picture.

The elite in Pakistan are divided into three categories. The first type is the traditional social elite, comprising of landlords, tribal *sardars*, *biradari* leaders, and the old-wealth rich. The second category is the positional elite, who derive power and prestige from their positions in state institutions. It is the authority vested in their offices that elevates them into the ranks of the elite. Military and civil officers, politicians, judges, journalists, etc. are among such elite. The top echelons of these positions form the national ruling elite. The middle-ranking officials, for example, mayors, councillors, magistrates, police superintendents, or lawyers, are the positional elite at the local level. The third category is the economic elite, such as corporate executives, industrialists, professionals, and businessmen. They are rich and economically influential but generally without a social base for political power.

Overall, Pakistan's elite derive power from the traditional structures of social as well as economic domination on the one hand, and from the positions vested with public authority on the other. These observations are elaborated and validated by the following historical accounts of the development of the three types of elite in the post-independence period.

Traditional elite

Historically, the ruling families and their feudal legatees, complemented by Islamic jurists, were the elite in the medieval Muslim societies of India. Tribal and caste/*biradari* leaders, and in cities leading merchants as well, were the local elite. Those selected by a king as his agents rose in status and power. The British patronized the historic elite, relying on them to maintain peace and order. In the colonial era, cities became centers of the emerging money economy and seats of administrative, educational, and health services. Thus, from cities emerged a small but influential group of lawyers, judges, and professionals who usually came from powerful clans and families. Together urban leaders, rural landlords, *biradari* and tribal leaders formed the elite strata of Muslim communities, nationally as well as regionally. The independence movement mobilized these elite groups and brought them into the political limelight.

The 1946 elections gave the Muslim League the mandate to represent Muslims and laid the groundwork for the partition of British India. The Muslim League's strategy for winning elections was to nominate local elite as its candidates and to seek the support of *sajjada nashins/pirs* (custodians and spiritual heirs of revered shrines), particularly in Punjab and Sindh.[8] This strategy consolidated the traditional elite's role as the powerbrokers in the new state of Pakistan.

The traditional elite have dominated the politics of Pakistan. During the periods of elected governments, provincial and national assemblies have been dominated by rural landlords and *biradari*/tribal leaders: Daultana, Gurmani, Khuhro, Talpur, or Hotis in period 1; Bhutto, Khar, Jatoi, Bughti in the 2; and Junejo, Leghari, Jamali, Maher in period 3, are among the names cropping up among elected rulers.

In times of military rule, the traditional elite were kept away initially, but they were co-opted sooner or later to gain legitimacy and consolidate their power base. Either as elected rulers or nominees of the military governments, the traditional elite have been the powerbrokers in the 55 years of Pakistan's history, one way or another.

At this juncture, a clarification of the term "traditional elite" is in order. The word "traditional" refers not to personal values and outlook but to their status in the social structure. Regarding personal lifestyle, as Chapter 6 points out, rural landlords seized opportunities arising from economic development.[9] They invested in industries and educated their children for administrative and military careers, thereby retaining their power base in the changing local economy. Unlike the modern economic elite, they have generally stayed rooted in their home territories even when they branched into new ventures. The traditional elite draw their power from their economic standing as well as their social base as heads of clans or ethnic communities.

Positional elite

The second category of elite consists of individuals who hold positions of public power. Military commanders, senior civil servants, chiefs of police or secret services, and judges have been among such elite at the national level. Regionally and locally, commissioners, police superintendents, and selected professionals such as doctors, lawyers, journalists, or even some corporate executives constitute the elite strata. Their status as elite, national or local, is tied to their positions. Individuals circulate in and out of the elite stratum, but positions continue to be the ladder for climbing to the elite ranks.

At the national level, the positional elite became political powerbrokers early in Pakistan's history. Ghulam Mohammad, an officer of the Finance Ministry, became the head of state in 1951, followed by Sikander Mirza and Mohammad Ali, two civil servants taking over the reins of the government in 1955. From these beginnings, the positional elite have gone on to become the "Establishment" that has ruled over Pakistan both directly for about 28 years of military rules, and indirectly as organizers and arbiters of elected governments. Stephen Cohen observes that Ayub's enduring legacy has been, "an informal political system that tied together the senior ranks of the military, the civil services, key members of the Judiciary and other elite…. dubbed as the Establishment."[10]

Since Ayub's coup, the military commanders have gained an upper hand within the "Establishment." The balance has tilted in their favor cumulatively through the three periods of Pakistan's history. By the 2000s, both serving and retired military officers were heading major economic, administrative, and even educational institutions.[11]

At the provincial and district levels, commissioners, magistrates, and police officers wield authority and dispense favors. They have had preeminent positions within local power structures. The 2001 system of elected district and city executives, *nazims*, has injected the traditional elite and political leaders into the roles of the positional elite. How this change will realign the local power structure is not yet clear after four years of the new local government system.

Two points should be noted about the positional elite. First, many such elite have used their positions to acquire land, build property, and establish businesses or industries. They have become rich and influential, independent of their positions. Sons and daughters of military commanders and civil servants have become leading industrialists, transporters, or corporate executives, thereby gaining a foothold among the economic elite.

Second, the social powers of both the traditional and the economic elite are reinforced by their connections with the positional elite. The positional elite exercise public authority and dispense services necessary for people. The political and economic elite depend on them for favors. In return, the positional elite need the help of the political and economic elite for their appointments, transfers, and promotions.[12] Thus, a system of power exchange ties various categories of elite together.

Economic elite

The phrase "twenty-two families" has become a metaphor for Pakistan's economic distribution. It was initially used by Dr Mahboob-ul-Haque, the chief economist of Pakistan's Planning Commission in 1968 to describe the pattern of economic distribution in the country, namely 22 families owned 66 percent of industrial, 70 percent of insurance, and 80 percent of banking assets.[13] It points to the economic elite of the modern sector who largely emerged after independence.

Nationally, Pakistan has a small but oligopolistic elite in the modern sector of the economy. This pattern persists, although membership of the elite families has increased and their composition has changed. Locally, the modern and traditional economic elite intertwine to some extent. For example, a leading landlord may also be the owner of a major factory in a town, or the owner of an IT firm could also be a notable of a powerful *biradari* in a city.

How has the composition of the national economic elite changed since the days of the "twenty-two families"? Shahid-ur-Rehman has tabulated the names of the top 44 family groups dominating the industrial and financial sectors, both in 1970 and 1997. Comparison of the two lists shows 24 new names in 1997 and the disappearance of an equal number from the 1970 list.[14] Adamjees, Noons, Karims, and Hyesons were among the economic elite in 1970, but their economic empires eroded through the splitting up of family assets and by the nationalization policies of the Bhutto government in the 1970s. They have been replaced by Ittefaq, United, Chakwal, Hashwani, and Servis groups, for example. The 44 families owned 43 percent of the nonfinancial companies listed on the Karachi Stock Exchange in 1995. They also collectively owned 370 unlisted companies.[15] Although their share of the national industrial assets has decreased slightly since 1970, they have continued to be a dominant force in Pakistan's economy.

Ethnicity and caste define even the economic elite of the modern sector. Imran Ali observes that two ethnocaste groups dominate Pakistan's big business: Gujrati-speaking Memons, Bohras, and Ismailis settled in Karachi and artisanal/ service castes of the Punjab, such as Chiniotis, Sheikhs, and Kakezais.[16] Karachi's economic barons dominated in period 1, but the balance tilted in favor of the Punjabi groups in period 3, as their close ties to General Zia's government gave them an advantage. While in 1970, 24 out of the top 44 families were from Karachi, by 1997 their number had fallen to 18, whereas the Punjabi groups increased from 12 to 24 families.[14]

The modern economic elite are the product not only of entrepreneurship and market forces but also of public subsidies, protected markets, and favorable loans. Particularly in period 3, dubiously obtained bank loans have financed the enterprises of politically well-connected families.[17] A form of savage capitalism of little public virtue has been the hallmark of the politicians and military and civilian officers who have founded new economic dynasties.[18] Some of them have built such a large network of businesses that they have joined the ranks of the 44 families.

Finally, this account of the economic elite is not complete without mentioning the business enterprises of the military and its various foundations. Army, air force, and navy have sponsored foundations such as Fauji, Shaheen, and Askari that own industries, airlines, farms, educational institutions, and real estate enterprises. Retired generals and colonels head these organizations, employing former military officers and managing near monopolies in businesses spread all across the country. These foundations are backed by the military and have privileges not available to their competitors. They are among the leading "big" businesses, with assets totaling billions of rupees. Their directors and executives are part of the economic elite although they are not the owners of these corporations personally.

Processes of elite formation

The formation of the elite is a process embedded in the social structure. One's *biradari*, caste, and ethnicity provide the social capital that, combined with individual enterprise and talent, lays the path for one's rise into the ranks of the elite. Inheritance and connections combine with an individual's achievements to open doors to power and riches. Independence and economic development have brought new opportunities but access to them is largely through the traditional paths. The blending of traditional privileges with modern materialism is the basis of elite formation.

The elites are not monolithic in structure and there are ups and downs in their fortunes. Individuals and families have risen and fallen out of the elite strata. There are many cases of rags-to-riches at the second and third tiers of the elite. At this juncture, the question to be asked is how does the elite affect the daily life of the ordinary citizen?

Elite privileges and daily life

In the late 1980s, a new phrase was added to the Pakistani narrative, namely VIP (very important person) culture. It refers to the special treatment influential persons expect and receive in the public sphere. By the late 1990s, the VIP privileges had to be graded to reflect the exceptional status of super elite such as prime ministers, presidents, military chiefs, etc. This led newspapers to coin the term VVIP (very very important persons). VVIPs' visits to a city are a citizen's nightmare, as roads are blocked, flights are delayed, and schoolchildren are taken in buses to form cheering crowds, even on a hot June afternoon. Such privileges override civic norms, and in many cases, public laws.

It is an everyday experience that to cash a check, book an air flight, or pay utility bills, ordinary citizens line up sometimes for hours, yet "important" persons routinely bypass queues to be solicitously served while the rightful wait. Trains and buses, sometimes even air flights, are delayed for late-arriving VIPs. The elite are ushered free to the choicest seats in cricket test matches, music concerts, or plays, while ticket-holders are shuffled around. These are not occasional happenings but daily experiences in Pakistan.

The daily life in Pakistan for ordinary citizens has little predictability and regularity. Every day has to be negotiated by some *ad hoc* arrangements. Almost any dealing with civic institutions requires beseeching, bribing, boasting (in the vein "you do not know who I am"), or seeking an influential person's intercession. Privilege and status are the currencies in public space. Those lacking in these assets have to put up with indifference and indignity. The elite subvert the institutional order by demanding special favors. Citizens' rights are violated routinely. Yet such violations seldom enter the narrative of democracy and human rights.

People used to accept elite privileges, but over time the public's tolerance has been wearing out and resentment is endemic. Newspapers take note of the brazen elite privileges or excessive public inconveniences. Occasionally, popular discontent has boiled over into protests and riots.[19]

Sites of segregation

Everyday life in Pakistan is a mosaic of intersecting circles of different lifestyles and separated circuits of activities. Differences are stark, visible in dress, food, language, gestures, working conditions, deportment, homes and neighborhoods, etc. Walking down a street, one may find men in *dhotis* (wrap-around cover for the lower body) and *kurta* (collarless shirt), *shalwar–kameez,* or pants and suits. Some may have turbans, many may be without any headgear, some others may have caps, a few could be sporting baseball hats. Women's dress does not vary as widely; *shalwar–kameez* and, to a lesser extent, a sari are the standard wear, but their social differences are signaled by how much of the head, face, or arms they bare and by the quality of the clothes. People's dress indicates their social class, cultural, and religious orientations and ethnic/regional background. By looking at someone's dress, one can tell where on the spectrum of the vernacular to global lifestyles she or he falls. Yet there is more to sociocultural differences than dress.

One way of describing the diversity of lifestyles and cultural orientations is to array them along a continuum ranging from vernacular/traditional on the one side, Islamic revivalist in the middle, and various shades of modern and global on the other end. Using common stereotypes by which Pakistanis characterize one another, sociocultural groups can be roughly divided into the following categories to highlight their lifestyles and outlooks.[20]

1 "Westernized," lately called Americanized, affluent who tend to be fashion-ably modernist, educated, and upper/upper-middle class;
2 *brown sahibs* (and their *mems*- wives) are high-status families affecting modernity but steeped in vernacular;
3 *ashrafs* (variously called Sayeds, Chaudhris, Khans, Maliks, Sardars, etc.) are local notables, upper class and powerful within their clans and communities, but traditional in outlook;
4 *babus* are low and middle-level white-collar workers mixing modest material modernity with literate traditions of indigenous cultures;
5 *safed posh* are traditional lower-middle classes involved in commerce, small industry, and providing services in rural as well as urban areas;
6 *mullahs* and *pirs* are clerics and spiritual guides and those following a pietistic but orthodox mode of living;
7 *Jamaatis*, this appellation was initially used to describe members of Jamaat-i-Islami, but it has been extended to all those of Islamic deportment and convictions; and
8 *dehatis* or *pandoos* are primarily rustic villagers and tribals, usually of poor and illiterate ancestry.

I must hurriedly add that these are typological categories or archetypes that high-light different modes of living. They overlap and fuse with each other, spinning out a wide array of sociocultural groups of distinct values and lifestyles. Some are identified with specific neighborhoods in cities and villages or regions.

The Westernized and their surrogates, *brown sahibs*, primarily live in modern suburbs and fashionable parts of cities, described in Chapter 5. Islamabad as a city is an emblem of their lifestyle, with its wide boulevards, bungalow estates of spacious lawns, tucked away servant quarters, air-conditioned shopping plazas, and trend-setting fashions. At the other extreme are *katchi abadis* that are places of migrant *dehatis* and low-status *babus*. Similarly, other groups cast imprints of their lifestyles and consumption patterns on the landscape.

Children of the upper classes of Western orientation attend schools, with names such as St Patrick or St Anthony, while *Jamaatis* have their Islamic academies that may, nevertheless, prepare students for the "A" and "O" levels of the Cambridge Secondary diplomas. In villages, there are public schools that do not have roofs, desks, or sometimes not even teachers.

Public schools offered a good education to children of both the rich and poor as well as the conservatives and modernists until they were swamped by the demands of exploding enrolments and Bhutto's nationalization of private schools in the 1970s. For example, I went to a government high school in Lahore in the early years of Pakistan. Among my school fellows were sons of governors, ministers, diplomats, and corporate executives on the one hand, and of carpenters and clerks on the other. This "mixing" of social classes and lifestyles has greatly decreased.

In the third period, privatization turned education into a lucrative business, spawning the "English medium" and vernacular schools of widely divergent quality. By the 1990s, private universities for professional and business studies sprouted all over the country. Some were of international standards, such as LUMS and GIK Institute; while others were just tuition centers selling nonaccredited degrees in business and computer studies. Each of these served different segments of society. All in all, education has become a mode of streaming youth into divergent social classes and cultural groups.

What neighborhood one chooses to live in; which school one can afford and prefer to send children to; where one goes for healthcare; and what one does for leisure have become expressions of one's social status and cultural orientations. In Pakistani society, such choices represent not only class but also cultural differences. Pakistan has become a society of compartmentalized life cycles, separating the rich from the poor and the folk (culture) from the Islamic and the modern.

Circuits of integration

Undoubtedly, the spatial and functional compartmentalization of sociocultural groups has not walled them off from each other. Social segregation in Pakistan may not rise to the level of racial and ethnic separation in New York, London, or Paris. There are structures and processes that scramble the boundaries between sociocultural groups. Nationalism and Islam are the two overarching structures that promote social integration at many levels: sociological, symbolic, and institutional. Extended family, *biradari*, *zat*, and tribe are the social institutions that link persons of divergent economic status, lifestyles, and locations into cohesive groups and communities. How do these circuits of integration work?

Anybody who has witnessed the riotous annual celebrations of Independence Day in Pakistan can appreciate the shared nationalist sentiments that momentarily unite people across class and ethnic lines. People's identity as Pakistanis is a force of social integration. Despite the social fragmentation and inequalities, Pakistani society has developed common memories, symbols, and sentiments that tie together, albeit frailly, its various segments into a national community.

To be a Muslim is even more directly a shared everyday experience. *Azan* (call to prayers) reverberating all across the land five times a day is a reminder of common bonds, regardless of whether one is an observant Muslim or not. While differentiated by sects, mosques and shrines are places where rich and poor, Pashtoons and Punjabis, old and young, and *ashrafs* and *dehatis* come together. Even at home, Muslims hold the Quran readings, *dars* (sermons), or collective prayers that breach boundaries of servant and master, high and low caste, acquaintances and relatives.

Islam's role as a crosscutting institution has grown over the three periods, but it has grown larger in the third period. Islamic youth organizations, *tablighi* (proselytizing) circles, and women's *dars* have spread in all sections of society. Paradoxically, Islamization has also heightened sectarian divisions while promoting feelings of Muslim brotherhood. On the whole, Islam's role as a "bonding" force is strongly felt.

Biradari, *zat*, and tribe are institutions of primordial identities and solidarity. They bring together persons of different occupations, educational backgrounds, and lifestyles. A marriage, funeral, or celebration is an occasion for obligatory socializing and customary gift exchanges among members of such groups. These bonds help breach barriers of class and lifestyle.

Finally, households and businesses in Pakistan operate as ecological systems wherein divergent elements are functionally linked together. Even households of modest means have casual help: a sweeper to clean the toilet, a poor neighbor or relative to shop, matchmaker for arranging marriages, etc. The elite are always in the company of servants who cook, clean, chauffeur, and keep watch over their children. In offices and businesses, they have peons, guards, and teaboys, apart from the clerical and professional staff. A family may shelter a widowed aunt or a distant relative who came to study in a local college. Although traditional in origin, such social obligations continue to hold sway despite mobility and development. They may even have grown over successive periods as urbanism has spread but institutions of public welfare have not evolved in parallel.

As pointed out earlier, neighborhoods and commercial areas have two sides, a facade of primary functions and an underside of complementary activities. Servant quarters at the back of bungalows, or porters and sales staff's teashops, eateries and shacks behind the bright lights of commercial centers are expressions of the physical proximity and functional interdependence of the rich and poor. Thus, in various ways, everyday life in Pakistan is based on proximity and face-to-face dealings of divergent sociocultural groups. It does not reduce social disparities, but it does bridge social distances.

Quality of everyday life

Quality of life is a concept indicating health, welfare, and environmental conditions of localities, regions, or nations that is used to highlight living conditions. I am adapting it to describe patterned behaviors in the public sphere, that is on the street, at work, and in public places. It particularly focuses on the degree of stability, regularity, satisfaction, security, and safety felt by people in public space. In sum, my aim is to outline common feelings and sentiments associated with everyday life outside the home. The change in these feelings over time will be pointed out with whatever direct and indirect indicators are available. I will begin with the description of work situations.

Work

The change in Pakistan's economy is reflected in its occupational profile. In 1961, an overwhelming majority of the labor force, two out of three workers (65.1 percent), were employed in agriculture. By 1998, about only one in three workers (34.7 percent) was engaged in farming, forestry, or fishing. On the other end of the spectrum, in 1961 only 1.1 percent of the labor force were in professional and technical occupations. Their proportion had increased to 7.7 percent by 1998, as their absolute number had increased tenfold since 1961. This growth in the professional labor force does not indicate that Pakistan has become an industrial society, but it suggests a notable shift nonetheless. What appears to have happened in the period 1961–98 is that rural labor shifted to the unskilled occupations in cities, which grew in proportion from 9.7 percent in 1961 to 33.9 percent of the 1998 labor force.[21] The majority of Pakistan's workers are in urban areas now and that is where post-independence work opportunities have developed.

Not only has the type of work changed but even the traditional occupations have new working conditions. Farming has become a commercial enterprise, using technological and chemical inputs and sensitive to market conditions, both nationally and globally. Farm work has come to involve operating machinery, applying chemical fertilizers, and pesticides. While in the 1960s, jobs advertised in newspapers were mostly for administrative assistants, stenos, spinning and weaving technicians, or heavy machinery operators, by the 1990s "positions vacant" were predominantly those of computer programmers, IT technicians, electrical engineers, and management and marketing professionals. While numerous new occupations have developed, particularly at the professional level, even established occupations require new skills and knowledge.

Both urban and rural occupations have been largely detached from their caste moorings. Carpenters' sons are doctors or army officers, whereas farmers' children may be carpet weavers. Occupations are increasingly based on personal capabilities and opportunities rather than on birth and inheritance, landlords being an exception. Unemployment stalks young workers and even engineers and doctors. This makes for a lot of insecurity, conformity, and ethnocommunal nepotism in workplaces.

Moving away from home has become almost a condition of working life. People move from villages to cities, and from one city to another in pursuit of work. Even the Pakistani diaspora has had a feedback effect on the job market in the country. Working in Dubai, Toronto, or New York has become a part of the ambition of young workers and for many it has become a crowning event in their careers. The brain drain has become so pervasive that it is affecting the quality of the workforce in Pakistani society. All these changes have come about incrementally. A date cannot be put on the beginning of such trends but the pace of their diffusion has quickened since the late 1970s, that is, the beginning of the third period.

Work environment, of course, varies by sector and industry. The bazaar sector is informal, lacking in explicit rules, and based on highly personalized dealings and *ad hoc* decision making. Owners of businesses work alongside workers for long hours in dusty and unhygienic conditions, while workers are, by and large, personal servants whose job security depends on the good will of owners. The modern sector, including public agencies, is organized in hierarchical ranks, divided into caste-like strata topped by "gazetted" officers, the middle layer made up of supervisors followed by clerks, teachers, journeymen, and the lowest rungs manned by drivers, peons, etc. These differentiations, common in modern organizations, are more rigidly followed in Pakistani workplaces, such as air-conditioned offices for officers, hot and drafty halls for clerks and workers. Workplaces recapitulate the patron–client structure of the social organization and have the informal substratum of ethnic, sectarian, or caste/friendship networks.

Work ethics take a back seat to socializing and personal obligations. Visit a public office, you will find staff chatting and entertaining visitors. Private corporations are a bit more focused on work, but visitors surround officers even there.

Vast armies of lowly workers live a life of bare subsistence. After long commutes from their crowded homes in villages and *katchi abadis*, peons, laborers, or *masis* (cleaning women) arrive at work exhausted with a full day's work ahead. The high point of their workday is a glass of tea or a little gossip with co-workers.

Except for the self-employed and a small class of professionals, artists, and high officers whose work is a calling or source of power, earning a livelihood and security are the primary motivations for work. Self-fulfillment and personal inclinations are secondary considerations in the choice of jobs and careers. The institution of work, like other social institutions, has divergent manifest and latent functions. The fissure dividing tradition and modernity also splits this institution.

Sense of community and trust

Travelers to Pakistan find its people warm, hospitable, and open, particularly the common folk.[22] People are generally approachable and easy to relate with, although different class segments have slightly different norms of relating to strangers. The modern and affluent segments are relatively more formal and distant toward others. Villagers and the urban lower and middle classes of the vernacular lifestyles are relatively more gregarious. Almost all groups observe the mores of deferring to age, sex and social status differences.

In a "lower class" carriage of a train or a country bus, it is not uncommon to share food and family stories with fellow passengers. An airplane ride or the "first class" car of a train does not offer such conviviality. People address each other as brother, sister, or uncle, signaling intimacy and deference of primary relations even in a passing contact. These patterns have changed little over time, although crowding and mobility have had an inhibiting effect on people's approachability in public.

Neighborhoods have been the setting for social networking, men visiting or meeting each other on streets, courtyards, or in corner tea shops. Women are the soul of neighborly relations. They visit one another, particularly during the day when men are away, keep an eye on each other's children, organize Quran readings, exchange food, and borrow money or goods from one another in times of need.

Traditionally, neighborhoods have a strong sense of community. Neighbors are fictive relatives and are treated as such. Often an older neighbor is expected to reprimand a child if the latter is found loitering or misbehaving. Such have been the norms of neighborliness. Villages have been all the more functioning communities with a strong sense of belonging. The honor and reputation of a village is a shared responsibility. This is the overall state of social relations in the old neighborhoods of cities and villages, but it should not suggest that these are communities of complete harmony. Undoubtedly, there are neighborly spats, kin strife, and community discords, but traditionally a sense of common destiny binds residents together.

Mobility, urbanization, and economic development have eroded the sense of community, although, as mentioned earlier, extended family and kin network remain strong. The attenuation of neighborliness is strikingly correlated with modernization and affluence. In cities, relations with neighbors weaken as the size of a house lot increases. In areas of large-lot bungalows, there is relatively little interaction among neighbors. Introductions are limited to encounters on the street and exchanges ritualized as sharing of sacrificial meat or *niaz* (prayers of thanks) offerings. Relatively speaking, women may have more visiting relations with neighbors than men, although similarity of lifestyles and class segments undergird such relations. Social interaction increases as the houses get smaller and lifestyles tilt toward relatively more traditional or vernacular norms.

These trends emerged in colonial times, with the residential segregation of the rich from the poor as well as of the vernacular and the modern. Yet they have blossomed successively in the three periods of post-independence development.

Overall, Pakistani society has had a high level of social trust historically, trust being manifest in interlocking interests and community solidarity. There was tolerance of social differences based on caste, religion, or sects. Over the three periods, social trust has gradually eroded as a result of divergence of interests, increasing disparities, and the state's failures to ensure safety and security for all citizens. By the 2000s, Pakistan has become a society of low trust.[23]

Security and safety

Historically, an average Pakistani, although poor, felt secure about life and property within home and locality. Crime was relatively rare and largely limited to feuds about land, money, or women, as the popular proverb suggests. Informal social controls of neighborhood, kin and *biradari* helped maintain order and peace. Over the 50 years of the post-independence period, this sense of security has gradually dissipated. Street crime, mob riots, bomb blasts, looting and burning of properties, and political, religious, and ethnic conflicts have multiplied, robbing people of their sense of security. Furthermore, hazards of daily life, be those traffic accidents, poorly built structures, polluted air and water, rain floods, etc., have increased with urbanization. Safety is a grossly neglected part of the development paradigm followed in Pakistan. In addition, changing community norms and growth of population have reduced the effectiveness of informal social controls. Altogether, there has been a threshold change in the feelings of security and safety in daily life.

Why have feelings of personal security and safety changed? This question draws us into examining the indicators of major crimes and public disorder. Data about these events are neither reliable nor readily available. Crime and accident data produced by the Federal Ministry of Interior are based on incidents reported to the police. There is an undetermined level of underreporting of crimes, due to the incompetence of police officials, reluctance to record crimes that show badly on their performance, or being paid off to ignore. Similarly, records of riots, bomb blasts, or floods are sketchy and inconsistent. Despite these limitations of data, I have developed some indicators of the trends in crime and other threats to life and property.

Data about murder are more reliable as it is an event that gets the media's attention and police tend to record it diligently. Thus, the trends in crime are observable from the reported murders per year. For riots, sectarian and ethnic clashes, and bomb blasts, etc., I have tabulated major yearly incidents from newspaper headlines for the 50-year period collected by Razi Razi and Shakir Shakir.[24] From these figures, a fairly good overview of the events affecting people's sense of security and safety can be gained.

The reported number of murders has steadily increased over the three periods of Pakistan's social history, although the year 1984 marks a watershed in the trend-line taking a sharp upward turn. In the first period (1948–70), the average number of murders per year was 2,848. The yearly average rose to 4,633, an almost 63 percent increase, in the second period (1971–7). In the third period, initially the average number of murders per year fell to 4,381 (1978–83), but in the latter part (1984–96) they shot up to 7,321 per year, about 67 percent increase since 1983. Taking the increase of population into account, the murder rate, computed as the ratio of one murder to number of persons, shows an increase in the first period, rising from 1 murder per 16,700 persons in 1951 to 1 per 13,907 in 1972. It fell to 1 murder per 17,790 persons in 1981, but rose back by the next population census in 1998 to 1 per 13,235. Overall, Pakistan's murder rate would be considered high as it approaches close to that of the USA (1 murder per 18,330 population in the year 2000), which is a country of high crime among the advanced countries. Other crimes, such as robberies, kidnapping, cattle rustling, child abduction, rapes, and that subcontinental shame, bride burning, have increased manifold over the 50-year period, as is evident from fragmentary data and media accounts.[25]

Based on the information culled from newspaper headlines, I have drawn two sets of graphs of the yearly incidents of riots, urban floods, bomb blasts, and ethnic strife (see Figures 9.1 and 9.2). One graph shows the number of respective incidents year by year, the other shows the number of deaths resulting from these events. The graphs show that: (1) spikes in riots coincide with years of political

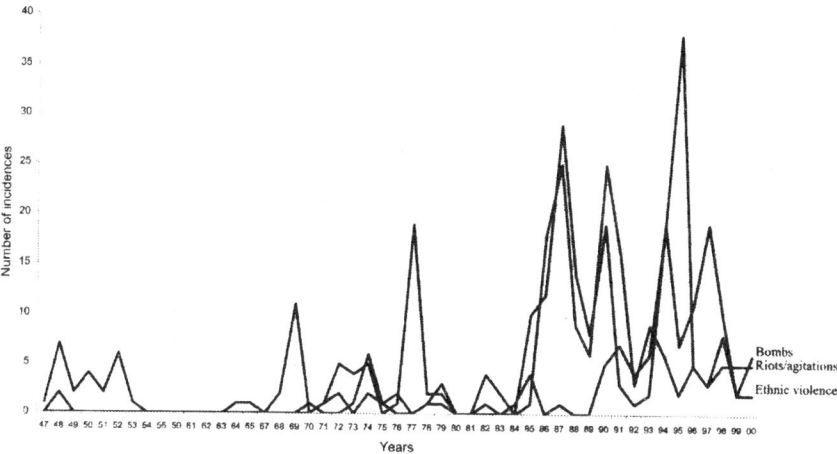

Figure 9.1 Number of incidences of violence, 1947–2000

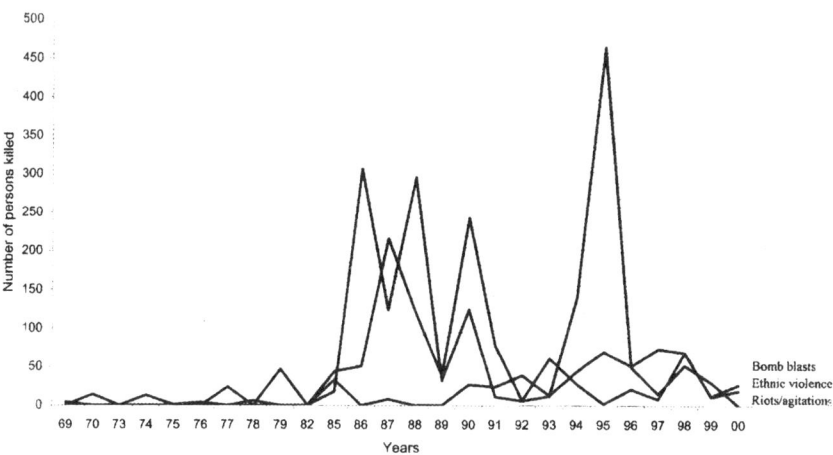

Figure 9.2 Number of persons killed in riots, bomb blasts and ethnic violence, 1947–2000

turmoil and agitations against the governments of the time; (2) ethnic or sectarian strife was a rare event in the first and second periods, but it burst on the public scene in full fury in the 1990s;[26] (3) bomb blasts became an epidemic from 1986 onward and continued into the early 1990s, remaining at the level of four to six incidents per year thereafter. Overall, the evidence is striking that by the third period, violence and disorder have become a condition of everyday life. Even if one is not personally affected by the violence, as millions have not suffered any direct loss, one is prone to feel anxious and uncertain about the unpredictable violence flaring up in one's surroundings. How have these feelings affected everyday life?

The tranquility and peace of the public space has diminished. In the 1950s and 1960s, one could be in a park or street late at night and be unconcerned about the possibility of being mugged or held up. There was seldom any anxiety about being in the "wrong place," for being a Pashtoon or Muhajir, Shia or Ahmadi, namely of different ethnicity or sect. Police may not have been friendly, but one was not apprehensive about the policemen's shakedown. This feeling of security began to erode in the 1970s, but by the 1990s one had to be careful about where one was and under what conditions.

Undisciplined traffic and murderous drivers have made roads and streets a daily threat to life and limb.[27] Even those in private cars are not immune from smash-ups. By the 1990s, almost every day newspapers carried accounts of trains derailing, buses turning over, pedestrians falling into sewer manholes, a protest march turning into a rampaging mob on a busy street, and mosques being attacked by sectarian terrorists, etc.[28] Sectarian riots, floods, or bomb blasts were occurrences over and above these daily events. The police were a hazard by themselves on account of their highhandedness and corruption.[29] They offered little protection and were themselves a source of anxiety.

Cumulatively, these factors have fostered defensive behavior. A large number of households keep guns. Security firms, almost nonexistent until the 1970s, have become a multibillion rupees industry. There is a trend toward building gated communities. A large number of urban neighborhoods and family compounds of the rich in villages have round-the-clock armed guards, as do many private homes and stores. Even modest homes have bars and grills on windows and doors. Various sect communities, *madrassahs,* and political parties maintain militias and vigilante gangs. Almost everywhere, there are reminders of looming violence.

Another marked but unacknowledged effect of rising crime and violence is that even the elite and powerful are not safe any more. It used to be that the victims of disorder were mostly from the poor and powerless. In the 1990s, commissioners, police superintendents, ministers, judges, and prominent public figures (for example, Hakim Saeed of Hamdard Foundation in 1998) were also victims of violence.[30] Being a member of the elite or a powerful public official was no more a guarantee of safety. Ethnic and sectarian violence, in particular, has spared no one.

Yet it should also be said that people have "accommodated" all these threats by being vigilant as well as fatalistic. Streets are choked with traffic, parks and restaurants are full, shopping plazas reverberate with the buzz of crowds at night. In Karachi, Lahore, or other metropolitan cities, there could be a bomb blast in one part, while life goes on undisturbed in other parts. This is the reality of Pakistan's everyday life. The distrust of strangers has increased. People have retreated into homes and private places for gatherings, parties, and socializing. Public space has shrunk.

The security and safety of minorities and women is a matter of a different order. Over and above the above-discussed threats to life and property, they are subject to harassment and loss of personal liberty. How these additional sources of violence have come to affect them will be briefly discussed below.

Minorities: marginalized and fearful

In Pakistan, "minority" is a code word for non-Muslims, such as Christians, Hindus, Ahmadis, and a minuscule number of Parsees, Sikhs, etc. Of course, there are ethnic groups who are in a minority numerically, but they are socially and constitutionally part of the majority community. About 96 percent of Pakistan's population is Muslim (1998 census), making the country overwhelmingly a society of Muslims. Minorities are numerically as well as socially and politically marginal to Pakistani society.

Numerically, minorities have grown at a slightly higher rate than Muslims. The population of minorities increased five times (400 percent), from 0.9 in 1961 to 4.9 million in 1998, compared with about four times (300 percent) increase of the Muslim population in 37 years. This difference in the rate of growth may be partially the result of the legislative reclassification of Ahmadis as non-Muslims in 1974. Pakistan has been "manufacturing" minorities by pushing out sects of unconventional beliefs from the Islamic community. Ahmadis were the first to be turned into a minority, but the politically inspired demands for excommunicating other sects continue to surface periodically. Islamic militants have occasionally demanded that Ismailis, Zikris, and some extremists have even asked that Shias, who are about 20–30 percent of the population, be declared minorities. Regardless of what the future brings for these sects, the fact that agitators are branding them non-Muslims makes these groups vulnerable and apprehensive.

Pakistan's constitution as well as public discourse has consistently maintained that minorities have full rights of citizenship and are entitled to the full protection of the law. Jinnah's address at the inaugural meeting of the new Constituent Assembly of Pakistan (August 11, 1947) was a call for the equal rights of all citizens, regardless of religion and creed. He said, "you will find in the course of time Hindu would cease to be Hindu and Muslim would cease to be Muslim, not in the religious sense...but in the political sense as citizens of the state."[31]

Successive military and civilian governments in Pakistan have not directly persecuted minorities, but they have often appeased Islamic militants for political gains. General Zia's Islamization policies made reciting of the *kalima* (the formal profession of Islamic faith), or use of Islamic symbols by Ahmadis cognizable offences. Islamization laws also laid the groundwork for the persecution of non-Muslims under the "blasphemy of the Prophet" provision, a charge punishable by death. The zealous *mullahs* and extremists have used the blasphemy ordinance to settle scores or harass individuals of Christian and Ahmadi faiths. The governments following General Zia's military rule offered little protection or justice to the accused.[32] Lately General Musharraf has attempted to reduce the scope for mischief under the controversial blasphemy law, by proposing a judicial review of accusations before the police may register a case against an accused. Yet even this procedural reform has provoked protests and threats from militant Islamists.[33] Hina Jilani observes, "Legislation and State policy have encouraged religious intolerance by accommodating religious extremism that has led to an aggressive hegemony of the majority religious group."[34] Public acts of omission more than those of commission have failed to prevent the terrorization of minorities. A person of minority faith lives a subdued life racked by fears. These conditions have crystallized in the third period; earlier there were isolated incidents of riots and violence but not a systematic persecution.

Undoubtedly, extremists blowing up churches or forcibly taking over Ahmadis' new town, Rabwah, and renaming it are events that grab headlines.[35] Yet the unacknowledged oppression that the minorities suffer in everyday life marginalizes them.[36] In a society where kin networks, *biradaris* and personal connections are necessary for getting jobs, promotions, or water supply to one's neighborhood, minorities are at a disadvantage. They are outsiders with an aura of disloyalty hanging over them. These feelings have grown in parallel with the rise of Islamism. In the 1950s and 1960s, Jinnah's admonishments and liberal Islamic values inhibited such sentiments.

By the 1980s, a person of minority faith could be easily intimidated with an anonymous letter or whispered rumor about her/his loyalty. One had to be careful about what one said, particularly about religion and politics. Pakistani discourse routinely blames others for national failures and Jews, Hindus, and lately Christians are the obvious suspects. This outlook oozes through newspapers, televisions, sermons, and political speeches. They foster attitudes of distrust toward minorities.

Paradoxically, on the personal level, people mix freely with persons of minority faith. Usually, there is considerable sympathy and warmth in such relations. Yet as a category of persons, Hindus, Christians, or Ahmadis are held to be unfaithful to Pakistan. This duality of attitudes permeates relations with minorities. They may be stereotyped as a community, but befriended individually. It also means that incidents of violence or discrimination against minorities do not stir a strong moral response from a majority of Muslims. There is often the unstated suspicion that minorities may have provoked such incidents.

Overall, rural communities have been generally more accepting of minorities, based on their spiritualist traditions, than cities and towns where denominational values reign. For example, Jonathan Addelton, son of an American missionary who lived in Shikarpur in the 1960s, narrates that his father found it easier to distribute biblical literature at village fairs and shrine *Urs* (annual gatherings of devotees) than in cities, where he frequently could not even set up a stall.[37] However by the third period, the viruses of violence and prejudice spread to small towns and villages, particularly in southern Punjab.

Pakistani leaders have a stock answer to the criticism of minorities' complaints. They maintain that Islam and Pakistan's constitution protect minorities and treat them as equal. Thus in the public discourse, the "ideal culture" is assumed to be the "real culture." In other words, idealized beliefs are counterposed to the reality in social life, a pervasive practice in Pakistan. However, such statements do not reassure minorities.

Harassment of women

The issue of security and safety takes a special meaning for women. Over and above the threats of crime, accidents, and violence, women have to contend with sexual harassment and religious zealotry in the public space. In streets, markets, and parks, women have to watch for that subcontinental malaise called "eve-teasing," namely overtly lecherous sizing up by men and touching and pinching by swarming young men. Women have to be extra vigilant walking, riding buses, going to crowded or lonely places, and even at work and play. It is only in the privacy of homes, surrounded by relatives and friends that women can let down their guard. This is a general condition of women's everyday life, although the rich and powerful are less affected by it.

The "honor" of a family is largely tied to its women. Thus, women bear the burden of upholding "honor" necessitating a lot of self-repression including limiting their participation in public life. Yet family and clan do not always provide security to women. As discussed in Chapter 8, honor killing and *karo kari* may be exceptional incidents, but they lurk in women's subconscious, limiting their liberty.

With rising Islamic orthodoxy, vigilantism to enforce the veil on women has grown, justified as a defense against Western *fahashi* (obscenity).[38] Periodically, zealots go about haranguing women about their make-up, dress, or mere presence in public places. Women used to play in national tennis tournaments, had field hockey competitions, and participated in athletics during the 1960s and 1970s. The modernization coming in the wake of economic development has aroused the reaction of the orthodox. General Zia banned the national women's hockey team. Mixed doubles in tennis have become a long-forgotten sport; women's athletics have gone behind *purdah*, screened from men's gaze. Public space for women has been shrinking. The MMA's (Islamic parties) provincial government in NWFP has practically banned profiling women in advertisements (2004–5).[39] All these sporadic events cumulatively jeopardize women's safety and civil rights.

Paradoxically, women's participation in the workforce has increased. In medical, teaching, and architectural professions, women have parity in numbers with men, if not the majority.[40] In the national, provincial, and local legislative bodies, about one-third of the parliamentarians are women under General Musharraf's initiated constitutional reforms (2002). The Islamic parties have also taken their share of women representatives. They now support women's representation and participation in electoral politics. Yet there is always a farther end on the right. Some *mullah* is always pronouncing women's voting or contesting elections to be un-Islamic. The point is that economic and political imperatives are bringing out women in public, yet social norms and practices are lagging behind, as are beliefs and values. This institutional lag, discussed earlier, has produced moral ambiguities and social tensions.

Not all women are equally affected by the threats to safety and liberty. Illustrative of the contradictions of social change, two culturally opposite groups have relatively more protection. First, there are the affluent and westernized that live and work in cocoons of guarded houses, air-conditioned cars, private clubs, and the corporate economy. Women of this class and segment escape by privatizing their activities. Second, the poor and traditional women that work in fields, factories, and homes side by side with men feel secure and confident in the public space.

Domestic workers, to take one example, commute long distances daily for work, riding in vans overflowing with men. This social segment has the protection of traditions backed by families and kin. It is the women of the middle-class segments who are more vulnerable to the hazards of public space in their daily life.

Again the trend toward breaking up a cohesive social organization into distinct sociocultural tracks is evident even around the issue of women's security and safety. Pakistani society has been fragmenting and its cohesion has been eroding. The fault lines in Pakistani society can be seen in its popular culture too.

Popular culture and the construction of everyday life

Before analyzing popular culture as the site where one can see how everyday life is constructed, the term "popular culture" needs to be clarified.[41] Popular culture is essentially the culture of the masses, that is, the culture of common people as distinct from that of the educated elite and intellectuals. It is reflected in crafts, arts, music, songs, media, festivals, entertainment, marches, sayings, and behaviors.[42] Classical anthropologists used to distinguish "low" culture of the masses from "high" culture of the literati, implying that the culture of the everyday is somehow less significant than the literary canons and courtly traditions.[43] This distinction has been erased in contemporary cultural studies. Now popular culture of everyday life is regarded as the text in which social and political realities are expressed. However, popular culture is not just a tablet over which the script of social life is written. It actively organizes perceptions, fosters attitudes, and channels communications that continually construct and reconstruct social organization and cultural institutions. Reading popular culture reveals the structure of society. If society is fractured, popular culture shows its chasms as well as bridges, its lines of separation and integration. This section is addressed to probing significant and persistent themes of popular culture in Pakistan and tracing their relation to social life in Pakistan.

Popular culture in Pakistan has its roots in regional communities, that is, Balochi, Pashtoon, Sindhi, Punjabi, Hunzawal, Balti, Kashmiri or even further down in their linguistic and cultural subgroups. The folk poetry, music, art, dress, spirituality, idioms, and mores of each of these communities have distinct configurations but are increasingly getting linked together by global and national institutions, knowledge and education, and the communication network. National institutions and ideologies are woven through them, producing common themes, expressions and symbols. I will focus on this layer of popular culture that courses through various regional cultural expressions.[44]

A theme of popular culture is the primacy of family and community in the life of individuals. An individual's desires and feelings are subservient to the demands of *samaj* (society or community). From ancient love legends, such as Heer–Ranjha or Sassi–Pannu to Bollywood songs, the message is unmistakable that the fate of lovers that defy caste and family mores is disappointment or tragedy. So strong are filial ties that Jagga Daaku (fearsome robber) cries like a child when missing his mother but kills his pursuers without batting an eyelash.[45] Caste, tribe, and family trump an individual's desires and goals. These notions and images are both expressions of social reality and instruments of indoctrination for tribal and *biradari* domination. Yet the loosening of primordial ties with mobility and urbanism has begun to be acknowledged in popular culture. The clash of old and new values and beliefs has become a common theme in songs and plays.

Starting in the 1970s, the drama serials of Pakistani television began presenting stories of conflicted families and the exploitative feudal values of clans and communities. The serial based on the famous novel of Shaukat Siddique, *Khuda Ki Basti* (God's Own Land), broke with the traditional images of family and neighborhood as nurturing and protective institutions. It was followed by other popular serials such as *Patjhar Kay Baad* (After Autumn), *Alif-Noon* (Alphabets), *Chand Grahan* (Moon Eclipse) challenging prevailing family values and kin solidarity. Television serials of the 1970s highlighted class conflicts and the clash of modern and traditional ways of life. Yet they stayed anchored to the ideals of the pristine past, straying not too far from projecting the family's primacy. They provided new notions about women's role as earners and urban living. Primordial ties were not repudiated, but the pursuit of personal goals, particularly of economic advancement and "clean" romance, was incorporated within family values. The television serials articulated the need for loosening the restrictive hold of the extended family.

The Islamization policies of the 1980s redefined the "ideal culture," emphasizing ritualistic pieties and religious observances as the core of social life. They also sanctified many folk traditions, particularly about women's role and deportment. A streak of joyless culture runs through the Islamic revivalist discourse. Islamists call for censoring music, painting, literature, and banning horse racing, drinking, dancing, or coeducation and the mixing of sexes. General Zia's Islamization had a lighter touch compared with what the MMA (Islamic parties) government of NWFP (2002–) has aimed to bring about. The MMA provincial government has introduced the *Hasba* Act, a legal measure to establish morality police for enforcing religious observances and promoting conformity to an Islamic code of conservative interpretations. It has cracked down on musicians, cinema owners, and cable television operators. Even circuses have not escaped their wrath.[46]

The point is that Islamic discourse has not only grown to be puritanical, but also restrictive of individual liberty. It has recast the folk order in a conservative mold, shedding its tolerant spiritualism and investing it with literalism. It is decidedly antimodern in the sociocultural sphere although willing to tap into the economic benefits of technology. The common refrain in the Islamic discourse is "Western technology without Western immorality." Yet in social life the material base comes with its own cultural and moral imperatives. One without the other produces only institutional contradictions and social incoherence. These themes are reflected in the popular culture.

The popular culture of Pakistan has developed a split personality. Of course, there has always been a distinction between the expressions of believed and lived forms of culture. Yet in the third period, this normal duality has evolved into divergent tracks of popular culture, namely ideologically approved and manifest versus latent and unrecognized but pervasive. Both coexist in Pakistani personality and culture. A few examples will illustrate my point.

Almost every public activity in Pakistan has come to begin solemnly with the recitation of the Quran, including air flights, public meetings, inaugural ceremonies for movies, or music concerts, and so on. Television and radio offer many hours of religious sermons, quiz shows about Islamic theology, and call-in programs for advice on Islamic norms. Quranic calligraphy adorns public buildings and Sadequain's calligraphic panels hang in airports, the Presidency, and in the living rooms of patrons of the arts. Although a typical middle class home may have few books, reading not being a favorite pastime, Islamic literature fills a book shelf. Interestingly, Islamic publications are the largest component of the publishing output in Pakistan.[47] *Allahamdo-Lila* (Praise be to God) and *Subhan-Allah* (Glory of God) have become figures of speech for even those who seldom follow religious observances. Islamic piety has emerged as the manifest popular culture. It is upfront but there is an underside that has thrived and grown in parallel.

At shrines all across the country, for ages whirling *Malangs* (Dervishes) have drawn crowds of men and women, segregated though, and *Qawwals* have belted out homage to Allah, the Prophet, and saints. The 1970s witnessed these folk spiritual tunes gaining the status of a national music, with the patronage of folk arts by the Bhutto government. This period also saw film music fused with Qawwali beats. Nusrat Fateh Ali Khan turned Qawwali into a global genre of fast beats and ecstasy. The fusion of folk and film rhythms created a new wave of popular music that has been embraced by all segments of society.

Buses decked with tape players blare Ataullah Iskhelvi's haunting Sariaki songs and Rahim Shah's Pashto ballads. Bhangra dance has been incorporated in *mehndi* ceremonies of marriage. Videos and Indian television have brought Bollywood movies into the family rooms of even the pious. Juhi Chawla's (popular Indian film actress) mega dance numbers are watched by whole families, wherever Zee TV is accessible. Despite Islamists' admonishments, music and songs have spread as people's demand for entertainment has grown and the youthful population has increased. This is the lived and unrecognized track of popular culture.

The political and ideological balance between the two cultural tracks tilt from one to the other, depending on whose votaries are in power. General Zia's Nizam-e-Mustafa restricted music and dancing. Nawaz Sharif in his drive to consolidate his rule through *Sharia* (1997) banned pop music and the long hair of musicians. Such bans primarily affected government-controlled television, radio, and public performances. Music, song, and even dance continued to flourish nonofficially, spread by audio and video technologies into far-flung villages.

The history of pop music in Pakistan is a metaphor for the diffusion of modern popular practices and the consequent reconstruction of cultural norms. Pop music began as a "culturally subversive" genre even in the West; its import into Pakistan was nothing less than a heresy. Yet starting from the so-called "spoiled" youth of the westernized class segment in the 1960s, it has almost become a part of mainstream music. In the process, it has been indigenized and immersed in spiritual symbolism. Today, Pakistani pop tunes bearing Urdu, Punjabi, or Sindhi lyrics are played on radio, television, and the web. Songs such as *Dil Dil Pakistan* (1987), *Shadi na Karna* (Don't Marry 1993), *Jazba-e-Junoon* (Passion of Ecstasy 1996), *Bilo De Ghar Janah* (Going to Bilo's Home 1997) blare from *khokhas* (roadside tea stalls), commuter vans, and marriage halls.

The journey of pop music from illicit to popular began with the Christian Youth bands of the 1960s. The disco craze of the 1970s was fed by Nazia and Zoheb Hasan's concerts, which in Naheed Akhtar's hands turned into Punjabi and Urdu bhangra by the early 1980s. With the rise of bands such as Vital Signs and Junoon, pop exploded in 1990s to become a vehicle for expressing patriotic sentiments and Sufi themes. It spread, evolved, and acquired a spiritual aura to incorporate the rising religiosity in Pakistan. Abrarul Haq burst on the pop scene in 1997 with a Punjabi beat that flaunted romance. Hadiqa Kyani (1998) successfully experimented with technofolk pop and rose quickly to be the new diva of the youth.[48] Pop music found a niche in the popular culture as a blend of Western rhythms and folk, Sufi and patriotic themes. It became the Pakistani version of the global youth culture. It sharpened the generation gap and bridged class and cultural divides. It spread in defiance of the official and religious establishment.

The role of technology in the transformation of popular culture in Pakistan should not be understated. The FM radio and satellite and cable television have not only brought distant and new messages into people's homes, but they have also eroded governmental capacity to control what the public watches or listens. The proliferation of media outlets has reinforced both tracks of popular culture. It has multiplied opportunities for the propagation of traditional values, Islamic sermons, and Quranic studies. Bearded men stoutly dressed in buttoned-up coats or neck-to-ankles coverall, heads covered with skullcaps or turbans, sermonize about sin, heaven, and hell. Women in *hijab* or *niqab* argue about the superiority of women's rights in Islam. Prayers from Mecca are telecast in real time and *azans* (call to prayers) are broadcast five times a day. Yet the multiplicity of media channels has also opened up the field for viewing Oscar ceremonies, pop concerts, political debates, human rights discussions, or the bombing of Afghanistan. Hip-gyrating dance numbers fill the television screen one moment and *mullahs'* fire-and-brimstone speeches the next. There is a surfeit of information and entertainment. The pietistic behaviors and religious orthodoxy are spreading at one level and the modernist/Western norms and practices at another.

On the surface, Islamic mores and eastern spiritualism are being subscribed to, but underneath coquettish pleasures, romance, and sex are crackling. When General Zia's Islamization disbanded the historic "red light areas" (neighborhoods of professional singers and sex workers), the call girl business took off transforming the sex trade, a shift that Fouzia Saeed calls "From Kothas to Kothi Khanas."[49] As movies were heavily censored to scrub suggestions of sex, cinemas started to insert blue clips (known as *totas* in the underground publicity channels) in the otherwise dull movies to draw crowds. Basant became a national festival of kite flying, parties, revelries, and abandon almost in complete defiance of *mullahs'* prohibitions. Restrictions on concerts, plays, and movies in the 1980s gave birth to the risqué *jugat* (lampooning) theatre catering to the bazaar merchants and young workers. These examples deliberately point out those aspects of the latent track that were for mass consumption. They do not refer to the modish subculture represented in the fashion pages of the *Herald* and *The Friday Times*.[50]

S. Zaidi finds the call-in shows of FM100 radio a metaphor for cultural change in Pakistan. He observes, "the flirtation on air between mostly female callers and male DJs" is often fun for the whole family, as "the phone is handed from one female to another, from daughter to mother, sister, or cousin." "In the age of openness and globalization, Pakistani society is now also more internationalized and westernized than it has ever been in the past."[51] These dual cultural pulls are tearing apart Pakistan's moral and institutional order. They underline the phenomenon of institutional lag that characterizes Pakistani society. This duality of themes in popular culture has a bearing on the Pakistani personality.

Mind-set: perceiving and apprehending the world

Mind-set is a term used to describe a complex of assumptions, concepts, and models that guide an individual, group, or society in perceiving, understanding, and explaining events and phenomena around them. It is the overall approach or the "system of logic" by which reality is grasped and explained. There are three dimensions of this notion. One, mind-set has common elements shared across a cultural group although individuals within the group may differ in their commitment to these elements. Two, societies cultivate distinct mind-sets, each reflective of its cultural themes. Three, the term mind-set overlaps with a host of other concepts that refer to the distinctness of the ways of thinking of a society, even of a civilization.

Other terms in vogue include worldview, ways of thinking, paradigmatic structure and, with a slightly different focus, national character. Worldview is a set of postulates or meta-assumptions about how life is organized. Epistemologists' term paradigm, a set of assumptions about the structure of the universe, parallels the notion of worldview.[52] Anthropologists maintain that worldview determines how a person, group, or culture as a whole apprehend and explain the events and phenomena around them.[53] They also, sometimes, refer to national character as a typical or average personality reflective of a culture, for example, the romantic French, pragmatic American, formal Japanese, etc.[54] From the perspective of our discussion, the common thread in all these terms is the distinct outlook and ways of thinking fostered by various societies and cultures. My objective is to observe the ways of thinking, in other words mind-set, of Pakistanis in their everyday life.

Antonio Gramsci called common sense, by which people live, "the philosophy of the nonphilosophers" and conceptions of the world inherited from society and culture.[55] Ideologies and socioeconomic conditions determine what notions, conceptions, or attitudes out of innumerable combinations available are chosen to be part of common sense and what are to be marginalized. Prevailing power structure is the agency that helps configure common sense.[56] Common sense is "what goes without saying" or, in Pierre Bourdieu's words, it is "doxa" or that portion of the world that seems self-evident.[57] It is common sense that forms a significant part of mind-set. Linguists maintain that language filters reality by focusing attention on some aspects and ignoring others. We see through the lens of our language and culture. Thus, our approach to observing the Pakistani mind is to identify assumptions and patterns of thought by which Pakistanis typically observe and explain reality.

I submit that Pakistanis as a sociocultural group have a distinct mind-set, which has been shaped by its historical forces and socioeconomic conditions. The Pakistani mind-set has a circular relationship with socioeconomic structures; it affects decision-making processes and through them influences socioeconomic structures that in turn feedback on people's ways of thinking and perceiving. A mind-set is not fixed for all times. It evolves, albeit gradually, as the social, economic, and political conditions change. What assumptions, concepts, and world-view constitute a Pakistani mind-set? This is the question that will be addressed in the following section.[58]

Pakistani mind-set

Pakistani ways of perceiving and apprehending reality have roots in the historical primordial community. They have been forged in the crucible of an agrarian economy and caste/clan relations. The colonial experience and the nationalist project have modified the historical mind-set and economic development; urbanization and Islamic resurgence have injected new assumptions and dispositions.

The idea of a Pakistani mind-set was almost nonexistent in the national discourse until 1972. It surfaced during the short-lived phase of soul-searching following the traumatic break up of Pakistan in 1971. One argument was that national misperceptions and misinterpretations of the conditions in East Pakistan were the "cause" of the crisis.[59] Since then it has remained a theme in modern circles, particularly among English language journalists. Khalid Ahmed refers to it as a factor in political conflicts of the 1990s.[60] Nasim Zehra, another distinguished correspondent, has written about Pakistani ways of thinking.[61] Many others, including some Urdu writers, have also occasionally used this notion for social commentary. Altogether mind-set is not a notion unfamiliar in Pakistan's intellectual circles.

Pakistani mind-set is an evolving structure of many different parts. Yet it has a core of fairly persistent assumptions. The following are its defining themes.

Personalizing the impersonal

A widely shared "mental model" of cause and effect in public life focuses on personalities who cause or thwart events. Whether the event to be explained is flood, poverty, truancy of one's child, or marital unhappiness, the explanation often is someone's manipulation, malevolent intentions, or in positive vein, goodwill. The prime mover of almost every event is a person(s). Social or economic processes, demographic trends, or even physical forces have a secondary role in the Pakistani narrative.

An illustrative example of this approach is the popular explanation for the breaking away of Bangladesh (erstwhile East Pakistan): it was Yahya Khan's, Mujibur Rehman's, or Bhutto's treachery; a slightly more institutional explanation ends up blaming Bengalis, India, or even the USA. The 1960s constitutional crisis of Pakistan, economic disparity, or the heavy-handed army action in East Pakistan remain at best secondary factors in Pakistanis' narrative, even almost 40 years later.[62] Pakistanis studying in American universities have a standard explanation if they fail a course: "my professor was prejudiced because I am a Muslim or coloured." Yet the cause of success is always one's unassailable superiority. Impersonal forces have little role in these mental models.

A variation of the anthropomorphic view of life prevails in Pakistan, where every occurrence, physical or human, has an identifiable human agent behind it. This viewpoint has been reinforced over time by the corruption, nepotism, and capriciousness of the state in Pakistan. Everyday life is based on *ad hoc* decisions and personalized dealings. No wonder the mind-set has evolved around the theme of personalizing the impersonal. There are two corollaries of this theme: (1) blaming others; (2) conspiracy theories.

Blaming others

As most of what happens in life is attributable to persons or groups, blaming the presumed enemies or ill-wishers for setbacks and failures is the first line of argument. It has been a persistent habit from colonial times, rather earlier, but it has been burnished into a philosophy since independence. From events of personal life to national affairs, someone malevolent is thought to be pulling strings. A few examples from different periods may illustrate the depth of this outlook:

- Pakistan Engineers Association blamed foreign consultants and the generalist administrator of WAPDA for the cracks appearing in the Tarbela Dam.[63]
- Zionists and Hindus ganged up to break up Pakistan (in 1971), because it is the "fortress of Islam."[64]
- "Hidden hand" (unseen enemies) is promoting terrorism and violence in Karachi.[65]
- NGOs are corrupting our women by visiting them at home on the pretext of teaching them.[66]

I have paraphrased just a sample of opinions expressed every day on widely different issues. This theme is the staple of news stories and social conversations. The "blame others" syndrome is deeply entrenched. Even in matters of personal performance, it is often others that bear the blame. If one did not get a promotion, its likely cause would be the stronger connections of the competitors or the ethnic prejudice of the bosses. The archetypical notions of the evil eye and hostile spirits may be the unconscious elements behind the blame-others theme.

Conspiracy theory

From blaming others to believing in active plotting by enemies, imagined or real, is a short step. The Pakistani mind-set is predisposed to presume conspiracy as the driving force of many events. Most happenings are thought to be the result of manipulation by others. This way of thinking is particularly applied to unusual events, which are frequent in a poor country like Pakistan. The conspiracy theory is the default explanation in personal matters but it is often the first cause presumed in national and international events.

The roster of conspiring agents varies with the ideological disposition of the proponent and with the political/social tenor of times. In the 1960s, India, Hindus, communists or the CIA were the presumed plotters against Pakistan. After the Arab–Israeli war of 1967, Jews or Israelis were added to the list of conspiring forces. India was the prime agent responsible for the debacle of East Pakistan. Bhutto in his waning days proclaimed the American conspiracy to punish him for Pakistan's friendship with China and for pursuing the "Islamic bomb." The 1980s brought the Soviet Union to Pakistan's doorstep and thus it became the provocateur of Pakistan's internal disorder. Afghan *jehad* spun a new strain of conspiracy theories that have morphed into the militant Islamists' creed of America "the perpetrator of the clash of civilizations." Ahmadis began to bear the blame for many problems early on in Pakistan's history. With the rising sectarian and ethnic differences, rival sects, Shia for Deobandis and Brelvis for Ahl-Hadith, provided fuel for conspiracy theories. I am not commenting on the veracity of these explanations; I am only pointing out their range.

My point is that the roster of conspirators in the Pakistani mind-set is not constant. It varies with the ideological orientation of the person(s) postulating such a position. One person's conspirator is a victim in another's account. It also changes from time to time, although conspiracy as a cause of events remains constant. The conspiracy theory is a packaged paradigm that can be slapped on any situation. Here is a sample of some bizarre conspiracy theories.

- The Pakistan People's Party, under the Bhutto family's leadership, is plotting to subvert Pakistanis' morality.[67]
- NGOs funded from abroad "exploit minorities and human rights issues" to promote foreign agendas.[68]
- Ethnic or sectarian strife is foreign inspired.[69]
- The Bank of Credit and Commerce International (BCCI) was bankrupted with the connivance of an influential Pakistani economist (presumably for the bank's Muslim credentials).[70]
- A traffic policeman is beaten by an army officer and the incident is raised in the provincial assembly. The Provincial Law Minister dismisses the question by branding it "as the conspiracy to defame army and the government."[71]

Conspiracy theories are common in all societies. President Kennedy's assassination, for example, spawned a veritable industry of spinning conspiracy theories, as has the tragedy of the 9/11 terrorists' attack on the World Trade Center. Yet in other societies conspiracy theories are marginal to the public discourse, seldom taken seriously. In Pakistan, they are in the mainstream of thought. Responsible opinion leaders propound them, public statements are laced with them, and school textbooks offer them as historical truths[72]

The conspiracy theory is an unconscious acknowledgment of one's impotence and a justification for inaction. It has become a barrier to objective and inductive thinking in Pakistan. Khalid Ahmed writes that, "a kind of suffocating militarist poultice is being applied to the Pakistani mind."[73] Nasim Zehra applies Ayn Rand's term "derivative mind" to Pakistanis: "we have become derivative in our thought process,… (do) not observe, collect and interpret facts and issues with reference to the realities of its own context."[74] An American correspondent comments that Pakistanis are warm and generous people, but "rumors and conspiracy theories are as commonly exchanged as rupee notes."[75]

Double-think

To hold opposing views is not unusual. Many situations do not lend themselves to consistent points of view. Yet in Pakistan, a habit of mind has emerged whereby one passionately holds an opinion or belief while simultaneously advocating the contrary position. In previous chapters, we encountered the pervasive dissonance between imagined and lived cultures. Double-think goes a step further. It is the internal contradictions of beliefs. The regularity with which contradictory viewpoints are held makes double-think a habit of mind.

People often strongly condemn extravagant marriage receptions as wasteful and even un-Islamic. Yet in the same breath defend big feasts and large dowries as necessary for a family's honor. It is a common theme that the Western way of life is immoral and corrupt, yet literally millions who subscribe to this belief aspire to migrate to America, Canada, or Europe. So desperate are people to emigrate that in the 2000s, thousands have been caught every year in Turkey and Greece illegally slipping across their borders on the way to northern Europe.[76] The road traffic in Pakistan is a vivid expression of double-think. Most drivers curse others for breaking traffic rules; yet at the same time they routinely run red lights, drive on the wrong side, or tailgate.

Compartmentalization of beliefs and actions

An extension of double-think is separating one's actions from one's beliefs. This is a very pervasive habit. A political leader may wax eloquently about the rights of minorities in Islam from a public platform, but agitate for removing Ahmadis or Christians from "important" positions. Films routinely portray a murderous robber who pays homage to a shrine before beginning his day. A Canadian reporter observed that a violent anti-America crowd protesting the US attack on Afghanistan was going on the same road where vendors were doing a brisk business in US visa lottery forms. What one believes and how one acts often bear little relation to each other.

The strongman syndrome

The archetype of *murd mujahid* (righteous fighter) is deeply embedded in the Pakistani psyche. Zulifiqar Gilani maintains that Pakistanis crave a savior, redeemer, or strong leader.[77] The mythologies woven around conquerors such as Mahmood Ghaznavi, Shahab-ud-din Ghuri, or Zahir-ud-din Babur, frame Pakistanis' outlook. A strongman charging across deserts and rivers at the head of an army is the archetype of a leader. This archetype predisposes Pakistanis toward authoritarian leaders and macho behaviors. The British cultivated the myth of martial races, the patrimony claimed by Pakistanis in general and Punjabis and Pashtoons in particular. That myth has reinforced Pakistanis' self-image as warriors and affects their approach to not only national affairs but also everyday life.

The notion of power in Pakistan is closely tied to the capacity to harm.[78] Clerics and feudals have the capacity to inflict physical violence, the former through exciting mobs and the latter by their agents and hangers-on. Both exert a strong influence in public life.[78]

The strongman syndrome, in particular, prompts two behaviors in everyday life, namely, associating with the powerful and name-dropping.[79] Introductions are made as the relative of that (famous) person or by one's job title/family status, and even degrees. One is seldom viewed just as an individual but mostly as someone who has power, connections, and high status. Flattery to be close to the powerful and boastfulness to intimate power are the two common expressions of the strongman syndrome in everyday life.

There is a "fix" for everything

In the post-independence period, the notion that the right connections, use of force, or money can fix anything has become the operating assumption of social life. This notion is reinforced by daily experiences. The rich and powerful often get away with breaking rules and flouting laws, be those small matters like lining up to see a doctor, or grave acts such as not paying taxes or being prosecuted for crimes. Such occurrences promote the idea that there is a fix for everything; one only has to find it. The pervasiveness of arbitrary and person-driven public policies has contributed to the rise of the belief in fix. Yet the pursuit of "fix" feeds back on the state making it all the more arbitrary.

The belief in fix breeds frustration and uncertainty in everyday dealings. If one's desire is not fulfilled, one has the gnawing feeling that one did not apply the right means. If one does not get a seat in a flight, it must be that one did not use the right channel for reservation; or if one's child could not get admission to a medical college, one could have pulled stronger strings. Such pervasive disappointments are the social costs of the "fix" mentality.

Entrepreneurship and go-getting culture

It was pointed out earlier that there has been a sociopsychological transformation of Pakistanis in the 50 years of independence. From a repressed and resigned (to fate) person, a typical Pakistani, a male in particular, has turned into an entrepreneur in pursuit of economic advancement. He is willing to leave home and village, change occupations, pursue new opportunities and pull strings to get ahead. Not all succeed and many fall by the wayside but most have the drive and ambition. This entrepreneurship of individuals has given rise to what has been called *challo* (push ahead) culture.[80]

People in pursuit of advancement of their personal as well as family fortunes have learnt to work hard and take risks. Farmers' children distinguish themselves in studies to graduate as doctors and engineers, craftsmen come to own workshops, clerks double as tutors to make ends meet, poor women and children labor at home weaving carpets, molding plastic toys, or making cardboard boxes.[81] Ambition and drive have become national traits. This entrepreneurial spirit is relatively new in Pakistani society. Yet it has also come with an attitude of using every available means, fair or foul, to advance one's fortunes.

Pakistani mind-set and everyday life

The above-described themes are the warp and woof of the Pakistani mind-set. They are the lenses through which a Pakistani may view the world. Yet a mind-set is not the sole determinant of people's behavior. It works in combination with motivations, values, and beliefs to guide actions. As a mode of thinking, a mind-set has different implications for behaviors of a personal scope than for those of collective interests.

At the personal level, conspiracy explanations or double-think do not inhibit people's drive and persistence. They may assume that they are confronted with intrigues and need a patron, but that spurs them to try harder, resort to further string pulling, or in other ways pursue their personal goals. Individually, their mode of thinking predisposes them to suspicions but not to despondency. They continue to search for "fixes."

Overall, the Pakistani mind-set at the personal level promotes enterprise and individualism. It is a different kind of individualism, not completely focused on the self but on taking along family and supporting as well as being supported by friends and relatives. Everyday life operates on the basis of exchange of favors and working the system. This is how the mind-set structures individuals' behavior at a personal level.

At the collective level, the Pakistani mind-set is predisposed toward sloganeering, packaged ideas and inability to act concertedly. Pakistanis' ways of thinking become barriers to inductive thinking and moral clarity. For example, in almost every home, evening discussions drift toward narratives of corruption and arbitrariness encountered daily. This cathartic condemnation of social and political ills is a feature of everyday discourse. It vents people's frustrations but seldom leads to communal action or a social movement.

A national columnist calls out in desperation, "we are a nation of hypocrites, divided by religious and Western extremism."[82] The host of a national affairs television program sums up his experience of the discourse he witnessed, "gift of verbosity being a national trait, most people are interested in making speeches than asking questions."[83] At the fiftieth anniversary of the Lahore Resolution, Iqbal Ahmed observed, "The most striking feature of our national life has been the equanimity with which our elite have experienced these disasters (loss of East Pakistan, poverty, political instability, etc.)... We are consumed by appetites of life and devoid of moral instincts."[84] These comments point to Pakistanis' penchant for self-criticism and their acute awareness of institutional ineffectiveness. The desire for change is acutely felt but as a collective people feel stymied. This is partially the outcome of the Pakistani mind-set.

Before concluding this section, it may be pointed out that the Pakistani mind-set itself is a social construct. It has been forged in the agrarian milieu of rural Pakistan and sustained by authoritarian ideologies and stultifying school curricula. Its contradictions have come into bold relief by the urbanization of society, rendering the traditional ways of thinking increasingly out of sync with the emerging reality.

Structure of everyday life

Everyday life in Pakistan is active and energetic but it appears chaotic to outsiders. It has an internal rhythm and structure instinctively understood by people. Standing on a roadside or by a street, one is struck by crowds hurrying past on foot, donkey carts, motor bicycles, cars and buses; by hawkers weaving in and out and pedestrians dashing across the unstoppable traffic, by the cacophony of sounds from horns, shouts, bells, and loudspeakers, and by the innumerable activities occurring simultaneously. Yet hundreds, in some cases thousands, negotiate this "chaos" every moment. There is an order behind the disorder. This typical street scene is a metaphor for everyday life. Are there patterns and processes that underlie everyday life? Yes, there are and those have been probed in this chapter.

Everyday life has changed with the changing society and culture. It was not always so pulsating with energy and activity. Even in the 1960s, everyday life was staid and rigidly defined, though not without fun. In about five decades, it has broken out of the traditional molds. It is simultaneously global and vernacular culturally, traditional and modern socially, and Islamic pietistic in beliefs but materialistic in behaviors. These divergent pulls have fragmented everyday life into different tracks, each representing the lifestyle of a particular category of people. The social cohesion of the "old" society has given way to the self-interests of split-up communities. These social trends have restructured everyday life. The following is a brief recapitulation of everyday life's patterns and processes.

- Class-segment is a social formation constituted by similarities of economic status, cultural orientation, lifestyles, and consumption patterns. It structures a person's everyday life. What one wears, where and how one works and lives, with whom one associates, how influential or helpless one feels, what one believes: on all these scores wide social differences have appeared in everyday life. One could be a globalist or *Jamaati*, in combination with low or high income; one's everyday life is circumscribed by one's class-segment.

- The fragmentation of sociocultural life has sharpened. It is reflected in the tracking and streaming of everyday life. Schools, homes, workplaces, neighborhoods, modes of transport, tastes and even the family life of people in different tracks diverge considerably. In the public space, the differences are vivid. Pakistani society has evolved from a historic dualistic social organization to a community of multiple lifestyles and (sub)cultures.

- Countering pulls of divergence are some overarching structures and processes, namely nationalism and Islam, and economic and social interdependencies. The shared memories and common destiny as a nation have taken root, even if they appear shallow at times. People of divergent class-segments and ethnicities move across territorial as well as social boundaries in large numbers. On the personal plane, there is an acceptance of diversity, except among ideologues of various stripes. The lived Islam, in distinction to the clerics' Islam, is also a force of social cohesion. People of widely different class-segments pray side by side, visit shrines and seek blessings of *pirs* together. Individually they are tolerant of denominational and ideological pluralism although they can be aroused to communal hatreds. Extended family, *biradari*, or tribe include the rich and poor as well as the orthodox and liberal. Everyday life is a web of interdependencies linking teaboys with executives, farm workers with landlords, and domestic servants with working wives. The social distances are bridged daily although social disparities continue to widen.

- Everyday life has changed strikingly in the 50-year history of Pakistan. There are many times more people and consequently more houses, greater traffic, crowded streets, and a different feel in everyday life. Occupations of yesteryear have disappeared and those that remain require new skills and different organizations. Skills, opportunities, and connections have largely displaced caste ascriptions as job qualifications. The duality of bazaar versus modern sectors permeates the world of work. Modern material products have been readily adopted by all segments of society. Islamic revival and entrenched traditions have offered little resistance to the modernization of consumption patterns. Sense of community and social trust have been eroded while pursuit of self and family interests have gained momentum. Security and safety have steadily become major concerns of everyday life. Minorities and women are particularly vulnerable to violence and discrimination. Negotiating the chores of daily life saps individuals' energy. The institutional infrastructure necessary for an urbanizing society is lagging behind galloping social needs.

- Islamic revivalism has institutionalized piety in everyday life. It has carved a niche in the public space, spawning an assertive Islamic lifestyle that combines material modernity with orthodox beliefs and practices.

- Lopsided social development has contributed to the emergence of the characteristic Pakistani mind-set, that is, ways of thinking and perceiving. Paradoxically, the Pakistani mind-set has cultivated an enterprising personality and go-getting culture, but it has inhibited moral clarity and social activism. Individuals and families are progressing but community and society are lagging.

- Everyday life is full of contradictions and uncertainties. The endemic poverty in combination with personalized and *ad hoc* dealings in the public space sap people's energies. The modernization of material culture has so increased people's needs that even middle-class segments are hard pressed to meet them, not to speak of the legions of poor. Public policy shortfalls have also contributed to raising the frustration quotient of everyday life.

10 Whither Pakistan?

Perspective

Pakistani society and culture have been changing and rapid change is likely to be a condition of life in the country for years to come. The preceding chapters unravel the story of these changes. In this concluding chapter, I want to compose an overall picture of the scope and direction of social change. Pulling together recurring themes and significant observations of the previous chapters, I hope to identify patterns of sociocultural change in Pakistan. What processes and structures underlie the evolving social institutions and cultural norms is the question addressed in this chapter. This question has been the starting point of the book. Here it is being revisited to recapitulate the main findings of this inquiry and to draw general conclusions about the directions of social change in Pakistan.

Presently, development and modernization are the conceptual yardsticks for analyzing the social and cultural transformation of Third World societies. These are also the criteria by which these societies themselves measure their progress, aiming to raise incomes, decrease poverty, increase productivity, facilitate techno-logical advancement, improve health, educational and nutritional standards, and promote responsive governance, representative government, equality, human rights, and freedom. Conceptually, modernization is a process that transforms these objectives into social institutions and cultural norms. In practice, their forms can vary but the meanings and functions remain the same. Third World societies also want to preserve their culture. Ostensibly, they do not want to become "second-hand" America or Britain. Thus, modernization ideals presumably will be clothed in indigenous dresses.

As discussed in Chapter 2, modernization ideals are universal in scope, such as technological mode of production, efficiency, organizations based on laws and reason rather than persons and customs, equality of opportunity, impersonalization of decision making, punctuality, enterprise and innovation, etc. The journey of a society toward fulfillment of these norms constitutes the process of modernization and their realization indicates a modern society.

Japan, China, Singapore and, to some extent, Turkey are examples of Asian societies that have incorporated modern norms and values within their distinct social organization and culture, just as America or France have forged different forms of modern Western societies. Yet being initially conceived in Western forms, these norms bear the stamp of westernization. It is not uncommon to equate modernization with westernization. Yet it need not be so.

Modernization is the functional necessity of societies that are growing, urbanizing, and developing. In Chapter 5, I have identified the institutional imperatives that are bearing down on the urbanizing and modernizing Pakistan. These imperatives are to: (1) make systematic provision of collective utilities and services for all, (2) organize space in urban modes, (3) develop civic order relevant for an urbanizing society, and (4) promote deliberated institutional development and cultural planning. These imperatives could be guidelines for Pakistan's social and cultural transformation.

Pakistan's modernization has taken a distinct form. It is manifestly recapitulating Western institutions and norms, without functionally realizing modernization ideals. The Western forms are adopted on the surface but often they serve traditional functions or are incorporated in historic structures. In addition, one part of an institution may tilt toward modern norms while other parts may be swept by Islamic mores, resulting in imbalanced development. Islamic revivalism has emerged as a parallel force of social change in Pakistan. Ideological and religious movements are driving social change almost as much as the technological and material advances. A troika of social processes – indigenization, modernization, and Islamization – underlie the dialectics of social change in Pakistan. How do the three processes interweave and what institutional structures emerge from their interactions? These questions point to the thrust of our discussion in this chapter.

Common threads

Underlying the kaleidoscopic social changes are geography, people, and Islam ensuring cultural continuity. The dynamics of change and continuity fall into fairly discernible patterns. Viewing them through the lens of modernization, it is obvious that Pakistani society has been incrementally moving along the path of modernism, largely in material culture and consumption patterns. Modern technology and goods have spread all across society, though not all social segments have benefited from material changes; nonetheless, everybody has been affected.

The mode of production in Pakistan has fundamentally changed. Pakistan is no longer an agrarian society, except in some remote rural pockets, and is no longer deeply steeped in occupational castes and the obligatory barter of goods and services of the *seypi* system. The largest force for change has been the monetization of the economy, which has transformed social relations. Beginning from almost no industries at the time of independence, Pakistan has developed a sizable consumer goods manufacturing sector, though the country is still in the early stages of industrialization.

What is striking is the unbalanced state of economic modernization. Some activities have leaped into the postindustrial phase, while many elementary goods and services continue to be produced in traditional modes. Pakistan is a nuclear state but hardly any city has an adequate sewerage treatment plant. Internet and cell phones have proliferated even in tribal areas but almost 70 percent of rural houses have no latrines (1998 census). Pakistan has been a strategic partner of the US in the cold war and the antiterrorism drive, yet at home "little mutinies" and ethnic and sectarian strife bubble not far below the surface.

Millions of Pakistanis live or work abroad. The Pakistani diaspora has linked remote villages with Europe, North America, and the Middle East. Globalization is a palpable presence in Pakistan. Yet cultural norms, beliefs and values, though not static, remain anchored to traditions and customs. This is the key pattern of social change. To a casual observer, Pakistani society appears to be full of contradictions and functioning on different planes for different purposes. Yet it has a logic of its own which can be described as its internal dynamics. Its defining characteristics are discussed below.

State and society

The state of Pakistan came first and the national society followed. The state has played a significant role in forging a national society on the base of ethnic and tribal communities. It has promoted economic development through five-year plans and by management of the economy. Its acts of commission and omission have determined the course of social development and cultural change.

From the beginning, more than one idea of Pakistan has defined the state and society, contributing to an ideological logjam and political instability. Ethnically and linguistically, Pakistan is a pluralistic society, but its state has pursued centrist and unitary policies. Islam has been used to justify the unitary character of the state. Thus state and ideology have been inherently in opposition to the pluralism of society. Although the state suppresses ethnoregional nationalism, periodically feelings of regional disparity boil over to shake governments with popular protests and occasional armed conflicts. Pakistani state and society have gone through cycles of political and social turmoil followed by periods of peace. The periodic crises of the state topped by military coups have swung the country from periods of strong state and weak society to short phases of strong society and weak state, as indicated by the overthrow of three entrenched governments through popular agitations.

Over a period of almost six decades, Pakistan as a society has evolved out of its traditional roots. It has shrunk geographically, with the breaking away of Bangladesh but expanded fourfold in population. Its four provinces – Northern Areas, tribal territories, and Azad Kashmir – have been strung together by national communication networks, transport services, trade and most of all by people's mobility. A national social formation has emerged over and above regional and provincial communities. Pakistani society is a living reality, though ethnic and linguistic communities continue to be vibrant and assertive.

Historically, a state has a critical role in processes of development and modernization. It organizes and directs the transformation from patrimonial order to a modern economy and constitutional rule. Even in the Western countries, Britain and Germany, for example, the state led in the transformation from a feudal to a modern society, particularly through the legislative initiatives of the nineteenth and early twentieth centuries.[1] In Pakistan, and other Third World countries, the state is the primary institution that can promote orderly social transformation and cultural change. The Pakistani state has steadily become less effective in this role from the first to the third period of its social history. Its political crises have given rise to imbalanced development. Social legislation and public action for reforming institutions have been lagging. Other institutional imperatives also remain neglected to varying degrees. Pakistan is turning into a weak state and a weak society. Is this an enduring condition or is another turn of fortune of state and society in the works? This remains an open question.

Institutional lags

Three major fissures have appeared in Pakistan's social institutions over the three periods, namely, (1) development of the material culture and underdevelopment of nonmaterial norms and practices, (2) disparity between private and public space, and (3) imbalance between imagined and lived culture. These divisions within the same structure on the one hand, and between one institution and some others on the other, have resulted in a lopsided modernization and unbalanced development. Let us look at each of these three types of imbalance.

The material elements of Pakistan's culture have changed rapidly and extensively, whereas the nonmaterial aspects have lagged behind, changing slowly and sporadically. Modern technology and consumer goods have been readily adopted by all sections of the society. From tea to television or Kentucky Fried Chicken to kidney transplants, modern products have spread readily. Yet mores of family planning, punctuality, or efficiency have not caught on. The nonmaterial culture continues to be tied to traditions while the material culture is galloping ahead in line with global trends.

This lag between the material and nonmaterial aspects of the culture has exacted high social costs. For example, motorbikes, cars, and other means of modern transport have spread far into society, but traffic laws and norms of road behavior have not evolved in parallel. Pakistani roads and streets have become one of the most hazardous places in the country. The daily toll of deaths and injuries, not to speak of smashed vehicles and broken roads, has been staggering. Yet no systematic and effective policies have been implemented to frame traffic laws relevant for local conditions or to educate people about the norms of the road. Inept and corrupt police compound the problem. This is an obvious example of the lag between material and nonmaterial cultures. Similar lags are observable in other aspects of social life, be it the green revolution, family and marriage, and Islamic practices (for example, the use of loudspeakers in mosques without corresponding norms of noise control for neighbors' convenience), etc.

The second fissure is between the private space of personal interests, social interactions and kin/community commitments, and the public space of common services, communications and discourses as well as the overarching moral order. In economic terms, private space corresponds to consumer goods, market exchanges and the public space relates to externalities, collective goods, laws, and policies. The phrase "space" in both terms refers not only to geographic or material aspects but also to nonmaterial and moral elements, to a greater extent.

Pakistan's development in the past six decades has steadily widened the chasm between private and public spaces. The development of private space has outstripped the evolution of public space. Expensive and well-appointed homes are surrounded by garbage-strewn streets, vividly contrasting the overdeveloped private space with the lagging public space. Over time, the private space of home has been secularized in the sense that family life is largely organized around the norms of material success and modern idioms of consumption, whereas public life has been Islamized, both in discourse and symbolism. Private facilities for medical treatment have exploded but mores of sanitation and medical ethics remain undeveloped. Marriages have steadily turned into extravagant affairs of lavish dowries, feasts, and status affirmation, while public regulations restricting the serving of food to large groups or excessive dowries are neither observed nor enforced. Public interest is trumped by private commitments. The disparity of private and public space is reflected in pervasive corruption and inefficiency.

Another fissure dividing Pakistan's society is that of imagined and lived culture. It divides people's views or images of how they live from the reality of their lived life. This division is observable at all levels, in social institutions, in personal behaviors, in moral conduct, and in community life. The society has been urbanized but it is imagined in rural idioms.

A clarification of the term "imagined" is in order. It does not mean an "ideal" that is intrinsically at variance from the real behavior. Imagined is the operational concept of what one thinks one is actually doing. It is commonly imagined that Pakistanis take care of elderly parents in joint families. Yet millions have moved away from their parental homes, leaving elderly parents alone. Lonely seniors are a living but unapprehended reality for a large section of the population. The imagined life of seniors is the blissful state of being surrounded by children and grandchildren. The situation of seniors is changing but its image remains stuck in the past.

Another example of the divergence between an imagined and a lived institution is the family. The imagined family is a joint family ruled over by a patriarch, living under one roof, but the lived family has many diverse forms. The emerging structure of family is a multi-household unit in which the parental household is the nucleus and grown children's often distant homes are satellites, linked together by obligatory bonds. These are just a few illustrative examples but the imagined and lived dichotomy is observable in all aspects of social life.

The theme of institutional lag has been documented in the preceding chapters. It is a structural condition of the changing Pakistan. It arises from the differences in the rate and direction of change of various components of culture and social organization. Social segmentation and cultural lag are the outcomes of these divisions.

Segmentation of caste and class

Social change does not occur uniformly in all parts of a society. Some groups and institutions change more than the others. In Pakistan, this process has taken a distinct form. It is splitting the society in segments or groups that differ from each other not only economically and materially, but also culturally and socially. In other words, social change has split relatively coherent classes and castes/tribes into groups of divergent lifestyles, economic standing, values, and ideologies. For example, a broad-based middle class is being split into groups of modern, traditional, and Islamic outlooks and lifestyles.

These cultural divisions partially arise from affiliations with different economic sectors, namely bazaar (informal), modern (formal, firm) and illicit. The process of differentiating the social strata into distinct economic/cultural groups may be called segmentation. This process can be better explained by concrete examples.

Long before independence, Pakistan's economy had begun to be divided into the modern (firm) and traditional (bazaar) modes of operation, though the latter sector dominated. Independence accelerated economic development and modernization. The modern sector has expanded to occupy commanding heights of the economy. Corporate businesses and industries have increased, the economy has been monetized almost completely, and internal and international trade has expanded. Pakistan has become very dependent on global financial institutions (World Bank and IMF) as well as foreign lenders. United Nations' treaties and conventions affect labor relations, environment, human rights, and governance, for example. All these developments have contributed to the expansion of the modern sector. The bazaar sector has also grown, by opportunistically changing and adopting new business practices, such as banking, currency exchanges, import–export rules, etc. Paralleling both, a sizable illicit sector has emerged in the forms of bribes, smuggling, black market, etc.

As discussed in Chapter 5, the critical difference between these sectors lies in their modes of operation and organization. The modern sector is organized around the specialization of activities and functions. Ostensibly, it operates by formal rules and impersonal dealings based on economic considerations, whereas the bazaar sector has overlapping functions and limited specialization of roles. Social ties and social capital permeates its economic transactions. The illicit sector has grown in the interstices of the other two sectors. Each of these sectors is vertically organized in upper, middle, and lower tiers or circuits replicating the economic strata.

Altogether, the economic organization is divided into segments of differentiated modes of operation and organizational culture. From a blacksmith shop of the lower circuit in the bazaar sector and a pirated video hawker of the illicit sector to a Toyota dealership of the upper modern circuit is an array of economically and culturally differentiated enterprises. The division of economic organization by sectors and circuits lays the groundwork for the segmented class structure that is then built upon by differences of lifestyle, values, and beliefs.

Class segments and social differentiation

Pakistan's social structure has been traditionally stratified in occupational castes and tribes/clans. In rural areas, this caste/clan hierarchy has coincided with land ownership, affluence, and power. In urban areas, castes/*biradaris* have overlapped but not fully corresponded to property ownership, income, or wealth. One could be rich but of lower caste, a commercially successful butcher or hide tanner, for example. Alternatively, somebody of high caste could be poor, for example, a Sayyed or Mughal could be a clerk in the provincial secretariat. Urban stratification has been based on combinations of income, caste, and profession. It is relatively more open, taking the characteristics of a class hierarchy, although rural caste structure has also begun to wear out.

Altogether, social class in Pakistan has always been defined by both economic and sociological criteria. Inherited attributes of caste, tribe, or kinship are also woven into economic classes. Economic development and social change have introduced new occupations and nontraditional sources of income and wealth. Mobility has released people from ascribed occupations and incomes. Remittances of carpenters working abroad have provided their families with living standards that village landlords cannot afford, for example. Such new opportunities of income and occupations have eroded the traditional caste underpinnings of the class structure but power and profession still matter.

How one earns a living has a bearing on one's class status. A small town *arhati* (commission agent) or rice-husking factory owner of the bazaar sector has more income but lower standing and prestige than a journalist or college professor of the modern sector, although both fall within the broad sweep of the middle class. More strikingly, *arhati* and professor not only differ by income but also by their lifestyles and cultural values despite being, sometimes, members of the same family or clan. This example illustrates the process of splitting of previously coherent social classes into segments differentiated by modes of earning livelihood as well as living.

Income and wealth lay the groundwork for social differentiation but differences of values and ways of living delineate class segments. Modernization is dividing the social classes into finely divided circles of distinct economic standings, lifestyles, and beliefs.

What do these class segments look like? Markers of class segments are sectoral affiliation, education, occupation, lifestyle, ideology, and interests. Class segments also reflect location along the ideological spectrum ranging from traditionalist, Islamist to modern liberal. They range from the global-westernized Muhajirs or Punjabis of middle-class standings on one side of the spectrum, for example, to Pashtoons of traditionalist or Islamic bent who are bazaar merchants or transporters on the other. Such class segments are narrowly defined combining in a myriad of ways, ethnicity, caste, class, and ideology. They are indicative of the social fragmentation within the broad sweep of economic classes.

The tripartition of social structure

Pakistan's society and culture have evolved from a dualistic to a tripartite structure since independence. The traditional and modern divide dates back to the colonial period, but the third component, namely institutionalized Islam, has evolved after independence. Its seeds were laid in the Objectives Resolution (1949) but it flourished in the third period. The tripartite division of social structure does not suggest three segregated organizations, but three parallel ideologies and systems of norms that, although autonomous, are nested together. In one sense, the traditional, modern, and Islamic modes of living are three subcultures, each with distinct values and lifestyle.

The tripartite division has permeated many social institutions. Education has come to have three systems of curricula, institutions, and approaches, respectively schools of English and vernacular mediums as well as seminaries and *madrassahs*. Vernacular medium schools cater to the lower classes and the traditionalists, particularly in rural areas, whereas the English medium schools are expensive, prestigious, and suited to the demands of upwardly mobile class segments. The Islamic institutions have historically trained imams (prayer leaders) and theological scholars, but in the third period, under the state's patronage, they have grown into an educational stream that trains students for religious as well as temporal roles.[2]

Similarly, three parallel but distinct types of femininity and gender relations have evolved, namely women of customary, modern, and Islamic outlooks and values. The tripartite division of women's role is especially visible in the public space. Traditional women largely stay at home and view their role essentially limited to the domestic sphere. Modern women aspire to be economically active and participate in the public sphere. Islamic women take part in the public life by carving segregated institutions, wearing full body *burqa*, face-hiding *niqab* or head-covering *hijab*, yet taking on jobs, and political and social leadership roles. Other institutions also manifest tripartite divisions such as three types of elite – communities, civil society, and economic organization.

Altogether, Pakistan's social structure shows a three-way cultural division in class segments. For example, in the middle class there are groups who are popularly, stereotypically, called westernized, *ashrafs, safed posh, babus or jamaatis* or *tablighis* (Islamists).[3] These groups could fall within comparable bands of income, wealth and/or clans/castes, but differ from each other in ideology, beliefs, personal orientation, women's role, and even dress and deportment. Similar tripartite class segments can be identified within the lower and upper classes. At this juncture, the question arises about the process(es) or agency that has brought about this tripartite structure and its segmentation. The next section addresses this question.

Processes of social change and cultural transformation

Development affects various institutions of a society in different ways. It seldom proceeds in one direction, contrary to earlier development theories. It has been rightly described as a dialectical process. These trends are observable in Pakistan's social change and cultural transformation. The tripartition of social structure and its segmentation into subcultural groups are indications of the growing internal differentiation of society and culture. Relative coherence of institutions and ways of life are giving way to a specialization of functions and diversity of cultural forms. Social change is carving parallel tracks within the economy and society, laying separate paths of development by class, mode of living, ideology, and occupation.

Pakistan has become a society with many differences. Its economic disparities are striking, reflected in the contrast between gated estates of villas and mud villages or *katchi abadis*. Its cultural diversity is visible in narrowly differentiated class segments, which separate even pietistic Islamists, for example, from liberal Muslims. This is the emerging structure of society, which has come about from processes of change as well as through the agency of state policies and interest groups as well as political parties. This interplay of structural processes and human agency has determined the direction of social change.

Historically, an agrarian order prevailed in the pre-British era. In this social order, caste specializations and customary norms were paramount. The material conditions and technology were largely based on animal power. Most of the population was attached to land in interlinked roles of landlords, peasants, and *kammis*.

The British built railways and roads, introduced industrial production, and organized a bureaucratic system of administration. Thus began a process of modernization that has continued to grow, reaching revolutionary proportions after independence, touching almost every aspect of social life but particularly transforming the material culture. Modernization created new occupations and modified social relations, laying the groundwork for a dualistic economy and society. Although carving their respective spheres, the modern and traditional modes of living were not entirely self-contained. For example, marriages or kinship/caste statuses continued to be primarily ruled by traditions, except for a small modernist segment of liberal values, while occupations have been increasingly influenced by modern norms of achievements and skills even within the bounds of caste ascriptions.

The dialectics of tradition and modernity are well known. I need not spend much time on it, except to reiterate that these two modes have led to the previously discussed institutional lags and social segmentation. In Pakistan, independence followed by a mass movement of the population, Kashmir and other disputes with India, alliances with the USA, and the Afghan revolution are some of the exogenous factors that have uniquely affected national development. Economic growth; changing mode of production; population explosion; mobility; spread of telephones, videos, and television; and urbanization are endogenous processes of social change that are common in the contemporary thrust of modernization.

A distinguishing characteristic of Pakistan's social change is its cultural roots in Islam and Muslim nationalism. Pakistan's national discourse has one constant, namely its commitment to Islamic identity. There may be disagreements about its meanings and scope. Yet this commitment *per se* is almost inviolate in the drive for social change. People have resisted westernization of social relations, particularly any westernization of family life and sexual morality. A puritanical Islamic model of life has been advocated and promoted in Pakistan as an alternative to westernization. The Islamic mode of living has grown into a lifestyle in Pakistani society. This point needs some elaboration.

Structure and agency of Islamization

Islamization has taken two forms in Pakistan. First, Pakistani society overall has been visibly Islamized. Islamic observances and pieties have spread to almost all segments of society, markedly in the third period. There is unprecedented attendance in mosques by young men. Television and radio devote many hours every day to sermons and prayers. Finding men praying in airports, hotel lobbies, or cricket matches has become an unsurprising sight. During the month of Ramadan, rarely can anyone be seen eating publicly and daily activities are in near suspension during the daytime. *Zakat*, a wealth tax, has been deducted compulsorily from Muslims' savings bank accounts since 1979.[4] The Islamization of social life has proceeded in parallel with the modernization of material culture and economic activities.

Second, Islamic normative order has been forged as a distinct social structure and (sub)culture. It has been offered as the third way, in contrast with socialism and capitalism. In Pakistan, some class segments have adopted the Islamic mode of life, creating an Islamic sector within society. An institutional framework for an Islamic mode of living was built during General Zia's rule.

Islamic banks offering presumably interest-free financial services now serve a significant segment of the population. Islamic studies are a compulsory part of educational curricula, even in medicine and engineering programs. In school textbooks, Islamic history, theology, or ideology has been injected in almost all courses. *Sharia* laws and *Shariat* courts have been introduced as a separate but parallel system of public laws. They include *Hudood* punishments for drinking, theft, and fornication as well as the *Qisas* and *Diyat* (blood money to compensate for murder) legislation. Islamic cultural institutions, administrative boards, and research bodies have multiplied.

A small but vociferous network of jehadist outfits has emerged, nurtured by the state initially for the Afghan resistance (1980) to the Soviet invasion but subsequently burnished in the Kashmir struggle. Offshoots of jehadists have morphed into terrorist gangs, carrying out sectarian violence as well as acts of sabotage within the country. Pakistan at the turn of century was a country where insecurity and anxiety were the pervasive feelings, arising from bomb blasts, random sectarian killings, and attacks on mosques.

After the 2002 elections, governments of Islamic parties in two provinces have aimed at enforcing *namaz* (five daily prayers) and other Islamic tenets through a new morality police. If implemented, such measures would severely curtail individual rights and liberties by bringing personal conduct, beliefs, and religious observances under the state's control. Vigilantism has increased targeting minorities and harassing small sects.[5] Local *mullahs* pronounce *fatwas* (juridical opinions) and dispense justice. The state, by and large, has allowed such institutions to flourish. All in all, Islamization has shaken customs and traditions and promoted social change of its own brand.

"Islam is a complete code of life." This belief is the bedrock of Islamic social order, both conceptually and historically. How can Islam accommodate the demands of modern life and technology? This question has occupied Muslim societies for almost a century, although the Islamic revivalist project of recent times has given it a new urgency.[6] I am not going to delve into this theoretical debate, because my focus is on how the lived social life is unfolding. How the Islamization process has fostered Islamic institutions and practices is the focus of this review.

Social life in Pakistan has been simultaneously evolving along two tracks, namely Islamization of the public space and modernization of the private space and economy. Within the limits of affordability, Islamists have been readily adopting fertilizers, tractors, cars and motorcycles, air travel, recent advances in medicine, flush toilets, concrete roofs, television, cell phones, or the pursuit of riches. The moral order of Pakistani society is cracking under the pressures of divergent pulls.

As a structure, the Islamic mode of living is a system of rules and values. This structure exists autonomously of any group or individual. Yet it has come about through a human agency. An idealized Islamic society has always been one of the ideas of Pakistan. After independence, *ulemas* and Islamic political parties, Jamaat-i-Islami in the forefront, pressed for the enactment of Islamic laws. They have resorted opportunistically to electoral politics, agitations, and even violence, whatever suited the moment. Maulana Maudoodi, the head of Jamaat-i-Islami, has been the preeminent theoretician and political guide of the Islamic movement. His puritanical vision of the Islamic order articulated in books, pamphlets, and speeches has appealed to the newly rising middle class. Islamists' electoral failures and General Ayub's military rule subdued the Islamic movement in the first period. Jamaat's failure in the 1970 elections drove it to the strategy of cultivating cadres of activist youth, professionals, and merchants.

Jamaat's student wing, Jamiat-i-Tulabah, became the nursery for young Islamists. It also organized a "ready to call" strong armed force to mount agitations and intimidate ideological opponents. Jamaat follows a well-tested military approach of binding new recruits into small groups for mutual support and sense of belonging. This strategy has served extremely well to recruit newly arriving village boys and girls lost in the crowd of new students in city colleges. For decades, it has dominated student union elections in universities and colleges, particularly in engineering, medicine, and science faculties. On graduation, these members of expanding professional segments bring with them the indoctrinations of Jamiat and lately *tablighis*. This is how Islamic segments of the urban middle class have been built from the bottom up. These segments are the driving wedge of Islamic revivalism in Pakistan. Students of *madrassahs* are not the vanguard of the Islamic movement.

Apart from Jamaat and its student wing, there are other organizations and move-ments, which have served as the human agency for building up the Islamic struc-ture. *Tablighis* as a social movement have contributed greatly toward increasing observances of Islamic tenets and cultivating pieties in everyday life. Another agency that has contributed to the building of the Islamic structure is General Zia's Islamic laws and policies.

So far I have discussed the internal elements of human agency behind the Islamic structure. External forces and organizations have also contributed to the strengthening of Islamic ideology and institutions in Pakistan. The USA encour-aged Islamic groups in Pakistan during the cold war as counterweights to the socialist influences of the "Godless" Soviet Union. Afghans' *jehad* against Soviet occupation in the 1980s was lavishly funded and armed by the USA through

Pakistan. Afghans' tribal Islam spilled into Pakistan planting sectarian violence and terrorism. More subtly but extensively, Pakistani workers in Saudi Arabia and the Gulf states brought back both Islamic conservatism and modern consumerism. Altogether, these internal and external elements have served as the human agency for the promotion of the Islamic structure in Pakistan.

Islamic revivalism is fundamentally an ideology of traditionalism and conservatism. It has shifted the national discourse toward politics of culture, beliefs, and practices. The festering national issues of social justice and class polarization have been sidetracked for the present.

Class polarization

A question lurks behind the foregoing analysis, namely what has happened to the class polarization that results from uneven development? I will briefly touch on this issue.

Liberal models of economic development assume that benefits and opportunities filter down from entrepreneurs and professionals to workers and peasants. Theories of welfare state as well as strategies of socialist development envisage rapid transformation of the economy and expansion of well-paying middle-level occupations, while the state promotes the floating up of working and unemployed poor into such opportunities. One way or the other, a bridging of social disparities is promised.

In Pakistan, 50 years of development have resulted in a modest improvement of the living conditions in general, but it still remains a poor country. The floor has been raised a bit, although not equally and sufficiently. Social disparities have become more biting and stark. Material needs have increased but incomes have not risen in parallel. About a third of the population is stuck in absolute poverty. Thus, the floating up or filtering down processes have been functioning for only some segments of the lower/middle classes and not across the board. The rich and well-connected have gained disproportionately. However, the salaried middle classes are always struggling to meet their needs. Financial stringency plagues the bulk of the population.

Class differences have sharpened. The concern about social justice for the poor peaked in the second period under Bhutto's populist egalitarianism but it practically dropped out of the national discourse during the third period. Public interest in reducing class disparities is now limited to the World Bank indebted poverty alleviation programs. It is voiced largely in international seminars in five-star hotels. Social rights of the poor and lower classes are not on the active national agenda any more and there is no political agitation. What has happened to the poor?

The poor have been always economically marginalized but since the 1980s, they have lost politically and socially. They have been rendered invisible, pushed out of public sight. The paradigm of development has shifted to market economy, privatization, and global competition. Globalization as the new face of modernization is more concerned with growth, competition, and free trade than with equality and economic distribution.

Islamic revivalism includes social justice as one of its ideals, but Pakistan's Islamic political parties are more concerned about covering women's faces or enforcing prayers and fasts than establishing a minimum wage. As pointed out previously, they have shifted the universe of discourse to cultural matters. The poor appear on Islamists' agenda primarily as objects of personal reforms. Other political parties, PML or PPP for example, pay lip service to reducing social disparities but when in power they advance the interests of landlords, businessmen, and officers. Segmentation and mobility have eroded working-class solidarity. Left-leaning activists have been scooped up by NGOs. All in all, political advocates and social organizers have abandoned the lower classes except to verbally sympathize about their conditions.

There is an acute sense of deprivation among the lower classes, but they are reduced to seeking personal solutions out of their class consciousness. Crime has ballooned. Suicides are at epidemic levels. A large floating population shuffles between villages and cities in search of work and shelter. Beggars crowd public places, road intersections, markets, and parks. Family seems to be the only social institution that shelters the poor, ill, and unemployed. Class polarization is palpable but public action has been ebbing in the third period.

Invention and reinvention of tradition

Social change erodes established values and norms, precipitating uncertainty of behavior in certain social situations. This condition has been called, a bit dramatically, normlessness or anomie. New values, beliefs, and norms eventually fill such a normative void, but they are seldom altogether new. They grow out of traditions, weaving traditional symbols and meanings into new functions and are the foundations over which the edifice of new values and norms rises.

That tradition and modernity are not mutually exclusive but complementary has been repeatedly demonstrated by the history of social change.[7] As a human practice, belief, value, or norm originating in the past, tradition is essentially defined by its age and history. It need not be unchanging. In fact, traditions are the invented or borrowed cultural traits that have aged. They are continually invented by linking new customs, beliefs, norms, and/or values to the real or imagined past. Linking new or revived norms and values with the presumed pristine past also reinvents traditions.[8] Pakistan's social change manifests both these processes.

The modernization process in Pakistan proceeds by inventing traditions. A few examples illustrate this point. Over time, marriage ceremonies have become more elaborate and expensive in all segments of society. Revival of *mehndi* (custom of coloring a bride's hands and feet with henna) and indulgences such as extravagant dowries and big feasts are new customs meant to fulfill "our" traditions and uphold a family's honor. Caste, clan, or tribal titles have been resurrected as surnames after they had begun to be abandoned in the 1950s and 1960s, to mark an individual's prestigious pedigree. Nepotism and corruption in modern bureaucracies reflect the incorporation of family values and kinship obligations in public activities. These few examples point out how traditional values and meanings are patched on new functions or structures.

Islamic revivalism is the most pervasive form of reinvented traditions. It promotes a puritanical vision of society organized around *Sharia* laws. Note that the traditional and modern versions of Pakistani culture are not un-Islamic but they have roots in folk/spiritual Islamic traditions of rural origins. The envisaged Islamic order is "modern" and urban in ethos, legalistic and textual in approach. It explicitly draws on the "uncorrupted" historical traditions and fundamental precepts of Islam. It calls for resurrecting institutions that its proponents interpret to be "original and eternal" in values.

As a social movement, Islamic revivalism parallels the contemporary evangelism in the USA and Europe and the messianic Judaism of Israel.[9] It offers a belief system and emotional sustenance for the recently prospering and largely urban class segments of professionals and merchants. Islamic revivalism is the ideology of those climbing out of an agrarian/feudal milieu into an urban/commercial order. Functionally, it resonates with the Protestant ethics that complemented the spirit of nascent capitalism in the Europe of the seventeenth or eighteenth century according to Max Weber's famous thesis.[10]

The revivalist project in Pakistan promotes social conservatism, emphasizing ritual pieties, women's segregation, rigid dress code, ascetic life routines, and a collectivist ethos. It consecrates profit-making and economic entrepreneurship and accepts modern technology by and large.[11] All in all, Islamic class segments in Pakistani society combine modern material culture with traditional norms and conservative values in an attempt to forge an Islamic model for an urbanizing society that needs a new social and moral order. So far this model has delivered little to improve everyday life.

Urbanizing society and agrarian moral order

Urbanization is one of the largest forces of social change in Pakistan.[12] It is not only that cities and towns have exploded and extended rural regions are reaching urban-level densities and population, but also that urban ways of living are spreading into rural areas. Urbanism as a way of life has swept Pakistan except in some tribal pockets in Balochistan, NWFP, southern Punjab, and western Sindh.

Television, radio, or telephones are accessible in villages although a large number of people are too poor to afford them. Villages that had nothing to buy until the 1960s now have tea shops and candy stores. Vans ferry day laborers and students to nearby towns. Farmers increasingly make business-like calculations in running their farms, a change from the tradition-bound and barter-based mode of operation. All in all, urban–rural differences are being bridged. Urban ways of life have spread deep into the social fabric. Rural migrants are swamping cities. Yet there is an aura of "the more things change, the more they remain the same," at least in form.

Urbanism has precipitated wide-ranging needs for institutional reforms and the provision of infrastructure and services. These imperatives of urban life remain unfulfilled, affecting the quality of life in large parts of Pakistan.

Villages and towns are bursting with population and choking with sewage and garbage for lack of organized services. Cities have a patchwork of utilities that have been largely appropriated by the rich and the well-connected even though the public health of some is indivisible from that of all in urban areas. Similarly, urbanizing places require modern land economy and property rights that balance community and individual interests, but such modern institutions exist largely in form, if they are found at all.

Urbanizing societies require impersonal dealings according to deliberated laws and mores. In urban areas, most of one's daily dealings are with strangers who are not kin or friends. This social milieu functions effectively with mutual trust, defined expectations, common values such as regularity and punctuality that are expressed through norms of modernization. A civic culture that cultivates such social conditions needs to be deliberately promoted. These are examples of how imperatives of urban life necessitate a new moral order which defines notions of good and bad and lays down ethical criteria that underpin social relations.

The prevailing moral order is not evolving in parallel with the urbanizing society. It is rooted in agrarian values. By its monetized economy, mobility, and achievement-based occupations, urbanism has eroded the interlocking obligations of mutual care among kin and in communities. Traditional ethics are weakening and the new moral order is slow to emerge. Economic and social disparities are increasing. People's interests are diverging and a sense of loss of community pervades.

In urbanizing societies, communities of interest and moral order of a civil society, formal and impersonal, normally replace communities of face-to-face relations and neighborly bonds. Pakistani society is experiencing the "loss of historic community" without the emergence of a "community of interest" typical of urban order. Public space continues to be appropriated by private privileges and kin loyalties, as is evident in widespread nepotism and the culture of connections. Emerging modern institutions have an aura of hollowness about them. They reproduce the form without the content and meaning of modernity. The moral and ethical foundations of the urbanizing society remain undeveloped.

The moral order promised by Islamic revivalism has so far not addressed the challenges of a society where pursuit of personal interests has outgrown the ethical and moral restraints of community and kin solidarity. It defines morals largely in terms of sexual mores, religious observances, and gender relations, remaining mostly silent about the challenges of impersonal relations, bureaucratic institutions, and the balancing of public and private interests, in short, the mass society of modern materialism. All in all, Islamic revivalism harks back to agrarian values and idealizes a moral order steeped in tribal/rural social organization. Pakistani society faces a moral and ethical void in its drive to material modernization.

Paradoxes of social change

Social change is known to be a process of imbalanced growth. Not all parts of a society change in equal measure; some progress, others remain static, and still others shift sideways. The diverging scope and direction of change among different institutions is a source of cultural paradoxes. This is also the situation of

Pakistani society. A brief recounting of the more striking paradoxes illustrates this point.

Pakistan is a poor country, which was even poorer 50 years ago. Its per capita income has increased about three times in constant currency since independence. This economic growth has sharpened social disparities. Apart from the poverty indicators, these disparities are etched in everyday life. Pakistani cities are choked with cars, yet on almost every major intersection half-clad small children besiege these cars, begging or selling flowers or snacks. A family's dinner at the Gymkhana Club costs more than the monthly salary of the doorman or security guard serving diners.

In the traditional village economy of barter, the occupational divisions of the *seypi* system complemented each other to form a system of mutual obligations. Money was scarce and poverty was the fate of almost everybody except landlords, and even they had little cash at hand. There were inequalities of power and status but poverty and impecuniosity were widely shared. One did not feel more deprived than one's neighbors.

Economic development over the past five decades has raised the floor in personal consumption. Even the poor have a better diet and clothes than they did 50 years ago. Of course, the rich inhabit a different world. The poor may be marginally better but their deprivations are also more painful. Money has become the measure of many things. The traditional entitlements have eroded and people are largely on their own without community support. Material progress has increased the vulnerability of individuals and reduced the welfare of the poor.

Cultural paradoxes are equally striking. People live, work, and travel far away from their ancestral homes. Yet subnational and ethnic identities have been resurgent. National feelings are stronger and Islamic unity is continually reaffirmed. Yet ethnic or regional "insurrections" have been raising their head with regularity and sectarianism has filtered down to small towns.

Modernization and development are supposed to transform social structures from caste to class system. Pakistan's modernization is carving a different path. As I have discussed in the preceding sections, in Pakistan, economic status combines with caste, ethnicity, subculture, and lifestyle to create a segmented class structure. Millionaire bazaar merchants live frugally in traditional ways while even the middle class of the modern segment fully imbibe Western consumerism. A nuclear engineer proposes to tap *jinns* to solve the energy crisis and other scientists hear him reverently.[13] A pious heart surgeon advises his patients to "sacrifice a black goat" for quick recovery. Such are the contradictions embedded in modernization.

Islamic revival itself is a movement for the modernization of religious beliefs and practices. The revivalist ideology has incorporated notions such as welfarism, social justice, and human rights within its puritanical philosophy. These notions are traced back to the original Islamic practices. Islamic parties have participated in elections and espoused democratic ideals. Puritanical Islam is displacing folk beliefs and spiritual/syncretic traditions of historic Islam in Pakistan. However, the high culture of Islamic revivalism has not noticeably affected everyday life even in the Islamic segments. Islamists observe social norms such as punctuality, efficiency, tolerance, or respect for rules as laxly as modernists and traditionalists. Such normative paradoxes have given rise to a characteristic Pakistani mind-set, whose contradictions are reflected in public as well as private behaviors.

Who gains and who loses?

What have groups, class segments, and individuals gained from the economic development and social change in Pakistan and who have lagged behind? This question brings up the distributional effects of material modernization and social segmentation.

Multiple paths have opened up for individuals and groups to advance economically and rise up the social ladder. Education and adoption of commercial and industrial occupations are the usual routes for most people, although such opportunities are not equally available to all. Obviously, these routes are laid by development and modernization. Groups that have access to education and are less tied to ancestral occupations have been the beneficiaries. Mobility has been a ladder for breaking out of the prison of poverty and dependence. Work abroad has changed the fortunes of millions.[14] Even migration to cities is the poor villagers' vote for the promise of a better life.

All in all, *kammis*, the landless, and those struck by misfortunes, namely widows, orphans, and the sick have been left behind by this sweep of occupational mobility. About one-third of the population that continues to be classified as poor, the majority being in rural areas, essentially lacks social assets for access to education and skills that help break the economic bondage. The remaining two-thirds of the population have gained, albeit unequally and in small doses, from incremental social progress. Among relative gainers are the urban middle and upper classes, landowning farmers, and rural craftsmen. For generations, lower and middle classes have looked at career jobs in the military and civil services as the route to respectability, power, and riches for officers.

Geographically, irrigated districts of central Punjab, lower Sindh, and Peshawar Valley are more prosperous and urbanized. They have been transformed by the entrepreneurial culture leading to greed. Dry lands of rain-fed agriculture in Sindh, western Punjab, much of Balochistan, and southern NWFP remain poor and backward. These regional disparities have fanned subnationality movements and periodic unrest.

Big landlords and *biradari*/tribal chiefs have retained their hold on power by opportunistically adapting to the changing economy, and not limiting themselves to income from land only. They own factories, urban properties, and businesses. By economic diversification, they continue to be rich and powerful in the emerging urban economy. Elections have repeatedly brought the scions of landlord families to assemblies and ministerial positions. Faces change but the same families continue to dominate the power structure, although some new dynasties, the Sharifs and Chaudhris of Punjab and Saif Ullahs of NWFP, for example, have also joined the ruling elite.

Military coups have catapulted army officers into the elite ranks. Every successive coup has further consolidated the military (serving as well as retired) officers' hold on power and consequently riches. Urban professions, such as law, medicine, and management have also become stairways to riches and prestige. The upper ranks of these professions are not as open to merit and personal achievement as the middle and lower ranks.

Islamization has opened another path to social power and prosperity. Leaders of Islamic parties have tasted success in elections and served as ministers during the third period. Heads of seminaries, imams of large mosques, and *ulemas* have come to control large properties and big followings.[15] They live in style, riding Pajeros (SUVs) with posses of armed guards and taking frequent trips abroad, all signs of high status and a good life. Their power lies in influencing public opinion through their *fatwas* (legal edicts) and Friday sermons. The Islamic elite have wedged their way into the power structure and enjoy its privileges.

The illicit sector offers its own path to riches and status. Corrupt officials, black market merchants, and unscrupulous contractors for example, amass fortunes which bring them respectability and the high life. Economic development has expanded opportunities and the scope for corruption. Illicit gains are now an instrument of gaining status.

Overall, Pakistani society has witnessed a considerable circulation of people up and down the social strata. The well-connected and powerful groups continue to enjoy a distinct advantage regardless. The elite have come to include some new groups, while the old establishment retains its position, both nationally and locally.

Social cohesion and functioning of society

How does Pakistani society hold together despite its ethnic divisions, segmented classes, and fragmented institutions? What are the processes that maintain its social cohesion? This two-part question raises a critical issue about some semblance of functional equilibrium of society.

Pakistan as a nation in general and state in particular has been described in grave terms, "a nation in turmoil," "a failed state," and "a divided society," for example.[16] Such descriptions are essentially a commentary on the political instability of Pakistan, reflected in its long military rules and repeated breakdowns of electoral democracy. Whether the country is really in such dire straits is questionable. Such comments are all the more inapplicable to society.

Ian Talbot rightly observes "reports of Pakistan's death have been greatly exaggerated."[17] Even a longstanding observer and critic of Pakistan's policies, Stephen Cohen, concludes that: "This is a state that is not likely to disappear soon."[18] Pakistan's divisions and differences reflect the divergence of social, political, and economic development, not unlike that of most other postcolonial societies. It may differ in the expression of such divisions and the challenge of managing them but not in the type of issues that these societies face.

There are many institutional bonds that hold society together. Family and kinship as institutions top the list. At the core of Pakistan's social organization are family and kinship. An individual derives her/his status, identity, security, and

opportunities initially from family and kin, even clan or tribe. On these foundations, one often builds a structure of personal achievements and self-fulfillment
without fully imbibing individualism. Bonds of family and kin interdependence
continue to keep one rooted in these institutions. Even if one gets rich and influential, one has to share the fruits of one's success by helping out relatives and
deploying one's power and status for the well-being of kin. Both these institutions
have incorporated demands of urbanism and development, documented in Chapter
8, but they continue to be the pivot of social organization. Of course, like all social
institutions, family and clan bonds carry social costs, such as promoting nepotism,
but they are a source of social cohesion.

Nationalism ties together people of all regions and ethnicities in a common
destiny. Despite simmering ethnic grievances and regional disparities, nationalism
entitles millions to move across regions and provinces to improve their life
chances. Normally, national unity reverberates below everyday life but it surfaces
strongly in times of crisis. It was articulated first in 1947 when refugees streamed
into the new state of Pakistan, later during the war of 1965 and the defeat of 1971
as well as in the periodic upheavals that bring down failing governments, such as
in 1969, 1971, 1977, and 1998. Almost every external threat, natural disaster, or
political crisis brings out the subterranean unity of the Pakistani nation. Pakistani
society rescues the state in crisis. It also holds the excesses of the state in check
through forceful expression of public discontent in a myriad of ways, including
violent agitations and insurrections. The people's nationalist commitments explain
why predictions of Pakistan's so-called demise have tuned out to be ill-founded.

People's faith in Pakistan can be gauged from an opinion survey in *Herald*
magazine on the fiftieth anniversary of Pakistan. It concludes from the response to
a question about choice to stay or migrate, "despite gloom and doom about the
future of country...massive 82 percent nationwide would like to stay on." In the
same vein, about 67 percent of respondents believed that their children "will have a
better life than themselves" in Pakistan.[19]

Islam is also a source of social cohesion. It unites spiritually and emotionally all
Muslims despite sectarian divides and differences of beliefs and practices. Its charities, mosques, and shrines are community institutions that contribute to people's
riding out personal as well as national crises. Islam also underpins Pakistan's
moral order, which despite being under strain from the challenges of modernization, nevertheless lays the common groundwork in Pakistani society. People have
strong faith in divine intervention to hold together Pakistan. A common refrain is
that only Allah's protection explains Pakistan's "muddling through" its challenges
and ills.

Apart from these institutions, Pakistani society has forged a number of coping
mechanisms, which maintain functional equilibrium, albeit inefficiently, in
society. These processes are undoubtedly two-edged swords. They maintain the
functional coherence. Yet they also contribute to inefficiency, exasperation, and
arbitrariness in everyday life. Presently I will concentrate on their contribution to
the functioning of society despite many odds, such as limited resources, poverty,
democratic deficit, and corruption.

First, Pakistan's hospitals, schools, telephone companies, judiciary, police or businesses – in sum almost all organizations and institutions – operate on the basis of connections, power exchanges, and ethnic and clan/community loyalties. Formal structures are overlaid with informal but persistent networks of personalized dealings, nepotism, or bribery and corruption. Even market transactions have an aura of personalized dealings. One is only assured of reliable dealings if one makes a personal connection to a storeowner. Trust is not generalized but flows along lines of familiarity.

A process of "personalizing the impersonal" lubricates the institutional and organizational gears. People have to pull strings for everyday transactions. This process is very wasteful and exasperating, but it inverts people's ire inward. "I did not have strong enough pull or I could not afford the bribe." This is a common refrain to explain one's failure. It is also the theme that sublimates people's desperations and inhibits them from coalescing into political movements for reform. These frustrations boil up periodically in popular agitations that have brought down three entrenched governments in Pakistan and shaken loose almost all others after a few years of rule. Personalized dealings diffuse people's exasperation and make them bear the inefficiencies of the system.

Second, mobility including migrating abroad has served as a safety valve. It offers a way out of unfulfilled expectations. A landless peasant in a village seeks a better future in the city's *katchi abadis*, or an unemployed doctor in the city solves his problem by taking a job in the Gulf countries, Europe, or the USA. Imagine the scale of political upheaval if all the hundreds of thousands of ambitious graduates had not migrated abroad! Similarly, millions of workers have migrated to cities in search of personal solutions to poverty and dependence in villages. Migration kindles hope and defuses desperation.

Third, Pakistani society has shown a great capacity to improvise on the spur of the moment. Whether it is a road accident or flood, seldom can any systematic and prompt public response be expected. Yet in all such situations, crowds gather and volunteers come forward to transport the injured in carts, on cots, or cars... whatever can be grabbed. Even in the 1965 and 1971 wars, neighborhoods improvised their own civil defense. Some of the remarkable but unrecognized innovations can be witnessed among the poor and afflicted. One only has to notice a handicapped person in a street wheeling himself on a piece of board, to appreciate the inventiveness of people.

It would not be an exaggeration to say that most of the indigenous innovations have been done in the lower circuits of the modern and bazaar sectors. Motor rickshaws run on a scooter's engine that can carry three to six passengers, and mechanics who can make automobile parts from discarded materials are living testimony to the raw ingenuity of people. Similarly, markets for recycled clothes, machines, and even imitation drugs are examples of the "make do" social capacity. I am not suggesting these activities have no ill effects but only underlining the social capacity to improvise in the face of challenges. As a coping mechanism, it helps keep society functioning.

This capacity to improvise on the spur of the moment is a recognized cultural trait. A common adage is "English plan decades ahead, Hindus plan years ahead, but Muslims plan as they go along."[20]

Fourth, the state is the default option. The Pakistani state has mobilized itself into effective actions in times of crisis or when confronted with exceptional situations. The state has acted as the backstop preventing society's slide. Periodically, the military intervenes to "stabilize" the country after a breakdown of political order or rampant corruption. At other times, civilian authorities have invited the military to control riots, supervise elections, carry out the long stymied census (1998), and crack down on electricity thefts, for example. Thus, state power is the backstop for the functioning of society. Pakistan's difficult moments have been smoothed by the momentary forceful actions of the state, although without changing the fundamental conditions that precipitate such crises.

I could add a few other factors that facilitate the functioning of societies and those in particular that have resonance in Pakistan. Yet the essential point is that societies once formed have internal compulsions to hold together. Pakistan's social organization is sustained by its people's faith in the idea and the reality of their nationhood. This faith combined with the web of daily interactions and discourses is the basis of social cohesion in Pakistan.

Theory

In conclusion, the theoretical insights gleaned from this book's narrative should be recounted to place Pakistan's experience in a broader context. This objective brings up two questions: (1) What theories or models, if any, explain the patterns of social change in Pakistan? (2) What modifications of such theories or new propositions are suggested by Pakistan's experience? This section addresses these questions.

As discussed in Chapter 2, modernization is currently the dominant paradigm for the analysis of social and cultural changes in the Third World. Since the 1970s, modernity has been dovetailing into globalization, thereby elevating some modern values and norms into universal measures of social change.[21] Be that as it may, from our perspective what is striking is that social change in Pakistan has followed a hopscotch pattern of modernization. It has not unfolded as an integrated process but as a compendium of divergent trends.

Pakistan's path of modernization presents a complex and contradictory picture. Material culture has been modernizing rapidly, consumption patterns and mass media have been more open to modern, in fact global, influences, but business practices, transactional norms, organizational culture, social relations, and the worldview have reinvented traditions and adopted modern forms without incorporating corresponding values and mores.

There is a moral and ideological resistance to modernization that smacks of westernization. Preserving "our culture and identity" is a strongly held value and Islamic revival promises the rediscovery of "equality, human rights, democracy, and scientific thinking in our heritage."[22] This cherry-picked modernization is not unique to Pakistan. Its form in the country is influenced by cultural particularities, but its structure is not unlike that of other countries.

Samir Khalaf labels similar patterns of social change in Lebanon as "adaptive modernization," wherein traditional institutions rearrange themselves in response to the challenges of material and economic changes.[23] The resurgent cultural identity and religious revival are movements for coping with tensions and discontinuities of social change. They may not necessarily resolve those tensions, but they revise and realign traditions. They are expressions of the process of indigenization of modernity. The theme of institutional lags, extensively discussed in this book, points to the imbalances and tensions arising from diverging directions of change in various components of culture. The point to be noted is that traditions are not stagnant and do not act as brakes to social change, but they evolve to maintain structural continuity.

Eric Hobsbawm's term, invention of tradition, and Manual Castell's notion of reflexivity, namely conscious reconstruction of institutions and identities, point to the ways in which traditions promote their own form of change.[24] Most theorists of modernization envisage a dialectical interplay between traditions and modernity.[25] They certainly do not subscribe to a singular process of modernization. It is the popular media that makes modernization out to be a one-directional process that sweeps away long established norms and values. Social change is messy and full of contradictions. That is why the state has a critical role in managing social change through the deliberate reconstruction of institutions. Social legislation and public reforms are the tools for such reconstruction. Of course, the Pakistani state has lagged behind in fulfilling this crucial responsibility.

The narrative of social change in Pakistan suggests that two parallel processes have unfolded: (1) the diffusion of modern materialism and consumerism, and (2) indigenization of technologies, products, and institutions. Islamization can be interpreted as a process of indigenizing political ideologies and moral values under the umbrella of Islam. Each of these processes is spawning a range of class segments and cultural groups. A traditionally organic society is being segmented into sharply differentiated groups of divergent lifestyles. Social distances are increasing and institutions are splitting. The fragmentation of society, without the common ground of an integrative moral order, is the challenge posed by the rapid social change in Pakistan.

From Karl Marx to Ralph Dahrendorf, a long line of conflict theorists point out that conflict among groups and institutions is the crucible for social change. Conflict has a positive function in society's progress. The competition for means of production, authority, and power in contemporary terms is the driving force in breaking age-old relationships of dominance. In Pakistan, the institutional lags and segmentation of society are symptoms of economic and material needs being in conflict with political and social norms and practices. The Pakistani state has been ineffective in initiating legislative and social reforms to reduce this conflict.

An ideological and moral gap has appeared with the increasing differentiation of society. Modernization and globalization do not offer a moral purpose and a fulfilling ideology; they threaten national identity. These ideological and moral gaps have widened since the collapse of socialist states in the 1980s. Islamic revivalism and the indigenization process carry an aura of purposeful life, although the potential of such a promise remains unrealized. They feed people's need for a national identity. They may not live up to the challenges of mass society and modernity, but in Pakistan no other ideological alternative has emerged yet to satisfy demands for national identity and modernity on "our terms." Similarly, a moral order that balances material modernism with cultural continuity is needed. This national agenda remains unattended, leaving cultural development wide open to revivalist movements. The challenge of social and cultural transformation is essentially moral in scope and has not been systematically addressed.

Notes

1 Changing Pakistan

1 For a detailed account of the emergence of Muslims' sense of community, see Jalal (2001: 78–101).
2 See Ahsan (1996: 413pp.).
3 See Qadeer (1999b: 1193–210).
4 This figure is quoted from The World Bank (2002: 21, table 2.2). Poverty estimates over time are often difficult to compare because of the different definitions and criteria. Yet there is clear evidence that over the 55-year period of independence, poverty has declined though the decline has been inconsistent, increasing in periods of economic stagnation and decreasing in times of high growth rates.
5 Source of data, Federal Bureau of Statistics (1998: 14, table 3.2).
6 See Afzal (1974: 20) and Federal Bureau of Statistics (2000: 51).
7 See Giddens (1982: 10).
8 There is an ongoing debate about whether Pakistan has a unitary national culture or a composite of cultures in which Punjabi, Sindhi, Pashtoon, and Balochi plus some others like Sariaki, Kashmari, Barouhi cultures are the components. In this book, I take a "layered" view of the structure of culture in which the national culture forms the top layer over the body of provincial and regional subcultures.
9 For a discussion of urbanization and urbanism, see Abu-Lughod (1991: 5–25).

2 Patterns of social change

1 For a quick overview of the contributions of these theorists, see Etzioni and Etzioni-Halevy (1973: 3–8).
2 See Rostow (1956: 25–48) and Marx and Engels (1932).
3 See Meier (1984: 6).
4 See Sen (1999: 3).
5 See Myrdal (1968: 59–61).
6 See Lerner (1966).
7 See Gusfield (1967: 351–62).
8 Khalaf (2001: 55–63) argues about the process of adaptive modernization by citing E. Gellener, C. Greetz, and J. Lewis.
9 See Shills (1981: 12).
10 "Invention" of tradition is a process of formalizing and ritualizing behaviors or practices by reference to the past. It does not mean something imagined anew (Hobsbawm and Ranger 1983: 4).
11 See Jinnah (undated: 9).
12 See Anderson (1983: 6–7).

13 Afzal (1974: 68, table 29) estimates that Pakistan had a net gain of about 1.8 million population over the 1941–51 period from international migration, largely from India at the time of partition.
14 The modernists in Pakistan were not entirely secularist. They leaned toward the liberal interpretations of Islamic precepts in line with the ideas of Sir Sayyid Ahmed Khan of the Aligarh Movement and the poet-philosopher Allama Mohammad Iqbal. They were content to call Pakistan the Islamic Republic and subscribed nominally to the religious symbolism and moral precepts.
15 See Waseem (1994: 299).
16 See Waseem (1994: 306).
17 Postindependence armies in the third world have been described as modernizers in the literature of the 1960s.
18 See Waseem (1994: 366).
19 Cohen (1998) maintains that the new army leadership had been raised on Islamic ideologies.
20 See Ziring (1997: 444).
21 Salariat is the term coined by Alavi (2002: 5) to describe "those who aspire to and depend upon careers in salaried employment, overwhelmingly in government in the absence of a large enough private sector." They rallied behind the demand for a separate homeland for Muslims.

3 Landscape of independence

1 See Kureshy (1977: 9).
2 See Linck (1959: 14).
3 See Environmental and Urban Affairs Division (EUAD) (1992: xvi–xvii).
4 This thumbnail sketch of the evolution of Pakistan's land tenure system is based on the accounts given in Khalid (1998: 1–48, 163–86).
5 Figures in this paragraph taken from Agriculture Census Organization (1960, 1980).
6 *Land Reforms Regulation 1972* and *Land Reforms Act II*, 1977.
7 See Khan (1981: 174, table 5.3; 188, table 5.5).
8 Data about land capabilities are drawn from Environmental and Urban Affairs Division (EUAD) (1992: 22–4).
9 For a full description of the informal land markets, see Alvi (1997), Hasan (1998: 171pp.), and Nientied (1987).
10 *The Friday Times* (July 4–10, 1997, p. 6) reported these figures from Justice Tiwana's inquiry.
11 There is a large and contentious body of sociological theories about urban ways of life and behaviors induced by city living. Two articles are seminal to this debate (Wirth 1938: 1–24; Simmel 1964: 409–24). They have been critiqued from the right as well as the left, yet any discussion of the issue reverts to their formulations. Savage *et al.* (2003: 107–52) give an overview and the critiques. Yet it has been acknowledged that the spatial concentration of population, division of labor, and specialization of social and economic roles, induced by the city, do necessitate social institutions that are more formal and impersonal than what obtains in villages organized around agrarian norms and clan structures.
12 Ruralopolis is the name coined for high-density rural regions. It is a mixture of urban settlements and rural activities (Qadeer 2000: 1583–603).
13 The figures of motorcycles and cars reported here are from the Federal Bureau of Statistics (1998: 163, table 10.9). These data are based on license plate registration data. The number of unregistered or spuriously tagged vehicles is said to be large, particularly since the 1980s with the arrival of Afghan transporters as refugees.
14 *Dawn*, June 6, 2003, p. 4, reported from the annual Pakistan Economic Survey 2002–3.

4 Nation and ethnicity

1 See, for example, Batalvi (1960: 700pp.), Qureshi (1965: 297pp.), Jalal (1985: 310pp.), Hasan (1993: 434pp.), and Sayeed (1967: 321pp.).

2 The term "imagined" here and in the rest of this book is used in the sense implied in Anderson (1983: 224pp.). "Imagined" means recreated from memories, records, and texts of those times and thus it is always an act of interpretation. Imagined does not mean that memories, images, or interpretations *per se* are false, concocted, or unreal.

3 See Jalal (2001: 139–59).

4 See Shaikh (1993: 81–7).

5 The partition of Bengal, the separation of Sindh from Bombay, a separate electorate, and religious personal laws have been cited as policies that widened the gulf between the two communities.

6 Jamiat-ul-Ulema-Hind and Brelvi Ulema of Thana Bhawan, Ahrars in Punjab were aligned with the Congress Party and they branded Jinnah and other Muslim Leaguers as *murtids* or *kafirs* (see Jalal (2001: 422–4)).

7 Maulana Sattar Niazi, Zafar Ali Khan, and Raja of Mahmudabad at various times proclaimed that Pakistan will be a state where Quranic laws will be enforced; whereas the manifesto of the Punjab Muslim League (1944) pledged agrarian reforms, civil liberties, and individual freedom (see Jalal (2001: 442–3)).

8 The All India Muslim League Central Committee staunchly resisted some Punjabi Leaguers' demand to oust Ahmadis from the community of Muslims. Jinnah pronounced many times both before and after independence that Pakistan was not going to be a theocratic state.

9 The image of women in Iqbal's poetry and Hijazi's novels is that of pious and inspiring mothers who nurture righteous and fearless sons.

10 See Isphani (2003: 22–3).

11 See Ahmed (1987: 87).

12 See Ahmed (1987: 95).

13 See Ahmed (1987: 121).

14 See *Constituent Assembly* (1949:1–2).

15 See Ahmed (1987: 141).

16 The election of the Islamic Alliance (Mutthida Majlis-e-Amal – MMA) as the main opposition party in the National Assembly and its success in forming provincial governments in NWFP and Balochistan provinces through the 2002 elections have brought Islamists to power for the first time by popular vote. Islamic parties these days are all for electoral democracy.

17 LaPorte (1999: 45–64) describes Pakistan as a nation still in the making after 50 years of independence.

18 See Abercrombie *et al.* (1984: 234).

19 Imran Khan was the captain of the national cricket team in the 1990s, Noor Jehan's songs thrilled the public for decades, Abida Parveen is a renowned singer of Sindhi Kafis and sufi songs, and Sattar Edhi is a social worker who has organized a national network of health and ambulance services.

20 See Waseem (1994: 242).

21 See Ahmed (1998: 1–11).

22 Karachi was thrown into a frenzy of Muhajir–Pashtoon riots by Bushra Zaidi's death, killed by a speeding van driven by a Pashtoon on April 5, 1985.

23 Since 1982 or so, bomb blasts in mosques and Imam Baras, and sectarian murders have rocked Pakistani cities and towns and those incidents are often intertwined with ethnic and sectarian violence.

24 Nawaz Sharif failed in his attempt to appoint Khwaja Zia-ud-Din as the army chief on October 19, 1999. General Musharraf pre-empted his move.

25 See Elfenbein (1966: 3, 10).

26 In the 2002 local and national elections the MQM and JI cadres fought pitched battles in colleges, schools, and streets.
27 See Bearak (2003a).
28 There is near-consensus among sociologists and political economists that social convergence is under way in Pakistan, in language, behavior, consumption patterns, and occupations (see Ahmed (1998: 261–8)).

5 Urban transformations

1 See Khaldun (1967: 273).
2 See Weber (1958a: 242pp.).
3 The distinction between Gemeinschaft and Gesellschaft was outlined in Tonnies (2001: 266pp.).
4 See Durkheim (1984: 352pp.).
5 See Simmel (1964: 409–24, original 1902, 1950).
6 See Wirth (1938: 8–20).
7 See Gans (1962) and Young and Wilmott (1962).
8 See Qadeer (2004: 6–9).
9 The Pakistan census defines urban places on the basis of their incorporation as municipal bodies, a status normally legislated if a place specializes in commercial/administrative functions and has some rudimentary infrastructure.
10 See Abu-Lughod (1991).
11 See Hasan (1999: 140).
12 See Savage and Warde (1993: 122).
13 For evidence of this four-part structure of a typical British-Indian city, see Qadeer (1983: 79–91), Lari and Lari (1996: 135–66), and King (1980: 9–16).
14 See Harris and Ullman (1945: 7–17).
15 See Suleri (1989: 54).
16 See Hasan (1999: 44–58) and Linden (1997: 81–6).
17 See The World Bank (1988: 16, table 3.1).
18 See Hasan (1999: 59).
19 Figures about *katchi abadis* should be taken as estimates which vary by differences in criteria and measuring procedures. For Lahore's estimates, see Lahore Development Authority (LDA) (1998: section 2–13).
20 See Balbo (1993: 24).
21 See Hussain (1998: 689–700).
22 Housing class is a concept advanced by Rex and Moore (1967: 330pp.) suggesting clusters of households having similar arrangements of living, such as poor who are renters, poor who are owners of modest means, luxury housing owners and squatters in the Third World. Housing classes are distinct from, though overlapg with, economic classes.
23 See Hasan (1999: 95).
24 See Geertz (1963: 246pp.) and International Labour Organization (ILO) (1972).
25 For a description of the structure of the informal or bazaar sector, see Kemal and Mahmood (1998: 24pp.).
26 About 51 percent of the GDP came from the underground economy in 1996. Its share had increased from 20 percent in 1973 (Iqbal *et al.* 1999: 20). Earlier one of the finance ministers of Pakistan, Dr Mahbubul Haq, estimated that Rs 20 billion a year had been misappropriated by public officials (*Pakistan and Gulf Economist,* April 12–18, 1986, p. 8).
27 See Santos (1979: 19).
28 See Hasan (1999: 64–5), Alvi (1997: 92), and *The Pakistan Times*, February 5, 1993, p. 5.
29 For the Punjab's industrial entrepreneurs and their clan affiliations, see Weiss (1991).

General Zia is said to have boasted that the *lohars* of Daska can copy even a missile; nothing is beyond their skills.

30 For a summary of the evolution of the notion of class, see Abercrombie *et al.* (2000: 49–54).

31 See Alavi (1989: 5–19) and Ahmed (1998: 249–52).

32 I carried out an informal demographic survey of a university campus in Lahore in 1990.

33 See Kaplan (2000: 244).

34 For a detailed discussion of the imperatives of urbanization, see Qadeer (1999b: 1199–206).

35 Categories and definitions of structural qualities of walls and roofs have changed from one housing census to the next and thus are not comparable. Even availability of indoor water supply and provision of electricity were not among the variables for which 1961 census data were collected. Yet they are relatively more reliable indicators for comparison over time.

36 *The Nation*, Internet edition, http://www.nation.com.pk/daily/July1998/13/index.php.

37 See Qadeer (1996: 449, table 3).

38 See Qadeer (1996: 455).

39 Housing lot production and distribution became an item on the political agenda of all prime ministers after 1970. Bhutto (1971–7) initiated the program for transferring land titles to *katchi abadi* residents and the distribution of 3 marla (75 sq yds) housing lots in rural areas. Junejo's Five-Marla Program followed it (1985–8). Nawaz Sharif's promised housing lots for workers and peasants (1990–3) were announced with great fanfare.

40 See Hasan (1999: 97), Lahore Development Authority (LDA) (1998: 18), and Zaidi (2000: 17).

41 See Federal Bureau of Statistics (1998: 130).

42 WAPDA's losses, mismanagement, and consumers' agitations have been a regular news item year after year. For example, see *The News,* Internet edition, http://www.jang.com.pk/thenews/index.html (accessed on June 2, 2003).

43 See Environmental and Urban Affairs Division (EUAD) (1991: 101).

44 Statement of Abida Hussain, Federal Minister of Population (*The Nation*, Internet edition, http://www.nation.com.pk/daily/May2-1997/index.php).

45 The significance and pervasiveness of the *nang* code in various forms is discussed in Ahmed (1988: 203–4).

46 The allusion to the preindustrial city is essentially to the model of such an urban life presented by Sjoberg (1960).

47 See Khalaf (2001: 55–9).

48 Reference to these theorists is notional to reflect old and new Western urban theories. It is not meant to be a critique of their works.

6 Development and the countryside

1 Muslims in subcontinental India–Pakistan are divided into castes that historically define social standings on the bases of presumed national origins, land tenure, and occupations, for example, Sayyids, Shiekhs, Mughals, Chaudhris, *lohars* (black-smiths), or *mochis* (cobblers). Unlike the Hindu caste system, their social standings are not religiously sanctioned. The boundaries are porous but respective groups are largely endogamous. Stern (2003: 74) uses the term "quasi castes" to describe Muslims social hierarchy.

2 See *Dawn*, Internet edition, www.dawn.com (accessed on July 24, 2004). Islamic punishments for adultery or fornication are adjudicated by strictly prescribed rules of evidence and jurisprudence.

3 See Ahmed (1988: 198–9).

4 See Rashdi (2003: 6).

5 See Imperial Gazetteer of India (1998: 59).

6 See Fabietti (1996: 11).
7 See Imperial Gazetteer of India (1991: 62).
8 See Khalid (1998: 181).
9 Mohenjo Daro, Harappa, and Taxila are archeological sites of the Indus Valley cities that date back to the BCE period. Even the existing cities of Lahore, Peshawar, Bhera, Shikarpur, Thatta are 1,000 or more years old.
10 The Jajmani system originated in ancient times. Upper-caste families had attached service castes, for example, barbers, cleaners, and cobblers, who ministered to their needs, in return for annual and ritual shares from harvest or gifts/payments. Among Muslims, the Jajmani system survived in villages in an attenuated form.
11 See Imperial Gazetteer of India (1998: 4).
12 Durkheim (1858–1917) and Weber (1864–1920) and other founders of modern sociology postulated an ideal type (model) of rural community by differentiating it from urban social organization. Theorists emphasizing social class as the defining social structure have questioned their postulated rural–urban differences. Recognizing that rural and urban communities are encased in the overarching national society and thus their respective quality of life are segments of the national living conditions, it is still valid to compare both rural–urban differences and convergences as a method of assessing their respective living conditions. See, for example, Giddens (1982) and Hodge and Qadeer (1983).
13 See Smelser (1973: 268–84).
14 See The World Bank (2002: i).
15 See The World Bank (2002: vii).
16 See Afzal (1974: 21).
17 See The World Bank (2002: viii).
18 These percentages are estimates derived from the weighted average of two types of *pacca* walls and roofs reported in the 1998 census.
19 See Zaman and Khan (1988: 31–2).
20 For a description of the *seypi* system, see Egler (1960: 32).
21 See Khan (1983: 136).
22 See Etienne (1995: 73).
23 See Khan (1983: 146).
24 H. Alavi concludes that the 'green revolution' had worsened the relative position of the poor in the old settled districts of Punjab, Balochistan, and NWFP (Alavi 1982: 33).
25 See Qadeer (1977: 71).
26 These figures come from Gotsch (1982: 64) and the Federal Bureau of Statistics (1998: 93).
27 See Federal Bureau of Statistics (1998: 93).
28 See Khan (1983: 138).
29 Some tenancy reforms were legislated, protecting occupancy and at-will tenants from arbitrary evictions and forced labor.
30 Figures for 1950 and 1976 have been taken from Khan (1983: 139, table 2) and for 2000 from the Agriculture Census Organization (2003: table 1.2).
31 In 2004, the military farm in Okara, Punjab, was continuing to be a site of unresolved dispute between the army and its long established occupancy tenants.
32 The housing minister's statement in the National Assembly, *The Pakistan Times*, April 2, 1976, p. 1.
33 *Viewpoint*, April 23, 1987, p. 32.
34 See Ejaz (1999).
35 Cases in point are biographies of Zulifiqar Ali Bhutto and Sherbaz Mazari (see Wolpert (1993) and Mazari (1999)).
36 This sketch is based on a number of cases that the author knows personally.
37 See Lerner (1965).
38 See Ali (1988: 241).
39 See Naseem (1981: 253).

40 Many army officers, soldiers, civil servants, and professionals either retire or hope to retire in villages where their relatives live. Retirees, particularly from the military, form a significant proportion of rural residents. The lore of the "peaceful and secure" life of the ancestral village has been strong in Pakistan.

41 A letter to the editor of *Akhbar-E-Jehan* pointed out that so many residents of Dera Ghazi Khan had migrated that about 20–25 buses left from the district for Karachi daily (*Akhbar-E-Jehan,* August 23–29, 2004, p. 3).

42 Waseem (1990: 219) points out that workers in Faisalabad's textile mills were divided into factions of Jhelum *biradari* versus Pindi *biradari* at one mill and between Arians and Rajputs at another.

43 See Werbner (1990: 48).

44 See Naseem (1981: 256).

45 After the September 2001 terrorist attack on the World Trade Center and the Pentagon in the USA, thousands of Pakistanis were rounded up as illegal immigrants and many more fled back to Pakistan or sought refuge in Canada. In the 2000s, there was regular news of the capture of boats or trucks loaded with illegal immigrants in Europe, South East Asia, and the Gulf. Almost invariably Pakistanis were among those caught in these incidents. In villages, young men were selling their ancestral land or borrowing money to pay for their legal or illegal emigration abroad. Such was the desire to emigrate.

46 *Overseas Pakistanis Foundation*, Government of Pakistan, www.opf.org.pk (accessed on December 11, 2004).

47 See Bilquees and Hamid (1981) and Naveed-i-Rahat (1990).

48 See Lefebvre (1999: 4).

49 Quoted by Lefebvre (1999: 200).

50 Quoted by Gardezi (1995: 114).

51 See Naseem (1981: 270).

52 See Fabietti (1996: 14).

53 See Lefebvre (1999: 262).

54 See Naveed-i-Rahat (1990: 110–11).

55 See Pervez (1998: 44).

56 See Pervez (1998: 26).

57 The author has read web postings from these two towns.

58 The author was struck by the names with which young boys playing cricket in a grassless field in Karimabad addressed each other in 1991. A good bat was Imran Khan and a bowler was Wasim Akram.

59 See Khan (2002).

60 See Edwards (1990: 66).

61 See Khan (2002: 145–7).

62 Another anthropology thesis at the Quaid-e-Azam University concludes from a study of diffusion of innovations in the Punjab that "media alone is not that much influential or successful in bringing about behaviourial (*sic*) or change in ideas. It works within the framework of interpersonal relations" (Muneeba 1991: 78).

63 F. L. Brayne the Deputy Commissioner of Gurgaon, a district in the East Punjab, started a district-wide program of rural reconstruction in the 1920s. The Punjab province intro-duced rural self-government through district boards in the 1930s and it was extended in the form of *punchayats* at the village level. Some efforts to extend this system in Sindh and the NWFP were also made.

64 For a succinct description and assessment of the V-AID program, see Khan (1998: 54–7).

65 See Qadeer (1977: 72), and Khan (1998: 65–6) also.

66 See Khan (1996).

67 See The Aga Khan Rural Support Programme (AKRSP) (1990: 5).

68 The NSRP was asked to return Rs 500 million in 1994 on the allegation that it was wrongfully allocated the sum by the previous government and rumors of kickbacks and financial improprieties stymied the program, see Khan (1998: 199).

69 See The World Bank (2002: 116).
70 See Khan (1998) and The World Bank (1995).
71 Surveys of the members of Basic Democracies and union councillors in the 1970s and 1990s bear out that largely the middle-class persons from villages occupied these positions. For example, the average basic democrat was 38 years old, not related to big landlords, and on average (59 percent) earned income from nonagricultural sources (Burki 1971: 188). A study of 1990s union councillors in NWFP showed that 50 percent had been associated with previous rural development programs (Rashid and Tunio 1990: 75).
72 Haider (1981: 124) observed that the local council elections had "initiated a process of slow but discernible transition of power".
73 The weaknesses of the Pakistani state are extensively documented and discussed (see Ziring (1997), Cohen (2004), and Waseem (1994)).
74 Year after year, letters to the editors of newspapers and weeklies such as *Akhbar-l-Jehan* (weekly) have almost the same pleas regarding water supply, absence of teachers, dilapidated schools, or police highhandedness.
75 *The Herald* (monthly) magazine has periodically reported a "who's who of dacoits" in Sindh. They were operating freely in many districts, abducting farmers and businessmen for ransom and invading villages (*The Herald*, May 1995, p. 40a; May 2002. pp. 59–64; September 2004, pp. 75–7).
76 *Jang,* Internet edition, www.jang.com.pk/jang/index.html, September 4, 2004.
77 See Ejaz (2002b).
78 See Khar (2003: 23).
79 See Barth (1981: 94–7) and Titus (1998: 666).
80 Weiss (2002) has documented how poor working women's daily life is circumscribed by notions of honor, as has Mirza (2002) for women office workers.
81 Note, for example, Abida Hussein's contrasting behavior in her village and in Islamabad or Lahore (see Duncan (1990: 100–1)). Ayesha Siddiqa, a civil servant and newspaper columnist was venerated as a *pir* by her tenants (see Haeri (2002: 169–74)).
82 See the Pakistan Human Rights Commission's annual reports for the 1990s.
83 For example, in nineteenth-century Europe, in the transition from agrarian to industrial societies, various countries enacted social legislations to regulate state and church relations, introduce educational and family reforms, define labor rights, and reorganize military and civil services. Relatively little has been done to bring about sustained social reforms in Pakistan. Whatever steps were taken in the first period were scrapped in the second period, correspondingly the initiatives of the second period were undone in the Islamization phase of the third period. Politics has trumped social reforms in Pakistan.
84 See Ahmed (1988: 30–45).
85 In the 1960s there was a sentiment for not using clan or caste identities as last names. Their use was declining then but since the 1980s, their use has come back.
86 See Malik (1992: 993).
87 See The World Bank (2002: 20–2).
88 See The World Bank (2002: 21, table 2.2).
89 See Malik (1992: 988) and The World Bank (2002: 21).
90 See Malik (1992: 988).
91 See The World Bank (2002: 39, box 2.4).
92 This situation approximates Durkheim's description of the shift from mechanical to organic solidarity, except that in Pakistan organic or legislative unity has not emerged, while the mechanical basis of solidarity has broken down.
93 Affluent villagers may have motorbikes, televisions, and houses with flush toilets, while the poor may be squatting on somebody's land, living without water and latrine, clad in tattered clothes and plastic slippers. Some households may be orthodox Islamists, while others could be nominal Muslims not knowing even *kalima*. Such

differences of beliefs, possessions, and lifestyles have appeared in recent times. Conventionally landlords and the landless consumed similar goods, except the former had those in plenty, while the latter took crumbs from the rich's tables.

94 More about sectarianism in a latter chapter.

95 A good example is the paradox of the popular leader of MQM, Altaf Hussain, commanding the authority and unquestioned submission of a *pir* from a majority of Muhajirs in Karachi, the most urbanized group in Pakistan. Person-centered organizations are also common in other cities.

7 Islam and social life

1 See Abercrombie *et al.* (2000: 180). For another definition of the term institution, see North (1989: 9, 1321) also.

2 See Lapidus (1998: xxii).

3 See Ikram (1997: 669).

4 Often customary practices contravened Islamic laws, such as in the case of a daughter's share from landed property. Customary practices precluded daughters from inheritance, whereas Islamic law allows a daughter half a son's share. Many landlords refused to follow Islamic laws of inheritance on the plea that customary practice precludes daughters from a share in property.

5 The status of a village *mullah* was only a notch above that of other *kammis* (workers attached to families). He was called to lead prayers, teach children the Quran, and perform religious rituals at birth, marriage, and burial in exchange for his family's keep.

6 See Jalal (2001: 69).

7 Justice Munir mentions that he heard the phrase "ideology of Pakistan" in 1953 in the hearings for the Court of Inquiry in Punjab Disturbances 1953. In the constitutional deliberations of 1962, Maulvi Bari's explanation that Islam equals the ideology of Pakistan was accepted. It has now become a stock answer to any public discussion about social values, national goals or constitutional issues (see Munir (1979: 25–6)).

8 See Qureshi (1980: 563).

9 See The Court of Inquiry (1954: 215).

10 See Nasr (1994: 28).

11 See Maudoodi (1952: 12).

12 See Callard (1957: 208–9).

13 Iskander Mirza, the governor general who initiated the military coup of 1958, explicitly said that one of the reasons for taking over the government was that "politicians were flirting with *mullahs*." Mirza's unpublished memoirs quoted by Nasr (1994: 145).

14 See Gauhar (1994: 35).

15 See Nasr (1994: 192).

16 The two models of Islamic state and society roughly correspond with Ahmed's "the sacred state excluding human will" and the "sacred state admitting human will" (see Ahmed (1987: 31)).

17 See Nasr (1994: 171).

18 Asad Gilani cited by Nasr (1994: 237, ch. 3, f.n. 31).

19 Urdu–Sindhi language controversy was exploited by the JI and JUP (1972) resulting in murderous riots in Karachi (see Waseem (1994: 318)).

20 See Wolpert (1993: 213).

21 See Wolpert (1993: 288).

22 Quoted by Wolpert (1993: 282).

23 The channeling of popular discontent into the struggle for *musawat-i-Mohammadi* (the Prophet's ordained equality) was a clever move by PNA.

24 Quoted by Nasr (1994: 189).

25 For a comprehensive account of the various components of General Zia's Islamization policies, see Waseem (1994: 380–385).

26 Police and magistracy were known to demand bigger bribes to spare accused from trials under *Hudood* laws.

27 See Iqbal (2003: 172).

28 Both these legislations have been widely protested by international human rights organizations, including Pakistan Human Rights Commission, UN Commission on Human Rights, etc.

29 *Dawn*, Internet edition, www.dawn.com/2002/07/19.

30 Salamat Masih, a Christian boy of 14 years, from the Gujranwala district was prosecuted for insulting the Prophet, but was acquitted by the High Court in 1995. Yet he had to flee the country to escape murder threats by local mobs, and the judge who acquitted him was later murdered. Dr Farooq of Gujranwala City was not so lucky. He was killed by a mob, whipped into a frenzy by the neighborhood *mullah*, for allegedly burning some pages of the Quran (April 1994). These two cases were widely reported in the press, many persons fell foul of the blasphemy law and lost their lives (see Human Rights Commission of Pakistan (1995: 38) and Khan (1994a: 44–54)).

31 See Khan (1994a: 46).

32 Eventually the Federal Shariat Court acquitted her, but the law's contradictions and antiwomen bias remained in the statue books (Waseem 1994: 381).

33 See Qureshi (1980: 571).

34 Hussain (1999: 264), in his literary biography, describes Gen Zia's getting up to say prayers (*namaz*) in the middle of a reception for journalists and writers and almost everybody dutifully lining up alongside him, while a similar observance was not followed by almost the same crowd the next day at the prime minister's reception.

35 Dr Israr Ahmed has been the head of his own Islamic Institute. For many years he has been on TV daily. His TV lectures included topics such as the Islamic justification of taking a vanquished enemy's women as concubines or the virtues of an Islamic Khalifat (nominated ruler).

36 See Abid (2002: 280).

37 In the period 1986–91, during the Afghan resistance against the Soviet Union, Pakistan has had about 100 incidents of major terrorist bombings. Most of these were presumed to be retaliatory strikes by the secret services of the Soviet Union and Afghan regime.

38 Qazi Hussain Ahmed organized youth wings, called Pasban, which were later renamed as Shabab-i-Milli, who staged riotous demonstrations and functioned as the *danda* (stick-wielding) force for the Jamaat.

39 See Nasr (1994: 195).

40 Brelvis' (a relatively liberal sect) annual gathering in Multan was emblazoned with the slogan "Soviet Russia sank in Afghanistan, next is America's turn. We will take Kashmir" (*The Friday Times*, November 7–13, 1997, p. 5).

41 See Nichols (1998: 123–4).

42 See Nichols (1998: 126–8).

43 Nasr (1993: 267) quotes a Jamaat leader "we were interested in Sirat al-Nabi (the path of the Prophet), while Zia was content with Milad al-Nabi (celebration of the Prophet's birthday)."

44 See Nasr (1993: 272).

45 The number of seats in respective elections have been estimated on the basis of the elected members' party affiliations, though they were elected under the banner of political coalitions.

46 See Jilani (1998: 58).

47 See Ahmed (1998: 108).

48 *Dawn*, Internet edition, www.dawn.com/2002/07/13.

49 Masood Khuderposh was an eminent civil servant who attempted to initiate a reform of prayers. He conducted *namaz* prayers in the mosque of Bagh-a-Jinnah, a park in Lahore in early 1960s. I witnessed the *namaz*.

50 For a description of these organizations, see *Newsline*, May 1998, p. 38.

51 How strong were Lashkar-e-Toyba and Jaish-e-Mohammad can be gauged from the

fact that the leaders of these organizations toured the country making speeches and proclaiming *jehad* in Kashmir, while the government claimed to have banned them. Jaish's leader Masood Azhar was sprung out of an Indian jail in exchange for the hostages in a hijacked Air India plane. While the government of Pakistan was denying knowing his whereabouts, he was openly addressing public meetings.

52 See Ahmed (1998: 110, 112).

53 See Khan (1994b: 27–31).

54 This estimate would be on the low side. Newspaper headlines report only major events and this bias affects my estimate. Although bombs are not always thrown in mosques and Imambarahs, most of the reported incidents were related to the Sunni–Shia mutual terrorism. Newspaper headlines from about 50 years have been compiled in Razi and Shakir (2001).

55 *The News*, Internet edition, www.jang.com.pk/thenews/index.html, February 7, 2004.

56 *The News*, Internet edition, www.jang.com.pk/thenews/index.html, June 3, 2003.

57 This reference is to the author's Master's thesis in sociology which though completed with the cooperation of leading *ulemas* (Maualana Maudoodi, Allama Ala ud Din, and Maulana Hanif Nadvi) irked Islamists for asking questions about beliefs and practices. The thesis was successfully completed but kept out of circulation by the university's administration (Qadeer 1959: 48).

58 From the late 1980s, members of various denominational organizations have started wearing turbans of different colors and other markers of dress to proclaim their religious affiliations.

59 *The News*, Internet edition, op. cit., November 17, 2003.

60 See Duncan (1990: 218).

61 For the role of *pirs* (spiritual guides and seers) and saints in rural Islam, see Lindblom (1990) and Gilmartin (1990).

62 See Ejaz (2002a).

63 See Ahmed (1984: 321).

64 For a temporal account of changing norms of *burqa*, see Qadeer (1999a: B.3).

65 Personal communication from Fayyaz Baqir, former president of the Nationalist Students Organization.

66 Tablighi Jamaat was founded by Maulana Ilyas in Delhi in 1941. It had a small nucleus of followers in Lahore. It gradually grew, but started gaining members in increasing numbers in the 1980s. For an account of the life and objectives of Maulana Ilyas and the Tablighi movement, see Khan (1986).

67 Tablighi Jamaat has attracted a large number of bazaar merchants, newly prospering urban professionals, and military and civilian officals, particularly retirees. Yet these same social classes are the primary purveyors of blackmarketing, overcharging and other ways of obtaining illegitimate financial gains. Typically in engineering colleges and universities, for example, there are hundreds of student members or sympathizers of Tablighi Jamaat. Yet on graduation, they behave not noticeably different from other engineers in adopting the corrupt practices of Pakistan's engineering professions.

68 *The News* reported that the annual gathering of Tablighis drew about a million persons (*The News*, Internet edition, op. cit., October 24, 2003).

69 Many professionals and officers take up the Tablighi lifestyle on retirement, after a long career of amassing wealth. For example, a retired general who became senior leader of Tablighi Jamaat was accused of embezzling millions as the chairman of the Evacuee Trust. He was not tried nor convicted for these accusations. There are many, many such cases.

70 The Islamization process of the Zia regime precipitated the issue of which *fiqh* (Islamic jurisprudence) was to be enforced through Islamic laws. Shias converged on Islamabad in 1980 to demand that the Fiqh-i-Jafarriya be applied on them for *zakat*, inheritance and *Hudood* laws. They partially succeeded and consequently Sunni *ulemas* started

apprehending that their *fiqh* would be sidelined. Such controversies grew into militancy (see Zaman (1998: 693–4)).

71   For an account of sectarian arguments within the Sunni school, among Brelvis, Deobandis, and Wahabis, see Jalalzai (1995: 36–45).

72   *The Nation*, September 1, 1994, p. 3. Later in 2004, the Punjab police listed 377 persons as active members of sectarian terrorist networks (*The News*, Internet edition, op. cit., February 7, 2004).

73   Based on tabulations of newspaper headlines as reported in Razi and Shakir (2001).

74   For a description of sectarian armed outfits, see Khan (1994b: 27–38).

75   Shia professionals were targeted individually in towns of southern Punjab, Lahore, and Karachi. For example, in 2003 about 70 Shia doctors were murdered in Karachi, driving many medical specialists out of the city.

76   For a detailed account of the Sunni–Shia conflict in Jhang district, see Zahab (2004).

77   *The Herald* (monthly), March 2002 profiled 14 "most wanted" sectarian terrorists. Almost all of them came from towns of southern Punjab, such as Multan, Layyah, Bahawal Nagar, and had affiliations with Sunni or Shia seminaries and militant organizations (Abbas 2002: 28–9).

78   See Ahmed (2004a).

79   See Salamon and Anheier (1997: 60).

80   Data on *madrassahs* is notoriously unreliable. Many are not registered; others are attached to mosques thereby falling out of statistical definitions. The figures for southern Punjab come from Zaman (1998: 710, table 1).

81   These are figures for *madrassahs* registered with the federal ministry (see *Dawn*, Internet edition, op. cit., July 28, 1999).

82   See Ahmed (2004b: 8).

83   *The Nation*, Internet edition, op. cit., January 1, 1997.

84   *The Friday Times*, October 17–23, 2003, p. 8.

85   Rhetoric here does not suggest vacuous talk or insincere language, but refers to ways of representing and articulating social objectives (Suleri 1992: 1–5).

86   My terms imagined and lived cultures overlap with, but also differ from, the ideal (what culture ought to be) and real (what it is) aspects of a culture.

87   Traffic in Pakistan is undisciplined and hazardous. Traffic accidents are numerous and take a very heavy toll of life, limbs and property every day.

88   See Maulana Maudoodi's views about the economy and the Islamic state, for example (Nasr 1996: 103–6). The Jamaat-i-Islami was also thought to be in sympathy with American international interests in opposition to the Soviet Union's goals.

89   See Hobsbawm and Ranger (1983: 4).

90   For example, Qazi Hussain Ahmed, leader of the Jamaat-i-Islami, was a multimillionaire, as were Maulanas Fazlur Rehman, Samiul Haq, Shah Ahmed Noorani, and Allama Tahirul Qadri (see Khan (2004: 62–3)).

91   See Aziz (1993) and Nayyar and Salim (2004).

92   These dates have been abstracted from newspaper headlines catalogued in Razi and Shakir (2001).

93   MQM raised the slogan "Muhajirs have not taken all upon themselves to sacrifice for Islam" during the 1990s. A veritable war was fought between the IJT and the Muhajir students organization in Karachi and Hyderabad colleges in 2003–4. Similarly, Baloch and Sindhi nationality movements rejected subordinating their goals to Islamic unity (see *The News*, Internet edition, op. cit., February 25, 2004).

8   Family, kinship, community, and civil society

1   Joint family is a two- or three-generation unit of blood relations living together, sharing property, child-rearing and elder-care, and usually maintaining one kitchen. Extended family is a loose federation of conjugal families or a social unit composed

of parents, children, and other kin, who may live under one roof or near each other sharing some functional responsibilities (see Chakraborty (2002: 20) and Abercrombie *et al.* (2000: 127)).

2 For an anthropological description of the Punjabi family, see Eglar (1960). For other regions, see Safdar (1997).

3 See Imperial Gazetteer of India (1998: 46).

4 For a theoretical discussion of the variations in Indian joint family, see Chakraborty (2002: 40–73).

5 See Parsons (1949).

6 These notions have not been found to be universally valid even in Western societies. Working-class families, immigrant households, and family corporations draw upon close-knit extended families for support and resources. See, for example, Young and Wilmot (1957), Goode (1963), and Gans (1962).

7 See Chakraborty (2002: 40–6).

8 See Korson (1975: 18).

9 Periodic Pakistan demographic and health surveys are the primary source of national data on family structures. Its 1990–1 survey, for example, documents that 61 percent of all marriages were among blood relatives. Zaidi (1998) observes that 50 percent of marriages in Punjab were with cousins

10 See Zaidi (1998) and Wahab and Ahmadi (1996).

11 The most popular narrative in Bollywood movies was lovers rebelling against family and caste restrictions. See, for example, *Awara, Barsat, Aan,* and *Anmol Ghari.*

12 Islami Jamiat-i-Tulba members have had many marriages among themselves. In annual meetings of Islamic political parties and missionary organizations, there is organized and informal "shopping" for like-minded mates. It is an organized activity in Islamic gatherings of Pakistanis and other Muslims in the USA, Canada, and Britain.

13 Two widely advertised marriage websites are mehndi.com and Shadi-on-line.com.

14 *Dawn,* Internet edition, www.dawn.com/2000/09/11.

15 See Government of Pakistan (1965: 14–17).

16 See Akram (2002: 21).

17 See Akram (2002: 21) and Khan (1996: 20–1).

18 Over time, peddling influence to get what normally should be a matter of market transaction or public utility for members of one one's family and kin has become a salient obligation.

19 A majority may not feel such conditions to be very restrictive, yet they have deleterious social consequences.

20 *The Herald,* 'What do Pakistani really want? Fifty years fifty questions', January 1997, p. 182.

21 See Qadeer (1999a: B3).

22 See Dawood (1999: 40).

23 *Dawn,* Internet edition, op. cit., July 24, 2002.

24 Women manage home usually and are responsible for major domestic decisions, including arranging marriages and dealing with relatives. See the life histories of women reported by Weiss (2002).

25 For example, a sick child in the city has to be taken to a doctor when men of the household are away. Similarly, women have to ride a bus or walk long distances, thereby coming in contact with strangers. These are the imperatives of urban living.

26 See Khuro (1981: 172).

27 For the history of Muslim women's political and social movements, see Saiyid (1998) and Mumtaz and Shaheed (1991).

28 See Patel (1991: 14).

29 National TV showed such scenes day after day during Bhutto's tours of Balochistan in 1976.

30 For discussion of the injustices perpetrated by this ordinance, see Patel (1991: 22–6).

31 See Zia (1991: 38).
32 In 1964, the author, working as an advisor in the Pakistan Planning Commission, found that female typists had been employed in the federal secretariat. So new was the presence of women in the lower ranks of the civil administration that there were no ladies' toilets and women had to be content with a toilet in the basement.
33 See Mirza (2002: 96).
34 *Dawn*, Internet edition, op. cit., December 20, 2002.
35 See Eglar (1960: 75), Korson (1975: 19), and Safdar (1997: 46–7).
36 Talbot (1998: 354) also recounts incidents in the elections of 1997 when many PPP leaders defected to the Muslim League of Nawaz Sharif bringing their *biradaris* with them and thus helping him win the elections.
37 See Ali (2002: 106–8).
38 Ghose (1969) wrote a novel, which weaves together themes of rich industrialists joining the corrupt administration to deprive poor farmers of their land. It is purported to have been inspired by this case.
39 See Waseem (1990: 218).
40 See Lindbolm (1990).
41 See Eglar (1960: 75).
42 See Hillery (1955: 777–91).
43 Lyon (1989: 5) has identified these common characteristics after reviewing various types of community studies and theories.
44 See Ejaz (2002b).
45 Such disputes have occurred throughout the history of Pakistan, but they seem to be multiplying in recent years. *Jirgas* (tribal/ village council of elders) have been revived in Sindh and even Punjab. They have been common in the tribal areas of NWFP and Balochistan, in the third period. The provincial government of Sindh was trying to promote *jirgas* to resolve village disputes in 2005.
46 Darling (1947: 67) writes "in 1922, for instance, in proportion to population nearly twice as many suits were instituted (in Punjab) as in the United Province".
47 See Cambridge University Asian Expedition (1962: 12–13).
48 See Qadeer (1975: 143).
49 See Jalazai (1998). The Islamic parties have consistently branded NGOs as promoters of alien values and Western culture. See, for example, *The News*, Internet edition, www.jang.com.pk/thenews/index.html (accessed on July 22, 2000). Even the general public regards many NGOs, particularly the development oriented, as self-serving organizations good only to hold seminars and write reports for foreign donors. Yet the community-based organizations that deliver direct services, such as schools and clinics are appreciated.
50 See Ahmed (1998: 249–60).
51 See Alavi (1998: 68–9).
52 The author grew up in the old city of Lahore. The dead-end street on which he grew up had nine houses and 17 households; some households doubled and tripled in small houses and only two households were exclusive occupants of their homes. A penniless widow was the neighbor of an affluent owner of a wood-sawing workshop. This was a typical residential street in the city.
53 See Naveed-i-Rahat (1990: 105–6).
54 See Mamdani (1996: 14–15).
55 See Cohen and Arato (1992: ix).
56 See White *et al.* (1996: 4).
57 Earlier the founding of Anjuman Himayat-Islam in Lahore, Sindh *madrassah* in Karachi, and Islamia colleges as well as schools in many cities was mentioned. These institutions became driving forces of Muslims' social and political advancement. Other examples include the Muslim Women's Conferences in 1916 and 1917 and literary clubs, particularly poetry recitation for arousing public awareness.

58 See Kayani (1977).
59 The anti-Ayub protests spread to small towns in east Pakistan as well as west Pakistan and thus were not easily controllable. Furthermore, they pitched professionals working in the government against administrators, chief engineers marched against their CSP bosses, doctors agitated for autonomy, bazaar merchants protested against industrial monopolists. Thus, a broad sociopolitical movement for political and social change was unleashed. Civil society was the vanguard of this movement.
60 *The Herald* reported that the Institute of Policy Studies, Islamabad, had estimated that there were 6,761 *madrassahs* and seminaries with one million students, whereas the Federal Ministry of Interior put the number of *madrassahs* at 20,000 with 3 million students (*The Herald*, November 2001, p. 18).
61 For the ideas espoused by the Islamic seminaries, see for example, Goldberg's (2000) account of the Madrassah Haqqania, Akhora Khattak describing it as a "*Jehad* factory."
62 See Banuri and Khan (1997: 62).
63 NGOs are continually blamed for living high on foreign funds and thereby serving Western interests. *Mullahs* threaten them with closing their offices and driving them away from their areas, particularly in NWFP and Balochistan. For example, see the news about the bombing of NGO offices in Karak, NWFP (*The News*, Internet edition. op. cit., July 19, 2001).
64 See Qadeer (1997: 758–9).
65 See Sadowski (1993: 16–19).
66 Gellner (1991: 91), for example, is one of many Western scholars who regard Muslim societies as lacking in vigorous civic traditions and political culture.
67 Current notions of civil society are based on the ethos of individualism and volunteerism. They do not regard social solidarity and normative structures as a necessary condition for civil society.

9 Everyday life

1 See Bowen and Early (1993: 1).
2 See Mines and Lamb (2002: 4).
3 Princess Amina was the *nom de guerre* of an Egyptian floor dancer.
4 He moved to Mansoora, a new and exclusive community built by the Jamaat-i-Islami for its leaders and workers.
5 See Reeves (1984: 30).
6 M. Ejaz has been a columnist in the *Daily News*. He has written about the social life in his ancestral village.
7 The definitions of elite and ruling elite have been derived from Abercrombie *et al.* (2000: 113–114).
8 See Talbot (1998: 69).
9 See Ali (2001: 109–10).
10 See Cohen (2004: 68).
11 During General Musharraf's rule, military officers, both retired and serving not only occupied the commanding heights of the civil administration, but were also appointed as administrators in districts. Almost all provincial governors, heads of public service commissions, vice chancellors of universities, chairs of metropolitan corporations, chiefs of public works and health agencies were military officers. most of these positions had been prized career jobs for civil servants (see Mir (2001: 3)).
12 Politicians and police depend on each other for favors. For example a police superintendent in Sahiwal was transferred five times because he was not obliging the politicians. This is not an uncommon experience (see Khalil (2005)).
13 These figures were revealed by Dr Haque in his speech to the Chamber of Commerce in Karachi (see Shahid-ur-Rehman (1998: 11)).
14 See Shahid-ur-Rehman (1998: 62).

15 See Shahid-ur-Rehman (1998: 56).
16 See Ali (2001: 108).
17 There have been numerous cycles of loan defaults by major businesses. Loans were obtained with political pressures and manipulations and given with little regard to their viability.
18 The term "savage capitalism" has been used by Mustapha Kamal Pasha to describe the entrepreneurship of the proto-nationalist class who adopt modern technology but not social and business values (Pasha 2001: 20–1).
19 In the 1990s, there were many incidents of riots at cricket matches when ticket-holders could not get seats.
20 I have used Urdu terms for describing these sociocultural groups, but acknowledge that there are Sindhi/Pashto/Baluchi and even Chitrali or Balti equivalent of these terms.
21 These figures are approximate as the census classification of occupations changed over successive censuses.
22 To cite just two out of many such accounts that are almost 40 years apart, Murphy (1995: 134) remarks about the "orthodox set" that in their households "one was being treated as a person rather than as a circus act." Warren (2003, reproduced on asiapeace@egroups.com) found the "Walled city" of Lahore a relaxed place where shopkeepers offered him tea or Coke and were curious about him as a foreigner and open to his queries.
23 *The Friday Times* (weekly) published a series of editorials and columns in January 2005 lamenting the erosion of trust.
24 About 53 years of newspaper headlines have been compiled in Razi and Shakir (2001).
25 The Human Rights Commission of Pakistan has published an annual "State of Human Rights" since the early 1990s. This publication documents well-known incidents of violence against women, minorities, and children, including abductions and trafficking. These reports show a continuing upward trend in these crimes.
26 *The Nation* (daily) reported in its Sunday magazine section that in the previous decade sectarian violence had escalated, with 1,104 incidents reported and 1,120 persons dead from those events (*The Nation*, Internet edition, www.nation.com.pk/daily May. 1997/11/index.php).
27 Bus and truck drivers are notoriously reckless and ill-trained. Vehicles are poorly maintained and traffic rules enforcement is compromised by the inadequacies and corruption of the police force.
28 Even ownership of mosques was widely contested by rival sects. In small towns and villages of Sindh, about 200 mosques were disputed by rival claims of Sunni Tehrik, Dawat-Islami and Ahle Hadith. About 1,000 policemen had to be deployed on Fridays to guard these mosques (*The News*, Internet edition, op. cit., February 26, 2002).
29 The newspapers regularly report police atrocities; incidents include accused persons dying during interrogations, beatings-up of innocent bystanders, bribes, and appropriation of properties by force.
30 I have deliberately not referred to highly publicized political murders or attempted murders, such as attempts on the lives of General Musharraf and Prime Minister Shaukat Aziz in 2004. What I want to point out is that influential persons not directly involved in any political, sectarian, or ethnic disputes were also victims.
31 See Jinnah (undated: 9).
32 Blasphemy accused have been locked away without trials and those who were tried but could not be convicted were refused acquittal for fear of retaliation against judges. One high court judge who acquitted a Christian youth accused of blasphemy was later murdered.
33 See Abbas (2005: 192–3).
34 See Jilani (1998: 128).
35 Attacks on churches in Bahawalpur and Taxila in 2001 resulted in many casualties and were said to be militants' revenge for Christian America's attack on the Taliban.

36 There are incidents of abduction and rape of Christian women, beating up of Ahmadis, etc. that remain unreported. Letters to editors highlight the police's indifference to such incidents. For one such protest of Christians against the dishonoring of their women, see *The Pakistan Times*, May 21, 1990, p. 5.

37 See Addleton (1997: 123–5).

38 Shabab-e-Millie, the youth wing of the Jamaat-i-Islami has periodically organized raids to smash or smear billboards showing women's faces and have harassed women for wearing dresses that bare the arms or show their hair. One organized spate of such incidents was in NWFP after the election of the MMA government (see *Dawn*, Internet edition, op. cit., October 9, 2003).

39 See *The News*, Internet edition, op. cit., January 29, 2005.

40 In medical colleges, architecture, and city planning programs women have outnumbered men since the 1990s, so much so that there are demands for setting aside admission quotas for men in medical colleges in reverse of the situation in the 1960s.

41 To confirm that popular culture lays the groundwork for the construction of everyday life, see Turner (1992: 6–7).

42 See Abercrombie *et al.* (2000: 267).

43 For a typical description of Pakistan's "high" culture, see Abbasi (1992).

44 This is a recognition of the tilt of this book toward national society and culture as evidenced in common institutions and themes.

45 This is a typical plot line of popular Punjabi movies such as *Maula Jat* and *Jagga Daaku*.

46 See Abbas (2005: 229).

47 Nasr (2004: 24) observes that Islamists wrote prolifically, dominating the public discourse.

48 This description of pop music's history draws on the *Herald's* retrospective of pop music (see *The Herald*, January 2005, pp.132–139).

49 See Saeed (2002: 181).

50 *The Herald* is the leading monthly magazine and *The Friday Times* is a weekly newspaper of liberal views.

51 See Zaidi (1996: 457–8).

52 See Kuhn (1964).

53 For example, anthropologists point out that food-gathering and -hunting societies view themselves as custodians of nature, whereas farming societies view nature as outside, something to be dominated (see Haviland (1999: 371–2)).

54 See Nakamura (1964: 3–4) and Haviland (1999: 148–9).

55 See Deshpande (2004: 4–5).

56 I am paraphrasing Deshpande (2004: 4).

57 See Deshpande (2004: 5)

58 I have given an elaborate account of the theoretical bases of the term mind-set, because it is a notion that has an imperialist history. For a long time distinctions were made between the "spiritualist and subjective" oriental mind and the "analytical and objective" occidental mind. Such dichotomous stereotypes are now rejected. Mind-set is not meant to resurrect ideological dichotomies. It is viewed as an expression of cultural modes of apprehending and defining reality, on a par with other cultural ways of thinking and observing. No notion of superior and inferior modes of thought is implied by this term.

59 My article on this topic was one of the first to explicitly raise the issue of Pakistani modes of thinking as contributory factors in the national crises. It was widely quoted and elicited a large number of letters (Qadeer 1972: 8).

60 See Ahmed (1997: 9).

61 See Zehra (2001).

62 See a typical narrative such as Ashraf and Bhutta (1991).

63 *The Pakistan Times*, September 2, 1974, p. 8.

64 This theme is a widely held explanation of the separation of East Pakistan and the defeat of the Pakistani army in 1971. It is a staple of public speeches and a common argument in individual discourses.

65 Specifically, this is Prime Minister Nawaz Sharif's statement to explain the wave of killings and student disturbances in Karachi in 1997 (*The News*, Internet edition, op. cit., July 6, 1997). Yet it could easily be from any other prime minister or president.

66 Statements of *ulema* and tribal leaders in Karak and Dir districts of the NWFP. Reported in *The News*, Internet edition, op. cit., July 19, 2001.

67 The speech by a PML leader, Saad Rafiq, at a panel discussion organized by the daily *Jang* and reproduced in *Pakeeza*, Toronto, June 26–July 2, 1996, p. 4.

68 See Jalalzai (1998: 90).

69 Such statements are common whenever there is an upsurge in ethnic riots.

70 Operating out of London, the Bank of Credit and Commerce (BCCI) was an international bank established and managed largely by Pakistanis. In 1991 it was accused of massive criminal fraud by the Bank of England and charged by the District Attorney of New York "as the largest bank fraud in world financial history," quoted by Coll (1994: 132). *Takbeer* (weekly), in its zeal to slam Dr Mehboob-ul-Haque spun the conspiracy theory making him the central character in the bank's demise (see *Takbeer* (weekly), May 31, 1997, p. 25).

71 *The News*, Internet edition, op. cit., November 1, 2003.

72 See Aziz (1993) and Nayyar and Salim (2004).

73 See Ahmed (1997) and Hoodbhoy (2000).

74 See Zehra (2001).

75 See Bearak (2003b).

76 See Gul (2005).

77 See Gilani (2001: 58).

78 See Ahmed (2003: 9).

79 See Gilani (2001: 55).

80 *Challo* culture is a term commonly used for the "no holds barred" drive for personal gains.

81 For accounts of poor women's conditions of work as piece workers at home, see Weiss (2002).

82 See Jillani (2004).

83 Mir (2000), a national newspaper columnist, anchors a TV show called "Dialogue." This quote is from his newspaper column.

84 See Ahmed (1990: 6).

10 Whither Pakistan?

1 For example, Britain between the 1870s and 1900, passed a raft of social legislations establishing voting rights, public health, compulsory primary education, and social security, which reformed the centuries-old church- and landlord-dominated social order. Similarly, Bismarck in the 1870s single-handedly consolidated Germany as a national state and transformed it into a modern welfare society through legislative and administrative measures. For an account of the British state's role in modernizing society, see Harris (1993: 180–219).

2 In the 2002 parliamentary elections, diplomas of seminaries were officially recognized as equivalent to college degrees, making *mullahs* eligible to contest elections while many veteran politicians did not qualify as they were not graduates.

3 For glimpses of the fine divisions within middle and upper classes by lifestyle and gender relations, see the life histories of Sajida Mokarram Shah, a widowed lawyer and Kishwar Naheed, a poetess and an official of the Information Ministry in Haeri (2002).

4 *Zakat* is a 2.5 percent annual levy on wealth collected from Muslims of the Sunni sect.

5 Usually Wahabi or Deobandi schools have been the primary inspirations for vigilantes and militant *mullahs*.

6 In India and Pakistan, the theme of reviving or reforming Islamic order has a long history. From Sayyid Ahmed Khan, Mohammad Iqbal, to Abul Ala Maudoodi is a long line of Muslim scholars and leaders who have envisioned various versions of Islamic order, ranging from modern/liberal to *Khalafat 'e-Rashda* (recreation of the order under the four righteous caliphs in eighth century).

7 Gusfield (1973: 333-41) debunked the notion of tradition being the opposite of modernity early in the debate about modernization. Recently even economic development theory has begun to acknowledge the culture (an expression of traditions) as "a constitutive part of development" and significant determinant of economic strategy (see Sen (2004: 39)).

8 See Hobsbawm and Ranger (1983: 1, 3).

9 The themes of the three movements are the same. Islamists say the Quran and Sunnah are their constitution, as evangelists hold the Bible and conservative Jews talk about the Torah as their constitutions.

10 See Weber (1958b).

11 Islamists go about railing against the "vulgarity" of television, Indian and Western movies, and music. They want to ban women's faces from advertisements and coeducation. These are elements of the lifestyle that they promise.

12 Urbanization is both a socioeconomic and geographic phenomenon. It combines numerous processes from population growth and increasing density to industrial production and interest-based social relations.

13 Pakistan's leading nuclear engineer, Bashir-ud-din Mahmood, read a paper at the Pakistan Science Conference about the tapping of *jinns* for energy supply.

14 About three million Pakistanis are sojourners or migrants abroad. Their remittances for family support expand the circle of beneficiaries to another 10–15 million persons.

15 *Jamia* (cathedral-like) mosques and seminaries such as Jamia Ashrafia in Lahore, Benori Mosque complex in Karachi, and Haqqania Madrassah and Mosque in Akhora Khatak are spread over scores of acres and enroll thousands of students each. Officials and teachers of these institutions are members of national and provincial assemblies and are courted by the media, governments, and foreign diplomats.

16 See for example, Samad (1995), Talbot (1998), and Cohen (2004).

17 See Talbot (1998: 372).

18 See Cohen (2004: 267).

19 *The Herald*, January 1997, pp. 143–4.

20 This was an adage often quoted during the communal riots at the time of partition. It was also cited often during the 1965 war with India.

21 See Mittelman (1996: 2–3) and Pasha and Samater (1996: 188–9).

22 Islamic movements claim that human rights, equality, rationality, and representative and consultative rule are values embedded in Islam. They were followed in the era of righteous caliphs but were violated by corrupt rulers of medieval times.

23 See Khalaf (2001: 62).

24 See Hobsbawm and Ranger (1983: 1) and Castells (1997: 11).

25 See for example Smelser (1973: 268–84), Gusfield (1973), and Eisenstadt (1973: 320–32).

Epilogue

Possible futures

Questions raised about Pakistan at family dinners or in academic journals revolve around the future of the society and state. Will it survive as an independent country? Will it be prosperous and stable? Invariably these questions concern the prospects of bringing about good governance, reducing poverty, fostering honest leadership, controlling corruption, and reforming legal and moral institutions. Furthermore, they lead to the discussion of the role of Islam in a country aspiring to development, modernization, and social justice. All these issues are tied to each other as strands of a spider's web. Obviously one individual or book cannot give informed opinions on all these topics. I certainly cannot claim expertise on all of them. My intention is to discuss only the strategic and futuristic implications of the findings of this book.

Obviously such a discussion is bound to be speculative in approach, hedged by assumptions about the internal and external conditions in the future. I have articulated two critical questions below about which I will speculate in the light of the conclusions of this book. Based on the foregoing narrative, I will delve briefly and directly into some possible future scenarios for Pakistan.

What could be the future of Pakistan as an independent state and society?

Pakistan will be around in 2050 although it will certainly be nightmarishly crowded (population projected to be 250 million in 2025 and 344 million in 2050), hyperurbanized, relatively poor, and reaching limits of land, water, and environmental resources. Undoubtedly, the land, people, and their communities will all be there. Those who will be the middle-aged and the elderly of 2050 are already born. They will be there in large numbers, many in positions of influence. What happens to them and what decisions they make in years to come will largely determine the future of Pakistan.

As discussed previously, the Pakistani state has shown resilience and an ability to muddle out of its crises. It has managed to survive wars, a break-up, and periodic political instability with wounds to show. In the twenty-first century, occupying and ruling other countries is so costly that it deters even the strongest countries. Any occupying country will find Pakistan's aroused and multitudinous population almost impossible to hold down for long. Similarly local or ethnic separatist movements are unlikely to find neighboring countries suitable homes to join with. Pakistan may linger in a state of continual turmoil but it is unlikely to fall apart. Appropriate policies accommodating ethnoregional rights and promoting efficient, fair, and accountable governance can bring stability and internal peace, erasing any potential for instability. The choice of a stable future is within the grasp of Pakistan's leaders and people.

Like all societies, Pakistani society is rooted in the community life of its people that has existed uninterrupted for thousands of years. There is no reason to think that social life will wither away. Ruling out possibilities of the dissolution of Pakistani society and state, the real question is what kind of social and political organizations they will be. Will they be just, peaceful, prospering, pluralist, effective, and responsive? Or will both the state and society be ill-governed, divided, doctrinal, stagnant, and inequitable? What future lies for Pakistan between these two polar possibilities?

Both scenarios lurk in the future of Pakistan. What will come to pass depends largely on the quality of leadership, institutional restructuring, and public policies, along with favorable external conditions.

State

To take the state first, its history has been unpromising. The Pakistani state has been locked in the cyclical pattern of short-lived democratic eras of person-centered political parties followed by long stretches of authoritarian military rule. There have been three such cycles in the 55 years of Pakistan's political history. Each phase of a cycle, political or military, wore out its credibility and was mortally shaken by popular discontent and violent agitations. The people of Pakistan have consistently shown the capacity not to tolerate arbitrary and corrupt governments too long. They are irrepressible in expressing their discontent and in their ability to shake entrenched governments. Military dictators do not last long and electoral democracy has not taken root. This is the dilemma of Pakistan and a source of its cyclical instability. Presently, there are no signs of any change in this pattern. This means the Pakistani state and society will continue to stagger from crisis to crisis and muddle along in the near future. This is the pessimistic prospect.

An optimistic scenario of the Pakistani state's future is not beyond the realm of possibility. It presumes some drastic changes in the present political culture, public institutions, and policies. Good governance that makes a visible difference in the lives of common persons is the ultimate legitimacy of a state. How it can be achieved given the specific conditions of Pakistan is the critical question.

What are considered to be some of the weaknesses of the Pakistani state could be turned into its strengths. Foremost among these qualities is people's low tolerance for the endemic corruption among rulers and administrators, and unfair policies. The periodic agitations that bring down governments are manifestations of people's acute awareness of their exasperation as citizens. This awareness can be harnessed for good governance and a rule of rules, the two fundamental conditions for stability and effectiveness of a state. Such a transformation will begin with what almost everybody in Pakistan insists is the precondition, namely honest and competent leadership at the national level. Pakistanis have been looking for a dedicated, national-minded, and intelligent leader. Jinnah, Bhutto, Ayub Khan, and for a short while even Musharraf, raised hopes of being such leaders. Jinnah did not live long, but the personal ambitions and self-serving policies of the rest betrayed them. A Pakistani Nelson Mandela (South Africa), Mahathir Mohammad (Malaysia), or Lee Kuan Yew (Singapore) could turn the trajectory of Pakistan's future.

An honest and competent national leader would have to immediately promote vigorous and wide-ranging institutional reforms. Rebuilding an accountable but secure bureaucracy, establishing an independent and competent judiciary, making policy-making processes transparent and equitable, promoting democratic political culture and citizens' rights, organizing a system of checks and balances to pre-empt abuse of power by individuals and institutions, ensuring fair distribution of resources, enacting provincial and regional rights to accord with social pluralism, avoiding the pitfall of personality cults, guaranteeing freedom of expression, enforcing the merit principle in public affairs, etc., are urgently needed measures that must be implemented, going beyond paying lip service to them. The Pakistani state has to focus on its internal structures and processes and reduce its external entanglements and dependencies.

In this spirit, resolving disputes with India and Afghanistan/Iran by realistically redefining objectives will release resources for economic and human development while reducing needs for large defense expenditures. I can go on listing many policies and reform measures but my objective is to illustrate the direction of reforms that will lay the foundations of good governance and a vigorous state. Such a reform agenda can be implemented in a span of 5–10 years. The results of this restructuring of the state must be visible as various measures unfold. This will help mobilize people behind a dedicated leader and her/ his goals. For concrete results, national policy changes must be complemented by management measures at a micro scale that improve everyday life.

As discussed in earlier chapters, failures of micro-level management which result in an ill-organized utility bills payment system, indifferent garbage collection, traffic rules that are tools of police shake-down, for example, have large adverse effects on citizens' quality of life. Alleviating such problems increases their trust of state. Institutional measures to reduce the humiliating and callous treatment that people have to bear every day should be simultaneously pursued with the national policy changes. Such improvements in people's lives largely require efficient and accountable management of institutions. They do not require large new investments of resources. Effective and fair use of existing resources through procedural and programmatic changes is the key to such reforms. I am trying to illustrate rather than prescribe the path of constructive change for the Pakistani state, the point being that a just and strong state is within the grasp of

Pakistan. It has to be worked at both from the top and bottom rungs of the state's structures.

Society

The balance sheet of social changes in Pakistani society over the past half century has both costs and benefits. Pakistani society has split into class-cum-lifestyle segments. Its social institutions do not dovetail into each other; instead fissures of institutional lag run through them. Its cohesiveness has given way to the fragmentation and the erosion of value and moral consensus. The traditional order has passed releasing people from geographic and (caste) occupational bonds. Expectations and ambitions of individuals have exploded, generating an ethos of a no-holds-barred personal drive. Social mobility has swept through all segments of society. Family and kin ties remain strong and may have even been reinforced. Material culture has been modernizing whereas nonmaterial norms and beliefs are tilting toward religious values and reinvented traditions. About a third of the population remains locked in abject poverty and for the rest too, social disparities have increased. There is no social security in this increasingly urbanizing society, whereas traditional systems of community charity and kin obligations for mutual care are breaking down. The national social contract has frayed.

Pakistani society is in transition. The pessimistic scenario is that it could continue to lose its moral bearings and social cohesion. People may be drawn inward to primordial structures based on kin, clan, and ethnic solidarities for security and (mutual) support which will be dysfunctional for an urbanizing society. While its social institutions are mired in premodern norms, Pakistan faces daunting challenges. Its population will almost triple in the next 40 years. Two new but densely packed Pakistans will have to be constructed despite scarcities of resources and a huge backlog of unfulfilled needs. Only an efficient state and a highly organized urban society can cope with these challenges. I have not even touched on external challenges.

Pakistan needs an urban moral order and universalistic values and norms, not particularistic mores of behavior. This is the true path of modernization, whereby formal rules, impersonal institutions, social values of equality, freedom of expression, nondiscrimination, efficiency, tolerance, pluralism, trust, and regularity of behaviors come to be the bases of social life. Historically in Europe, North America, Japan, and to some extent China and Russia, such norms and values have been promoted through social legislation. Thus the state by its enactments, policies, and behavior fosters a modern-urban ethos. As discussed above, the Pakistani state has so far given little guidance to society. If this situation continues, as it appears presently, Pakistani society will remain weak and steeped in an agrarian social order. A reformed state can help build a strong and vibrant society.

If the Pakistani state can enforce, not just enact, family reforms, a modicum of old-age and unemployment security, labor rights, citizens' rights that empower individuals and groups against the arbitrariness of public bureaucracies and corporations, equality of all citizens including women and minorities, etc., its society will be transformed. I am again trying to be illustrative of the direction of intended social change and not presenting a plan of action. As in the case of state, national legislation must be accompanied by micro policies that concretely express the new urban ethos. For example, sweeping away the pervasive privileges of influential persons, such as allowing those with connections to bypass long queues of waiting patients in a hospital or eliminating quotas of housing lots for army officers, will foster a rule of rules.

Moral values emerge from such everyday acts and mutual communications. They can also be deliberately promoted through reform policies, social movements, and examples set by leaders. These processes are operating in Pakistan, but presently they are discursive and lacking in focus. Public guidance can string them together into a mutually reinforcing reform strategy. Building the foundations of an urban moral order is the task of social development in Pakistan. Progress on that score will raise hopes of an optimistic future.

All in all, given the challenges of population explosion and resource limitations, the only hope for a stable and strong society lies in the drastic and deliberate reorganization of the state and society. Without such restructuring in the not too distant future, Pakistan faces prospects of staggering from crisis to crisis. There is no real option but to reform the state and society.

Can modernization be integrated with Islamic revivalism in urban Pakistan?

On the ideological plane, this is the most pressing question today in Pakistan, and in other Muslim countries. Islam is woven into the identity and nationalism of Pakistan. Another force that holds Islam central to Pakistani culture and society is its role as the religion of the overwhelming majority of Pakistanis. Pakistani Muslims have become progressively more religious in their beliefs and practices in the past 30 years. Islam remains at the core of their spiritual and community life. These facts do not suggest that Pakistan is destined to be a theocratic state and puritanical society.

While Islamic revivalism has swept social discourse and politics, economy, consumption patterns, and social relations are modernizing even westernizing, both in form and function. The imagined culture is being Islamized but the lived culture is increasingly tilting toward modern materialism. The imperatives of development and urbanization are driving a wedge between everyday life and norms and values espoused by Islamists. A large gulf is appearing between the beliefs and practices of a vast majority of people. This gulf is not some insidious plot of modernity or the West that will be overcome with more strict enforcement of Islamic pieties and codes, as Islamic revivalists argue.

The moral challenges arising from development and urban living have not been addressed by the reinvented traditions of agrarian and tribal origins. Experiments of Islamization in Pakistan, Iran, Afghanistan, and even Saudi Arabia have not yielded societies of high morals, efficiency, prosperity, equity, or even cleanliness or peace. Saudi Arabia and Iran are lucky to have oil that continues to fuel their relatively better standards of living although with increasing disparities and corruption. The point is that Islam as a religious institution can potentially be integrated with modernization as much as Christianity, Judaism, or Hinduism. It is the Islamic revivalist project that diverges from the imperatives of an urban society and modernizing economy.

Islamic precepts have always been a matter of interpretation. There is not a singular model of Islamic society but the revivalist discourse tends to sweep the diversity of views under the rug to advance a particular ideology. Within the spectrum of recently tried Islamic orders, the Taliban's envisioned society differed greatly from Iranian, Saudi, or Pakistani Islamization models. As discussed in preceding chapters, there was more than one version of the idea of Pakistan in its formative period, each assigning a different role, albeit important, to Islam in Pakistan's polity. All in all, the revivalist project is as much a political ideology as liberalism or socialism. It also aims at using the state's authority to settle doctrinal differences.

Modernization has coexisted with religion as is evident in Judeo-Christian America and Europe as well as Judaic Israel. Despite numerous ideological contradictions and legislative zigzags, these societies have managed to maintain a dynamic moral equilibrium under the supremacy of legislature and with the independence of the judiciary as well as open public debate. The necessary condition for maintaining a balance between religion and other social institutions is that the religious establishment should not have a veto right over others. It should not be privileged over civil society and legislative bodies. Different ideologies should have a fair opportunity to influence people's choices.

Islamic revivalism is as much a drive for power and authority by *ulemas* and Islamists as a movement to advance their ideological visions. By claiming to be the exclusive agency for interpreting divine edicts in human affairs, *ulemas* and Islamists assert a veto right over legislative, social, and political processes. It is this assertion of the right to be exclusive interpreters of Islamic laws that is the source of tension between modernity and Islamic revivalism. What needs to be institutionalized is a process that intrinsically allows all Muslims, *ulemas* as well as modernists, to interpret and apply universal Islamic precepts to contemporary problems. The process of interpreting Islam needs to be democratized and the supremacy of the people's choice through legislative bodies should be constitutionally guaranteed.

The revivalist movement has a wide range of ideologies. In Pakistan, it includes Islamic political parties currently following the electoral route to power, although they opportunistically also use violence to pursue their goals. It also includes freelance *mullahs* who proclaim Islamic rule in a locality, issue *fatwas* (juridical opinions), persecute nonconformists and challenge the state's authority. Farther to the right in the revivalist tent are *jehadis,* sectarian purists and self-proclaimed enforcers of Islam, who terrorize citizens for "un-Islamic behavior," particularly women and minorities. They have caused mayhem and violence to the extent that Pakistan's peace and security are jeopardized. Various Islamists tend to outdo each other in extremist or fundamental interpretations of Islam. Pakistan as a state and society will continue to be in moral confusion and raked by violence as long as these groups operate with relative impunity. It will be a society living on the brink of social breakdown. This is the pessimistic scenario.

The optimistic scenario is premised on the assumption that the supremacy of the public will and the legislative process should prevail. Groups and individuals should be able to advocate Islamic measures but they should not be able to impose their interpretations of Islam without due process. Islamic moral order and religious values should be enacted through legislative and judicial processes reconciling a variety of interpretations. Any one section of society, including Islamists, should have neither privileged standing nor should they be excluded from the public discourse. Singular legislative and judicial bodies should form the apex of the Pakistani state structure. The present trend toward separate *Shariat* courts and parallel Islamic institutions is a source of social contradictions. My point is that Islamic revivalists should not be the exclusive custodians of Islamic ideology and have veto power over public decision making. Ultimately parliament and other legislative bodies, whose members are bound to be Muslims overwhelmingly, should be the final arbiters of laws and policies. Islamic revivalism as a platform for grabbing power needs to be discouraged.

Islamic order admits many interpretations and thus requires wide-ranging public discussions to develop a consensus. Islamic scholars have long held that *ijtehad* (interpreting universal Islamic precepts for current applications with the use of precedents and reason) is the way of reconciling Islam and modernity. By lodging interpretive functions in legislative and judicial bodies, Pakistan can integrate Islam and modernity.

At the level of everyday life, ideologies provide only the broad principles. It is security, peace and decent living conditions with dignity and equal opportunity that are the primary concerns of people. By improving the economic and social conditions of living, Pakistani society's preoccupation with theoretical questions of Islam and modernity can be bypassed and a dynamic equilibrium between ideals and reality can be struck. Pakistan should focus on people's everyday problems and not be frozen in esoteric ideological debates. Ideology that helps fulfill people's needs commands their commitment.

Bibliography

Abbas, A. (2002) 'Pakistan's most wanted', *The Herald*, March.

Abbas, H. (2005) *Pakistan's Drift into Extremism*, Armonk, NY: ME Sharpe.

Abbasi, M. (1992) *Pakistani Culture*, Islamabad: National Institute of Historical and Cultural Research.

Abercrombie, N.; Hill, S.; and Turner, B. (1984) *The Penguin Dictionary of Sociology*, 4th edn, London: Penguin Books.

Abid, A. (2002) *Safar Adhi Sadhi Ka* ('Journey of Half a Century'), Karachi: Adara Maaraf Islami.

Abu-Lughod, J. (1991) *Changing Cities: Urban Sociology*, New York: HarperCollins.

Addleton, J. (1997) *Some Far and Distant Place*, Athens, GA: University of Georgia Press.

Afzal, M. (1974) *The Population of Pakistan*, Islamabad: Pakistan Institute of Development Economics.

The Aga Khan Rural Support Programme (AKRSP) (1990) *Briefing Notes*, Gilgit: The Aga Khan Rural Support Programme.

Agriculture Census Organization (1960, 1980) *Agricultural Census of Pakistan*, Karachi: Statistics Division, Government of Pakistan.

—— (2003) *Agricultural Census 2000*, Lahore: Government of Pakistan, Pakistan Report.

Ahmed, A. (1984) 'Religious presence and symbolism in Pakhtun society', in A. Ahmed and D. Hart (eds), *Islam in Tribal Societies*, London: Routledge & Kegan Paul.

—— (1988) *Pakistan Society. Islam, Ethnicity and Leadership in South Asia*, Delhi: Oxford University Press.

Ahmed, F. (1998) *Ethnicity and Politics in Pakistan*, Karachi: Oxford University Press.

Ahmed, I. (1987) *The Concept of Islamic State*, New York: St. Martin's Press.

—— (1990) 'View from the top', *The Pakistan Times*, March 23.

Ahmed, K. (1997) 'The Pakistani mind', *The Friday Times*, May 23–29.

—— (2003) 'Leadership and power in Pakistan', *The Friday Times*, August 29–September 4.

—— (2004a) 'Second opinion: have religion will travel', *Daily Times*, Internet edition, www.dailytimes.com.pk, September 4.

—— (2004b) 'Who threatens General Musharraf?', *The Friday Times*, January 23–29.

Ahmed, M. (1998) 'Revivalism, Islamization, sectarianism and violence in Pakistan', in C. Baxter and C. Kennedy (eds), *Pakistan 1997*, Boulder: Westview Press.

Ahsan, A. (1996) *The Indus Saga and the Making of Pakistan*, Karachi: Oxford University Press.

Akram, A. (2002) 'Weddings: from dreams to themes', *The Friday Times*, June 21–27.

Alavi, H. (1982) 'The rural elite and agricultural development', in K. Ali (ed.), *Pakistan. The Political Economy of Rural Development*, Lahore: Vanguard Publications.

—— (1989) 'Formation of the social structure of South Asia under the impact of colonialism', in H. Alavi and J. Harris (eds), *Sociology of Developing Societies*, London: Macmillan.

—— (1998) 'Pakistan and Islam: ethnicity and ideology', in F. Halliday and H. Alavi (eds), *State and Ideology in the Middle East and Pakistan*, London: Macmillan.

—— (2002) 'Social forces and ideology in the making of Pakistan', *The Friday Times*, December 6–12.

Ali, I. (1988) *The Punjab Under Imperialism, 1885–1947*, Delhi: Oxford University Press.

Alvi, I. (2001) 'Business and power in Pakistan', in A. Weiss and S. Gilani (eds), *Power and Civil Society in Pakistan*, Oxford: Oxford University Press.

—— (1997) *The Informal Sector in Urban Economy*, Karachi: Oxford University Press.

Amir, A. (2001) 'Passion for verbosity', *Dawn*, Internet edition, www.dawn.com, May 11.

Anderson, B. (1983) *Imagined Communities*, London: Verso.

Ashraf, A. and Bhutta, C. (1991) *Ashub-e-Pakistan* ('Travail of Pakistan'), Lahore: Bisat-e-Adab.

Aziz, K. (1993) *The Murder of History*, Lahore: Vanguard Publications.

Balbo, M. (1993) 'Urban planning and the fragmented city of developing countries', *Third World Planning Review*, 15/1.

Barth, F. (1981) 'Ethnic processes on the Pathan-Baluch boundary', in *Features of Persons and Society in Swat: Selected Essays of Fredrik Barth*, vol. 2, London: Routledge & Kegan Paul.

Batalvi, A. (1960) *Iqbal ke Akhari Doo Saal* ('Iqbal's Last Two Years'), Lahore: Iqbal Academy.

Bearak, B. (2003a) 'Pakistan is a failed state...' *New York Times Magazine*, Internet edition, www.balochvoice.com/reports/Pakistan, December 7 (accessed on June 17, 2005).

—— (2003b) 'Pakistan is a great hub of duplicity', *The New York Times Sunday Magazine*, December 7.

Benuri, T. and Khan, S. (1997) *Just Development: Beyond Adjustment with a Human Face*, Oxford: Oxford University Press.

Bilquees, F. and Hamid, S. (1981) *Impact of International Migration on Women and Children Left Behind: A Case Study of a Punjabi Village*, Islamabad: Pakistan Institute of Development Economics, Research Report No. 115.

Bowen, D. and Early, E. (eds) (1993) *Everyday Life in the Muslim Middle East*, Bloomington: Indiana University Press.

Burki, S. (1971) 'Interest group involvement in west Pakistan's rural works program', *Public Policy*, XIX (Winter).

Callard, K. (1957) *Pakistan*, London: George Allen & Unwin.

Cambridge University Asian Expedition (1962) *The Budhopur Report*, Lahore: Social Sciences Research Centre, University of the Punjab.

Castells, M. (1997) *The Power of Identity*, Oxford: Blackwell Publishers.

Chakraborty, K. (2002) *Family in India*, Jaipur: Rawat Publications.

Cohen, J. and Arato, A. (1992) *Civil Society and Political Theory*, Cambridge, MA: The MIT Press.

Cohen, S. (1998) *The Pakistan Army: With a New Foreword and Epilogue*, Karachi: Oxford University Press.

—— (2004) *The Idea of Pakistan*, Washington, DC: Brookings Institution Press.

Coll, S. (1994) *On the Grand Trunk Road*, New York: Times Books.

The Constituent Assembly of Pakistan Debates (1949), vol. 5.

The Court of Inquiry (1954) *Report to the Enquiry into the Punjab Disturbances of 1953*, Lahore: Government Printing, Punjab.

Darling, M. (1947) *The Punjab Peasant in Prosperity and Debt*, London: Oxford University Press (original 1925).

Dawood, A. (1999) *Sindhi Aurat ki Kahani* ('Sindhi Woman's Story'), Karachi: Ceen Publisher.

Deshpande, S. (2004) *Contemporary India*, New Delhi: Penguin Books.

Dogar, R. (2000) *Asli Zia-Ul-Haq* ('Real Zia-Ul-Haq'), Lahore: Deed-Suneed Publishers.

Duncan, E. (1990) *Breaking the Curfew*, London: Arrow Books.

Durkheim, E. (1984) *The Division of Labour in Society* (translated by W. Halls), London: Macmillan (original 1893).

Edwards, D. (1990) 'Frontiers, boundaries and frames. The marginal identity of Afghan refugees', in A. Ahmed (ed.), *Pakistan. The Social Sciences Perspecitive*, Karachi: Oxford University Press.

Egler, Z. (1960) *A Punjabi Village*, New York: Columbia University Press.

Eisenstadt, S. (1973) 'Breakdowns of political modernization', in A. Etzioni and E. Etzioni-Halvey (eds), *Social Change*, New York: Basic Books.

Ejaz, M. (1999) 'A microcosm of Pakistan', *The News*, Internet edition, www.jang.com.pk/ thenews, December 19.

—— (2002a) 'Pakistan's new liberal spirit', *The News*, Internet edition, www.jang.com.pk, thenews, April 14.

—— (2002b) 'The narrowing urban–rural divide', *The News*, Internet edition, www.nation.com.pk/daily.march.2002/12/index.html, March 17.

Elfenbein, J. (1966) *The Baluchi Language: A Dialectology with Text*, vol. 27, London: Royal Asiatic Society Monographs.

Environmental and Urban Affairs Division (EUAD) (1991) *The Pakistan National Conservation Strategy*, Karachi: Government of Pakistan and The World Conservation Union.

—— (1992) *The Pakistan National Conservation Strategy*, Islamabad: Government of Pakistan.

Etienne, G. (1995) *Rural Change in South Asia*, New Delhi: Vikas Publishing.

Etzioni, A. and Etzioni-Halvey, E. (eds) (1973) *Social Change*, New York: Basic Books.

Fabietti, U. (1996) 'Equality versus hierarchy: conceptualizing change in southern Balochistan', in P. Titus (ed.), *Marginality and Modernity. Ethnicity and Change in Post Colonial Balochistan*, Oxford: Oxford University Press.

Federal Bureau of Statistics (1998) *50 Years of Pakistan Volume 1*, Karachi: Manager of Publications, Government of Pakistan.

—— (2000) *Statistical Pocket Book of Pakistan*, Islamabad: Government of Pakistan.

Gans, H. (1962) *The Urban Villagers*, New York: Free Press.

Gardezi, H. (1995) *The Political Economy of International Labour Migration*, Montreal: Black Rose Book.

Gauhar, A. (1994) *Ayub Khan*, Lahore: Sang-e-Meel Publications.

Geertz, C. (1963) *Peddlers and Princes: Social Development and Economic Change in Two Indonesian Towns*, Chicago: The University of Chicago Press.

Gellener, E. (1991) 'Civil society in historical context', *International Social Science Journal*, 129 (August).

Ghose, Z. (1969) *The Murder of Aziz Khan*, New York: John Day.

Giddens, A. (1982) *Sociology*, New York: Harcourt Brace Jovanovich.

Gilani, S. (2001) 'Personal and social power in Pakistan', in A. Weiss and S. Gilani (eds), *Power and Civil Society in Pakistan*, Oxford: Oxford University Press.

Gilmartin, D. (1990) 'Shrines, succession and sources of moral authority in the Punjab', in A. Ahmed (ed.), *Pakistan. The Social Science Perspective*, Karachi: Oxford University Press.

Goldberg, J. (2000) 'The education of holy warriors', *The New York Times Magazine*, June 25.

Goode, W. (1963) *World Revolution and Family Patterns*, London: Collier-Macmillan.

Gotsch, C. (1982) 'Tractor mechanization and rural development in Pakistan', in K. Ali (ed.), *Pakistan. The Political Economy of Rural Development*, Lahore: Vanguard Publications.

Government of Pakistan (1965) *Report of the Commission for Eradication of Social Evils*, Karachi: Ministry of Health, Labour and Social Welfare.

Gul, I. (2005) 'Statistics reveal horrors of human smuggling', *Daily Times*, Internet edition, www.dailytimes.com.pk, March 10.

Gusfield, J. (1967) 'Tradition and modernity: misplaced polarities in the study of social change', *American Journal of Sociology*, 72/4.

—— (1973) 'Tradition and modernity: misplaced polarities in the study of social change', in A. Etzioni and E. Etzioni-Halevy (eds), *Social Change*, New York: Basic Books.

Haeri, S. (2002) *No Shame for the Sun*, Syracuse: Syracuse University Press.

Haider, S. (1981) *Social Change and Development in Pakistan*, Lahore: Progressive Publishers.

Harris, C. and Ullman, E. (1945) 'The nature of cities', *Annals: American Academy of Political and Social Science*, 242.

Harris, J. (1993) *Private Lives, Public Spirit: Britain 1870–1914*, London: Penguin Books.

Hasan, A. (1999) *Understanding Karachi*, Karachi: City Press.

Hasan, M. (ed.) (1993) *India's Partition Process, Strategy and Mobilization*, Delhi: Oxford University Press.

Haviland, W. (1999) *Cultural Anthropology*, Fort Worth: Harcourt Brace College Publishers.

Hillery, G. (1955) 'Definitions of community: areas of agreement', *Rural Sociology*, 20.

Hobsbawm, E. and Ranger, T. (eds) (1983) *The Invention of Tradition*, Cambridge: Cambridge University Press.

Hodge, G. and Qadeer, M. (1983) *Towns and Villages in Canada*, Toronto: Butterworths.

Hoodbhoy, P. (2000) 'What are they teaching in Pakistani schools?', *Chowk*, Internet magazine, www.chowk.com, April 10.

Human Rights Commission of Pakistan (1995) *State of Human Rights in 1995*, Lahore: Human Rights Commission of Pakistan.

Hussain, I. (1999) *Charagon Ka Dohan* ('Lamp's Haze'), Lahore: Sang-e-Meel Publications.

Hussain, S. (1998) *Alam Mein Intekhab – Peshawar* ('The One and Only – Peshawar'), Toledo: Literary Circle of Toledo.

Ikram, S. (1997) *A History of Muslim Civilization in India and Pakistan*, Lahore: Institute of Islamic Culture.

Imperial Gazetteer of India (1991) *North–West Frontier Province*, Lahore: Sang-e-Meel Publications (original undated).

—— (1998) *Punjab Volume 1*, Lahore: Sang-e-Meel Publications (original undated).

International Labour Organization (ILO) (1972) *Employment, Income and Inequality: A Strategy for Increasing Productive Employment in Kenya*, Geneva: ILO.

Iqbal, J. (2003) *Apna Girban Chalk* ('Opening My Heart'), Lahore: Sang-e-Meel Publications.

Iqbal, Z.; Qureshi, S.; and Mahmood, R. (1999) *The Underground Economy and Tax Evasion in Pakistan: A Fresh Assessment*, Islamabad: Pakistan Institute of Development Economics, Research Report No. 158.

Isphani, M. (2003) 'Pakistan: the cauldron', *The Friday Times*, June 27–July 3.

Jalal, A. (1985) *The Sole Spokesman: Jinnah, the Muslim League and the Demand for Pakistan*, Cambridge: Cambridge University Press.

—— (2001) *Self and Sovereignty*, Lahore: Sang-e-Meel Publications.

Jalalzai, M. (1995) *Sectarianism in Pakistan*, Lahore: AH Publishers.

—— (1998) *The NGOs Conspiracy in Pakistan*, Lahore: Classic Books.

Jilani, H. (1998) *Human Rights and Democratic Development in Pakistan*, Lahore: Human Rights Commission of Pakistan.

Jillani, M. (2004) 'Evoking old promises', *The News*, Internet edition, www.jang.com.pk/ thenews, January 1.

Jinnah, Mohammad A. (Quaid-i-Azam) (undated) *Speeches as Governor General of Pakistan 1947–48*, Karachi: Government of Pakistan.

Kaplan, P. (2000) *Soldiers of God*, New York: Vintage Books.

Kayani, M. (1977) *A Judge May Laugh*, Lahore: Pakistan Writers' Co-operative Society.

Kemal, A. and Mahmood, Z. (1998) *The Urban Informal Sector of Pakistan: Some Stylized Facts*, Islamabad: Pakistan Institute of Development Economics, Research Report No. 161.

Khalaf, S. (2001) *Cultural Resistance*, London: Saqi Books.

Khaldun, I. (1967) *The Muqaddimah* (translated by F. Rosenthal and abridged by N. Dawood), Princeton: Princeton University Press.

Khalid, A. (1998) *The Agrarian History of Pakistan*, Lahore: Allied Press.

Khalil, A. (2005) 'How politics promotes police corruption', *The News*, Internet edition, www.jang.com.pk/thenews, February 5.

Khan, A. (1994a) 'The blasphemy law. The bigot's charter', *The Herald*, May.

—— (1994b) 'The rise of sectarian mafias', *The Herald*, June.

—— (1996) *Orangi Pilot Project Reminiscences and Reflections*, Karachi: Oxford University Press.

Khan, F. (2002) *Viewing Television*, Unpublished, Master of Science thesis, Islamabad: Department of Anthropology, Quaid-e-Azam University.

Khan, M. (1981) *Underdevelopment and Agrarian Structure in Pakistan*, Lahore: Vanguard Publications.

—— (1983) 'Classes and agrarian transition in Pakistan', *The Pakistan Development Review*, 22/3.

—— (1986) *Tablighi Movement*, New Delhi: The Islamic Centre.

—— (1998) *Climbing the Development Ladder with NGO Support: Experiences of Rural People in Pakistan*, Karachi: Oxford University Press.

—— (2004) 'Poor little rich boys', *The Herald*, February.

Khan, R. (1996) 'Marrying in style', *The Friday Times*, October 31–November 6.

Khar, S. (2003) 'Letter from Muzzafargarh', *The Friday Times*, March 14–20.

Khuro, H. (ed.) (1981) 'Muslim political organization in Sind, 1843–1938', in *Sind Through the Centuries*, Karachi: Oxford University Press

King, A. (1980) 'Colonialism and the development of the modern Asian city, some theoretical considerations', in K. Ballhatchet and J. Harrison (eds), *The City in South Asia*, London: Curzon Press

Korson, H. (1975) 'Modernization and social change in the family in Pakistan', in W. Wriggins (ed.), *Pakistan in Transition*, Islamabad: University of Islamabad Press

Kuhn, T. (1964) *The Structure of Scientific Revolutions*, Chicago: The University of Chicago Press.

Kureshy, K. (1977) *A Geography of Pakistan*, Karachi: Oxford University Press.

Lahore Development Authority (LDA) (1998) *Integrated Master Plan for Lahore, Draft Report*, Lahore: National Engineering Services Pakistan (PVT).

Lapidus, I. (1998) *A History of Islamic Societies*, Cambridge: Cambridge University Press.

LaPorte, R. (1999) 'Pakistan: a nation in the making', in S. Harrison, P. Kreisberg, and D. Kux (eds), *India and Pakistan. The First Fifty Years*, Cambridge: Cambridge University Press.

Lari, Y. and Lari, M. (1996) *Karachi*, Karachi: Oxford University Press.

Lefebvre, A. (1999) *Kinship, Honour and Money in Rural Pakistan*, Richmond: Curzon Press.

Lerner, D. (1966) *The Passing of Traditional Society: Modernizing Middle East*, New York: Free Press.

Linck, O. (1959) *A Passage through Pakistan*, Detroit: Wayne University Press.

Lindblom, C. (1990) 'Leadership categories and social processes in Islam: the case of Dir and Swat', in A. Ahmed (ed.), *Pakistan. The Social Sciences Perspective*, Karachi: Oxford University Press.

Linden, J. (1997) 'In a culture of patronage; patrons and grassroots organization in a sites and services project in Hyderabad, Pakistan', *Environment and Urbanization*, 9/1 (April).

Lyon, L. (1989) *The Community in Urban Society*, Prospect Heights: Waveland Press.

Malik, S. (1992) 'Rural poverty in Pakistan: some recent evidence', *The Pakistan Development Review*, 31/4 (Part 11).

Mamdani, M. (1996) *Citizen and Subject*, Princeton: Princeton University Press.

Marx, K. and Engels, F. (1932) *Manifesto of Communist Party* (translation), New York: International Publishers.

Maudoodi, A. (1952) *Hamare Mutalibe* ('Our Demands'), Lahore: Central Publications Jamaat-i-Islami.

Mazari, S. (1999) *A Journey in Disillusionment*, Karachi: Oxford University Press.

Meier, G. (1984) *Leading Issues in Economic Development*, 4th edn, New York: Oxford University Press.

Mines, D. and Lamb, S. (eds) (2002) *Everyday Life in South Asia*, Bloomington: Indiana University Press.

Mir, A. (2000) 'The kill-joy spirit', *Dawn*, Internet edition, October 27.

—— (2001) 'Soldiers monopolize top civilian posts', *The Friday Times*, March 9–15.

Mirza, J. (2002) *Between Chadder and the Market. Female Office Workers in Lahore*, Karachi: Oxford University Press.

Mittelman, J. (ed.) (1996) 'Dynamics of globalization', in *Globalization: Critical Reflections*, Boulder: Lynne Rienner.

Mumtaz, K. and Shaheed, F. (1991) 'Historical roots of the women's movement: a period of awakening 1896–47', in F. Zafar (ed.), *Finding Our Way*, Lahore: ASR Publications.

Muneeba (1991) *Diffusion of Innovations and Its Impact on the Life of Villagers*. Unpublished, Master of Science thesis, Islamabad: Department of Anthropology, Quaid-e-Azam University.

Munir, M. (1979) *From Jinnah to Zia*, Lahore: Vanguard Books.

Murphy, D. (1995) *Full Tilt*, Hammersmith: Flamingo.

Myrdal, G. (1968) *Asian Drama Volume 1*, New York: Pantheon.

Nakamura, H. (1964) *Ways of Thinking of Eastern People* (translated by P. P. Wiener), Honolulu: University of Hawii Press.

Naseem, S. (1981) *Underdevelopment, Poverty and Inequality in Pakistan*, Lahore: Vanguard Publications.

Nasr, S. (1994) *The Vanguard of the Islamic Revolution*, London: IB Tauris.

——— (1996) *Mawdudi and the Making of Islamic Revivalism*, New York: Oxford University Press.

Nasr, V. (1993) 'Islamic opposition to the Islamic state: the Jamaat-I-Islami, 1977–88', *International Journal of Middle Eastern Studies*, 25.

——— (2004) 'Escaping the wasteland', *The Friday Times*, June 25– July 1.

Naveed-i-Rahat (1990) *Male Outmigration and Matri Weighted Households*, Delhi: Hindustan Publishing.

Nayyar, A. and Salim, A. (2004) *The Subtle Subversion: The State of Curricula and Textbooks in Pakistan*, Islamabad: Sustainable Development Policy Institute.

Nichols, R. (1998) 'Challenging the state: religious movements in the north–western frontier province', in C. Baxter and C. Kennedy (eds), *Pakistan 1997*, Boulder: Westview Press.

Nientied, P. (1987) *Practice and Theory of Urban Policy in the Third World*, Amsterdam: CHD.

North, D. (1989) 'Institutions and economic growth; an historical introduction', *World Development*, 17/9.

Overseas Pakistanis Foundation (2004) Government of Pakistan, www.opf.org.pk (accessed on December 12).

Parsons, T. (1949) 'The social structure of the family', in R. Nanda (ed.), *The Family: Its Functions and Destiny*, New York: Harper and Brothers Publishers.

Pasha, M. (2001) 'Savage capitalism and civil society', in A. Weiss and S. Gilani (eds), *Power and Civil Society in Pakistan*, Oxford: Oxford University Press.

——— and Samater, A. (1996) 'The resurgence of Islam', in J. Mittelman (ed.), *Globalization: Critical Reflections*, Boulder: Lynne Rienner.

Patel, R. (1991) *Socio-Economic Political Status and Women and Law in Pakistan*, Karachi: Faiza Publishers.

Pervez, N. (1998) *Pakistan Television Drama and Social Change*, Karachi: Department of Mass Communication, Karachi: University of Karachi.

Qadeer, M. (1959) *A Study of Changes in Religious Attitudes of Male College Lecturers in Lahore*. Master's thesis, Lahore: Department of Sociology, Punjab University.

——— (1972) 'The Pakistani mind: the root of crisis', *Dawn*, November 12.

——— (1975) 'Some indigenous factors in the institutionalization of professions in Pakistan', in W. Wriggens (ed.), *Pakistan in Transition*, Islamabad: University of Islamabad Press.

——— (1977) *An Evaluation of the Rural Development Programme*, Islamabad: Pakistan Institute of Development Economics.

——— (1983) *Urban Development in the Third World*, New York: Praeger.

——— (1996) 'An assessment of Pakistan's urban policies, 1947–96', *The Pakistan Development Review*, 35/4.

——— (1997) 'The evolving structure of civil society and the state in Pakistan', *The Pakistan Development Review*, 36/4 (Part 11).

——— (1999a) 'Silence of burqa', *The Montreal Gazette*, September 21.

——— (1999b) 'Urbanization of everybody, institutional imperatives, and social transformation in Pakistan', *The Pakistan Development Review*, 38/4 (Part 11).

——— (2000) 'Ruralopolis: the spatial organization and residential land economy of high density rural regions in south Asia', *Urban Studies*, 37/9.

——— (2004) 'Urbanization by implosion', *Habitat International*, 28.

Qureshi, I. (1965) *The Struggle for Pakistan*, Karachi: University of Karachi.

Qureshi, S. (1980) 'Islam and development: the Zia regime in Pakistan', *World Development*, 8, no. 7/8.

Rashid, A. and Tunio, G. (1990) *Socio-Economic Change Through Union Councils*, Peshawar: Pakistan Academy for Rural Development.

Rashdi, P. (2003) *Sindh Ways and Days*, Karachi: Oxford University Press.

Razi, R. and Shakir, S. (2001) *Pakistan's 53 Years*, Lahore: Sang-e-Meel Publications.

Reeves, R. (1984) *Passage to Peshawar*, New York: Simon and Schuster.

Rex, J. and Moore R. (1967) *Race, Community and Conflict: A Study of Sparkbrook*, Harmondsworth: Penguin.

Rostow, W. (1956) 'The takeoff into self-sustained growth', *The Economic Journal*, LXVI, 261.

Sadowski, Y. (1993) 'The new orientalism and the democracy debate', *Middle East Report*, July/August, no. 18.

Saeed, F. (2002) *Taboo*, Karachi: Oxford University Press.

Safdar, S. (1997) *Kinship and Marriage in Pakhtoon Society*. Lahore: Pak Book Empire.

Saiyid, D. (1998) *Muslim Women of the British Punjab*, Houndmills: Macmillan Press.

Salamon, L. and Anheier, H. (1997) 'The civil society sector', *Society*, January/February.

Samad, Y. (1995) *A Nation in Turmoil*, Karachi: Oxford University Press.

Santos, M. (1979) *The Shared Space*, London: Methuen.

Savage, M. and Warde, A. (1993) *Urban Sociology, Capitalism and Modernity*, 1st edn, London: Macmillan.

Savage, M.; Warde, A.; and Ward, K. (2003) *Urban Sociology, Capitalism and Modernity*, Houndsmills: Palgrave Macmillan.

Sayeed, K. (1967) *The Political System of Pakistan*, Boston: Houghton Mifflin.

Sen, A. (1999) *Development as Freedom*, New York: Anchor Books.

—— (2004) 'How does culture matter?' in V. Rao and M. Walton (eds), *Culture Change and Public Action*, Stanford: Stanford University Press.

Shah, M. (1992) *Sardari, Jirga and Local Government Systems in Balochistan*, Quetta: Qasim Publishers.

Shahid-ur-Rehman (1998) *Who Owns Pakistan?* Islamabad: Aelia Communication.

Shaikh, F. (1993) 'Muslims and political representation in colonial India: the making of Pakistan', in M. Hasan (ed.), *India's Partition Process, Strategy and Mobilization*, Delhi: Oxford University Press.

Shills, E. (1981) *Tradition*, Chicago: The University of Chicago Press.

Simmel, G. (1964) 'The metropolis and mental life', in K. Wolff (ed.), *The Sociology of Georg Simmel*, New York: Free Press.

Sjoberg, G. (1960) *The Preindustrial City; Past and Present*, New York: Free Press.

Smelser, N. (1973) 'Toward a theory of modernization', in A. Etzioni and E. Etzioni-Halevy (eds), *Social Change*, New York: Basic Books.

Stern, R. (2003) *Changing India*, 2nd edn, Cambridge: Cambridge University Press.

Suleri, S. (1989) *Meatless Days*, Chicago: The University of Chicago Press.

—— (1992) *The Rhetoric of English India*, Chicago: The University of Chicago Press.

Takbeer (1997) 'Pakistan's mysterious political character – Dr. Mahboob ul Haque', May 31.

Talbot, I. (1998) *Pakistan, a Modern History*, New York: St. Martin's Press.

Titus, P. (1998) 'Honor the Baloch, buy the Pushtun: sterotypes, social organization and history in western Pakistan', *Modern Asian Studies*, 32/3.

Tonnies, F. (2001) *Community and Civil Society* (translation), Cambridge: Cambridge University Press (original 1887).

Turner, G. (1990) *British Cultural Studies An Introduction*, London: Routledge.

Wahab, A. and Ahmad, M. (1996) 'Biosocial perspective of consanguineous marriages in rural and urban Swat, Pakistan', *Journal of Biosocial Science*, 28.

Warren, D. (2003) 'Lahore: on the Islamic gale', *Commentary*, 115/2.

Waseem, M. (1990) 'Urban growth and political change at the local level', in A. Ahmed (ed.), *Pakistan. The Social Sciences Perspecitive*, Karachi: Oxford University Press.

—— (1994) *Politics and the State in Pakistan*, Islamabad: National Institute of Historical and Cultural Research.

Weber, M. (1958a) *The City* (translation), New York: Free Press (original 1921).

—— (1958b) *The Protestant Ethic and the Spirit of Capitalism* (translated by T. Parsons). Mineola: Dover Publications (original 1904–5).

Weiss, A. (1991) *Culture and Development in Pakistan*, Lahore: Vanguard Publications.

—— (2002) *Walls Within Walls*, Karachi: Oxford University Press.

Werbner, P. (1990) *The Migration Process*, New York: Berg.

White, G.; Howell, J.; and Xiaoyuan, S. (1996) *In Search of Civil Society. Market Reform and Social Change in Contemporary China*, Oxford: Clarendon Press.

Wirth, L. (1938) 'Urbanism as a way of life', *American Journal of Sociology*, 44: 1.

Wolpert, S. (1993) *Zulfi Bhutto of Pakistan: His Life and Times*, New York: Oxford University Press.

The World Bank (1988) *Pakistan Urban Development Project*, Washington, DC: Country Document, World Bank.

—— (1995) *Pakistan: Poverty Assessment*, Washington, DC: World Bank, Report No.14397-PAK.

—— (2002) *Pakistan: Poverty Assessment*, Islamabad: World Bank, Document Report No. 24296-PAK.

Young, M. and Wilmott, P. (1957) *Families and Kinship in East London,* New York: Free Press.

—— (1962) *Family and Kinship in East London*, Harmondsworth: Penguin.

Zahab, M. (2004) 'The Sunni-Shia conflict in Jhang', in I. Ahmed and H. Reifield (eds), *Lived Islam in South Asia*, Delhi: Social Science Press.

Zaidi, A. (1998) 'Phuppi ki beti, Mamoon ka beta', *Chowk*, www.chowk.com/universityAve/azaidi_march 6.

Zaidi, S. (1996) 'Radio as social metaphor', *Economic and Political Weekly*, February 24.

—— (2000) *Urban Environment*, Balochistan Conservation Strategy Background Paper, Quetta: IUCN.

Zaman, K. and Khan, M. (1988) *Socio-Economic Change in Punjab Villages*, Lahore: Punjab Economic Research Institute, no. 247

Zaman, M. (1998) 'Sectarianism in Pakistan: the radicalization of Shi 'i and Sunni', *Journal of Asian Studies*, 32/2.

Zehra, N. (2001) 'Pakistan's second handers', *The News*, Internet edition, www.jang.com.pk/thenews/index.html July 5.

Zia, S. (1991) 'The legal status of women in Pakistan', in F. Zafar (ed.), *Finding Our Way*, Lahore: ASR Publications.

Ziring, L. (1997) *Pakistan in the Twentieth Century*, Karachi: Oxford University Press.

Index

jehadis: and Islamization 172–3, 305; sent to Kashmir 181
Jehan, Noor 283
Jinnah, Mohammad Ali 1, 23, 61–2, 63, 71; equal rights 241
joint family 190–2, 292–3, *see also* family

Kalashnikovs 223, *see also* guns
Kalat 84
Karachi 5, 39, 89; development 47; flooding 102; migration 76; and national economy 82; Pir Ilahi Bux Colony 41; planned communities 88; population 81, 82, 83; population explosion 40, 50; sewerage 101–2; squatter colonies 41, 87, 130–1; urban structure 91; water supplies 91
Karachi Electric Supply Company (KESC) 103
Karakoram highway 43, 56
karo kari 148, 198, 243
Kashmir: *jehadis* in 181, *see also* Azad Kashmir
katchi abadis 41, 48, 50, 55, 87–8, 130–1, 232; and traditional lifestyles 89, 108, *see also* cities; urbanization
Khan, Ayub, General 25–7, 64; deposition 97, 213; land reform 45; secular constitution 161–2
Khan, Imran 283
khel 203–5, 207
Khuderposh, Masood 172, 290
kinship 203–5, 222; and nepotism 205
kinship bonds 149, 275–6
Kohat 84
kundas 104

Lahore 39, 40, 82–3, 89, 286; migration 76; planned communities 88; population 50, 81–3; squatter colonies 41, 88, 130–1; tea houses 221, 223; traditional social structure 89–90; Walled City 220–2
land area 5
land reform 45
land tenure 43–6; agriculture 124–6; British rule 43, 112–13, 114–15; tribal 114–15
landholdings, size 44–5
landlords, economic advancement 274
landscape 5–6, 38, 55–6
languages 7–8, 62, 64, 66
legal systems 60
Libya, relations with 29
life expectancy 7, 119
lifestyle: *mullahs* 232; and social class 224–6; traditional 89, 108
lions, hunting 38

literacy 10, 118, 118–19, 119
Local Government Ordinance 142
love marriages 193, 197, 226

madrassahs 184; increase 180, 214
man, nature of 61
Mangla dam 41–2, 47
manufacturing industry, growth 32–3, 259
Mardan 84
marriage 192–4, 204, 217; arranged 193–4, 197, 226; cousins 192, 194; and ethnicity 76; restrictions on 71, *see also* love marriages; matchmaking; weddings
matchmaking 193, 293
material culture 261, 278
Maudoodi, Maulana 268
megacities 81–3, *see also* cities; urbanization
mehndi 270
men, television watching 138–9
migration: financial effects 133–4; internal 132–3; international 131–2, 133, 277; into cities 76, 98–9, 128–31, 277; and partition (of India) 24; and social change 13–14, 16, 24; social impacts 133
military: business activities 230; and the "Establishment" 229, 295
military officers: in civil administration 32; economic advancement 274–5
military rule 25–6, 31–3, 35, 228, 301
mind-set: definition 248; and everyday life 254–5; Pakistani 249–55, 256
minivans 53; and rural mobility 129
minorities 241–2
mobility, and modernization 128
modern economy 92–5, 263
modernization: adaptive 278–9; agriculture 122–4, 235; and British rule 266; and cities 79–80, 109; driving forces 218; economic 259–60; Europe 20; General Pervaiz Musharraf 35; and indigenization 279; and invention of traditions 270–1; and Islamic revivalism 184–5, 259, 304–6; material culture 278; North America 20; and social change 15, 20–1; and tradition 21–2; and urbanization 79–80, 271–2; and westernism 20–1, 259
Mohenjo Daro 286
monetization, economic transactions 121, 259
moral order: and social change 148–9, 288, 303; urban 271–2, 303–4; villages 148–9, 153
morality *see* public morality
morality police 245
mortality 7, 10; infants 10, 119, 192
mosques, ownership 296
motorcycles 11, 53, 129